Projecting Imperial Power

Projecting Imperial Power

New Nineteenth-Century Emperors and the Public Sphere

HELEN WATANABE-O'KELLY

OXFORD

UNIVERSITY PRESS

OXFORD
UNIVERSITY PRESS

Great Clarendon Street, Oxford, OX2 6DP,
United Kingdom

Oxford University Press is a department of the University of Oxford.
It furthers the University's objective of excellence in research, scholarship,
and education by publishing worldwide. Oxford is a registered trade mark of
Oxford University Press in the UK and in certain other countries

© Helen Watanabe-O'Kelly 2021

The moral rights of the author have been asserted

First Edition published in 2021

Impression: 1

Published in the United States of America by Oxford University Press
198 Madison Avenue, New York, NY 10016, United States of America

British Library Cataloguing in Publication Data
Data available

Library of Congress Control Number: 2020952996

ISBN 978-0-19-880247-1

DOI: 10.1093/oso/9780198802471.001.0001

Printed and bound in the UK by
TJ Books Limited

For Ekkehard

Acknowledgements

While researching this book, I had the good fortune to spend five months from September 2018 to the end of January 2019 as a Fellow of the Institut des Études Avancées de Paris. The IEA not only provided me with a beautiful place to work but with facilities which enabled me to begin this book. I am deeply grateful to its staff, especially Simon Luck, to the Class of 2018 for many stimulating conversations, and to Christophe Duhamelle of the École des Hautes Études en Sciences Sociales (EHESS) in Paris for his comments on my early ideas for this book. I also owe a great debt of gratitude to the Leverhulme Foundation, which awarded me an Emeritus Fellowship for 2017–19. This covered much of my travel in Europe, India, and Mexico, paid for some research assistance, and financed many of my illustrations and picture permissions. Five colleagues and friends gave generously of their time and expertise and read portions of the book while it was in the making: Pierre Béhar, William Godsey, Philip Mansel, Hamish Scott, and Toshio Watanabe. Their comments were invaluable in helping me to think my arguments through, they recommended works that I had missed, they prevented me from making errors in areas in which they are much more expert than I, and they encouraged me in the writing of such a wide-ranging book. I should also like to thank Jayashree Thirumaran and Bhavani Govindasamy for their meticulous care in guiding this book through the production stages.

My greatest debt of gratitude, however, goes to my husband Ekkehard Henschke. He accompanied me on all my journeys and took many of the photographs. Himself a historian, he read the manuscript, discussed it with me daily, read relevant works himself, and recommended further reading. He supported me in every imaginable way, personally and academically. I dedicate this book to him.

Contents

List of Illustrations

Cover illustration. Friedrich Wilhelm III and Friedrich Wilhelm IV, kings of Prussia, followed by the three German emperors, Wilhelm I, Friedrich III and Wilhelm II. Queen Luise leads the procession and Empress Auguste Viktoria brings up the rear. Mosaic in the Gedächtniskirche, Berlin. Detail. Photo © Ekkehard Henschke

List of Plates (for full details see the List of Illustrations)

A Note on Proper Names

Napoleon I and Napoleon III are so well known under the English form of their names that it would be pedantic to refer to them as Napoléon. All other names, however, are spelled as in the original language, so Agustín, Karl, Franz, and Wilhelm, not Augustine, Charles, Francis, and William; Elisabeth and Auguste Viktoria, not Elizabeth and Augusta Victoria.

Introduction

This is not a book about empire, on which there is an enormous literature, but about emperors, specifically about the newly proclaimed emperors of the nineteenth century and their symbolic power. The group begins with Franz II, Holy Roman Emperor, who proclaimed himself Franz I, emperor of Austria, in 1804 and with Napoleon I, elected as emperor in the same year. It continues with Agustín I of Mexico and Pedro I of Brazil who took the title of emperor in 1822 when they achieved the independence of their territories from Spain and Portugal, respectively. Napoleon III was elected emperor of the French in 1852 and Maximilian of Austria arrived in Mexico in 1864, having also been offered the title of emperor. Wilhelm I, king of Prussia, was invited by the German princes to become German emperor in 1871, while the British Parliament awarded Victoria, queen of Great Britain, Ireland, and India, the title of empress of India in 1876.

That the new nineteenth-century emperors and the means by which they projected their imperial status would repay study was the result of a visit to the Schatzkammer in the Hofburg in Vienna. This is the Imperial Treasury where the insignia, robes, and relics of the Habsburgs are displayed. One of the first objects the visitor sees on entering is a full-length red velvet cloak, richly embroidered with gold thread. The label on the glass case explains that this is the cloak of the emperor of Austria, that it was made in 1830 for Franz I and designed by Philip von Stubenrauch (1784–1848), the leading Viennese theatre designer of his day. Two questions immediately presented themselves: why did Franz need a *new* imperial cloak when he had been Franz II, Holy Roman Emperor, since 1792? And why, if he had proclaimed himself emperor of Austria in 1804, did he not need new robes until 1830? The answer turned out to be that, when he was sixty-two, he decided to designate his eldest son Ferdinand as his official heir and so had him crowned 'junior king' of Hungary in 1830 (Franz himself had been crowned king of Hungary in 1792). Franz could not take part in the ceremony wearing the robes of a Holy Roman Emperor, for he had abolished this title in 1806, nor could he wear the robes of the king of Hungary on this occasion, nor would the robes of the Order of the Golden Fleece or of the Order of Leopold, in both of which he had had himself portrayed, have been appropriate. He needed robes specifically as emperor of Austria, and he turned to a theatre designer to design them.

This underlined the importance of clothing as a signifier of rank and office.[1] It led me to ask: if Franz I, emperor of Austria, needed a new cloak as the outward sign of his new imperial dignity, what about Napoleon Bonaparte when he

Projecting Imperial Power: New Nineteenth-Century Emperors and the Public Sphere. Helen Watanabe-O'Kelly, Oxford University Press (2021). © Helen Watanabe-O'Kelly. DOI: 10.1093/oso/9780198802471.003.0001

crowned himself emperor of the French in 1804? What did the emperors of Mexico and Brazil wear? How was Victoria's new title as empress of India marked? This led to the further question as to what other appurtenances of power the new emperors needed to create in order to project their imperial status, to demonstrate that they were not merely royal but imperial. Did they have a coronation or an acclamation? How did they use courts and costumes, portraits and monuments, ceremonial and religion, architecture and town planning, international exhibitions and pageants, festivals and museums, to project themselves as emperors to the elite within their kingdoms, to the wider mass of their subjects, and to the international public? What traditions did they invent in order to support all this image-making?

Then there was the question of dynasty and succession. Both Mexican emperors were executed and had no imperial successors. All the other emperors initiated imperial dynasties. Napoleon I was followed after an interval of thirty-seven years by his nephew Napoleon III (r.1852–71). Franz I was succeeded by his son Ferdinand (r.1835–48), and then by Ferdinand's nephew Franz Joseph I (r.1848–1916) and his grandson Karl I, the last-named ruling for only two years from 1916 to 1918 before renouncing the throne. Pedro I of Brazil (r.1822–31) was succeeded by his son Pedro II (r.1831–89). Wilhelm I was briefly succeeded by his son Friedrich in 1888 and in the same year by his grandson Wilhelm II, who ruled until he was forced to abdicate in 1918. Victoria (r.1837–1901) was succeeded by Edward VII (r.1901–10) and by George V (r.1910–36) as king-emperors. George V's eldest son Edward VIII was never crowned and abdicated after less than a year, so George VI (r.1936–52) was the last emperor of India and ruled as such from 1936 up to Indian Independence in 1947. Dynasty also reminds us that, though the emperors in the six different territories frequently made war against each other, they were often interconnected by ties of blood. Napoleon I's second wife and empress of the French was Marie-Louise of Austria, daughter of Franz I. Her sister Leopoldine was the first empress of Brazil. Her son Emperor Pedro II was therefore Franz Joseph of Austria's first cousin. Franz Joseph's brother Maximilian became the second emperor of Mexico. Maximilian's consort, Charlotte, was the daughter of Leopold of Saxe-Coburg-Saalfeld, who became Leopold I, King of Belgium, and was therefore a cousin of both Queen Victoria and of her husband Prince Albert. This meant that Charlotte was also a cousin of their daughter Victoria, consort of Friedrich III, German emperor. Auguste Viktoria, consort of Emperor Wilhelm II, was a great-niece of Queen Victoria, while Wilhelm II was Queen Victoria's grandson.

The emperors also moved in the same international cultural sphere, with artists, architects, and composers moving between courts and capital cities. This is a subject that deserves a book all to itself, but one painter and one composer may serve to illustrate the point. Franz Xaver Winterhalter (1805–73) painted the portraits not only of Queen Victoria and her family, but also of Charlotte of Belgium, empress of Mexico; of Napoleon III and Eugénie, emperor and empress of the French; of Wilhelm I of Prussia (later German emperor); and of Franz Joseph, emperor of Austria, and his consort Elisabeth. The operas of Richard Wagner (1813–83) were performed in the principal opera houses of Paris, Berlin, and Vienna and, at the Delhi durbar of 1877, after the chief herald had read out the proclamation of Queen Victoria's new title of empress, the band played the march from Wagner's *Tannhäuser*. The year before, Emperor Pedro II of Brazil had attended the first performance in Bayreuth of Wagner's *Rheingold* as part of the *Ring* cycle. Of course, too, the emperors and their families visited each other, which also led to mutual influence. The impetus to install a Ruhmeshalle or Hall of Fame in the Armoury in Berlin in 1875, for instance, came about because Wilhelm I had visited the hall of the same name in the Arsenal in Vienna in 1873.

The trajectory of this book takes us, therefore, from Napoleon I and Franz I in 1804 to the demise of the Austrian and German empires in 1918 and then to the independence of India in 1947. These rulers were emperors, but were their territories empires? Jürgen Osterhammel presents eight criteria by which we can distinguish between an empire and a nation state.[2] An empire brings together a conglomeration of different national identities and languages under one ruler and is therefore heterogeneous. It sees itself as the heir to previous empires and is ruled by an imperial elite at the centre, which has a common language and cultural assumptions that are not necessarily shared by those at the periphery. It rules from above and the rights and duties of its inhabitants are assigned to them from above. The nation state, in contrast, is united by one language and is therefore homogeneous. It is made up of citizens, who have the same rights and duties as each other, and its power is legitimated from below. Osterhammel freely admits that there is no such thing in reality as a typical empire. He regards Napoleon I's France, for all its short life, as exhibiting the typical characteristics of an empire, for instance, the creation of an imperial elite that was placed in positions of power all over Europe and an extreme cultural arrogance, but he sees Austria, from 1867 Austro-Hungary, as 'an extreme borderline case',[3] for it is a conglomeration of territories which are not colonies and which are held together by 'the symbolism of the monarchy and a multi-cultural officer corps'.[4] He then moves on to imperialism as colonialism and, though he has many interesting things to say about the workings of colonial systems, the focus of this present book is different. Whether they had colonies or not—Brazil and Mexico did not—, whether they had a constitution or not, whether they ruled over territories with a significant minority or minorities that spoke a different language—the German and Austrian empires—or over teeming millions, all of whom had a lingua franca imposed on them—British India—, whether the ruler was elected by plebiscite—Napoleon I and III—, or ascended the imperial throne by dynastic succession—Pedro II of Brazil, Franz Joseph, and Karl of Austria—, all the rulers of the six territories analysed here bore the title of emperor and used imperial symbols which they developed and extended during the period of the empire in question.

Symbolic Power

To be an emperor meant to perform emperorship, just as Louis XIV, King of France, and the monarchs of the *ancien régime* performed kingship.[5] This meant creating symbolic power, which 'is defined in and through a fixed relationship between those who exert power and those who submit to it'. The monarch has 'to make people see and make people believe, to confirm or transform the vision of the world'.[6] The creation of symbolic power, therefore, involves two parties: actor and audience. Election or dynastic succession, followed by coronation or acclamation, were only the beginning of a performance that created symbolic power, which was necessary whether the emperor had real political power or not. Indeed, it could be argued that an emperor had to take more trouble to create symbolic power, the less actual power he had. As Timothy Blanning puts it: 'The greater the doubts about the stability or legitimacy of a throne, the greater the need for display', so that, in David Cannadine's words, the monarch sometimes elevated himself to an 'Olympus of decorative, integrative impotence'.[7]

Does this mean that the new emperor had to have charisma, famously defined by Max Weber in *Wirtschaft und Gesellschaft* as the quality that leads a ruler's subjects to believe in him and be led by him?[8] The charismatic ruler by definition has extraordinary qualities and is recognized as a leader because of his miraculous achievements. He creates an emotional community with those he leads ('eine emotionale Vergemeinschaftung') and his power is the opposite of traditional bureaucratic everyday authority. He turns the past on its head and is therefore a revolutionary. According to Weber, the charismatic leader is filled with the sense of mission, of vocation, of destiny, and the example he gives is Napoleon I. Gérard conveys something of these qualities in his depiction of Napoleon in his coronation robes (Figure 1). Edward Berenson shows how late nineteenth-century explorers became charismatic figures by expanding 'the limits of human possibility',[9] by fulfilling a contemporary need for manliness and virility, and by 'exemplify[ing] the aspirations and beliefs already held by his or her audience'.[10]

Clifford Geertz developed Weber's idea of the charismatic ruler further, basing his ideas on those of Edward Shils which, he said,

> encourage us to look for the vast universality of the will of kings (or of presidents, generals, führers, and party secretaries) in the same place as we look for that of gods: in the rites and images through which it is exerted. More exactly, if charisma is a sign of involvement with the animating centers of society, and if such centers are cultural phenomena and thus historically constructed, investigations into the symbolics of power and into its nature are very similar endeavors.[11]

Figure 1 François Gérard, *Napoleon I in his coronation robes*. Oil on canvas. Château de Versailles, France/Bridgeman Images

Thinking of the seventeen emperors in this study, among them four Habsburgs, three Hohenzollerns, two Braganzas, and four from the House of Hanover/Saxe-Coburg-Gotha/Windsor, the only two conceivable candidates for the title of charismatic ruler, apart from Napoleon I, are Agustín I of Mexico and Napoleon III, so, while personal charisma in Weber's sense may be helpful in creating symbolic power, it is not actually necessary. One emperor who saw himself as charismatic and tried to project himself as such was Wilhelm II, German emperor, but his performance by no means convinced everyone. Already in 1892, only four years into his reign, Baroness Hildegard von Spitzemberg (1841–1914), that well-connected and acute observer of the Berlin court from the 1860s to the outbreak of World War I, writes of him in her diary: 'the leadership role which he is confident he can play is so coloured by mysticism and so blown out of proportion that one feels great foreboding.'[12]

Nonetheless, the role that most of the seventeen emperors and one empress played in the national life of their territories was accepted by most of their subjects most of the time. The theatrical metaphors that Erving Goffman uses, in discussing social interactions in everyday life, are helpful here because they are even more applicable to something as consciously theatrical as the performance of emperorship, as Goffman realizes. He elaborates the notion of 'front', conveyed by setting, insignia denoting rank, clothing, posture, speech patterns, facial expressions, and gestures.[13] He discusses the mechanism of social distance as a way to generate awe, stressing that 'the real secret behind the mystery is that there is no mystery; the real problem is to prevent the audience from learning this too.'[14] In another statement that can usefully be applied to the performance of emperorship, he writes that 'the object of a performer is to sustain a particular definition of the situation, this representing, as it were, his claim as to what reality is.'[15] Reflecting on the emperors this book discusses, we see that five of them were forced to abdicate (Napoleon I, Napoleon III, emperors of the French; Ferdinand I, emperor of Austria; Wilhelm II, German emperor; and Pedro II, emperor of Brazil), while two more had to renounce the throne (Karl I, emperor of Austria, and George VI, emperor of India) and two were executed (Agustín and Maximilian of Mexico). This was, of course, in large measure due to external factors such as lost wars, revolutions, and political demands, but the moment when their subjects no longer believed in their emperors' performance hastened their demise or departure, for 'the impression of reality fostered by a performance is a delicate, fragile thing.'[16]

The question remains as to why a populace was ever convinced by a regal or imperial performance. In his analysis of the British political system, *The English Constitution*, which dates in its first version to 1867, Walter Bagehot explains that this is because people need a king or emperor. He distinguishes between what he calls the 'dignified' and the 'efficient' parts of government. The efficient parts are those by which the system 'works and rules', but it is the dignified parts 'which excite and preserve the reverence of the population'.[17] He goes on to explain what he means by the dignified parts of government:

> The elements which excite the most easy reverence will be the *theatrical* elements; those which appeal to the senses, which claim to be embodiments of the greatest human ideas—which boast in some cases of far more than human origin. That which is mystic in its claims; —that which is occult in mode of action; that which is brilliant to the eye; that which is seen vividly for a moment, and then is seen no more; that which is hidden and unhidden; that which is specious, and yet interesting—palpable in its seeming, and yet professing to be more than palpable in its results—this, howsoever its form may change, or however we may define it or describe it, is the sort of thing—the only sort which yet comes home to the mass of men.[18]

Monarchy for Bagehot is the system that best provides these theatrical, mystic, and brilliant elements which are a necessary concomitant to the prosaic business of government. He begins his chapter on the monarchy by explaining why it is that the everyday actions of 'a retired widow and an unemployed youth' (Queen Victoria and the Prince of Wales, the future Edward VII, respectively!) are worthy of report and claims that this is because they make government intelligible to the mass of the people:

> When you put before the mass of mankind the question, 'Will you be governed by a king, or will you be governed by a constitution?' the inquiry comes out thus—'Will you be governed in a way you understand, or will you be governed in a way you do not understand?' The issue was put to the French people; they were asked, 'Will you be governed by Louis Napoleon, or will you be governed by an assembly?' The French people said, 'We will be governed by the one man we can imagine, and not by the many people we cannot imagine'.[19]

Imagination is the key term here. The people had to be able to imagine the monarch—in Bagehot's example Napoleon III, emperor of the French—, for the point of a monarch was to be an imaginative construct which would awaken reverence and provide colour and mystery. As Barbara Stollberg-Rilinger explains:

> Every institutional order must be embodied in symbol and ritual; it rests on fictions in which both sides believe. 'Fiction' means in this context that every social order is based on a social construction and on a collective assignment of meaning. [...] An institutional order [...] consists fundamentally in nothing more than the permanent reciprocal expectations of those who take part in it [...] Social order functions on the basis of 'expectations of expectations'.[20]

Note that the power both of Weber's charismatic leader and of Bagehot's 'retired widow' rests on their ability to arouse the emotions of their followers or subjects in what Werner Telesko calls 'emotionalised patriarchalism'.[21]

For the social construct that was a new emperor to be accepted, he needed to appear *as* an emperor, which usually began with a coronation or acclamation. This was to demonstrate that he was an elevated being with a divine mandate, though the ceremony was sometimes combined with a constitutional oath to show that he also had a mandate from the people. Having been crowned or acclaimed, the emperor then had to surround himself with a hierarchically organized and minutely regulated imperial court in which members of the elite were bound to the emperor by a system of court offices, honours, and decorations that made them part of the imperial performance. As Geertz puts it, the members of the governing elite, 'justify their existence and order their actions in terms of a collection of stories, ceremonies, insignia, formalities, and appurtenances that they have either inherited or, in more revolutionary situations, invented'.[22] These 'insignia and formalities' were laid down in the rule books which each court produced and which regulated every aspect of ceremonial and laid down rules of precedence for visiting dignitaries, officeholders, and the bearers of titles and decorations. The elaborate regulations on dress to be worn at court and in the emperor's presence were a vital part of the imperial performance and served three purposes: the dress code distinguished those who moved in the emperor's orbit from ordinary citizens, made rank and office visible, and enabled the emperor to exert control over all who came into contact with him by compelling them to dress in a certain way. This included the huge number of servants who ensured the smooth running of all aspects of ceremonial and daily life. Imperial dress and an imperial court were not enough, however. It was essential for the emperor to curate his image and, if he could not be visible to his subjects in person, to make sure that this image was widely disseminated. From the mid-century on, any successors to the first emperor or empress intensified imperial display by further developing imperial iconography, increasing the size of the court, making rules of dress and ceremonial more complex and detailed, and using new media to disseminate the emperor's image.

Each of the emperors—and the one empress—performed emperorship in a different way. Franz I and Pedro II presented themselves as princes of peace, though Pedro II fought a war against Paraguay from late 1864 to March 1870 with huge loss of life; Franz Joseph and Wilhelm II saw themselves as *reges christiani*, publicly engaging in religious ceremonies, while Queen Victoria was mother of the empire, 'wrapping Britain's far-flung colonies in her nurturing embrace'.[23] The role of warrior hero was one that Napoleon I made his own, but Pedro I and Wilhelm I played this part too. Fatally for them, so did Napoleon III and Wilhelm II, whose reigns came to an end because they were defeated. Other emperors liked to present themselves as the servants of their people—witness the depictions of Napoleon I, Franz I, and Wilhelm I at their desks and the dutiful way that George V and George VI carried out their duties. But whether they saw themselves as heroic figures or not, most of them regarded themselves as divinely mandated, as emperors by the grace of God, and all of them saw their elevation as the working out of destiny.

Legitimation through Tradition

In order to underpin this appeal to destiny, the emperors called on a distant past to legitimate their reigns and to present themselves as the heirs to an ancient tradition. Hans-Siegbert Rehberg explains that in the process of institutionalizing the monarchy, symbols are needed to connect present time with past time, present space with distant space, and observable phenomena with invisible phenomena. The monarch has to lay claim to permanence and uses images to engage the power of the imagination in order to do so—images, of course, always being fictional constructs.[24] Napoleon, with no royal or even convincingly aristocratic antecedents, presented himself as the heir to Charlemagne and the Merovingians. When his nephew Napoleon III celebrated the extension of his term of office as president with a Te Deum in Notre Dame on 1 January 1852, he had paintings of Charlemagne, Saint Louis, and Louis XIV placed above the entrance, and both Napoleons drew on the iconography of the Roman emperors. The Hohenzollerns frequently recurred to the Hohenstaufen dynasty and presented themselves as the heirs of Friedrich Barbarossa, Holy Roman Emperor from 1155 to 1190, who supposedly lay sleeping deep in the Kyffhäuser mountain, waiting for a worthy successor to restore his empire. This myth was depicted in prominent locations such as the mosaic at the base of the Siegesäule (the Victory Column) in Berlin, on the stage, and in many other genres and settings. The Habsburgs' foundational myth began with Rudolf I, Count of Habsburg, in the thirteenth century, who was the first Habsburg to be elected Holy Roman Emperor. Episodes from his life were depicted again and again, for instance in the pageant performed in Vienna in celebration of Franz Joseph's Diamond Jubilee in 1908. The Habsburgs also performed their own myth for themselves, for instance, in the six scenes and an epilogue performed privately by the imperial family on 22 April 1879 in the residence of Archduke Carl Ludwig, the emperor's brother, on the occasion of the Silver Wedding of Franz Joseph and Elisabeth.[25] In this pageant, Franz Joseph's son and heir Prince Rudolf played the part of Rudolf I, as shown in Figure 2, and other family members presented key scenes from the history of the dynasty of Habsburg-Lorraine.

Agustín I, emperor of Mexico, claimed that his empire was heir to the Aztec empire of Anáhuac in 1822, and Maximilian of Austria did the same when he arrived forty-two years later. The British monarchs who bore the title of empress and emperor of India presented themselves as the heirs of the Mughal emperors whose court in Delhi they destroyed and whose ruler they tried and sent into exile.[26] When New Delhi was being planned in 1912, Lord Hardinge, the viceroy, insisted that one principal avenue should lead to the Purana Qila, the sixteenth-century Mughal fort, and another to the Jama Masjid, the seventeenth-century Mughal mosque, both major focal points in Old Delhi, thus making visible the connection between the British present and the Mughal past.[27]

The Emperors and Modernity

At the same time as the emperors were appealing to an age gone by and presenting the foundational myths of the dynasty and the nation to generations of schoolchildren in history textbooks and to their parents on the stage and in history paintings, the territories they were ruling over were engaged in extraordinarily rapid social and economic change and modernization. As discussed in

Figure 2 Crown Prince Rudolf dressed as his ancestor Rudolf I in 1879. Photograph. Wikimedia Commons

chapter VII, their capital cities underwent exponential growth during the period: between 1825 and 1900 the population of Paris grew almost fourfold, that of Vienna almost fivefold, and that of Berlin almost elevenfold.[28] The population of Rio de Janeiro was 137,000 in 1838 and 300,000 in 1880. The newly expanded cities needed clean water, sanitation, and lighting, so pumping stations, water towers, gasometers, and electricity stations are typical features of the nineteenth-century cityscape. Grand railway stations bear witness to increased mobility, linking far-flung corners of a territory or continent and bringing workers from the land into the new factories in the cities. The railway also made the distribution of mail faster. In 1860, runners and horses still distributed the majority of the mail in India, but by 1900 the longest runners' line from Calcutta to Madras had been supplanted by the railway and 863 runners had lost their employment.[29] The laying of telegraph cables across huge distances both overland and under the sea, to be followed by wireless telegraphy towards the end of the nineteenth century, speeded up communications again. Before the transatlantic cable, it took thirteen days in 1865 for news of the assassination of President Lincoln to reach London but only twelve hours in 1881 for the attempt on Tsar Alexander II's life to be reported there.[30] Post and telegraph offices were being built in ever-increasing numbers from the 1860s on, and the increased availability of news led to a huge growth in the numbers of newspaper titles published and sold. Where the *Augsburger Allgemeine*, the biggest German-speaking newspaper in the first half of the nineteenth century, sold barely 10,000 copies, the *Berliner Lokal-Anzeiger*, founded in 1883, rapidly reached sales of 100,000 copies, even though the competition was much greater.[31] *Le Petit Parisien* sold a million copies by the end of the century. It was only possible to print so many copies because of developments in the production of paper and of machines to speed up the printing process. New technologies also made it possible to print illustrations cheaply. Since the engineers and inventors driving technological innovation needed to be trained, new polytechnics and technical colleges were built, alongside colleges of art and music to train artists and composers. New museums made collections of art and antiquities, of natural science and technology, available to a wider public. Last but not least, the parliament in Vienna, inaugurated in 1883, and the Reichstag in Berlin, opened in 1894, bear witness to the constitutional changes that characterized the era, just as new stock exchange and bank buildings remind us of the role of capital.

Some of the emperors engaged with this new, fast-moving world more than others and associated their regimes with technological progress. The first central station in Rio de Janeiro dating to 1858, the Estaçao Central do Brasil (pulled down in the 1930s), was opened by Emperor Pedro II; the enlarged Gare du Nord in Paris was inaugurated by Napoleon III in 1860; the extended Anhalter Bahnhof in Berlin, at that time the biggest railway station in Germany, was inaugurated in 1880 by Emperor Wilhelm I and Chancellor Bismarck. The magnificent Victoria Terminus in Bombay, built in the Gothic Revival style, was completed in 1887 in time for Queen Victoria's Golden Jubilee.[32] The first Blackwall Tunnel under the Thames in London was opened by the Prince of Wales, the future Edward VII, in 1897 and he was often asked to inaugurate projects relating to the new technology (Figure 3). His nephew Wilhelm II was extremely interested in technology, to a degree unusual in a man of his class, but it was a selective interest, as Wolfgang König shows.[33] Canal and naval engineering, air transport, electronics, radio telegraphy, and photography aroused his enthusiasm and he promoted them, whereas machine manufacture, the chemical industry, and railway construction held no interest for him, and this at a time when Berlin was a leading light in some of these industries. Imperial involvement in urban planning and in international exhibitions are analysed in chapters VII and VIII, respectively.

The Structure of the Book

Chapter I analyses Napoleon's coming to power, his coronation, and the new imperial iconography he created which gave him legitimacy. His coronations in Paris and in Milan were crucial in creating round him an imperial and sacral aura. His noisy image-making is contrasted with Franz I's quiet insistence on his

Figure 3 Edward VII and Queen Alexandra speaking into an electric arc, experiment at Armstrong College, Newcastle, UK, drawing by Arthur Garratt, from *L'Illustrazione Italiana*, Year XXXIII, No 37, 16 September 1906. Veneranda Biblioteca Ambrosiana, Milan, Italy De Agostini Picture Library/Bridgeman Images

Habsburg lineage, which he demonstrated in the Franzensburg, the small neo-Gothic castle he began to build in 1798 as a dynastic monument. Napoleon's defeats in 1814 and 1815 meant that Franz was again *the* emperor, and it was he who hosted the sovereigns of Europe at the Congress of Vienna which redistributed territory after the end of the Napoleonic wars.

Chapter II explains how three new imperial titles came into being in territories outside Europe: Brazil, Mexico, and British India. The two Braganza emperors of Brazil, Pedro I and Pedro II, and the first emperor of Mexico, Agustín de Iturbide y Arámburu (1783–1824), are the only emperors anywhere, after Napoleon I, to have had an imperial coronation. Victoria's new title as empress of India—'Kaiser-i-Hind'—was celebrated in Delhi in 1877 at what was called the Imperial Assemblage or Durbar, a ceremony invented by Lord Lytton, the viceroy at the time.

Chapter III deals with the court, with dress, and with the honours system. In playing his role, the emperor needed a court and courtiers, whose behaviour and costume were highly regulated according to manuals of ceremonial and dress, which often evolved into a rigid and immoveable system. The medals, honours, and decorations that were handed out in such numbers throughout the whole period were also part of the court system of reward and control.

Chapter IV discusses one of the key figures in the court system, the empress, who had to play her role during a period when the place of women in society was changing. She had to fulfil the usual duties laid down for the consort: give birth to an heir, usually male, and, if possible, at least a 'spare', be an icon of beauty and fashion, and engage in charitable activities. Some empresses nonetheless made lasting contributions to the development of medical training and care and to women's education. Whether the empress was able to exert political influence or not depended on local circumstances. It is here, in the discussion of Empress Elisabeth of Austria's political involvement, that the establishment of the dual monarchy of Austro-Hungary is discussed.

Chapter V is concerned with the central question of image. Seeing and being seen is the glue that cements the relationship between ruler and ruled. The ruler was expected to present him or herself to the public gaze in person, but an image of the ruler was an important substitute. The different types of official portrait are discussed, as well the changes brought about by photography.

Chapter VI discusses how religion was used by imperial regimes to demonstrate their divine mandate. Napoleon I used the church as a tool of legitimation on such grand occasions as his coronation and the christening of his son, while wrestling with Pope Pius VII as spiritual and temporal ruler throughout his entire reign. Napoleon III took over the festival of Saint-Napoleon from his uncle and used it to woo the populace. For Franz Joseph of Austria, Catholic piety was part of his self-understanding as well as his public persona and he demonstrated that piety publicly on certain important religious feast days. The Hohenzollern emperors created for themselves the role of guardians of the Reformation and defenders of Protestantism in Europe and ultimately the world. Church-building was a major activity of the reign of Wilhelm II.

Chapter VII shows how the emperors redesigned the urban landscape by creating grand ceremonial avenues and erecting monuments. At the same time, these cities were given clean water, modern sanitation, gas, and electric lighting. Maximilian of Mexico had grand plans for how to transform Mexico City on the lines of Vienna, Paris, and Brussels, but was executed before he could accomplish them. Pedro II created the town of Petrópolis in the hills above Rio de Janeiro as an imperial summer residence. London was the latecomer, only beginning to rethink its urban layout in the early twentieth century.

Chapter VIII discusses how emperors used international exhibitions to promote themselves and their empires. The 'Expositions Universelles' held in Paris in 1855 and 1867 and promoted by Napoleon III are contrasted with the 'Weltausstellung' staged in Vienna in 1873. Pedro II played an important role in displaying and selling the empire of Brazil and its products at four international exhibitions in London in 1862, in Paris in 1867, in Vienna in 1873, and in Philadelphia in 1876.

Chapter IX shows how Britain invented an imperial identity for India in the twentieth century through imposing architecture and two durbars, held in Delhi in 1903 and 1911 respectively. For the Coronation Durbar in 1911, a new Imperial Crown of India was specially made. The grand new imperial capital of New Delhi was inaugurated in 1931. The British public also had to be convinced of their imperial mission, which is what the Festival of Empire in 1911 and the British Empire Exhibition in 1924 were designed to do, accompanied each time by a huge pageant performed by amateurs projecting this message.

Chapter X analyses some examples of how theatre and pageants were used in imperial myth-making in the Austrian and German empires, at a time when fewer and fewer of the populace accepted the will of a divinely anointed ruler. Those in power needed to persuade them that the nation's destiny, and therefore their own, was tied in an indissoluble bond to the emperor who ruled over them by the grace of God.

Chapter XI gives a brief overview of the wars and appalling loss of life which were the result of imperial ambition. It describes how the six empires came to an end and goes on to ask how they are remembered today. It describes how the imperial city has been repurposed for use by democratic governments on the one hand and for tourism on the other and then analyses some of the fates that awaited imperial statuary after the end of an imperial regime.

Sources and Scholarship

Writing this book has been as pleasurable as it has been challenging. It involved reading the memoirs, diaries, and letters listed in the bibliography which brought personalities, places, and periods to life; searching contemporary newspapers for both the official version of events and a critical or satirical viewpoint; reading literary authors who painted a vivid picture of the imperial regimes that they were living through. It involved a great deal of travel on three continents to see all the cities, palaces, paintings, buildings, and monuments that I discuss. I had fortunately visited the Paço de São Cristovão in Rio de Janeiro before it burned down in 2018. Before the corona pandemic made travel impossible, I had visited the Imperial Palace in Petrópolis and Maximilian's castle of Miramar at Triest; I had gone up the Hooghly River from Calcutta to see the statues of the Raj in their retirement at Old Flagstaff House and stood dwarfed by the architecture of New Delhi. When the pandemic closed libraries in March 2020, I had already done my research in the Archivo General de la Nación in Mexico City, in the Haus- Hof- und Staatsarchiv and the Österreichische Nationalbibliothek in

Vienna, the Staatsbibliothek and the Ibero-Amerikanisches Institut in Berlin, the Bibliothèque de la Sorbonne in Paris, and the Bodleian Library, Oxford. I thank the archivists and librarians of these institutions for the work that they do for all scholars. I am also deeply grateful to the Internet Archive, the Hathi Trust, the scholarly publishers who made publications available online, and the many libraries that digitized their holdings for enabling research to continue during the closure of libraries and archives. Were it not for them, I would have had to put my work on this book on hold indefinitely.

One of my greatest pleasures has been to read the work of other scholars—specialists on empire, on the invention of tradition, on ceremonial, on portraiture and photography, on town planning and sculpture, and on theories of symbolic power, and to peruse the magisterial biographies of so many of the principal actors in each of the six territories with which this book is concerned. Readers will see from the bibliography, which is above all a list of cited works, who my mentors were. Without them I could not have attempted to write this book and I thank all these colleagues, so many of whom write so well and so inspiringly, from the bottom of my heart.

Notes

1. Mansel, *Dressed to Rule*.
2. Osterhammel, *Die Verwandlung*, pp. 607–10.
3. Osterhammel, *Die Verwandlung*, p. 628.
4. Osterhammel, *Die Verwandlung*, p. 625.
5. Blanning, *The Culture of Power*, pp. 29–52.
6. Bourdieu, 'Sur le pouvoir symbolique', p. 410.
7. Blanning, *The Culture of Power*, p. 32; Cannadine, 'The British Monarchy', p. 116.
8. Weber, *Wirtschaft und Gesellschaft*, pp. 140–2.
9. Berenson, 'Charisma', p. 25.
10. Berenson, 'Charisma', p. 184.
11. Geertz, 'Centers, kings, and charisma', p.124.
12. Spitzemberg, *Tagebuch*, p. 298.
13. Goffman, *The Presentation*, pp. 14–15.
14. Goffman, *The Presentation*, p. 46.
15. Goffman, *The Presentation*, p. 53.
16. Goffman, *The Presentation*, p. 36.
17. Bagehot, *The English Constitution*, p. 7.
18. Bagehot, *The English Constitution*, p. 9.
19. Bagehot, *The English Constitution*, p.38.
20. Stollberg-Rilinger, *Des Kaisers alte Kleider*, p. 9.
21. Telesko, *Geschichtsraum Österreich*, p. 153.
22. Geertz, 'Centers, kings, and charisma', p. 124.
23. Giloi, *Monarchy, Myth*, p. 342.

24. Rehberg, 'Weltrepräsentation und Verkörperung', p. 8.

25. Gaul, *Lebende Bilder*.

26. Dalrymple, *The Last Mughal*.

27. Davies, *Splendours*, p. 224.

28. Kos et al., *Experiment Metropole*, p. 13.

29. Bonea, *The News of Empire*, p. 46.

30. Osterhammel, *Die Verwandlung*, p. 1026.

31. Telesko, *Das 19. Jahrhundert*, pp. 235–6.

32. In modern-day Mumbai it is officially called Chhatrapati Shivaji Terminus, though it is still known to many simply as VT.

33. König, *Wilhelm II. und die Moderne*.

I

Creating Myth, Asserting Dynasty

Napoleon I and Franz I of Austria

The series of new nineteenth-century emperors that this book analyses began in 1804 with two figures who could hardly be more different and who exemplify two contrasting methods of projecting imperial power. One of them, Napoleon Bonaparte, concentrated his efforts on creating a myth and a huge panoply of power to compensate for the fact that he was a parvenu. The other, Franz I of Austria, formerly Franz II, Holy Roman Emperor, quietly asserted his ancient lineage and reminded his people of his dynastic claim to imperial glory.

Napoleon and his Imperial Coronation in 1804

The military achievements of the Corsican army commander and First Consul of France Napoleon Bonaparte (1769–1823) caused the French people, in 1804, to choose him as hereditary emperor, thereby according him supreme power and making him the founder of a new dynasty. In 1806 Louis Dubroca began his 364-page history of the French dynastic tradition by explaining that his work would

> do homage to the great character of the august founder of the French empire, present a picture of the immense blessings he has brought and represent the powerful motives for national recognition that have accorded him supreme power and have made him the hereditary head of his family.[1]

Dubroca is emphasizing that Napoleon did not just ascend the throne, as a king would have done, by agnatic patrilinear succession; instead, he was elected by the people. The imperial dignity was conferred on him, as in the Roman Empire, as a reward for outstanding merit. Dubroca's frontispiece bears the caption 'Dix-Huit Brumaire', the date of the *coup d'état* on 9 November 1799 that led to the young army commander being proclaimed First Consul of France. It depicts Napoleon raising up the armoured personification of France, while a winged figure holds a shield surmounted by an eagle bearing the words 'la dynastie de Napoléon' and extends a crown over Napoleon's head. In a cave under his feet lie the shattered remains of similar shields representing the superseded dynasties of Clovis from the fifth and sixth centuries, Pepin from the eighth, and Hugues Capet from the

Projecting Imperial Power: New Nineteenth-Century Emperors and the Public Sphere. Helen Watanabe-O'Kelly, Oxford University Press (2021). © Helen Watanabe-O'Kelly. DOI: 10.1093/oso/9780198802471.003.0002

tenth, who, according to Dubroca, founded the Capetian dynasty that ruled until the execution of Louis XVI. Dubroca relates how, when the Second Consul Cambacérès was sent to Napoleon as an emissary by the Senate after they had decided to offer him the title of hereditary emperor, Cambacérès, already addressing Napoleon as 'Votre Majesté', speaks of 'the love and recognition of the French people' and proclaims

> Happy the nation which, after so many troubles and uncertainties, finds in its bosom a man capable of calming the storm of passions, of reconciling all the different interests, and of reuniting all voices.[2]

The Senate proclaimed him emperor on 18 May 1804. The turmoil that Cambacérès mentions refers not just to the period of the Revolution and the Terror that succeeded it but to the fact that the Directory had lost political and economic control before Napoleon came to power. Napoleon's *coup d'état*, organized with Charles-Maurice de Talleyrand-Périgord (1754–1838) and Emanuel-Joseph Sieyès (1748–1836), led to a new constitution in which he became First Consul, alongside Jean-Jacques-Régis de Cambacérès (1753–1824) and Charles-François Lebrun (1739–1824). This was ratified by a plebiscite in January 1800, in which the votes were manipulated by Lucien Bonaparte, Napoleon's brother. In a more accurate reflection of popular opinion, 3.2 million voters agreed in 1802 to make Napoleon First Consul for life and 2.5 million voted to elevate him to rank of hereditary emperor in 1804. It could therefore be claimed that it was the people themselves who had chosen this man to lead them in their hour of need, even if fewer voted for the rank of emperor than for that of consul for life. The French had deposed and then publicly executed their hereditary king in 1793, but an elected emperor could not only be linked to the republican principles of the French Revolution but could also endow France with some of the glamour of ancient Rome and of the *ancien régime* without restoring the Bourbon monarchy. Stability could only be guaranteed through an office holder at the head of a constitutional state and then only if that office was hereditary. This would ensure that the system outlived one man, which is why the Empire won support among the political and military elites as well as among the people.

Napoleon's coronation as Emperor of the French in Paris on 2 December 1804 is an object lesson in how to project imperial power.[3] There were three problems that had to be solved: how to give a new coronation ceremony legitimacy; how to organize a coronation only eleven years after the execution of the previous Bourbon king Louis XVI; and how to invest the coronation with an aura of the sacred that would convey to the people that this emperor was divinely sanctioned.

Napoleon tackled the first of these three challenges by linking his coronation ceremony to ancient tradition and by presenting himself as the heir to mythical and historical figures from the past. All monarchs connect themselves to an ideal past, to the origins of their dynasty, and to that end often employ genealogists and historians who can demonstrate their unbroken descent from their heroic fore-bears. Napoleon could not do this because he was a parvenu. Had he been born eighteen months earlier he would not even have been French, as Corsica belonged to the Republic of Genoa up to 1768 and therefore only became French a year before the child known as Napoleone Buonaparte was born. His grandfather had become a member of the 'noblesse de robe' only eleven and a half years before Napoleon's birth. The Buonapartes were not rich and Napoleon owed his rise to his military successes, his manipulation of the facts so that disasters appeared as successes—for instance, during the Egyptian campaign in 1798–1801[4]—and his ruthless will to power. Once proclaimed emperor, in less than six months he created an imperial iconography from scratch with the help of the Grand Master of Ceremonies, Louis-Philippe, Count de Ségur (1753–1830). It was clear that a new symbol was needed for the Empire and this was discussed for the first time in the Conseil d'État on 12 June 1804.[5] The first suggestion was a cock and then a lion, but the minutes of the meeting next day recorded an 'aigle déployée', that is, an eagle with spread wings, which was both a reference to ancient Rome but also to Charlemagne. In a decree of 10 July 1804, Napoleon defined the new imperial coat of arms, to be designed by Jean-Baptiste Isabey (1765–1855), as consisting of the aforementioned eagle in antique gold on a blue ground, holding a bolt of lightning in its claws.[6] Both the eagle and the lightning are a reference to Jupiter, emphasizing the Roman origin of the imperial idea. From this point on, eagles featured prominently in every Napoleonic context and, as we shall see, Napoleon built the second, military, part of his coronation ceremonies round them.

On the coat of arms, the eagle was surrounded by bees, because brooches in the shape of bees (or cicadas) were found in Tournai in 1653 in the tomb of Childeric I, the founder in 457 CE of the Merovingian dynasty and the father of Clovis. From this point on, bees were embroidered on many Napoleonic robes and furnishings, replacing the fleurs de lys of the Bourbons. Napoleon was making a link to a distant age before that of the Valois and the Bourbons, promoting himself as the successor not only of Clovis but also of Charlemagne. The painting by Jacques-Louis David (1748–1825) entitled *The First Consul Crossing the Alps at the Great St Bernard Pass* (1801) shows the names of Bonaparte, Hannibal, and Charlemagne carved into the stones at the feet of Napoleon's leaping steed, so Charlemagne was already woven into the Bonaparte legend. Thierry Lentz draws attention to political writings of the period in which the parallel was also drawn.[7] On 2 October 1804, Napoleon had visited Aachen (Aix-la-Chapelle) and taken part in a solemn procession in which the relics containing the skull and arm of Charlemagne were carried into the cathedral there. It seems that he even saw himself as a latter-day Charlemagne: 'je suis Charlemagne', he wrote to his uncle Cardinal Fesch on 14 February 1806.[8] When he entered Notre-Dame for the coronation, he did so through a temporary porch which had two main pillars.

On one of them was the statue of Clovis, on the other the statue of Charlemagne, 'fondateurs de la monarchie française', as the official printed accounts of the coronation put it.[9] As he processed up the aisle, Napoleon wore a wreath of golden oak and olive leaves like a Roman emperor and carried a sceptre, to indicate that he had already been made emperor by the will of the French people and that the coronation was only confirming it. At the ceremony, the officers of state placed on the altar the imperial crown—a replica of Charlemagne's—, a sword also supposed to be Charlemagne's but which came from Philippe III le Hardi from the thirteenth century, the hand of justice, also a copy, the sceptre of Charles V from the fourteenth century with a statuette of Charlemagne on top, the emperor's cloak embroidered all over with golden bees, a ring, the chain of the Legion of Honour, and the imperial orb (see Figure 1). The crown, cloak, and ring of the Empress were also placed on the altar. Napoleon is legitimating his imperial dignity by connecting himself to the founder of the Holy Roman Empire in the year 800.

While it is possible to speak in French of a coronation or 'couronnement', the term usually used is 'sacre', the anointing, which emphasizes the religious nature of the ceremony. The anointing of a sovereign reminds us that the monarch is God's representative on earth; that he (or in rare cases she) is divinely mandated and rules as God's instrument. Napoleon could have staged his *sacre* on the Champ de Mars where he had held other ceremonies and where the Revolutionary festivals had taken place, but he chose instead to hold it in a great cathedral. He distanced himself from the Bourbon kings, however, by choosing not Rheims where they had customarily been crowned, but Notre-Dame. Then, in a direct challenge to the Holy Roman Emperor, Franz II, who was still in power, he brought Pope Pius VII (Barnaba Niccolò Maria Luigi Chiaramonti, 1742–1823) from Rome to officiate, making a link with the last Holy Roman Emperor to be crowned by the pope, namely Charles V in 1530. On 15 July 1801, Napoleon I had signed a concordat with Pius VII, bringing to an end the persecution of the church and of the clergy brought about by the French Revolution. The pope hoped, by agreeing to be present in Paris, that he could improve its terms, a hope destined to be dashed.[10] But Napoleon's efforts during his entire reign to make the pope do his bidding were also ultimately unsuccessful, as discussed more fully in chapter VI. Another challenge to Franz was the attendance of a number of German princes at the coronation: the Margrave of Baden, and the Princes of Hesse-Darmstadt and Hesse-Homburg being the most important.

Napoleon's coronation took place during a Mass that was not only presided over by the pope, but also by the archbishops of Paris and Milan, and twenty-four other bishops, as well as supporting clergy. At this ceremony, the confessed unbeliever, who did not take communion as coronation ceremonial demanded, submitted himself to an elaborate ecclesiastical ritual, allowing the pope to anoint him and pronounce him emperor and to bless the insignia which had been so carefully designed as symbols of his power. Napoleon entered Notre-Dame garbed as an emperor to indicate that it was the people who had chosen him, and he swore a constitutional oath at the other end of Notre-Dame as the final act of the coronation, but the religious ceremony presented him to the people as God's representative on earth, a divinely sanctioned being to whom loyalty and obedience were also due because of his divine mandate. God had chosen him as emperor, not merely the two and a half million citizens who had voted for his new dignity.

Six of the Latin prayers spoken by the pope were taken from the coronation ceremonial prescribed by the *Pontificale Romanum*.[11] This had been codified by Clement VIII in 1596, with additions by Urban VIII in 1644 and by Benedict XIV in 1752. There were some unique variations at Napoleon's coronation, however. It was usual, for instance, for the monarch, prior to the coronation, to swear an oath in the words laid down in the *Pontificale* promising to serve God, to rule justly, and to protect the church and his people. At Napoleon's coronation, however, it was the pope who called on Napoleon to make these promises, whereupon Napoleon, placing both his hands on the gospels, simply answered with the one word: 'Profiteor' (I promise).[12] There followed prayers, exhortations, litanies, and blessings, again from the *Pontificale*, but when it came to the anointing of the Empress and the blessing of the imperial sword, the rings, and other insignia, the prayers were taken from the *Cérémonial du sacre des rois de France*,[13] since there was no precedent for this in the *Pontificale*. The prayers for the presentation to Napoleon of the sword and hand of justice were also taken from the *Pontificale*, those for the presentation to emperor and empress of the sceptre and the rings from the *Cérémonial*, from which five prayers in all were taken. Napoleon gave the order for the anointing to proceed, so that he could speak afterwards of an act of 'self-unction',[14] and he famously took the crown from the pope and crowned himself. Then he crowned Joséphine de Beauharnais, his consort, as recorded in David's famous painting, but it is the pope whose words proclaim Napoleon emperor by the power of God:

> God confirms you in this imperial throne and Jesus Christ Our Lord, King of Kings, and Lord of Lords, who lives and reigns eternally with God the Father and the Holy Spirit causes you to reign with him in the eternal kingdom. Amen.[15]

Then, as the *Pontificale* lays down, the Pope kissed Napoleon on the cheek and proclaimed: 'Hail to the Emperor in Eternity.' Only fifteen years after the Revolution had turned France from a monarchy into a republic, the religious ceremony at Napoleon's coronation takes up where Bossuet, in a work published in 1709, left off: 'God established the kings as his representatives and reigns over the peoples through them and all power comes from God.'[16]

Figure 4 Louis Le Coeur, Napoleon I swearing the constitutional oath at his coronation in Notre-Dame Cathedral on 2 December 1804. Hand-tinted engraving. Private Collection The Stapleton Collection/Bridgeman Images

After the religious ceremony was over and the pope had left the altar to disrobe, Napoleon processed down to the west end of Notre-Dame, where his Great Throne stood on a dais positioned high above the nave under a huge triumphal arch the whole width of the nave and reaching almost to the roof of the cathedral (Figure 4). The arch was surmounted by eagles and bore the legend 'Napoleon Emperor of the French' across the top and beneath it, on either side, 'Honneur' and 'Patrie'. In the centre, over the throne, hung draperies depending from an imperial crown. Here the presidents of the Senate, the Legislature, and the Tribunate were presented to the newly crowned emperor and the most senior of the presidents of the Council of State gave him the text of the constitutional oath. Raising his right hand and placing his left on the gospel this is what he swore:

I swear to maintain the integrity of the Republic; to respect and to cause to be respected the laws of the Concordat and the freedom of worship; to respect and to cause to be respected equality before the law, political and civil liberty, the irrevocability of the sale of national property; not to raise any duty or establish any tax except by law; to maintain the institution of the Legion of Honour; to govern solely in the interest of and for the happiness and glory of the French people.

If the first part of the coronation ritual was designed to show that Napoleon was a legitimate ruler in the eyes of God, the second part confirmed that he had a mandate from the people and was a constitutional monarch.

David's depiction of Napoleon crowning Joséphine, begun in 1805, was completed in January 1808 and exhibited in the Salon in that year. It is a gigantic composition, almost ten metres wide by six metres high. Pope Pius VII is a central figure, but also present, and depicted by David, were the Archbishop of Milan, Cardinal Giovanni Battista Caprara Montecuccoli (1733–1810), who, a year later, crowned Napoleon King of Italy, Jean-Baptiste de Belloy, the ninety-five-year-old archbishop of Paris, and twenty-four other bishops. Clearly recognizable in the painting are ten members of Napoleon's family, including his mother who was not actually present, many marshals and generals of France, foreign diplomats, and all the important functionaries of his court, including Ségur, Talleyrand, Géraud-Christophe-Michel Duroc (1772–1813), and Louis-Alexandre Berthier (1753–1815). Napoleon's fellow consuls, Lebrun and Cambacérès, are also shown, as are Joséphine's ladies in waiting. This painting, therefore, portrays his court at the beginning of the imperial reign. Louis-Léopold Boilly, in his painting of 1810, *The Public Viewing David's Coronation of Napoleon at the Louvre*, shows people of all ages crowding round in front of it, with at least one couple consulting a guidebook to work out who all the notables depicted are.

The thirty-nine colour plates by Isabey and by the architects Charles Percier (1764–1838) and Pierre-François-Léonard Fontaine (1762–1853) give us the most vivid impression of how elaborate the coronation and the accompanying festivities were.[17] Between them these three artists were responsible for the outward appearance of the whole event, with Isabey designing the costumes and Percier and Fontaine the ephemeral architecture. The plates begin with seven depictions of the course of the coronation, from Napoleon's departure from the Tuileries, through his arrival at Notre-Dame, his anointing by the pope, his self-coronation, the Offertory Procession during the mass, his constitutional oath, and then the setting for the distribution of the eagles, the moment at which the army was included in the ceremonial. The other thirty-two plates are of the costumes designed for the emperor and empress but also for the pope, princes and princesses, great officers of state, officers of the imperial household, judges, ministers, colonels of cuirassiers, dragoons, hussars and the light cavalry, pages, heralds at arms, senators, counsellors of state, members of the legislative body and of the Tribunate, mayors, and presidents of cantons. The display of jewels, velvet, lace, and silk, the embroidery and plumes, the shakos and bearskins were set off by the red draperies with their gold fringes in which Notre-Dame was swathed.

Napoleon came to power through his military exploits and the clever way he promoted them for propaganda purposes, so the army was and remained central to his power. It was therefore only to be expected that it should play a central part at the initiation of the Empire. Point 2 of the decree of 10 July 1804 (21 Messidor An XII) announcing the coronation decreed that, as part of the ceremonial, new imperial standards would be distributed to the army on the Champ de Mars. This took place on 5 December 1804. Napoleon set out in detail what these standards should look like in a letter to Maréchal Berthier that he dictated on 27 July 1804 from his headquarters at Pont-de-Briques, making it plain that what were envisaged were standards, surmounted by eagles, based on those borne by the Roman legions. The eagles were to have the same form as the eagle on the imperial seal and the standards should say that the eagle was presented by the emperor to such and such a regiment.[18] Deputations from all the regiments were to gather and exchange their old Republican standards for the eagles, swearing an oath of allegiance to the new emperor. David was again commissioned to paint the scene. The title of his painting, completed in 1810, is 'The Oath sworn by the Army to the Emperor after the Distribution of the Eagles on the Champ de Mars' (Figure 5). Under a blue sky, in the right-hand half of the picture, officers representing several different regiments are pressing forward with their standards, falling over each other in their enthusiasm to approach their commander-in-chief. Some of the eagles are pointing down, but most are raised aloft. On four of the banners, we can read which regiment they belonged to, for instance, on the foremost which is dipped downwards, we can see the words 'L'Empereur des Français au 1er Regiment de Ligne'. On the back were the words 'Valeur et Discipline', so it was this exhortation that the troops were looking at as they marched behind their standard. The left-hand side of the picture shows the richly

Figure 5 Jacques-Louis David, *The Distribution of the Eagle Standards, 5 December 1804*, detail. Oil on canvas. Château de Versailles, France/Bridgeman Images

decorated structure that was erected in front of the École Militaire. This consisted of a high dais under a richly decorated canopy with galleries extending on each side adorned with red draperies and red carpets and with pillars surmounted with huge golden eagles. Each of the galleries was divided into eight sections representing the sixteen cohorts of the Legion of Honour. In David's painting, Napoleon, in coronation robes, crowned with his golden wreath and holding the sceptre, stands in the middle of the dais and stretches his right hand out to the standard-bearers rushing towards him. Behind him and to the side are Joséphine, Louis and Joseph Bonaparte, Eugène de Beauharnais, and such members of the court as Cambacérès and Duroc. Between them and the officers rushing forward are the newly minted marshals of France, raising their batons in a gesture which mirrors that of the standard-bearers. Ten of the eighteen marshals created in 1804 can be discerned, among them Augereau, Bernadotte, Berthier, Lannes, Masséna, and Murat.

The painting is another exercise in myth-making and does not correspond to the reality. On the day, it rained so heavily that the official account speaks of 'torrents of water' mixed with a terrible cold which was very hard on the troops who had been lined up since six o'clock that morning.[19] Not only that. Many of the eagles were not ready in time. This is not surprising when one realizes that, to equip the imperial guard, the infantry, the cavalry, the artillery, the veterans, the *gendarmerie*, the Garde de Paris, the navy, and the Garde Nationale, as well as those battalions stationed overseas, 1,100 eagles were needed. The eagle, twenty centimetres high, was designed by Antoine-Denis Chaudet (1763–1810) and cast in gilded bronze by the leading *bronzier* of the day, Pierre-Philippe Thomire (1751–1843), who had produced exquisite objects for Marie-Antoinette and continued to produce others throughout the Empire and the Restoration. Naturally Thomire could not make so many eagles so quickly, so not every regiment got one. Some regiments received the wrong eagle, others had not received theirs four months later.[20] According to Général Teste, then a captain, quoted by Regnault, the deputations from the various regiments were told to leave their old standards on the ground at the ceremony on the Champ de Mars and to line up to receive their eagles, but the crowd behind them began to toss and trample on the flags, whereupon the soldiers broke ranks to recover their old Republican standards. Another problem with the eagles was their weight, so that they were replaced with a lighter version in 1810. When Napoleon III, nephew of Napoleon I, picked up the symbolism of the eagles again, he had an electroplated and an aluminium version produced which was much lighter again.[21]

On the sixth, seventh, and eighth of December, that is, on the three days after the distribution of the eagles, Napoleon, seated on his throne in the Tuileries and wearing his imperial robes, received all the various groups that exercised authority in the state: archbishops, bishops, ministers, senators, presidents of electoral colleges in the départements and in the arrondissements, prefects, judges, deputies from the colonies, and, on the final day in the gallery of the Louvre, 7,000 representatives of the army and the navy, of the national guard, and of the guards of honour. Another important festivity was the formal banquet given by the city of Paris to the emperor and empress on 16 December. These official events were embedded in a whole series of other festivities lasting several weeks, both popular amusements for the people in the streets and squares of the city and formal banquets and concerts organized by such bodies as the Senate and the generals and stretching on into what was called Nivôse in the Revolutionary calendar, that is, late December and early January. The Protestants even performed an oratorio in honour of the coronation in the church of St Louis du Louvre on 28 December.

Napoleon's Coronation as King of Italy in 1805

This was not Napoleon's only coronation. Six months later, on 26 May 1805, he had himself crowned king of Italy in Milan, linking himself again to Charlemagne, king of the Lombards.[22] As Caiani explains in his authoritative account, the provinces of Lombardy and Emilia, made up of five ancient duchies and principalities, had been recovered from Austria in 1802 and were governed as a separate satellite republic whose capital was Milan. When France became an empire, the

Consulta di Stato offered Napoleon the Italian crown. He did not accept immediately, hoping to instal either his brother Joseph or his other brother Louis on the
throne. They refused, as it would have meant renouncing their rights to the French
succession, so when a delegation offered Napoleon the crown in front of the
French Senate on 17 March 1805, he accepted and agreed to travel to Milan in
May 1805 for the ceremony, at which, he decided, he would not be anointed but
only crowned. For this purpose, the Iron Crown of Lombardy was specially
brought to Milan from Monza, so that Napoleon could emulate Charles V, Holy
Roman Emperor, the last ruler who had been crowned with it. The Iron Crown
was not just a royal symbol, but a sacred relic supposed to contain one of the nails
from the Crucifixion. A complex ceremonial was invented for the coronation
actually involving four crowns: that of Lombardy, the French imperial crown
which was brought from France together with the other imperial insignia, a
modern replica of Charlemagne's crown, and a new diadem commissioned for
the Kingdom of Italy. The coronation was based on the imperial coronation of
1804 but with many adjustments to take account of local sensitivities and power
structures. Great efforts were made to accommodate the local elites and local
customs, for instance, using the Ambrosian liturgy which was usual in Milan. As
in Paris, a coat of arms had to be created, as well as costumes, canopies, and
draperies of all kinds in a period of less than two months. For lack of time, the
costumes had to be based on those designed for the Paris coronation, but green
was used instead of blue as the prevailing colour. The Comte de Ségur arrived in
Milan in early April to oversee the complex arrangements and issue the invitations
to ecclesiastical, legal, and aristocratic figures of all kinds, and Cardinal Caprara
hurried from Paris to Milan to officiate at the coronation mass. Eugène de
Beauharnais, Napoleon's stepson, who was to be the new viceroy, had already
been there since early March.

Napoleon, accompanied by Joséphine and his sister Elisa, Princess of Piombino,
made his triumphant entry into Milan on 8 May 1805 and the Iron Crown arrived
from Monza on 23 May. Two days later, as the highpoint of a complex ceremony
involving all the various crowns and sets of insignia, Napoleon crowned himself
king of Italy. Caiani comments:

> The crowning of Napoleon in Milan's Duomo was, for the French Empire, what
> the Delhi Durbars were to be for the British Empire. This was a prime moment to
> flaunt and display the cultural diversity that imperial power had mastered.[23]

Caiani also reads the coronation as an attempt to 'establish shared affinities' with
the Italian elites.[24] On 5 June 1805, Napoleon instituted the Order of the Iron
Crown, and between then and 1814, more than 1,500 Italians were invested with it
in the classic gesture of attempting to bind persons thought to be important or
useful to the monarch. Surprisingly, when the territory was recovered by the

Austrians, they renamed this order the Austrian Imperial Order of the Iron Crown, and it existed until 1918.

Napoleon had many other strategies that enabled him to project his imperial power, not least to himself. He owned forty-four palaces, many of them such as the Tuileries, Fontainebleau, and Compiègne taken over from the Bourbons, others acquired as part of his conquests in Italy and the Low Countries.[25] Many of the French palaces had suffered during the Revolution and had been emptied of furniture. Napoleon had them restored, redecorated, and furnished under the supervision of Duroc and Fontaine, thus enabling many important luxury industries to survive and flourish. By 1813, they had all been redecorated and furnished.[26] This meant that everywhere one looked, the eye alighted on golden eagles, bees, and the letter N. The throne room at Fontainebleau, which still survives, is just one example.[27]

It was at Fontainebleau that Napoleon learned that the French Senate had dethroned him on 3 April 1814, so that he was forced to abdicate. This was ratified by the French Senate in the 'Acte de dechéance de l'Empéreur'. Napoleon was forced into exile on the island of Elba off the Italian coast. Though he returned to France and again raised an army during the hundred days that he was at large, he was finally defeated in 1815 at the Battle of Waterloo by the British, the Prussians, and the Dutch. His reign as emperor finally came to an end with his second abdication and imprisonment on the inhospitable island of St Helena, far away from Europe in the Atlantic Ocean. Here he insisted on being addressed as 'Sire' and on his attendants wearing court dress in his presence. Still attempting to project power through outward signs, he died there in 1821.

Franz II/I—From Holy Roman Emperor to Emperor of Austria

When Napoleon and his team were inventing coronation ceremonies, they were well aware of what an imperial coronation based on ancient tradition looked like. The senior monarch of the day, the Holy Roman Emperor from the House of Habsburg Franz II (1768–1835), only a year older than Napoleon, had been elected, anointed, and crowned in 1792 according to such a ceremonial laid down in the year 1356 in a document known as the Golden Bull. Franz stood in a line of Holy Roman Emperors going back to Charlemagne who, in the so-called *translatio imperii*, had founded the Holy (that is, Christian) Roman Empire in Rome on Christmas Day in the year 800. Franz could therefore truly claim to be Charlemagne's successor with a great deal more justification than Napoleon could, and could also claim to be heir to the Roman emperors.

Franz was born Franz Joseph Karl, Archduke of Austria, in Florence on 12 February 1768. His uncle, Emperor Joseph II (1741–90), had no sons, so Franz was brought to Vienna in 1784 to be prepared, as the designated successor, for his future role as emperor. When Joseph died in 1790, Franz was thought too young to become emperor, so his father Peter Leopold was elected and crowned Holy Roman Emperor in Frankfurt as Leopold II.[28] Leopold had only just begun to bring order into the chaotic tangle of partially failed reforms initiated, often against the will of his subjects, by Joseph II, when he died unexpectedly on 1 March 1792, having reigned for only just over two years. Franz, the third emperor in three years, had therefore to succeed his father much sooner than expected. He was crowned King of Hungary on 6 June 1792 in Ofen (Buda) and on 9 August 1792 King of Bohemia in Prague. Between these two royal coronations, also celebrated according to ancient ceremonial, he was elected King of the Romans on 5 July 1792, followed on 14 July 1792 by his anointing and coronation in the collegiate church of St Bartholomäus in Frankfurt as Franz II, the twenty-seventh Holy Roman Emperor.[29] The date was chosen to assert the authority and status of the Holy Roman Emperor precisely because it was the third anniversary of the storming of the Bastille. During the coronation mass, Franz prostrated himself in the shape of a cross before the altar like a priest about to be ordained and committed himself to loyalty to the pope, to the Catholic and Apostolic Church, to the realm, and to the poor. Then he was anointed, before retiring to be clothed in the alb, stole, gloves, stockings, and shoes which formed part of the coronation insignia. These miracles of textile art were thought to be Charlemagne's but are in fact medieval. Then Franz was wrapped in the imperial cloak, made in Palermo in 1133–34 and falsely believed for a long time also to be Charlemagne's. He was invested with the sword, the lance, the sceptre, the orb, and the ring, was crowned with the imperial crown, and ascended the throne. Napoleon's mixed bag of replicas and ancient objects could not compete with the hallowed insignia and garments used in the ceremony. Franz then swore another oath and took communion, which Napoleon did not do.

Because of the constitutional importance of the election, anointing, and coronation of a Holy Roman Emperor, great importance was attached to the imperial insignia—Charlemagne's sword, the jewelled casket containing the blood of St Stephen the Martyr, and the jewelled gospel book. These were kept in Aachen (Aix-la-Chapelle) and were sent for on 23 June 1792. Equal importance was also given to the coronation insignia—the crown, sceptre, orb, sword, cloak, gloves, and slippers—which had to come from Nürnberg where they were kept. These hallowed objects were necessary for the coronation to be valid and, because of their high symbolic and auratic value, they could not be allowed to fall into Napoleon's hands, who was well known for acquiring art objects from the lands he conquered and transferring them to Paris. The insignia were, therefore, moved to Vienna, where they can still be seen in the Schatzkammer (Treasury). Elements of Napoleon's two coronations were clearly designed to emulate and compete with the original imperial ceremonial. The constant references to Charlemagne, the presence of the pope in Notre-Dame, and the use of the Iron Crown of Lombardy for Napoleon's coronation as king of Italy have already been mentioned. Another is the presence in Notre-Dame and afterwards at the banquet, seated at the emperor's own table, of Karl Theodor von Dalberg (1744–1817), Archbishop of Mainz and Arch-Chancellor of the Holy Roman Empire.[30] Since 1494, it was customary, after a Holy Roman Emperor had been crowned, for the herald to ask in a loud voice: 'Is there no Dalberg here?'. A member of the Dalberg family would then step forward in full armour and be the first to be knighted by the new emperor. This happened at the coronation of Franz II, and Napoleon too could say that at his coronation there was a Dalberg present. Karl Theodor von Dalberg, however, in Peter Wilson's estimation, eventually 'helped to make it impossible for Austria to retain the Imperial title' because Dalberg 'needed French support [...] to safeguard his own position as arch-chancellor'.[31] He was outmanoeuvred by Napoleon, and one cannot help seeing him as a well-intentioned or perhaps a greedy minnow getting too close to a shark.

No one could have predicted that Franz's coronation of 1792 was to be the last ever coronation of a Holy Roman Emperor, that the Empire itself, founded by Charlemagne on Christmas Day 800, was shortly to come to an end after a thousand years, and that this coronation spelled the end of *ancien régime* Europe. A month after Franz's coronation, on 13 August 1792, Louis XVI was arrested. The French monarchy was abolished on 21 September 1792, and on 21 January 1793, Louis, Franz's uncle by marriage, was beheaded. When the French Senate ratified the new constitution, which created Napoleon hereditary emperor of the French on 18 May 1804, Franz and his ministers felt impelled to act. On 11 August 1804, in the proclamation called the 'Allerhöchste Pragmatikalordnung', he created himself the hereditary emperor of Austria as Franz I.[32] As he explains in that document, he felt it incumbent upon him, 'as the ruler of the house and monarchy of Austria' to maintain equal status with the Russian Tsar and the new sovereign of France, a personage he does not deign to name. His imperial title is justified, he says, by the ancient glory of his dynasty, and by the large size and population of his dominions. From 1804 to 1806, Franz was both Franz II, Holy Roman Emperor, and Franz I, emperor of Austria. In 1804, Franz had no intention of giving up his imperial title—he referred to himself at this time as 'erwählter Kaiser' (elected emperor). By 1806, however, he was forced into it by circumstance. On 1 August 1806, the German states belonging to the Confederation of the Rhine declared their exit from the Empire, Franz finally abdicated on 6 August 1806 and brought the Holy Roman Empire of the German Nation to an end just over a thousand years after its foundation.[33]

The period running up to this abdication is a low point in Austrian history, one in which Austria was not only defeated but humiliated over and over again. The Austrian forces were defeated by France at the Battles of Marengo and Hohenlinden and had to sign the Treaty of Lunéville in February 1801, allowing the French to extend their control to the left bank of the Rhine. In September and

October 1805, Napoleon defeated the army of Karl Mack von Leiberich (1752–1828) at Ulm, marched into Vienna in November, and comprehensively defeated the Austrian and Russian forces at the Battle of Austerlitz on 2 December. In Vienna, Napoleon occupied Franz's palace of Schönbrunn. Austria had to conclude the Treaty of Pressburg with France on 26 December 1805, giving up Venetia to Napoleon's Kingdom of Italy and ceding Tyrol to Bavaria. In the dignified but regretful statement announcing his abdication and dissolving the Holy Roman Empire, Franz stated that the terms of the Peace of Pressburg made it impossible for him to keep the promises he had made at his election as Holy Roman Emperor and that, furthermore, the withdrawal of a number of German territories from the Empire in order to form the Confederation of the Rhine made the Empire obsolete. Many of the smaller territories had ceased to exist as independent entities in any case, once France had taken over their territories on the left bank of the Rhine in 1803. Franz was also, of course, afraid that Napoleon would convince or compel the German princes to elect him Holy Roman Emperor. This was not fanciful, for in 1808 in Erfurt, at the meeting between Tsar Alexander I and Napoleon, the kings of Bavaria, Saxony, Württemberg, and the newly created kingdom of Westphalia, as well as thirty-four German princes swore allegiance to Napoleon. Franz refused to attend. The imperial insignia and the imperial garments were now museum pieces, relics of an empire that had ceased to exist. Though Archduke Karl (1771–1847), the emperor's brother and a gifted military commander, inflicted his first defeat on Napoleon at the Battle of Aspern in late May 1809, Napoleon comprehensively defeated the Austrian army again at the Battle of Wagram in early July 1809 and entered Vienna, again taking up residence in Schönbrunn. Austria was forced to sign the Treaty of Schönbrunn on 14 October 1809, accepting particularly harsh terms, losing its access to the sea and ceding c.100,000 square kilometres of territory with a population of about three and a half million people to France and its allies. Austria also had to pay France an indemnity of 85 million francs, accede to the Continental blockade against Britain, and reduce its army to a mere 150,000 men.

Having divorced his first wife Joséphine de Beauharnais on the grounds that she was too old to bear him the son he needed to continue the Bonaparte dynasty, Napoleon was looking around Europe for a bride. In spite of his military victories, the court he had called into being, and the traditions he had invented, what he did not have and could never acquire was royal descent. He was very aware that the one thing that could not be fabricated was a royal bloodline: a person either did or did not have the blood of the Habsburgs or of the Bourbons running in their veins. His bride therefore had to belong to one of Europe's old-established ruling houses. The Austrian Foreign Minister, Count Clemens von Metternich (1773–1859), fearful that Napoleon would chose a Russian Grand Duchess and that the ensuing alliance would split Europe into a French Empire in the west and a Russian one in the east, with Austria a power of the second rank, had various diplomats drop hints at the French court that the Habsburg princess Marie-Louise (1791–1847) would make a suitable Empress of the French.[34] By marrying Marie-Louise, as he did in 1809, Napoleon ensured that the son she bore him a year later was at least half a Habsburg.

Austria was not just in trouble on the military front, but financially, and its bureaucracy was simply not fit for purpose.[35] Ludwig von Cobenzl (1753–1809), vice chancellor for foreign affairs from September 1801, and Franz von Colloredo-Wallsee (1736–1806), 'Kabinettssekretär' and confidant of the emperor,

> agreed that the finances were a shambles, that the military in its present state was incapable of mounting an effective defense, that officials were lax in carrying out their duties, and that the government in general had reached such a state of lethargy and incapacity that it might have become impervious to improvement.[36]

While Napoleon was dominating Europe and creating an ever more magnificent and glamorous court, Franz I, by temperament a quiet, unshowy, unheroic person, most often to be seen in a black frock coat just like his subjects or at most in military uniform, carried on fulfilling his daily duties, sitting in his study, as depicted in Johann Stephan Decker's painting of 1826, the very model of the administrator king (Figure 6).

Figure 6 Franz I, emperor of Austria, in his study. Engraving after the oil painting by Johann Stephan Decker. A. Dagli Orti/De Agostini Picture Library/Bridgeman Images

He liked to postpone difficult decisions, being particularly loth to make them in front of others. He preferred to read the paperwork after a meeting and did nothing with any urgency. Because of his work habits, no one else felt any urgency either, and the bureaucracy had practically ground to a halt. The chief elements in his public persona were the peacemaker, the family man, and the father of the nation, who was perceived as behaving towards his subjects with charity, simplicity, and respect. Cobenzl, however, felt that Franz should cut much more of a dash and should 'show himself to his people with sufficient fanfare and representation for his dignity'. Instead of travelling in a two-horse carriage, 'he should have at least six horses with at least four Hungarian guards in their flashy red uniforms and on their white horses and perhaps a carriage or two full of chamberlains trailing behind.'[37] In other words, what was missing was spectacle, what Walter Bagehot in 1867 called 'the dignified element' of government.[38]

The Franzensburg

Franz, however, was not Napoleon. Certainly, only eleven days after the proclamation of the Austrian Empire, on 22 August 1804, he ordered his Chief Building Inspector Vinzenz Freiherr von Struppi (1733–1810) to begin the construction of a new 'Zeremoniensaal' or grand reception room according to the plans of court architect Louis de Montoyer (1749–1811),[39] and, as Werner Telesko points out, some of the stucco reliefs by Augustin Robatz depicted scenes from the reign of the wise ruler Franz.[40] But this could not be considered a projection of power on the Napoleonic scale. Dynasty and ancient descent, not outward show, were Franz's unbeatable advantages over his French adversary, for in those areas a Bonaparte, no matter how great his military might, could never trump a Habsburg. From 1798 on, Franz began to invest time and his own money in a project that emphasized his ancient Habsburg lineage. This project was the construction, furnishing, and decoration of a mock-Gothic castle called the Franzensburg, set in a medieval landscape laid out in a beautiful park next to the summer palace of Laxenburg just outside Vienna (Figure 7). The building was a retreat from the city, surrounded as it was by trees and, from 1807, by water, when the lake was enlarged and the castle could only be reached by means of a short ferry ride. To provide the appearance of an ancient building, two chapels at Klosterneuburg, the 'Capella speciosa' dating to 1222 and the Kreuz- und Sebastianikapelle from 1421, were torn down to provide building material.[41] Franz's project manager Michael Sebastian Riedl (1763–1850), custodian of the emperor's privy purse from 1800 and then commandant of the Franzensburg, was commissioned to travel all over Lower and Upper Austria, seeking out and acquiring real medieval panelling, wooden ceilings and doorways, wall hangings,

Figure 7 Franzensburg, Vienna, exterior view. Photo © Ekkehard Henschke

paintings of saints, furniture, and other objects in convents and abbeys such as Säusenstein and Waldhausen, Melk, Kremsmünster, Zwettl, Klosterneuburg, Heiligenkreuz, Schlierbach, and Wilhering, in castles such as Greillenstein, Rappottenstein, Pöggstahl, and Rosenburg, and even in Salzburg Town Hall, from where a coffered ceiling and leather hangings were taken.[42] All these elements were integrated into the castle, as was stained glass from the church of Maria am Gestade in Vienna, from the castle church of Pöggstall, and from the Carthusian monastery of Gaming. Riedl took away six cartloads of material from the town of Eger (now Cheb in the Czech Republic).[43] All this was to give the Franzensburg an authentically medieval 'feel'. That it should visibly represent the German style was just as important during this period when French Empire style began to sweep Europe. Its political symbolism is in keeping with the 'Old German dress' introduced for special events from 1806 by Franz's consort, Maria Theresa of Naples and Sicily (1772–1807).[44] Maria Theresa's father may have been a Bourbon, but her mother was the forceful Habsburg princess Maria Carolina and her grandmother was Maria Theresia.

There had originally been a plan to build a ruined copy of the original 'Habsburg', the eleventh-century fortress situated on a mountain ridge in Canton Aargau in Switzerland to which the dynasty owed its name. This structure was to have been placed on a rock near the Franzensburg, with a grotto underneath to house the life-size statues of important Habsburgs by Peter and Paul Strudel, carved between 1696 and 1714. This plan was given up and the figures were instead placed in the Habsburg Hall in the Franzensburg, discussed below. The castle was conceived as a museum to which the public would have access and, when the first phase of construction was finished on 15 October 1801, it was immediately opened to the public. Two days after the official opening, the visitor's book records that court servants and local craftspeople visited the castle.[45] A second building called the 'Knappenhof', containing accommodation for the guards and storerooms was to be joined to the castle, with the building work beginning in 1809, but the war and subsequent bankruptcy of the Austrian state brought construction to a complete halt. It was not until 1822 that work began to join the two buildings together. The Franzensburg was finally finished in 1835, the year of Franz I's death.

The castle is a dynastic monument which presents the Habsburgs down the ages but also reflects on their place in history, embodying what Werner Telesko calls 'reflektierte Vergangenheit'.[46] Almost at the beginning of the visitor's progress through the castle nowadays is the Habsburg Hall ('Habsburger Saal'), a rotunda containing seventeen life-size figures of the Habsburg emperors, going back to Rudolf I (1218–91), the first Habsburg emperor, and ending with Maria Theresia (1717–80) (Figure 8). Above each figure is a lunette which shows an important episode during that emperor's reign, for instance, the unification of the

Figure 8 The Habsburg Hall in the Franzensburg. Photo © Ekkehard Henschke

imperial crown with the crowns of Hungary and Bohemia over the statue of Albrecht II, Charles V's crusade to Tunis in 1535 to rescue the Christian slaves over the figure of Charles, or Ferdinand III signing the Peace of Westphalia in 1648. After proceeding through a suite of rooms decorated in the medieval style, we come to the Austrian throne room, installed as early as 1800 and commemorating Franz's coronation as Holy Roman Emperor. Two large oil paintings by Johann Baptist Hoechle (1754–1832) from 1801 depict the coronation in Frankfurt and the banquet that followed. On the floor above is the Lorraine Hall ('Lothringer Saal'), celebrating the combined dynasty of Habsburg-Lorraine which began with Franz's grandfather Franz Stephan, Duke of Lorraine and Holy Roman Emperor (1708–65), the husband of Maria Theresia. In this room, twenty life-size portraits present nineteen male members and one female member of this branch of the dynasty—emperors, kings of Hungary, grand dukes of Tuscany, and Grand Masters of the Teutonic Order. There is a Viceroy of Lombardy-Venetia, a Palatine of Hungary, and an Archbishop of Olmütz (Olomouc). Gorgeously robed, these figures represent the glory of the dynasty and of the Habsburg family at the time of building. Next to it is an anteroom, whose walls are covered with five large paintings depicting episodes from Habsburg history that exemplify Habsburg piety. Examples are the entry of Emperor Friedrich into Rome in 1452, the meeting of Leopold I and Jan III Sobieski, King of Poland, after they have defeated the Turks outside Vienna in 1683, and the myth of Count Rudolf of Habsburg in 1268 giving his horse to a priest to enable him to cross a flooded river and bring the sacrament to a dying man. On this floor too is the Hall of the Hungarian Coronation. Paintings here depict the coronation as queen of Hungary of Franz's fourth wife, Caroline Auguste, in 1825 and the coronation ride of his son and successor Ferdinand (1793–1875) as King of Hungary in 1830, while the stained-glass windows depict Hungarian towns. The Franzensburg continued to be expanded at intervals up to the death of Franz I, and everywhere the eye alights on elements that document the fact that the Habsburg dynasty will go on into the future: stained-glass windows depicting the emperor and his second wife surrounded by their children or the emperor and his two sons, portraits of Franz's third and fourth wives. While statues, portraits, and paintings confront the viewer with Austrian history entwined with the ruling dynasty, the medieval furnishing of such rooms as the dining hall, the reception rooms, or the chatelaine's bedroom projects an atmosphere of timeless continuity.

Franz, the Emperor of Peace

On 16 June 1814, after Napoleon had been defeated and banished to the island of Elba off the coast of Italy, Franz was welcomed back to Vienna from Paris as the 'Emperor of Peace', and it was in Vienna that the crowned heads of Europe and their representatives met to sort out the new political order.[47] Franz was their host from 18 September 1814 to 9 June 1815 and, as the head of the House of Habsburg, the senior European dynasty, took precedence over all of them, just as he had done before the advent of Napoleon. As a projection of imperial power, it could scarcely have been bettered, and there was a constant round of festivities, plays, balls, military reviews, concerts, operas, and banquets.[48] Austria, Britain, Prussia, and Russia, the victors in the struggle against Napoleon, were joined already in the autumn of 1814 by France. But Portugal, Sweden and Spain, Denmark, Naples, and Sardinia, the Netherlands, the Vatican, and Switzerland, along with over thirty sovereign German territories, were also among those represented. Brian Vick points out that it was the Congress of Vienna that first brought crowned heads together 'with the expectation that it might promote lasting peace rather than imminent war', and he shows how conducive the various social events were in bringing the delegates together.[49] At the Congress, chaired by the Austrian Foreign Minister Clemens Wenzel Fürst von Metternich (1773–1859), territorial borders were redrawn and Austria had much of its territory restored. At the Congress too, the 'German Federation' (Deutscher Bund) of thirty-eight, later thirty-nine sovereign German states and free cities came into being. Its purpose was mutual defence and security, and its assembly met in Frankfurt with an Inner Council chaired by Austria. Austria joined Prussia and Russia in the so-called Holy Alliance.

Franz was not so self-effacing as not to want to make his victory over Napoleon visible. In the heart of his capital city, he had a substantial five-arch stone gate constructed by his soldiers, the 'Äußeres Burgtor'. Work was begun in 1818 and it was finally inaugurated on 18 October 1824 on the anniversary of the Battle of Leipzig, the so-called Battle of the Nations in which Franz had taken part, at which the tide really began to turn against Napoleon. On outer side of the gate is the inscription FRANCISCUS I. IMPERATOR AUSTRIAE MDCCCXXIV (Franz I, emperor of Austria 1824) and on the side towards the Hofburg can be read Franz's motto: 'IUSTITIA REGNORUM FUNDAMENTUM' (Justice is the foundation of kingdoms).

Franz was succeeded by three generations of emperors of Austria—his son Ferdinand, his grandson Franz Joseph, and his great-grandson Karl, so that the Habsburgs ruled uninterruptedly until 1918. Karl's eldest son, Otto von Habsburg (1912–2011), who might have succeeded as emperor of Austria, as king of Hungary and as king of Bohemia, died in 2011 at the age of ninety-eight. He had a huge ceremonious funeral through the streets of Vienna and, like his mother Empress Zita, princess of Bourbon-Parma, is buried in the Habsburg Imperial Burial Vault, the Kapuzinergruft in the centre of the city. Napoleon I's dream of a dynasty outlasting him was destroyed by death. His only son—the putative Napoleon II who was known to his Habsburg relatives from 1818 as the Duke of Reichstadt—died of pneumonia in 1832. Though Napoleon I's nephew

Napoleon III revived the Bonaparte dynasty first as President of France in 1848 and then as emperor in 1852, the Second Empire came to an end in 1870 when Napoleon III was forced to abdicate. His son, Napoléon Eugène Louis Bonaparte, known as the Prince Impérial (1856–79) but whom some Bonapartists called Napoleon IV after his father's death in 1873, was killed fighting for the British in Africa in the Anglo-Zulu War. He is buried in Farnborough in England. Dynasties have always depended on good luck and good health.

Notes

1. Dubroca, *Les Quatre fondateurs*, p. vi.
2. Dubroca, *Les Quatre fondateurs*, p. 319.
3. Oesterle, 'Die Kaiserkrönung Napoleons'; Dwyer, 'Citizen Emperor'.
4. Dwyer, *Napoleon: The Path to Power*, pp. 372, 399, and 400.
5. Regnault, *Les aigles impériales*, p. 19.
6. https://www.napoleon.org/en/history-of-the-two-empires/the-symbols-of-empire/
7. Lentz, 'Napoleon and Charlemagne'.
8. Napoléon, *Correspondance générale*, vol. 6, p. 118.
9. Dusaulchoy de Bergemont, *Histoire du Couronnement*, pp. 143–95.
10. Porterfield and Siegfried, *Staging Empire*, p. 7.
11. *Pontificale Romanum*.
12. Dusaulchoy de Bergemont, *Histoire du Couronnement*, p. 167.
13. Alletz, *Cérémonial du sacre des rois de France*.
14. Dwyer, *Citizen Emperor*, p. 165.
15. Dusaulchoy de Bergemont, *Histoire du Couronnement*, p. 182.
16. Bossuet, *Politique*, pp. 71 and 72.
17. Isabey, *Le sacre de S.M. l'Empereur*.
18. Regnault, *Les aigles impériales*, p. 20.
19. Dusaulchoy de Bergemont, *Histoire du Couronnement*, p. 207.
20. Regnault, *Les aigles impériales*, p. 26.
21. Lefort, 'Les Aigles'.
22. Caiani, 'Ornamentalism in a European Context?'.
23. Caiani, 'Ornamentalism in a European Context?', p. 47.
24. Caiani, 'Ornamentalism in a European Context?', p. 68.
25. Mansel, *The Eagle in Splendour*, pp. 61–78.
26. Mansel, *The Eagle in Splendour*, p. 70.
27. Vittet, *L'appartement de Napoléon Ier*.
28. Weber, *Merkwürdigkeiten*; Jäger, *Vollstaendiges Diarium*.
29. Hattenhauer, *Das Heilige Reich*.
30. Dusaulchoy de Bergemont, *Histoire du Couronnement*, p. 151.
31. Wilson, 'Bolstering the Prestige', p. 726.
32. Allerhöchste Pragmatikal-Verordnung vom 11. August 1804.https://de.wikisource.org/wiki/Die_Siegel_der_deutschen_Kaiser_und_K%C3%B6nige_Band_5/Beilagen#Beilage_2

33. *Bey der Niederlegung der kaiserlichen Reichs-Regierung.* Decree of 6 August 1806. https://de.wikisource.org/wiki/Die_Siegel_der_deutschen_Kaiser_und_K%C3% B6nige_Band_5/Beilagen#Beilage_3

34. Palmer, *Metternich*, pp. 73–5.

35. Roider, 'The Habsburg Foreign Ministry'.

36. Roider, 'The Habsburg Foreign Ministry', p. 165.

37. Roider, 'The Habsburg Foreign Ministry', p. 178.

38. Bagehot, *The English Constitution*, p. 7.

39. Benedik, 'Der Zeremoniensaal'.

40. Telesko, *Geschichtsraum Österreich*, pp. 149–50.

41. Bürgler et al, *Die Franzensburg*, p. 37.

42. Telesko, *Geschichtsraum Österreich*, pp. 174–86.

43. Telesko, *Geschichtsraum Österreich*, p. 177.

44. Schneider, 'Herkunft und Verbreitungsformen'.

45. Bürgler et al, *Die Franzensburg*, p. 38.

46. Telesko, *Geschichtsraum Österreich*, p. 175.

47. *Feyerlichkeiten bei der Rückkehr.*

48. Grossegger, *Der Kaiser-Huldigungs-Festzug*; Grossegger, 'Du kannst Dir keinen Begriff machen'; Hilscher, 'Antonio Salieri'.

49. Vick, *The Congress of Vienna*, pp. 21–65.

II

Adopting the Imperial Idea
Beyond Europe

During the Napoleonic period, what we might call 'the imperial idea' was spreading to colonial territories far from Europe. Having seen the splendid coronation
that Napoleon I organized in 1804 to inaugurate and legitimate his reign as elected
emperor at a time of national turmoil and uncertainty, we might expect that all
new emperors would follow suit, but in fact Mexico and Brazil were the only
territories, not only outside Europe but anywhere, where an emperor was crowned
and anointed in a cathedral on the Napoleonic model. There were only three such
coronations: that of Pedro I (1798–1834) in 1822 and of his son Pedro II of Brazil
(1825–91) in 1841, and of Agustín I of Mexico (1783–1824) in 1822. These
coronations used elements taken from European ceremonial, which also provided
the model for the courts, costumes, honours, and decorations of these new
emperors.

In India, the third colonial territory that gave its ruler an imperial title, the
British invented a completely different ceremony which, if we try to find a
European parallel, resembled an acclamation or 'Huldigung'. The British called
this ceremony a 'durbar', that is, a ceremonial meeting between a ruler and his
nobles, and used it to try to ensure the loyalty of the Indian princes. Lord Lytton,
who invented the 1877 durbar, called it 'the Imperial Assemblage'.

Apart from Agustín and Maximilian of Mexico and Napoleon III of France, all
the other nineteenth-century emperors came to the throne by dynastic succession,
including Pedro II, the second emperor of Brazil. Some emperors had been
crowned as monarchs before they acquired the imperial title. Victoria, of the
House of Hanover, had been anointed and crowned queen of Great Britain and
Ireland in London on 28 June 1838, long before she was acclaimed as empress of
India in 1877. The Hohenzollern Wilhelm I had been anointed and crowned king
of Prussia in Königsberg on 18 October 1861 and was not acclaimed as the first
German emperor until ten years later, on 18 January 1871 in the Palace of
Versailles. Neither his son nor his grandson, both of whom succeeded him in
1888 as kings of Prussia as well as German emperors, were crowned, though
Wilhelm II had a crown made for himself, the so-called Hohenzollern crown, and
hoped for an imperial coronation. The Habsburg Franz I of Austria had already
been anointed and crowned in Frankfurt as Franz II, Holy Roman Emperor, in
1792, long before he constituted himself emperor of Austria in 1804, and in the

Projecting Imperial Power: New Nineteenth-Century Emperors and the Public Sphere. Helen Watanabe-O'Kelly,
Oxford University Press (2021). © Helen Watanabe-O'Kelly. DOI: 10.1093/oso/9780198802471.003.0003

same year he was also crowned king of Bohemia and king of Hungary. His successor Ferdinand I was crowned king of Hungary in 1830, king of Bohemia in 1835, and king of Lombardy-Venetia in 1838. Though articles 12 and 13 of the new Austrian constitution of 4 March 1849 stated that the emperor of Austria would be crowned and though the then Foreign Minister Alexander Bach (1813–93) planned a coronation in 1854, it never took place because of the constitutional difficulties it would have caused in an empire containing territories with such different traditions and ancient rights.[1] Franz Joseph was finally crowned king of Hungary almost twenty years into his reign in 1867 to seal what is known as the Hungarian Compromise of that year which called into being the so-called Dual Monarchy. The emperors of India continued to be crowned kings of Great Britain and Ireland. To repeat: the only territories, therefore, where imperial coronations took place were the colonies of Mexico and Brazil, where the creation of the imperial title was associated with independence from their European overlords, Spain and Portugal respectively. The paradox is that, in order to give themselves legitimacy as they shook off the colonial yoke, the emperors of Brazil and Mexico adopted the time-hallowed ceremonial of European coronations.

How Brazil Became an Empire—Pedro I

The two Brazilian emperors were members of the House of Braganza, a noble family since the end of the fourteenth century from which the kings of Portugal had been drawn since 1640. In 1807 Napoleon invaded the Iberian peninsula, which led to the flight to Rio de Janeiro of Queen Maria of Portugal (1734–1816), her son João (1767–1826), and her grandson Pedro (1798–1834). Their embarkation was assisted by the British and they were accompanied on the arduous sea voyage to Brazil by their entire court and their officials.[2] Thirty vessels with at least ten and perhaps as many as fifteen thousand people set off on 29 November.[3] When they arrived in Rio de Janeiro some seven weeks later, that city only had a population of about 60,000, of whom more than 40 per cent were slaves of African descent. This influx of Europeans changed Brazil profoundly, a change that was recognized when what had been eighteen separate 'captaincies' or regions were united in 1815 in the new Kingdom of Brazil.[4] Rio de Janeiro developed from being simply one port among several to being the capital of the new kingdom. Queen Maria, who had been mentally impaired for many years, died in 1816, and her son, who had acted as regent since 1792, succeeded her as João VI, king of Portugal and Brazil. The acclamation that was customary for the Braganza monarchs took place in Rio de Janeiro on 6 February 1818.[5] Meanwhile, during the thirteen-year absence of monarch and court, Portuguese politics had changed significantly. On 24 August 1820, an uprising at Porto called for a constitutional monarchy, and this was the spark that eventually led to Portugal and Brazil splitting into two separate states. Roderick Barman, in a chapter entitled 'Stumbling into Independence', describes the complicated process by which the vast territory of the Brazilian provinces became one nation ruled over by Crown Prince Pedro with the title of emperor.[6]

In 1821, the Lisbon government demanded that the Cortes be elected according to the Spanish constitution of 1812.[7] D. João, a born procrastinator, now had to consider whether to return to Portugal himself, as he had promised to do in 1807, or whether to allow his son, the twenty-two-year-old Crown Prince, to return to Portugal as regent, with the risk that he might usurp the throne. On 10 February 1821 there was an uprising in Salvador, followed on 26 February by a rebellion of three Portuguese army units in Rio de Janeiro in support of the Porto uprising. D. Pedro calmed the rebellion and induced his father to accept a constitution for Brazil to be drafted by the Cortes in Portugal and to replace his ministers and senior civil servants in Brazil with men acceptable to the military. D. João finally sailed for Portugal on 26 April 1821, after another abortive coup which attempted to keep him in Brazil was put down. D. Pedro was declared regent of Brazil with sweeping powers, though his authority was far from secure either in the provinces or in Rio itself.

Since 1808, Brazil had experienced what it was like to be the centre of the Portuguese Empire but, after D. João's return to Portugal in 1821, it was the Portuguese Cortes which had the authority to decide what governmental and administrative structures were appropriate for Brazil. Portuguese rule over Brazil was always complicated by the fact that it took six to eight weeks for news from one territory to reach the other. In September 1821, the Cortes decreed that each Brazilian province should be ruled by an interim governing council until the new constitution should be enacted, thus decentralizing the country again and under-mining the administration in Rio. A second bill decreed that the regency of D. Pedro was no longer necessary and instructed the king to recall him to Portugal. A further bill proposed the abolition of such institutions as the higher courts and other governmental structures which had been established in Rio during the years since 1808. This caused a number of different groups in Brazil, all of whom had much to lose if these demands were carried out, to unite in begging D. Pedro to remain: Radicals, Masons, and so-called Luso-Brazilians (that is, Brazilians who had studied at Coimbra in Portugal). On 9 January 1822, D. Pedro acceded to the demands of a petition signed by some 8,000 people and agreed to stay, and Portuguese troops were ousted from Rio. The Cortes continued to deny self-government to Brazil, so that the months of May and June of that year brought about an open rupture between homeland and colony. The Cortes voted to send fresh troops to Brazil, which seemed to indicate that it wished to subdue Brazil by force, and it then proposed bringing criminal prosecutions against the members of the São Paolo junta who had invited D. Pedro to remain in Brazil and against the ministers at Rio who had summoned a Council of Delegates. The consequence of this was the famous 'Grito de Ipiranga' or 'Cry of Ipiranga', uttered by D. Pedro on the bank of a small river near São Paolo on 7 September 1822. On horseback and with drawn sword he proclaimed:

> Friends, the Portuguese Cortes wishes to enslave and persecute us. As from today our bonds are ended. No ties join us anymore...Brazilians, let our watchword from this day forth be 'Independência ou Morte'![8]

The role that Leopoldine, Pedro's consort, played in Brazil's evolution towards independence from Portugal is discussed in chapter IV. Once D. Pedro had decided to stay in Brazil, the territory now had to decide what sort of political system it would adopt, maintaining its independence from the Cortes but at the same time its respect for the Portuguese king. The solution adopted was to retain the title of king for the Portuguese monarch, but to give D. Pedro the title of 'constitutional emperor'. At his acclamation on 12 October 1822, his twenty-fourth birthday, D. Pedro publicly accepted the title of constitutional emperor and defender in perpetuity of Brazil. Some six weeks later he was crowned and anointed. His coronation was originally planned for 25 November, as the archival documents show,[9] but it was postponed until 1 December, the date on which the Braganzas first became kings of Portugal in 1640 when João IV (1604–56) freed Portugal from Spanish rule. On that date, therefore, in 1822 in the Cathedral of Our Lady of Mount Carmel in Rio de Janeiro D. Pedro was anointed and crowned Emperor Pedro I of Brazil.[10]

The Austrian ambassador at the time, Wenzel Philipp Leopold, Freiherr Mareschall von Bieberstein (1785–1851), writing to Metternich back in Austria, thought that the coronation was based on Napoleon's,[11] whereas in fact, gesture for gesture and word for word, the actual ceremony used the time-honoured ritual and prayers laid down in the *Pontificale Romanum*. Where Napoleon had combined parts of the *Pontificale* with other elements as necessary, in Brazil it was followed exactly. The organizing committee for the coronation was led by the de facto prime minister José Bonifácio de Andrada e Silva (1763–1838) and consisted in addition of Friar Antonio de Arrábida (the emperor's tutor), José Egydio Alvares de Almeida (Baron of Santo Amaro), José Caetano da Silva Coutinho (Bishop of Rio de Janeiro), and Monsignor Duarte Mendes de Sampaio Fidalgo (Canon of the Cathedral of Rio de Janeiro and Rector of the Seminary of Our Lady of Lapa). On the day of the coronation, the court drove down to the cathedral in a carriage procession from the Palácio da Boa Vista, situated on the hill above the city. The imperial insignia consisted of the sword, the staff, the keys, the imperial cloak, the sceptre, and the crown.[12] D. Pedro wore military uniform with tall riding boots (Figure 9). The imperial cloak, of green velvet lined with yellow silk and embroidered with gold stars, was modelled on the ponchos worn by the

Figure 9 Jean-Baptiste Debret, *The Coronation of Emperor Pedro I of Brazil*. Oil on canvas. Universal History Archive/UIG/Bridgeman Images

indigenous Brazilians. Over this D. Pedro wore around his shoulders a wide collar of orange toucan feathers.[13] After the anointing, he descended from his throne and was presented with the imperial sword and then crowned. This first imperial crown of Brazil consisted of a green velvet cap surrounded by a diadem of gold, with eight palmettes alternating with pearls and decorated with diamonds. Eight hoops set with pearls rose up from the diadem and were joined at the top, surmounted by a globe in the shape of an armillary sphere, with the cross of the Order of Christ, one of the Portuguese knightly orders, on top of that again. In his right hand, Pedro held the immensely long imperial sceptre—some two metres in length—surmounted by a wyvern sejant, one of the symbols of the House of Braganza.[14] This long sceptre is the one element that is reminiscent of Napoleon's coronation.

Romero de Oliveira surmises that the coronation was designed to assert the power of D. Pedro vis-à-vis the General Assembly in Brazil, since the power of an anointed monarch came from God, not from the people, and that it was also intended to legitimize his rule in the eyes of his father and of the Portuguese Cortes.[15] We might add that he also needed to legitimize it in the eyes of his father-in-law Emperor Franz I of Austria and other European monarchs, who at first refused to recognize the new nation, on the grounds that Pedro had rebelled against his own father.

Jean-Baptiste Debret (1768–1848) opens a fascinating window onto Brazil in the period between 1816 and 1831 in the three-volume work entitled *Voyage pittoresque et historique au Brésil* and published in Paris between 1834 and 1839.[16]

Debret, a pupil of Jacques-Louis David to whom he was related, came to Brazil in 1816 as part of a French artistic mission whose purpose was to found an Academy of Fine Arts in Rio and to raise the general level of art and architecture in Brazil. On his return to France in 1831 he published his depiction of the landscape, flora and fauna of Brazil, the customs of its indigenous inhabitants, many scenes from the society of Rio de Janeiro in which every white family had its slaves, and, as official painter to Pedro I, representations of the court, its festivals and ceremonies. It is thanks to Debret that we have depictions of the acclamation of João VI, of the coronation of Pedro I, of the arrival of Leopoldine of Austria, the bride of Pedro I, and of her funeral cortège. The 153 plates are accompanied by detailed texts giving the political and historical context of the depictions, as well as explaining the plates themselves.

Though Pedro I was crowned emperor in 1822, it took until 29 August 1825 for a treaty of recognition and friendship between Brazil and Portugal to be agreed, which was ratified by D. João in November of that year. This finally secured diplomatic recognition for the empire of Brazil from the other European monarchies A male heir, the future Pedro II, was born in that same year on 2 December. A year later, D. João died, which meant that Pedro I of Brazil was now also king of Portugal; however, he abdicated in favour of his daughter Maria II (1819–53) with his brother Miguel as regent. Pedro saw himself as a Napoleonic hero with ultimate authority over the whole state of Brazil and he clashed repeatedly with the General Assembly to which the constitution had given equal authority. Constant and irreconcilable differences led him to abdicate as emperor of Brazil in 1831 in favour of his six-year-old son Pedro II (1825–91) and to sail for Portugal in order to rule as king there.

From Consolidation to Abdication—Pedro II

According to the constitution, Pedro II was not supposed to come of age until his eighteenth birthday in 1843. However, the regency was so unstable that the date was advanced by three years. D. Pedro was declared of age and took the oath of office in the Senate House in Rio de Janeiro on 23 July 1840 and was crowned and anointed on 18 July 1841.[17] Though he had grown up in seclusion up to this point, he was not unknown to his subjects throughout the vast territory of Brazil. In 1838, when he was thirteen, his portrait had been sent out to all parts of the country.[18] It was, however, the coronation that really presented him to his people. The grandeur of the ceremonial and of Pedro's own appearance were designed to confer legitimacy and sacral power on a very young man who had succeeded to the throne of a nation that was only slightly older than he was.

The most important architectural element specially built for the coronation was the sixty-three-metre-long veranda, designed by Manoel de Araújo Porto Alegre, constructed along the west side of the Palace Square. Rather like the structure built in front of the École Militaire in Paris for the distribution of the eagles at Napoleon's coronation, it had a central 'temple' and two side pavilions. On top of the nineteen-metre-high temple was a quadriga bearing the genius of Brazil, wearing a laurel wreath and holding an imperial sceptre. Inside the temple was a throne room where, after the newly crowned emperor had shown himself to the people in his regalia, he held a *beija-mão*, literally a kissing of hands, the traditional ceremony of obeisance. On the ceiling over his head was a depiction of his father bequeathing the thrones of Portugal and Brazil to his sister and to him respectively, while large medallions represented the other great emperors Charlemagne, Franz II (I), Napoleon, and Peter the Great. Franz II/I was Pedro's grandfather and Napoleon his step-uncle. The side galleries, called respectively Amazon and Plata, contained the names of illustrious men of Brazil.[19] The Palace Square had been enlarged, the African and Afro-Brazilian food sellers had been cleared away, the streets were spread with mango leaves, houses had been white-washed, and, at night, their front windows were illuminated.

The celebrations lasted for a week with firework displays, a theatre gala, and a huge ball. All over the city, ephemeral monuments had been erected which were lit up at night. The Temple of Harmony at the intersection of São Pedro and Direita Streets consisted of an arch with the figures of Hercules and Mars on either side.[20] On top of this was a classical temple in which musicians could play. On the pediment were the imperial arms and on top of the roof the figure of Fame with a trumpet. Another arch at the point where Direita Street joined the Palace Square bore portraits of Pedro and his sisters and of the discoverers of Brazil and of Rio. Other structures such as arches and obelisks were scattered throughout the city. There was a Chinese pavilion on Constitution Square and an arch resting on forty elephants at the intersection of São Pedro and Quintana streets. Another elaborate monument on the road from the São Cristóvão Palace was a Gothic structure with fourteen windows and a portico in which stood an effigy of Pedro II in his regalia. Hand in hand with the elaboration of imperial ritual was the revival of an impressive court, such as had existed in the time of Pedro I.

D. Pedro reigned for forty-nine years and, as time went on, became because less and less willing to take part in ceremonial and more and more withdrawn into his own world of scholarship, spending long periods abroad from 1871 on. He was a conscientious and hard-working monarch, but he was tired of the burden of rulership which had been his since his childhood. He had no male heir, his two sons having died in childhood, and he did not consider that his daughter Isabel could succeed him as empress, even though the constitution allowed it. During the

Figure 10 Pedro Américo de Figueiredo e Melo, *Pedro II, emperor of Brazil, at the state opening of parliament, 3 May 1872*. Oil on canvas. Imperial Museum of Brazil. Wikimedia Commons

1870s, he began to reduce the ceremonial aspects of his reign.[21] In 1872, on his return from Europe, he made the ceremony of the *beija-mão* voluntary. On his return from another journey in 1877, he abolished the palace guard with their colourful uniforms and halberds. He only wore his robes of state at the opening and closing of the legislative assembly, as shown in Figure 10, he only held grand receptions at court (*días de grande gala*) on such occasions as his birthday, and he and the empress ceased to be the social centre of the city. If one of the most important functions of a monarch is to be a single, simple-to-grasp figurehead who can awaken reverence, provide colour and mystery, focus the popular imagination, and be a magnet for his people's emotions, then D. Pedro saw less and less point in engaging in the ritual that would have ensured this. He began to be lampooned and caricatured in the local press.[22] On 15 November 1888, a Republic was announced after a *coup d'état*, and on 17 November the imperial family left for Europe. His wife died soon after arrival in Europe and D. Pedro himself died in Paris on 5 December 1891.

The First Mexican Empire and Independence

At the same time as Brazil was moving more or less peacefully towards independence from Portugal, between 1810 and 1821 Mexico was battling its way towards independence from Spain. Fighting on the side of the royalists and against such freedom fighters as José Maria Morelos (1765–1815) was the creole, that is Mexican-born, officer, Agustín de Iturbide y Arámburu (1783–1824).[23] The war was brought to a temporary halt in 1817, when the insurgents accepted an amnesty from the then Spanish viceroy, Juan Ruíz de Apodaca (1754–1835). However, in 1820, Colonel Iturbide, as he then was, proclaimed a new rebellion on behalf of what he called the Plan of Iguala, which he promulgated on 24 February 1821 and which Vicente Guerrero (1782–1831), the main rebel leader in the south of the country, accepted after a short interval. Iturbide claims in the document known as the *Manifiesto* found on his body after his death that the Plan of Iguala was his work alone.[24] Others are of the opinion that it may have been the work of several hands.[25] Whichever is true, it had four main articles: Mexican independence (strictly speaking, at this stage, autonomy); a constitutional monarchy with the Spanish king Ferdinand VII or another member of the Bourbon dynasty at its head; the Catholic religion as the only religion of Mexico; and the unity of all inhabitants of Mexico, no matter what their origin, ethnicity, or social class. Benedict Anderson points out, with reference to Peru, the novelty of the newly independent nation in not distinguishing between ethnic groups but in declaring all of them 'children and *citizens* of Peru'.[26] Here Mexico did exactly the same thing. These articles were boiled down to the so-called Three Guarantees: independence, religion, and unity (or union). This was a compromise that creoles and Spaniards, the church and the landed aristocracy, the rich and the poor alike, could all accept, and so independence from Spain was achieved without bloodshed. Until a Congress or Cortes could be formed and a new monarch chosen, it was decided that a provisional council would rule with a regency and that a new army, called the Army of the Three Guarantees ('el Ejército Trigarante'), led by Iturbide would implement the provisions of Iguala.

The next step towards Mexican independence occurred when Juan O'Donojú y O'Ryan (1762–1821) arrived from Spain with the title of Superior Political Chief of the Province of New Spain ('jefe político superior de la provincia de Nueva España'), more or less the successor to the viceroy, as set out in the Spanish Constitution of 1812. O'Donojú arrived to find a fait accompli: Iturbide had an army of 30,000 men and nearly every city and town had gone over to him. Though he had no authority to do so, O'Donojú had no choice but to sign the Treaty of

Córdoba on 24 August 1821, confirming Mexican independence. O'Donojú believed that, since it called for a member of the Bourbon dynasty to be the new monarch, by signing the Treaty he was preserving an important colony for Spain, and he also thought that the Cortes had already agreed to the plan. On 27 September 1821, Iturbide entered Mexico City. On the following day, amid general euphoria, the Act of Independence was signed and the Provisional Governing Council ('Junta Provisional Gubernativa') and the Regency were inaugurated. Iturbide was made president of the Regency and acted in this capacity from September 1821 until May 1822. Legislative powers were vested in the Junta, but its members had been picked by Iturbide and they gave him such sweeping powers that he could have made himself a dictator if he had wished to do so.[27] After the Spanish king rejected the Treaties of Córdoba, Iturbide was repeatedly offered the throne in the autumn of 1821 and the spring of 1822, but he refused. He finally acquiesced, however, in May 1822, when a demonstration led by some of his troops arrived outside his residence in Mexico City, the Moncada Palace, and demanded that he accept the crown. Congress debated the matter and sixty-seven members out of eighty-two voted to make him emperor immediately, while fifteen voted to refer the matter to the provinces. Two days later he swore before Congress to defend the Catholic religion, to act for the good of the nation, to obey the decrees of the Congress, not to deprive anyone of his property, and to respect the political liberty of the nation and of every individual. He was crowned Agustín I on 21 July 1822, the only native-born monarch in the Americas before Pedro II of Brazil. From this point on, things began to go wrong, and the manner in which Iturbide projected his power as emperor and his inability to satisfy conflicting demands led to widespread dissatisfaction. One element much criticized was his overspending. His court consisted of 134 persons and imperial expenditure was reckoned to be five times that of the former Spanish viceroy. One and a half million pesos were allotted to the imperial house in the budget announced in December 1822. At the same time, because there was no money in the treasury, the army and government officials were forced to take a pay cut of up to 20 per cent, and there was a property tax of 40 per cent. Large amounts of paper money were printed, and officials were forced to accept a third of their salaries in this useless currency. Criticism was freely voiced in the press, which led to attempts to curtail its freedom, and military tribunals were introduced. At the same time, crime rose. Agustín's conflicts with Congress became so insoluble that he dissolved it on 31 October 1822 and decreed that it should be replaced with a 'Junta Nacional Instituyente', with deputies chosen by himself from the members of the now defunct Congress.[28] In so doing, he broke the oath he had sworn at his coronation to obey Congress. After a series of uprisings against him in which he lost control of the army and the country began to fracture into separate provinces, he abdicated on 19 March 1823. He went into exile in Livorno in the Grand Duchy of Tuscany, but returned to Mexico on 14 July 1824, not realizing that he had been outlawed in his absence. He was captured and executed by firing squad on 19 June 1824. His rule had lasted for only eighteen months in total, ten of them as emperor.

How did it come to pass that the title given to Iturbide was that of emperor? Timothy Anna points out that 'Mexico became a monarchy because the Plan of Iguala and the Treaties of Córdoba, upon the basis of which independence was achieved, re-created the supposedly legitimate empire of Anáhuac, or the Mexican Empire'.[29] This is confirmed by one of the documents setting out the ceremonial for Agustín's coronation, in which he and his wife are referred to as the emperor and empress of Anáhuac.[30] The Plan of Iguala envisaged a member of the Spanish royal house arriving as monarch but, once that suggestion was rejected in Spain, the Mexicans felt free to choose their own monarch. The adoration bestowed on Iturbide in the first months after independence made him not just into a hero but into a demi-god, as even the most cursory glance at the flood of pamphlets, laudatory poems and dialogues, published in Mexico in 1821, confirms.[31] The mobilization of support for him in his native province of Yucatán can be seen in the entry of his wife Ana Huarte y Muñiz (1786–1861) into his home town of Valladolid in that province on 21 August 1821, just before the Treaty of Córdoba was signed.[32] This entry was in effect that of a queen.

Figure 11 *Solemn and Peaceful Entry of the Army of the Three Guarantees into Mexico City on 27 September 1821.* Oil on canvas. Museo Nacional de Historia, Castillo de Chapultepec, Mexico/Bridgeman Images

A month later, on 27 September, Iturbide's thirty-eighth birthday, he and his army of ten thousand men entered a decorated and illuminated Mexico City to scenes of great rejoicing in which some sixty thousand citizens of all classes took part (Figure 11). Iturbide, with Juan O'Donojú at this side, reviewed the troops from the balcony of the Viceregal Palace. At a ceremony in the cathedral, he sat in the viceroy's chair. From this point on, and even before he was declared emperor, he was already developing a public festival culture to celebrate independence and the new governmental structures.[33]

Another month later again, on 27 October 1821, the oath of independence was sworn, and it was decreed by the Regency that this should be celebrated throughout the entire country with dances, illuminations, cockfights, and bullfights. In Mexico City, the oath was sworn in the main square where a kind of colonnaded pavilion was constructed in front of, and covering, the statue of the Spanish monarch, Carlos IV. This was decorated with allegorical figures symbolizing Mexico's independence. Some of the main buildings were hung with canvases also displaying allegories, for instance, the canvas covering the building called the Casas Consistoriales depicted Mexico City flanked by Liberty and Peace. The imperial standard, which commemorated the banner born by Hernán Cortés and was the symbol of Spain's power in Mexico, was paraded through the streets that evening with the mayor proclaiming Mexican independence to the four quarters of the globe. The next day there was a solemn mass and a bullfight, and on the third day Iturbide received the homage of the corporations. On each of the three nights, the city was illuminated. Religion played a central role in promoting the legitimacy of Iturbide's power. As explained in chapter VI, the anniversary of each notable date in his campaign for independence was celebrated with a mass or a religious procession.

Once Agustín had been created emperor, there were many other occasions which could be singled out for public rejoicing. On 16 and 27 of September there were festivals to mark the dates on which the fight for independence was begun and concluded respectively. Other important dates were 19 May, the date on which Congress elected Iturbide emperor, 26 August, which was Agustín's saint's day, and 27 September, which was his birthday. Yet another important date was 30 September, the birthday of the imperial prince (the title of emperor was automatically hereditary), while 12 December, the feast day of the apparition of the Virgin of Guadalupe, was also declared a court festival. The feast of St Hippolyte, the patron saint of Mexico City, which fell on 13 August, continued to be celebrated in the city, even though this date commemorated the Spanish conquest of New Spain and ceased to be celebrated in other regions. Iturbide also took part in the Corpus Christi procession held in 1822 on 6 June. All of these festivities were occasions for popular rejoicing on which Iturbide could present himself to the people.

The high point was Iturbide's coronation and anointing on 21 July 1822 as Agustín I, 'by Divine Providence and the National Congress, First Constitutional

Figure 12 *Portrait of Agustín de Iturbide, emperor of Mexico, in his coronation robes.* Oil on canvas. 1822. De Agostini Picture Library/Bridgeman Images

Emperor of Mexico' (Figure 12).[34] Agustín wore a red fringed cloak embroidered with eagles and the letters A and I over a white garment embellished with stars that came to below the knee. An ermine collar, a lace jabot and gold-laced Roman boots completed the costume. He is usually depicted holding a marshal's baton, and a crown adorned with pearls can be seen behind him. That he was emperor by the grace of Congress was made clear not just in his title but because it was the president of the Congress who actually crowned him in the cathedral. Spanish monarchs were not anointed and crowned but rather sworn in and acclaimed, so there was no Spanish precedent that could be adopted. As in the case of Brazil, the religious ritual and the prayers in the Cathedral were taken from a shortened version of the *Pontificale Romanum*, but with some details based on Napoleon's coronation.[35] Agustín and Ana were taken in procession the short distance from the Viceregal Palace to the Cathedral, accompanied by ushers, kings at arms, and pages and with three generals bearing the crown, ring, and mantle of the empress and four the crown, sceptre, ring, and mantle of the emperor. Emperor and empress were met at the door of the cathedral by two bishops and, as in Notre Dame in 1804, processed up the aisle under a baldachin. As at Napoleon's coronation, there were two pairs of thrones set up in the cathedral—smaller ones for the emperor and empress before the coronation and larger ones for afterwards. Once emperor and empress were seated on their smaller thrones and the princes, princesses and the emperor's father were seated near them, the consecrating bishop struck up the hymn *Veni Creator*. The insignia were placed on the altar and then the bishop asked the emperor to swear to serve God, to rule justly, and to protect the church and his people by putting to him the question 'profiteris ne', whereupon Agustín answered 'profiteor' with his hands on the gospel, just like Napoleon at his coronation. The bishop then said three prayers from the *Pontificale*, and the president, vice-president, and secretaries of the Congress approached so that Agustín could swear an oath to uphold the agreement made with Congress on 21 May. Then the Mass began and Agustín and his wife were led to the altar to be anointed on their lower right arms. The bishop blessed the insignia and the president of the Congress placed the crown on Agustín's head, addressing him with the caveat: 'do not forget that this great power which the nation has put into your hands is limited by the constitution and the laws', saying that, if he did anything to the detriment of the nation, these powers could be taken from him.[36] Once invested with the other insignia, Agustín then crowned his wife, as Napoleon had done, and the bishop said the prayer 'In hoc imperii solio confirmet vos Deus' before pronouncing the words 'Vivat imperator in aeternum'. Neither of these are taken from the *Pontificale* but from Napoleon's coronation ceremony.[37] At this moment, the kings at arms positioned outside the cathedral scattered coins to the populace. The Mass then proceeded. Once it was over, the chief king at arms pronounced in a loud voice: 'the most pious and most august first constitutional Emperor of the Mexicans Agustín is crowned and enthroned. "Viva el Emperador!"' and after that 'viva la Emperatriz.'[38] The princes and all the officials present signed the 'proceso verbal' (the official account of the proceedings) and the clergy conducted the imperial couple out of the cathedral again under a baldachin.

The provinces were also urged to celebrate the new emperor and two examples are the celebrations held in 1822 in Guadalajara, 550 kilometres distant from Mexico City, and in Durango, some 800 kilometres distant. The Governor of Guadalajara, Don Antonio Basio Gutierrez y Ulloa, organized a celebration on 27 and 28 August 1822 for the coronation of the 'Héroe Americano', as the official printed notice called him.[39] The houses of the town were to be decorated and illuminated on both evenings. On 28 August, in the evening, there was to be a grand serenade of military music, followed by fireworks. Then the leading officers of the Regimiento de Infantería Nacional Local, together with the other leading citizens, were to carry the portrait of the beloved emperor in a torchlight procession to their quarters, after which there would be more fireworks. Next day there were to be three salvos of artillery and at 8.30 in the morning at the door of the cathedral a company of the regiment already mentioned consisting of five officers and twenty-five men was to let off a salvo at the start of Mass, at the elevation of the host, and at the end of the service. There were then to be more marching and a serenade on the second evening. All shops were to be closed on 28th as it was declared a public holiday. Processing through the streets with the portrait of the ruler was a custom carried out elsewhere in the Spanish colonies to honour the king of Spain.[40]

In a decree dated 29 August 1822, the 'Gefe Político' or Provincial Governor of Durango, Ignacio del Corral y Romero, decided to honour the emperor's Saint's Day.[41] The cathedral was to be decorated with banners and a hanging, and illuminated on the vigil and on the day itself. The houses of the town were also to be illuminated. A mass was to be said in the cathedral, but three theatrical performances were also to be staged on three consecutive evenings, the first two to be dedicated to their imperial majesties, 'and the third in grateful memory of the benefits which the nation is enjoying', and all inhabitants were called to celebrate the 'Héroe libertador'. Twenty songs were to be printed, presumably so that the populace could sing them together, and there was to be a military parade and fifteen cannonades.

Once Agustín had dissolved parliament on 31 October 1822, however, rebellion began to break out in various places and Santa Anna already proclaimed a Republic some weeks later. Agustín, who had gone to Puebla to put down the revolt, returned to Mexico City, and his government decided to stage a triumphal entry. Three days of celebration were to be held on 14, 15, and 16 December 1822.[42] It had been intended that a portrait of the emperor be pulled through the city on a triumphal car on 15 December but, since these dates were too close to the traditional and important festival in honour of the Virgin of Guadalupe on 12 December, it was decided to link Iturbide's image to that of the Virgin. The Virgin of Guadalupe was then and is now the patron of Mexico, and she was associated with the struggle for independence from the beginning, with Miguel Hidalgo y Costilla (1753–1811), the priest who led a revolt against the Spanish, putting her image on the banners of his troops. It therefore conferred great legitimacy on Agustín to place himself under the protection of the Virgin of Guadalupe, so priests and other notable citizens pulled a chariot through the streets bearing the image of the Virgin with Agustín's portrait placed at its base. On the next evening there was another procession, but this time only Agustín's portrait was drawn through the streets in a triumphal car under nine triumphal arches, and the Viceregal Palace on the Plaza Major, now the official residence of the emperor, was hung with painted canvases displaying, for instance, *Union fleeing from Discord* and personifications of Liberty and América.

These festivals could not save Agustín's reign. He need not have died, however, if communications between Mexico and Livorno had been swifter, preventing his return. On his body, between his shirt and his sash, covered in blood stains, a paper entitled *Manifiesto al Mundo de Agustín de Iturbide* (Statement to the World by Agustín de Iturbide) was found after his death.[43] It is addressed to Lord Burgersh (General John Fane, Lord Burgersh, Eleventh Earl of Westmorland (1784–1859)), the British envoy to the Grand Duchy of Tuscany from 1814 to 1830, and is a justification of all Agustín's actions up to the time of writing. In it he expresses deep disappointment at the defection of some of his chief supporters such as Santa Anna. It is a moving document that spells the end of the first Mexican Empire and provides a strange foretaste of the end of the second, that of Maximilian I in 1867, in his case after a slightly longer reign of only three years.

The Second Mexican Empire and Maximilian of Austria

The Second Mexican Empire from 1864 to 1867 came about for quite different reasons than the first. Mexico had gone through a very turbulent period as a republic in the four decades since the First Empire of Iturbide, with frequent changes of president and constant armed struggle. One of the low points of this period was the Treaty of Guadalupe Hidalgo in 1848, in which Mexico had to cede half its territory to the United States. In 1857, a group of liberal republicans led by the lawyer, judge, and politician Benito Juárez (1806–72), at that time president of Mexico (a post he held with interruptions until 1872), introduced a radical new constitution under the heading of 'La Reforma'. This called for the separation of church and state, the sale of church lands, freedom of conscience, of the press and of assembly, and equality of all citizens before the law, thus reaffirming the abolition of slavery. This led to the three-year civil war known as the War of the Reform, in which the conservatives, led by the church and by the aristocracy who had the most to lose, fought against the liberal republicans. The republicans were initially successful, and Juárez and his troops entered Mexico City in 1861. The conservatives thought that, by installing a foreign monarch whom they could control, they could bring Juárez's republic to an end, inaugurate a period of peace and stability, unify the country, and bring about economic recovery. This was only possible with the assistance of a foreign army. Napoleon III, emperor of the French, had been thinking of intervening in Mexican affairs since 1856.[44] Various considerations motivated him—prevention of US expansion into Latin America, access to Latin American markets and to Mexican silver, the acquisition of a springboard for further conquests in the region being the most important. Napoleon III first sent troops to Mexico in 1861 when, together with Britain and Spain, the French invaded. The pretext was to recover a debt: Mexico was in such economic and financial trouble that Juárez had ordered a two-year moratorium on the payment of interest on monies owed by Mexico. Britain and Spain soon withdrew, however, when they realized that Napoleon's goal was to conquer and colonize Mexico, thus breaking the London Convention that they had all signed. The French continued the invasion alone, seizing the chance afforded by the American Civil War (1861–65). This meant that US attention and resources were focused elsewhere, so that they were unable to enforce the Monroe Doctrine, opposing European interference in the Americas. The best way to control Mexico, it seemed to Napoleon, was to instal a puppet monarch. As Erika Pani has pointed out, the Mexicans who rallied to Maximilian and served in his government were not traitors or negligible figures but 'Mexicans of relatively diverse social and ideological or partisan backgrounds, distinguished in the fields of law and culture, with experience in high-level politics since the 1840s.'[45] They had studied governmental systems abroad and were well versed in political theory and believed that an empire, backed by a major foreign power, was the only solution to Mexico's problems and that it would make Mexico stronger and more powerful.

The figure who was chosen as emperor was Ferdinand Maximilian, Archduke of Austria (1832–67), an intelligent, enlightened, and intellectually curious man, who had the misfortune to be born the younger brother of the Austrian Emperor Franz Joseph I (1830–1916).[46] (See Figure 24 below.) He was a distinguished commander of the Austrian Navy and had served as viceroy of the Kingdom of Lombardy-Venetia from 1857 to 1859. However, his views were too liberal for his older brother and Franz Joseph removed him from office in 1859. In any case, Austria had to relinquish Lombardy to France in 1859 after its defeat at the Battle of Solferino. Maximilian and his wife Charlotte of Belgium (1840–1927) retired to Trieste where he built and furnished the castle of Miramar overlooking the sea, laying out its gardens and furnishing the interior with exquisite taste. Already in 1859, he was approached by members of the conservative Mexican aristocracy, asking him to become emperor of Mexico. In 1861 he was again offered the crown.[47] Believing that he would have continuing French support, he swore an oath accepting the crown on 10 April 1864, on condition that the Mexican people elected him in a plebiscite. This condition was only fulfilled by means of a fudge, but Maximilian did not know that.[48] He and Carlota, as she was henceforth known, set sail for Mexico with an entourage of eighty-five people and landed at Veracruz on 29 May 1864. Maximilian created a government and an administration and passed a number of laws which in many cases were as liberal as those of Juárez, which displeased his conservative backers. Napoleon III realized a couple of years after Maximilian's arrival that the 'Expédition du Mexique', as it was called in France, was a mistake and that he needed his troops at home to fight the Prussians. The French army withdrew from Mexico in 1866 and, with the end of the American Civil War in 1865, the US was now able to provide Juárez with arms. Maximilian was captured and, together with two of his generals, Miguel Miramón (1832–67) and Tomás Mejía (1802–67), was executed by Juárez's firing squad in Querétaro on 19 June 1867 and the Mexican Republic was restored.[49]

A 368-page account entitled *Advenimiento de SS. MM. Maximiliano y Carlota al trono de México* (The Accession—or Arrival—of Their Majesties Maximilian and Carlota to the Throne of Mexico) relates not just their accession in a legal sense but their actual arrival, the steps that led to Maximilian's acceptance of the throne, the journey of the imperial couple across the seas from Trieste to Mexico, and then their two-week journey overland from the port of Veracruz to Mexico City.[50] The work is a compendium of various documents—an account of the delegation to offer Maximilian the throne in 1863 by the Mexican diplomat who headed it, José María Gutierrez de Estrada (1800–67), who also contributed a biography of Maximilian, letters describing the sea journey and the stopovers in Gibraltar and Martinique by a Mr Chauveau, an account of the imperial couple's stay in Rome, and their audience with the pope by another of the diplomats accompanying them, Ignacio Aguilar y Marocho (1813–84). Then follow reports from all the local newspapers of the reception of the imperial couple in the various Mexican cities on their route, with laudatory poems and engravings of the triumphal arches. The culmination of the journey and of the account is the imperial couple's reception in the capital and the celebrations there. The account conveys the sense of a chivalrous monarch, leaving his home and voyaging over the seas to come and save Mexico in her hour of need, bringing peace, progress, and civilization. On his arrival Maximilian began his proclamation on 28 May 1864 in Veracruz with these words:

> Mexicans: You wanted me! Your noble nation, through a spontaneous majority, has designated me, from this day forward, to watch over your destiny [...] The Almighty, through you, has assigned to me the noble task of dedicating all my strength and heart to a people which, exhausted from battles and disastrous struggles, sincerely desires peace and well-being.[51]

The speech goes on to mention 'the civilizing banner of France, raised to such a height by its noble emperor, to whom you owe the rebirth of Order and Peace'.

There was surprise that the imperial couple did not leave Veracruz more quickly since a vomiting disease had gripped the town, but they drove through the town in an open carriage and admired the triumphal arches before moving on, successively, to the towns of Córdoba, Orizaba, and Puebla. It took them two weeks to achieve this journey (which would take a total of about five hours on modern roads), partly because of the difficult terrain—we read of travelling by the light of torches, the axle breaking, the rain coming down, arriving at 2.30 in the morning—but also because in each place they were received with great jubilation and spent between one and three nights. Triumphal arches, illuminations, fireworks, gun salutes, banquets, and loyal addresses were the order of the day in each town and there was always a mass and often a Te Deum. The imperial couple also took time to visit hospitals, orphanages, and schools to which they always donated money. In Orizaba, Maximilian set off on his own with only one companion to visit the prison unannounced,[52] and in Puebla they visited the Academy of Fine Arts. He also visited a hacienda to observe textile production. The couple's simplicity is mentioned again and again in the account, evinced by their walking among the people and Maximilian giving his wife his arm and holding an umbrella over her when it came on to rain.[53] Their piety is also remarked on, as is their democratic behaviour, inviting two indigenous alcaldes to dinner and refusing to have the ordinary people kept back when they were out in public. In Córdoba some people were apparently heard to say: 'estos son los redentores de México' [these are Mexico's saviours].[54]

The indigenous inhabitants lined the roads between the towns with arches of flowers and vegetation of which the total was estimated as 1,500. On the outskirts of Mexico City, the couple made a detour to visit the shrine of the Virgin of Guadalupe and hear Mass there. Then they drove down into the centre of the city, along streets decorated with flags and impressive arches, to the cathedral where they were received by three archbishops, by the cathedral chapter, and by all the clergy of the capital. They were then led under a baldachin to their thrones, where a Te Deum was sung. After that, they walked to the palace nearby, where there was the usual series of loyal addresses, appearances before the people on the balcony, illuminations, firework displays, a dinner, and visits to charitable organizations. Since this was the capital, however, there was also an operatic performance in the imperial theatre and a grand ball in the Colegio de la Minería.

The French backing for the Second Empire was visible everywhere and was recognized by the Mexicans. They could hardly overlook it, when the French troops were omnipresent. The French generals Auguste-Henri Brincourt (1823–1909), Ernst-Louis-Marie de Maussion (1817–87), and Pierre-Joseph Jeanningros (1816–1902) accompanied the imperial couple on the road to Puebla, which the commander-in-chief of the French forces, General François-Achille Bazaine (1811–88), had captured only the year before after a siege, a feat that led to his being created a marshal of France. The account mentions how much Puebla had suffered in what are called 'the Republican Wars',[55] and the French victory is emphasized when General Brincourt reviewed the French and Mexican troops in front of the cathedral in Puebla as part of the celebrations for the entry of Maximilian and Carlota. The Mexicans themselves were very conscious of the role of France and of her emperor, picking out the names of Napoleon and Eugénie as well as those of Maximilian and Carlota in coloured lights in Puebla, erecting busts of all four on the Arco de la Paz in Mexico City, and placing portraits of the French imperial couple in the throne room in the palace in Mexico City, where Maximilian and Carlota received the congratulations of Marshal Bazaine. The laudatory poetry too praises the role of the French. A poem to Carlota, for instance, ends with a couplet addressed to each member of the French imperial couple.[56]

Maximilian has often been dismissed in older historiography as a naïve and vainglorious simpleton who devoted too much time to marginal matters such as court etiquette, ceremonial, festivals, and uniforms. It can certainly be argued that he was naïve to put so much faith in his French backer and not to realize that Napoleon did not care about Mexico for itself, but only wanted whatever advantage he could get for France. Once Mexico became a liability, Napoleon withdrew his troops and Maximilian's empire was doomed. From the beginning, however,

Maximilian was determined to do his best for his new subjects and concerned himself with matters of government, administration, education, culture, and the economy. On his journey to the capital, he projected his power through his courtesy, his respect for Mexicans of all kinds, and his charity. He also made great efforts to get to know his empire and travelled extensively throughout the country.[57] However, he knew that, as an emperor, he also had to create a court and an imperial aura, and this is discussed in chapter III.

He also set in train the refurbishment of the Viceregal, now Imperial, Palace in the centre of Mexico City and that of the fortress of Chapultepec, which was then on the outskirts of the city. He began the construction of a ceremonial boulevard called the Paseo de la Emperatriz, running from Chapultepec to the centre of the city, and had other plans to make his capital an imperial city on European lines, as discussed in chapter VII. All this was, of course, very costly, and it is estimated that the imperial court spent 1,700,000 million pesos annually compared to the 71,000 pesos that the presidency had cost in 1860.[58]

To claim legitimacy as Mexican emperor, it was also necessary for Maximilian not just to 'mexicanize' himself, which he and Carlota did by always speaking Spanish, sometimes dressing in Mexican costume and eating Mexican food, but also to insert himself into the native tradition.[59] One of the ways he did this was to celebrate pre-Hispanic culture, as for instance in his inaugural address to the newly founded Academia Imperial de Ciencia y Literatura, inaugurated on his birthday in 1865.[60] It was far more difficult to decide how to insert himself into the story of Mexican independence. He could have simply promoted himself as the heir to Agustín I, as the second emperor who was taking up where the first had left off. This would have been a highly contentious choice, seeing that Agustín had been shot because of his high-handed and authoritarian attitude towards Congress and particularly among republicans. As Robert Duncan relates, one of Maximilian's first problems was to decide on the date for Independence Day.[61] On 16 September 1810, Miguel Hidalgo, the priest who began the struggle for independence, uttered his famous cry, the 'Grito de Dolores', in the small town now known as Dolores Hidalgo. This date was first commemorated in Mexico City in 1825. The President of the Republic re-enacted Hidalgo's Grito an hour before midnight the evening before, Hidalgo's manifesto was read out, and there were all kinds of other celebrations. Independence was actually achieved by Agustín de Iturbide, as we have seen, and the date of his entry into Mexico City with the Army of the Three Guarantees on 27 September 1821 was also commemorated. From 1837, both days were celebrated, but from the period of the Reforma on, only 16 September was marked as a public holiday. In 1863, during the regency, both days were again celebrated. It was therefore a highly symbolic act to choose one date over the other. Maximilian's choice was 16 September, but his intention was to celebrate both Hidalgo's beginning and Iturbide's conclusion of the independence process on that date.

He wanted to be present in Mexico City on 16 September 1864, the first independence celebration of his reign, but, because of a throat inflammation, he could not get back to the city in time. Instead he visited Dolores Hidalgo, stayed overnight, and at eleven o'clock at night on 15 September he uttered the famous cry for independence from the window of Padre Hidalgo's own house, and gave a speech glorifying the struggle for independence from the Spanish monarchs—from whom he himself was descended!—and referring to Mexico as Anáhuac. He also signed a visitor's book placed in Hidalgo's house by Juárez, and ordered a marble plaque to be put up. This went down well with republicans and with ordinary Mexicans but offended the conservatives who had supported him for emperor, for in his speech in Dolores Hidalgo he did not even mention Iturbide.

Supporters of the imperial couple wanted to erect a monument to Carlota in the centre of Mexico City, but Maximilian convinced them to use the marble for a monument to independence, which would contain statues of such heroes as Hidalgo, Morelos, and Iturbide.[62] The ground was broken on 16 September 1863 in Maximilian's absence, with Carlota laying the first stone. For the second anniversary of independence, Maximilian gave further details of what the independence monument would look like: it would be of white marble with a granite dado, and bronze statues of Hidalgo, Iturbide, Morelos, and Guerrero would stand in the four corners. A porphyry column 137 feet high would rise in the middle, with a golden garland bearing the names of other independence heroes spiralling round it and with a gilded Mexican eagle on top. For lack of money this monument was never built, though Maximilian did manage to have a statue of Morelos erected on the hundredth anniversary of his birth in 1865. By 1866, Carlota had returned to Europe but celebrated Mexican independence at Miramar with a banquet and a reception. Maximilian did honour Iturbide by transferring the casket containing his ashes in the cathedral in Mexico City from a modest tomb to an elaborate bronze sarcophagus and, since he and Carlota were childless, by adopting two of the grandsons of Iturbide, one of whom, Agustín, was only two years old.

As Luz María Hernández Sáenz has shown in her analysis of El Diario del Imperio, the official publication which appeared five days a week from Monday to Friday, the range and intensity of Maximilian's efforts on behalf of his people was enormous.[63] Getting up every day at 4.30 in the morning, he tried to implement his vision of a huge territory linked by improved communications—rail and roads between the towns, steamers between the ports—and by an extended telegraphic web; of a country in which foreign companies would invest, founding two banks to enable trade and commerce, and to which Europeans would want to emigrate; of a country in which education at all levels was improved, as well as public health; and which had in its capital city theatres of a high standard, an Imperial Library, and an Imperial Academy of Sciences and Literature.

The *Diario del Imperio* is full of decrees establishing these things, theoretically projecting the power of the emperor. Many of them could not bear fruit, however, given the disunity of the country, the state of the Mexican finances, and the shortness of Maximilian's reign. The *Diario* is, however, also full of court news: the appointment of ladies of the bedchamber to the empress, soirées, and other gatherings at court and, extremely often, the distribution of honours. Like the bearers of ancient royal titles, all of the new emperors dispensed honours— membership of knightly orders or orders of merit—but in their case the new emperors first had to create them. These are discussed in detail in chapter III.

The Delhi Durbar of 1877

Victoria, named Empress of India in 1876 in the Royal Titles Act after consider- able controversy in Parliament and in the British press, never set foot in her empire, which at that date consisted of modern-day India, Pakistan, Bangladesh, and Burma.[64] She had, as pointed out above, been crowned and anointed queen of Great Britain and Ireland in 1838 and named Queen of India in 1858 in the Government of India Act after the suppression of the Indian Uprising of 1857. At that time, British dominion over India was taken away from the East India Company and the last Mughal emperor, Bahadur Shah Zafar II (1775–1862), was tried and exiled, his reign was brought to an end, and his capital city destroyed.[65] Because the title of empress was controversial in Britain, Victoria's passage from queen to empress of India—or 'Kaiser-i-Hind'—twenty years later needed to be marked in some extraordinary way in India, and the man chosen by Prime Minister Disraeli to organize the ceremony was the diplomat Robert Bulwer-Lytton, First Earl of Lytton (1831–91), viceroy of India from 1876 to 1880.

Writing to Queen Victoria in 1876, Lord Lytton promised 'to give every possible éclat to the Queen's assumption of a title, which conspicuously places Her authority upon that ancient throne of the Moguls, with which the imagination and traditions of your Majesty's Indian subjects associate the splendour of supreme power'.[66] Because Victoria was to be seen as the successor to the Mughal emperors, the ceremony of proclamation took place in Delhi, the site of their now destroyed court, and Delhi then became the site of the two succeeding ceremonies in 1903 and 1911 respectively, even though the capital of British India was still Calcutta, 1500 kilometres away. Though Lord Lytton called the ceremony he organized 'the Imperial Assemblage', it was based on the Indian ceremonial tradition of the durbar, the formal meeting between a ruler and those over whom he had authority. As Bernard Cohn explains, the person to be honoured by the ruler offered *nazar*, gold coins, or *peshkash*, valuables, to the prince and in return was given a *khelat*, which usually meant a set of clothes or accoutrements: 'the recipient was incorporated through the medium of the clothing into the body of the donor.'[67] The durbar ritual was meant, therefore, to be a ceremony of incorporation, not, as the British saw it, of subordination. Furthermore, the British misconstrued the offering of *nazar* and *peshkash* as bribery and saw the relationship, therefore, as an economic one.

Lord Lytton took the idea of the durbar, that is, the meeting of a ruler and his lords, but combined it, in David Cannadine's words, with 'an improvised pseudo-medieval spectacular of rank and inequality'.[68] The purpose of the Imperial Assemblage, taking place less than twenty years after the 1857 Uprising (which the British called the Mutiny), was not only to proclaim the empress's new title but to bind the Indian princes to her and to recognize the loyalty of those who had supported Britain. One third of India was governed by between 500 and 600 princes with inherited titles, lands, and wealth, ruling their own states under the British Raj. Referred to by the British as the 'feudatories of the Empire' and as 'the Indian Chiefs', they were considered one of the pillars of the Raj and were to be simultaneously both honoured and brought into line at the 1877 Assemblage.

The memory of the Uprising was an important component in this durbar and in the two later ones held in 1903 and 1911 respectively, for they took place on the very Delhi ridge from where the British had pounded the city in August and September 1857.[69] Lord Lytton and each of his successors set up a huge, tented city here, larger at each successive ceremony. According to the official account of the first durbar, 'Englishmen and Natives were meeting as friends on the spot where they had fought as foes. They were feasting and making merry on the ground where shots were flying, shells were bursting, and the work of slaughter and destruction was going on night and day.'[70] The British may now have considered the loyal Indian princes as their friends, but they made sure to emphasize who were the victors in 1857. The viceroy arrived by rail from Calcutta on 23 December 1876 and was received at the station by various high-ranking British officials and the sixty-three Indian Chiefs (as the British called the various Indian princes) who were attending the Assemblage. Mounting an elephant, he then made a three-hour triumphal progress through the conquered city along streets lined with British troops and with the Indian princes and their retinues lined up at intervals to salute him. The procession 'went along the Ridge so gallantly held by British troops during the height of the troubles in 1857. It passed the monument erected to those who fell...[and] the house of Hindu Rao, which was so bravely defended throughout the whole siege.'[71] Note that the Indian princes did not themselves process, but merely made 'the profoundest obeisance' to the viceroy as he passed.[72] During the week between this entry and the main ceremony, the sixty-three Indian Chiefs were received individually by the viceroy and each was presented with a huge banner, medieval and European in appearance, depicting a coat of arms specially designed for him by Robert Taylor, a Bengal civil servant (Figure 13).[73]

Figure 13 Lord Lytton receiving the Nepalese deputation in front of the full-length portrait of Queen Victoria at the Imperial Durbar in Delhi in 1877. Engraving. Collection Look and Learn/Illustrated Papers Collection/Bridgeman Images

The main ceremony, the Imperial Proclamation, took place on 1 January 1877. The sixty-three Indian princes and important officials sat in two semi-circular tented galleries 800 feet long. The princes had their banners behind them, and they faced a red and gold hexagonal Throne Pavilion in which the viceroy, dressed in the mantle of the Grand Master of the Star of India, sat under a portrait of the queen. Other blocks of seating had been constructed for ambassadors and spectators. After a fanfare of trumpets, the Chief Herald Major Osmond Barnes, a veteran of the Uprising, read out the Empress's Proclamation, which was followed by the march from Wagner's *Tannhäuser*. The Assemblage ended on 5 January with a parade of the troops. This included any retainers that the Indian princes had brought with them, but they were vastly outnumbered by the 13,462 men, 430 officers, and artillery that the British could muster. Any doubt that another uprising might topple the British Raj was surely dispelled by this show of military might.

The well-known painter Valentine Cameron Prinsep (1838–1904) was commissioned to paint the scene, and the painting, to which the princes were expected to contribute, was conceived as a gift to the empress. The enormous canvas, *The Imperial Assemblage held at Delhi, 1 January 1877*, 304.8 × 723 cm, is now in the Royal Collection in London. The extremely colourful work was a kind of group portrait for which Prinsep travelled all over India in the course of a year painting as many princes as he could from the life. It was not completed until 1880 and was received very negatively in London when it was unveiled. Sean Willcock's explanation for the rejection of the painting is that 'the aesthetic discord of the painting flew in the face of the visual grammar that had been established in Victorian Britain to picture stable forms of governance...'. Prinsep's 'representational difficulties...registered a wider British inability to envision (and perhaps even administer) the multi-racial Raj as a viable political entity'.[74]

Prinsep came from a so-called 'Indian family', having been born in Calcutta before being sent back to England. His father and six members of that generation were in the Indian civil service, as well as two of his own brothers. In 1879, he published his informal journal of his attendance at the durbar and his travels round India to paint the Indian princes, and in it he contrasts the exquisite Mughal architecture he sees in Delhi with what he considers the tastelessness of the ephemeral durbar structures:

> This morning I have been up again, and went on to the place of assembly. Oh, horror! What have I to paint? A kind of thing that outdoes the Crystal Palace in 'hideosity.' It has been designed by an engineer, and is all iron, gold, red, blue, and white. The daïs for the chiefs is 200 yards across, and the Viceroy's daïs is right in the middle, and is a kind of scarlet temple 80 feet high. Never was there such Brummagem ornament, or more atrocious taste.[75]

Four days later he goes to see this structure again:

> First acquaintance does not tend to change in any way my first opinion. They have been heaping ornament on ornament, colour on colour, on the central or Viceregal daïs, till the whole is like the top of a Twelfth cake. They have stuck pieces of needlework into stone panels, and tin shields and battleaxes all over the place. The size—which, by the way, will make painting it impossible—gives it a vast appearance, like a gigantic circus, and the decorations are in keeping.[76]

Perhaps, as Willcock suggests, this was intended to disarm criticism before his own painting was unveiled, but it certainly provides a corrective to the eulogistic official account.

On a more positive note, Miles Taylor points out that the British aimed, through the Assemblage, 'to fold the Indian aristocracy into their own monarchical order, not separate them', that 'there was less submissiveness on the part of the princes than is often claimed', that 'none of them made any public show of obeisance to the viceroy', and that the princes 'returned to their territories with their authority and status validated'. Lytton's Delhi show 'was as much a catalyst for catapulting Indian princes into modernity as it was a throwback to an imagined feudal past', he claims.[77] This may have been the case in 1877, but by the time of the two twentieth-century durbars, which are discussed in chapter IX, Indians were demanding a greater say in their own affairs. In 1911, one of the most important princes, Sayajirao III (1863–1939), the Gaekwad of Baroda, staged a small protest at the most formal moment of the durbar by bowing to the king-emperor George V as one monarch to another, rather than prostrating himself, and then by turning his back and trotting off down the steps of the dais. No one thought foresaw it in 1877, but this empire only lasted for seventy years and came to an end in 1947.

Notes

1. Stickler, 'Die Herrschaftsauffassung Kaiser Franz Josephs'.
2. Wilcken, *Empire Adrift*.
3. Rui Vilar, 'A transferência', p. 13.
4. Barman, *Brazil*, p. 44.
5. *Um novo mundo*, pp. 159–73.
6. Barman, *Brazil*, pp. 65–96.
7. Barman, *Brazil*, p. 68.
8. Barman, *Brazil*, p. 96.
9. Schubert, *A coroação*.
10. Romero de Oliveira, 'O império da lei'.
11. Mareschall von Bieberstein, 'Correspondência'.
12. Schubert, *A coroação*, p. 21.
13. Debret, writing at the time, says that they were toucan feathers, but Moritz Schwarcz (*The Emperor's Beard*, p. 53) says that they were the feathers of the indigenous bird known as the cock of the rock and that toucan feathers were substituted in the 1860s.
14. A wyvern has only two legs and a coiled serpent's tail; 'sejant' means that it is erect and resting on its haunches.
15. Romero de Oliveira, 'O império da lei', p. 147.
16. Debret, *Voyage pittoresque*, vol. 3, plate 48.
17. Barbosa Oriente, *Pedro II*; Barman, *Citizen Emperor*.
18. Barman, *Citizen Emperor*, p. 65.
19. Kraay, *Days of National Festivity*, pp. 96–111.
20. Kraay, *Days of National* Festivity, pp. 104–7.
21. Barman, *Citizen Emperor*, p.309.
22. Moritz Schwarcz, 'The Banana Emperor'.
23. Anna, 'The Rule of Agustín' and *The Mexican Empire of Iturbide*.
24. *Manifiesto al mundo*. In the notes, the name of the addressee Lord Burgersh is misread as Bunghest.
25. Rodriguez O., 'Los caudillos', p. 322.
26. Anderson, *Imagined Communities*, p. 50.
27. Anna, 'The Rule of Agustín de Iturbide', p.82.

28. Archivo General de la Nación (AGN), Gobernación, Sin Sección, caja 29, exp. 1.

29. Anna, 'The rule of Agustín', p. 82.

30. *Orden del accompañamiento desde Palacio*, AGN, Gobernacion, Sin Sección, caja 27, exp. 2.

31. Rodríguez Moya, 'Agustín de Iturbide', p. 211.

32. *Entrada pública en Valladolid*.

33. Vázquez Mantecón, 'Las Fiestas para el Libertador', p. 46. Since this article appeared, the AGN has renumbered the boxes ('cajas') containing the documents cited, increasing them in each case by five, so that, for instance, caja 22 is now caja 27.

34. *Proyecto del ceremonial*, AGN, Gobernación, Sin Sección, caja 30, exp. 10; Carbajal López, 'Una liturgia de ruptura'.

35. *Ceremonias de la Iglesia*.

36. *Proyecto*, p. 10.

37. Dusaulchoy de Bergemont, *Histoire du Couronnement*, p. 182.

38. *Proyecto*, p. 13.

39. AGN, Gobernación, Sin Sección, Caja 44, exp. 6.

40. Alberro, 'Los efectos speciales', p. 855.

41. AGN, Gobernación, Sin Sección, Caja 34, exp. 3.

42. Vázquez Mantecón, 'Las Fiestas para el Libertador', p. 68.

43. *Manifiesto al mundo*.

44. Pruonto, *Das mexikanische Kaiserreich*.

45. Pani, 'Dreaming of a Mexican Empire', p. 4; Ibsen, *Maximilian*.

46. Barta, *Maximilian von Mexiko*.

47. Gutierrez de Estrada, *Méjico*. See Pruonto, *Das mexikanische Kaiserreich*, pp. 110–12.

48. Duncan, 'Political Legitimation', p. 32.

49. Kühn, *Das Ende des maximilianischen Kaiserreichs*; Villalpando, *El juicio de la historia*.

50. *Advenimiento*; Pani, 'El proyecto de Estado'.

51. *Advenimiento*, pp. 155–6.

52. *Advenimiento*, p. 211.

53. *Advenimiento*, p. 192.

54. *Advenimiento*, p.176.

55. *Advenimiento*, p. 214.

56. *Advenimiento*, p. 299.

57. Ratz and Gómez Tepexicuapan, *Los viajes de Maximiliano*.

58. Pani, 'El proyecto de Estado', p. 425.

59. Duncan, 'Embracing a Suitable Past'.

60. Pani, 'El proyecto de Estado', p. 443.

61. Duncan, 'Embracing a Suitable Past', pp. 258–9.

62. Duncan, 'Embracing a Suitable Past', pp. 268–9, and Pani, 'El Proyecto de Estado', pp. 444–5.

63. Hernández Sáenz, *Espejismo y realidad*, pp. 41–100. The CD accompanying her book contains a digitized version of the *Diario del Imperio*.

64. Taylor, *Empress*, pp. 167–71.

65. Dalrymple, *The Last Mughal*.

66. Quoted from Taylor, *Empress*, p. 172.

67. Cohn, 'Representing Authority', p. 168. In *Colonialism*, Cohn spells these terms *nazr* and *khilat* respectively.
68. Cannadine, *Ornamentalism*, p. 46.
69. Goyle, 'Tracing a Cultural Memory'.
70. Wheeler, *The History of the Imperial Assemblage*, p. 47.
71. Wheeler, *The History of the Imperial Assemblage*, p. 56.
72. Wheeler, *The History of the Imperial Assemblage*, p. 54.
73. Taylor, *The Princely Armory*.
74. Willcock, 'Composing the Spectacle', p. 135.
75. Prinsep, *Imperial India*, p. 20.
76. Prinsep, *Imperial India*, p. 29.
77. Taylor, *Empress*, pp. 180–1.

III

Performing Emperorship

In 1909 Thomas Mann published his second novel *Königliche Hoheit* (Royal Highness). In it he describes the life of Klaus Heinrich, the young prince of an impoverished territory who has taken over the symbolic duties which his older invalid brother Albrecht is both unable and unwilling to perform.[1] Klaus Heinrich has no skills, not even those of a soldier, and has learnt nothing during his studies, but the one thing he does know how to do is to play the part of a prince conscientiously, always appearing in the correct uniform, wearing his medals, and saying the right thing. At the same time, he has no knowledge of real life and little real contact with human beings. His withered left arm and hand, which he conceals behind his back or by resting both hands on his sword, are a clear reference to Wilhelm II, German emperor and king of Prussia at the time Mann was writing, shown in Figure 14 wearing the uniform of the Prussian Garde du Corps with its distinctive eagle helmet. Klaus Heinrich goes to a great deal of trouble to make his regal performance convincing by learning just enough about the place he is about to visit or the event he is about to grace to satisfy the locals that he cares about them. The creation of symbolic power involves two parties: actor and audience. Thomas Mann writes: 'wherever he appeared it was a red letter day, the people celebrated themselves in the festival, and the humdrum everyday was transfigured and became poetry.'[2] The performance fulfils a need in the audience. If that need ceases to exist or if the performer is no longer interested in satisfying it, the emperor is suddenly unmasked, and criticism and mockery take the place of veneration. At that point he can no longer count on the support of his subjects. In 1870, at the end of the five-year Paraguay War, Pedro II of Brazil became the frequent subject of satirical caricatures. The war, with its loss of life, damaged his image; the emperor began to withdraw from politics and to absent himself from Brazil on long journeys abroad, and there was a great expansion of the satirical press in Brazil. As Lilia Moritz Schwarcz comments, 'these caricatures [...] were clear evidence of his fragility as a public figure, who, having lost (or relinquished) his divine representation, was no longer a convincing "citizen monarch"'.[3]

What is so revealing about Thomas Mann's analysis is that, though many of the emperors this book discusses did have a sense of destiny, their power was quite often more façade than reality.

Projecting Imperial Power: New Nineteenth-Century Emperors and the Public Sphere. Helen Watanabe-O'Kelly, Oxford University Press (2021). © Helen Watanabe-O'Kelly. DOI: 10.1093/oso/9780198802471.003.0004

Figure 14 John Watson Nicol, Wilhelm II, German emperor. Colour lithograph. Private Collection Peter Newark Pictures/Bridgeman Images

Court Society and Courtiers

If emperorship was a performance, the fellow actors who prevented the emperor from standing alone on an empty stage were the members of his court. Apart from the imperial family and the imperial household, they consisted of a strictly regulated elite coterie of aristocrats who formed 'court society'. Some of the male members of this group played a part in the wider world if they were appointed government ministers or diplomats, but, as the role of parliaments and of the press grew and as the franchise widened during the nineteenth century, the centre of national political life was no longer to be found in the court. The overlap between politicians and courtiers diminished as the century progressed. At the beginning of the century, Charles-Maurice de Talleyrand-Périgord (1757–1838) functioned as both Minister of Foreign Affairs under Napoleon from 1804 to 1809 and as Napoleon's Grand Chamberlain, which was not a purely ceremonial post. In the second half of the century, although Otto, Prince Bismarck (1815–98), had constant access to Wilhelm I, to Crown Prince Friedrich Wilhelm (later, briefly, Friedrich III), and to Wilhelm II, no one would ever have thought of this Federal Chancellor and Chancellor of Prussia as a courtier who could be asked to 'ensure that the stars of the Emperor's orders were sewn onto his coats in the correct manner', something that Talleyrand did.[4] The aristocratic members of court society had exchanged the independence and power that they might have had in an earlier age as political actors for the status conferred on them by their access to the monarch and for the glamour of participation in ritualized court celebrations. How many people were members of any court society and how closed that society was varied from territory to territory. It depended at least in part on the personality of the emperor who was at its head and how open he was to newly ennobled wealthy industrialists or bankers.

To become a member of court society under the Habsburgs, a man or woman had to be 'hoffähig'—that is, to have sixteen quarterings on his or her coat of arms, indicating sixteen noble great-great-grandparents. At Vienna it was the 'Oberstkämmerer' (the Lord Chamberlain) and his staff who researched family trees and checked that there had not been any marriages with commoners in the last four generations.[5] At Vienna, in the pre-Lenten period every year, there were two official balls: the so-called 'Hofball' (the court ball) and the 'Ball bei Hof' (the ball held at court).[6] Individual invitations to the 'Hofball' were not issued. All those who were considered 'hoffähig' were admitted to it, as were officers garrisoned in Vienna, and the whole of the diplomatic corps, which meant that some two thousand people attended. There was a lot of waiting around, and the ball was so crowded that actual dancing was more or less impossible. At the 'Ball bei Hof', on the other hand, the three or four hundred families who made up the real court society were invited individually, so that seven hundred people usually attended this event, the emperor and empress dined with their guests, and there was more dancing. It was not enough simply to be 'hoffähig', one had to know exactly where one came in the table of precedence, which depended on how ancient one's family was and whether the family had been 'reichsunmittelbar', that is, whether it had so-called 'imperial immediacy', meaning that it had stood directly under the authority of the emperor before the Holy Roman Empire came to an end in 1804. To come from an 'immediate' family put one ahead of all others at court, though even among this group there were two different grades.[7] These rules of precedence, based not on merit but on birth, constituted a straitjacket which was gladly worn by the Austrian aristocracy right up to the end of World War I, as Brigitta Hamann shows and as is confirmed by the memoirs of Prince Erwein Lobkowicz, a member of one of the oldest families and therefore of this inner circle.[8] So strict were the rules that Countess Sophie Chotek (1868–1914), though a member of the high Bohemian nobility, could only become the morganatic wife of Archduke Franz Ferdinand, the putative future emperor, and was not allowed to appear at her husband's side on any court occasion nor be buried in the Habsburg burial vault in the Kapuzinerkirche in Vienna.

It was possible in Austria to be ennobled for service to the state and given the title of Privy Counsellor. This honour was accorded to prime ministers, for instance. If other persons such as industrialists or high state functionaries were honoured, they could only appear at the Viennese court if given the title of 'Truchsess', that is, Steward. Lest it be thought that Vienna was unusual in its observance of numerous gradations, Rudolf Vierhaus tells us that Prussian court society in Wilhelm II's day had fifty-six classes of aristocrats.[9] As well as the wider group that made up court society, there were all kinds of court appointments which themselves conferred additional status, of which the most important at the Viennese court were the heads of the four major departments: the Obersthofmeister (Lord High Steward), the Obersthofmarschall (the Lord Marshall), the Oberstkämmerer (the Lord Chamberlain), and the Oberststallmeister (the Master of the Horse). These departments formed the household of the emperor, and similar court officers formed the household of the empress and other members of the imperial family. The *Hof= und Staats=Schematismus des österreichischen Kaiserthums* published each year from 1813 lists for each of the male members of the imperial family their privy counsellors, gentlemen of the bedchamber, pages, and officers of the guard; and for each of the female members ladies of the bedchamber, mistress of the robes and so on.

This official handbook for 1814 tells us that the imperial family consisted of almost fifty people, but even if we add up all the members of the various households of these fifty Habsburgs, we would still not arrive at the true figure of all those who formed part of the imperial household. We learn that fifteen hundred to two thousand people formed part of the household of Franz Joseph, emperor of Austria, at any time during his reign from 1848 to 1916. This figure can only be reached if we count all the persons who worked as clerks in the court administration, guarded the imperial family, administered the royal collections, looked after furniture and clothing, said Mass in the imperial chapel, sang in the choir, groomed the horses, tended the gardens, waited on the courtiers, cooked the food, and cleaned the rooms. An Austrian emperor was at the very top of a vast pyramid of people who served his needs but who, in their turn, had to be organized, administered, paid, fed, and clothed. This is true *mutatis mutandis* of all emperors.

The Austrian emperor was continuing a system that had evolved over the previous centuries. It is instructive to examine those courts that had to be created from scratch when a new empire came into being or after an interregnum. The courts of Napoleon I, of Pedro II of Brazil, and of Maximilian of Mexico are revealing examples. As early as May 1797, after a long and hard campaign in Italy, Napoleon rested for ten weeks in the Villa Crivelli at Mombello near Lake Como, and here he created a court around him with strict rules of etiquette, what Broers calls 'a proto-royal court'.[10] He dined in public like a sovereign, allowing Italians to watch from the galleries, and he no longer permitted those close to him to address him as 'tu'.[11]

As emperor, Napoleon created a new nobility and saw to it that those members of his court who no longer knew or had never known the manners of the *ancien régime* should receive instruction.[12] His own imperial title was conferred on him by plebiscite, but, since it was hereditary, his successors would come to the throne by dynastic succession, and a monarchy was thereby re-established. At the time of his coronation in 1804, Napoleon conferred the title of prince on eight close family members. In 1806 he re-established the title of duke and in 1808 those of count, baron, and knight. A special category was the so-called 'victory titles', conferred on successful commanders in Napoleon's many wars. Louis-Nicolas Davout (or Davoust, 1770–1823) is a typical example. He was created Marshal of France in 1804, one of fourteen generals honoured at that time. In 1806, after distinguishing himself in many military encounters, he won the Battle of Auerstädt against the Prussians and was created Duke of Auerstädt. In 1809 he took part in the Battle of Eckmühl and was created Prince of Eckmühl. In the same way, Marshal Berthier was created Prince of Wagram and Marshal Masséna Prince of Essling. When Napoleon's son was born, he was named Napoleon II (1811–32) and was given the titles of Imperial Prince and King of Rome, to mirror the title of King of the Romans traditionally conferred on the son of the Holy Roman Emperor. In this way, Napoleon created an elite round him, a context within which he could perform his imperial role. In April 1806 he published a handbook setting out a system of strictly regulated etiquette for his court.[13] Just like the handbook of Louis XIV's court, *L'État de la France*,[14] Napoleon's handbook begins with the court chapel and the Grand Almoner, that is, the bishop who headed the chapel, and then lists the clerics who were to serve there, detailing the services and even the seating arrangements. Napoleon I's handbook was reprinted by l'Imprimerie nationale in July 1852 at the beginning of the Second Empire.

Roderick Barman describes how, after the regency between the departure of Pedro I of Brazil for Portugal in 1831 and the coronation of his son Pedro II in 1841, a court had to be created more or less from scratch.[15] This involved filling the major ceremonial posts such as Lord High Steward (*mordomo mor*), Grand Chamberlain (*mordomo e porteiro da imperial câmara*), Master of the Horse, Mistress of the Robes, and Grand Almoner. Gentlemen of the Bedchamber were also appointed in some numbers (*gentis-homens da imperial câmara*). Barman describes how the Grand Chamberlain, Paulo Barbosa da Silva (1790–68), had to refurbish the two palaces and order various elegant appurtenances from Europe such as a dinner service, coaches, and barouches. The Austrian envoy Leopold Baron von Daiser-Silbach represented Pedro II's grandfather Franz I in Rio de Janeiro and, clearly appalled by the lack of a proper system of court etiquette and ceremonial, wrote to Vienna at the end of 1840 for a copy of the regulations in force there, for, he said, here 'there exists only confusion and a capricious arbitrariness which at times causes embarrassment and will cause even more in the future.'[16] Action was taken in Rio to regulate access to court based on lineage and office, and it was stipulated which court uniforms were to be worn on formal occasions at court when the emperor took part in the ceremony of obeisance known as the kissing of hands, the *beija-mão*. At this time too, Barman tells us, the knee breeches of Pedro I's day gave way to 'trousers of white cashmere with a gold strip down the leg',[17] resembling in other words the trousers worn by other monarchs as part of their dress uniform.

Maximilian of Mexico, who had grown up in Vienna, also understood the importance of a court to bind an elite to him by structuring court society hierarchically. These persons then came into personal contact with the emperor because they were invited to social events at his newly created court in Mexico City. As Erika Pani observes, 'the court resembled a theatrical apparatus by means of which the imperial government expressed its power and the dignity of the monarchs.'[18] She explains how he and his wife, Charlotte of Belgium, chose who should fill various court offices. She points out that their choice fell on some members of the ancient indigenous nobility, those who were most involved in bringing them to Mexico in the first place, those related to Agustín de Iturbide, the previous emperor, and then those people who could be most useful to them from an economic, political and social point of view.[19] She explains how the festivities organized at court represented a neutral space in which those who represented different shades of political opinion in a divided country could meet.[20] Women were officially invited for the first time, though they apparently found the intellectually curious and better educated Charlotte—or Carlota, as she was always known in Mexico—, something of a trial.

Maximilian arrived in Mexico with a book of etiquette and ceremonial for his new court, the *Reglamento para los Servicios y Honor de la Corte*.[21] He was extremely proud of this lengthy document with its 328 printed pages of text, telling his brother Karl Ludwig in a letter of 24 February 1865 how perfect it was.[22] This book of rules for life in the palace is exactly the kind of step-by-step guide that was needed, if there were to be a dignified and orderly court society in a country that had only briefly had a court more than forty years before and could no longer remember the era of the Spanish viceroys. The *Reglamento* lays down who is in charge of what aspect of the imperial service, what their duties are, when they are to carry out certain tasks, how they are to be dressed, what occasions are to be celebrated, what is the precise choreography for interactions with the emperor and empress both in daily life and on special occasions. Maximilian's strictures on the vulgarity of Napoleon III's court are well known, as well as his perception of the latter as a *parvenu*.[23] The court in Mexico City should, by contrast, have the dignity of the imperial court in Vienna where he grew up.

As well as the text, the *Reglamento* includes twelve diagrams, showing the imperial apartments, seating plans for services in the royal chapel, and charts of how courtiers and visitors are to move through and round the main rooms in the palace on the occasion of court festivals and ceremonies. In its detail on the make-up of the court and its various departments headed by such officers as the Grand Chamberlain and the Lord Steward, its table of precedence, its exact instructions on who is to wait on the emperor and the empress on all possible occasions, the ceremonial to be observed on every occasion from visits to the theatre to religious festivals, and its table of what costume is expected from whom on what occasion, it is clearly Vienna transposed to Mexico City. This is particularly marked in the detailed instructions for the celebration of Holy Week—Palm Sunday, Maundy Thursday, Good Friday, Easter Saturday—, and for the celebration of Corpus Christi. It is also reminiscent of the court of Franz Joseph, Maximilian's older brother, in the repetition at the end of every chapter, in the passages setting out the duties of various court functionaries, that they shall only see the emperor if sent for, that they shall never speak to him about anything outside of their designated duties, and that if they need to communicate with him they must write to him. Maximilian, like Franz Joseph, by regulating the behaviour of his household so rigidly, thereby cut himself off from spontaneous pieces of information or from what might have been useful warnings. The *Reglamento* illustrates, as nothing else could, not only how vitally important for the performance of emperorship a regulated and ceremonial court was considered to be, but also how it could be a hindrance.

The corresponding work for the Prussian court, *Ceremonial-Buch für den Königlich Preussischen Hof*, was composed by Baron Rudolf Maria Bernhard von Stillfried-Alcántara (1804–82) and published in 1877. It is rather different in tone from Maximilian's book of instructions. Stillfried-Alcántara was not just the *Ceremonienmeister* and later *Oberceremonienmeister* at the Prussian court for almost four decades but was also a historian who edited historiographical works relating to the Hohenzollerns and even acted as a diplomat on occasion. The voice of an experienced courtier and genealogist speaks to us from his pages, and his book is meant to be a how-to manual which will answer all those questions that he and his department at court were always being asked. As he says at the beginning of his preface:

> The present book is not a manual of ceremonial theory but a compilation of regulations long in existence and in constant force at the Royal Prussian court; it is a handbook for those persons who belong to this court or who wish to appear there.[24]

Of course, this *Ceremonial-Buch* addresses questions of precedence, etiquette, ceremonial, and clothing, but it is an advice manual, not a dry and intimidating book of rules. Incidentally, where it also differs from Maximilian's *Reglamento* is in its two lengthy final sections on mourning and funerals.

The Viceregal Court in India

If it is important to codify rules for court ceremonial and ritual in which the emperor himself plays a central role, it is even more essential to do so when the sovereign is thousands of miles away and is represented by a viceroy. Lord Curzon (George Nathaniel Curzon, 1859–1925), viceroy from 1899 to 1905, puts this very clearly in his two-volume work *British Government in India*, published just before his death:

> From the days when the East India Company acquired the government of India, and appointed a Governor General, the incumbent of that high office has always been expected to maintain a considerable degree of state, to follow a very strict ceremonial observance, and to entertain on a lavish scale. Such a practice was not only in exact harmony with Indian tradition, which associated sovereignty with splendour, but it was also demanded by the British population of Bengal, who expected the head of the Government, and the representative of their own Monarch, to deal with the native Rajas and nobles and with themselves on a footing not merely of equality but of vantage, and to hold a Court in Calcutta that should more than reproduce (because of the special requirements of the Orient) the etiquette and dignity of the Court at home. Whatever strictures might be passed upon the habits or tastes of individual Governors or Viceroys, that this standard should be upheld has been a proposition of universal acceptance in India. And while those who have ostentatiously risen above it have excited good-humoured criticism, those who have fallen below it have been severely condemned.[25]

At all times, the viceroy in India had to embody the might of the empress, and the only way to do this was through ceremonial pomp and architectural splendour. Mary Curzon, arriving in India with her husband in December 1898, writes vividly to her family in the United States about the special white train in which they travelled from Bombay to Calcutta, about their reception in Calcutta by enormous crowds before going to Government House where the outgoing viceroy Lord Elgin and the three maharajahs of Patiala, Scindia (that is, Gwalior), and Kashmir stood to receive them at the head of the Grand Staircase, covered in jewels.[26] In *British Government in India*, Lord Curzon devotes chapters IV and V of volume I to a description of this mansion as it was during his tenure and illustrates his account with photographs. By coincidence, it was based on his own ancestral home of Kedleston Hall in Derbyshire, largely designed by Robert Adam. Curzon's account gives a good impression of the size and magnificence of the state rooms. The Marble Hall consisted of a central space with side aisles separated by pillars. It was paved with grey marble and could seat 120 guests at a state dinner. Larger than life-size marble busts of the twelve Caesars were ranged along the walls of the side aisles. From the Marble Hall the guest then passed through curtains into the Throne Room. At one end of this room the viceroy's throne was placed under a velvet embroidered canopy:

> It was primarily the Throne Room where Durbars were held, Princes received, and Addresses presented, and where the Levées and Drawing-rooms took place. But it was also the Dining Room on all ordinary occasions, i.e. for parties of not more than fifty, and on the occasion of larger banquets, the meeting room in which the guests were assembled in a row all round the room, before the viceroy and his wife came in for the introductions that preceded the entry into the Marble Hall for dinner.[27]

Mary Curzon's letters also indicate that a dinner for fifty people was indeed quite 'an ordinary occasion' and that grand dinners for 120 were regular events. Lord Curzon also describes the Ball Room and the Council Room and relates that in his time, 'the number present at the Levées (confined of course to men) was, as a rule, over 1600, and on one occasion over 2000; at the State Evening Party, mainly given for Indian guests, it was 1500; at the State Ball 1600 of both sexes.'[28] During the three months of each year that the viceroy spent in Calcutta (six were spent at the summer capital of Simla and three travelling round India), he was obliged to entertain lavishly and frequently, simply as part of his duty to represent the empress and the Raj to both British and Indians, and these duties consisted of:

> two Levées, Drawing Room, State Ball, State Evening Party, Garden Party; together with several balls of five hundred to six hundred persons, and a weekly dance in addition; Official Dinners of one hundred to one hundred and twenty, and smaller dinners two or three times in the week. The principal outside functions were the Proclamation Parade of all the troops in the garrison held on New Year's Day on the Maidan, the annual Convocation of the Calcutta University of which the Viceroy was the Chancellor, the review of the Body Guard at Ballygunje, and countless minor ceremonies or functions.[29]

Lord Curzon describes the two 'great silver chairs of State' which were used 'on State occasions, such as the Levée, the Drawing-room, or official Durbars', and he illustrates this with a photograph.[30] One of these magnificent thrones had lion armrests, the Star of India on the back, and the imperial crown on a lotus flower rising up above the back of the throne. The other, used by the Prince of Wales on his visit to India in 1875–76, had the Prince of Wales's feathers on top at the back. All these huge receptions, dinners, and balls were not, however, Lord Curzon's favourite among his official functions. He writes that 'the Durbar or reception of some great and powerful Indian Chief, who came to pay his respects to, or to be entertained by, the Viceroy', was for him the most impressive ceremony.[31] No one but the retinue of the visiting Indian prince and the viceroy's staff, or his personal guests concealed behind a screen as Mary Curzon once was, were present at this ceremony held in the Throne Room. Her account, addressed to her mother and sisters on 12 January 1899, and his account twenty-six years later tally exactly. 'Each Maharaja', writes Mary, 'comes in the Viceroy's State carriages and escorted by the Bodyguard.'[32] Behind the throne where her husband is to sit 'stood red-clothed chaprasses [attendants] holding peacocks' tails, yak tails with silver handles and huge maces, quite twenty of them, and the big Hall was lined by the guard of Honour'. The viceroy waited for his guest, standing on the dais in front of the canopied throne. The band could be heard playing outside, the crunch of wheels announced the arrival of the prince, he and his retinue mounted the marble staircase whereupon the guns thundered out from the Fort. When the guns stopped, the prince advanced through the Marble Hall and into the Throne Room, where the viceroy either came down from the dais to meet him or waited for him in front of the throne, as befitted his rank. The two groups of officials sat down on either side of the throne, whereupon 'the Chief then rose, came forward while everyone stood, bowed low and presented the *nazar* or ceremonial offering of one or more gold *mohurs* [gold coins] laid upon a white silk handkerchief, which were touched and remitted by the Viceroy.' The members of the Chief's retinue were presented and there was some conversation.

> At the end the Viceroy's turn for the offer of ritual hospitality came; and from a silver gilt platter, presented to him for the purpose, he took the *pan*, a small triangular packet containing a composition of the areca nut cut up in small pieces powdered with lime and wrapped in a leaf of the betel (a small pepperplant) covered with gold leaf. This he handed to the chief who accepted it in the hollow of his hand. Next the Viceroy sprinkled a few drops of attar of roses from a gold and silver flagon on the extended handkerchief of the guest. The Foreign Secretary offered the like compliment to the principal Sirdars [important officials].[33]

This was a ceremony of obeisance by a native ruler towards the empress of India, with the viceroy standing in for the empress. It only took fifteen to twenty minutes, Lord Curzon tells his readers.

The rank of the visiting chief or prince has just been mentioned. It was the British who decided on the relative status of Indian rulers, of whom there were between 500 and 600. It was clear that a ruler as grand and as wealthy as the Maharajah of Mysore or the Nizam of Hyderabad should be treated with as much respect as a European king, but there was a question as to how many of the lesser princes should be recognized. The Indian princes and their titles are listed in *The Golden Book of India*, compiled by Sir Roper Lethbridge and published in two editions in 1893 and 1900. In his preface Lethbridge makes clear that it is the British government which decides if a title, no matter how ancient, can be recognized or not:

> Indian titles are officially defined to be, either by grant from Government, i.e. a new creation by Her Imperial Majesty the Queen Empress through her representative; or 'by descent, or by well-established usage.' The Government alone can be the judge of the validity of claims, and of their relative strength, in the case of titles acquired by 'descent' or by 'well-established usage.'[34]

Because, Lethbridge says, there is no central authority which can openly and transparently authorize Indian titles, this gives rise to great injustice. Lethbridge simply lists all the Indian rulers in alphabetical order, but there was a strict order of precedence, jealously enforced by the Indian princes themselves. One of the ways that precedence was marked was by the system of gun salutes. Of the 500–600 princes just mentioned, only 103 so-called 'salute states' were accorded gun salutes and the number of guns fired in the salute denoted the importance and rank of that territory. The five most important territories—Hyderabad, Gwalior, Mysore, Kashmir, and Baroda—were accorded twenty-one-gun salutes, while the others were given nineteen, seventeen, fifteen, thirteen, eleven, or nine guns respectively. The empress or emperor, by contrast, was given the so-called Imperial Salute of 101 guns and the queen the Royal Salute of thirty-one guns. Looked at from one angle, the gun salutes, like the award of honours and medals to Indians, were acts of respect and recognition; looked at from another, they were acts of condescension.

It was not, of course, only Indian princes who were ranked as to their status. Two thirds of India were ruled directly and, after the proclamation of Queen Victoria as empress of India, an order of precedence for members of the British government and administration in India was laid down on 1 November 1877 and amended on 10 February 1899. At the top of the hierarchy was the governor-general and viceroy of India, and at the bottom at number 78 were the 'Officers in the Third Class Graded List of Civil Officers not Reserved for Members of the Indian Civil Service', a definition one only hopes that the members of this category understood.[35] Hand in hand with this list went stipulations about dress for the various ranks on all conceivable occasions. These, set out over seventeen pages in Herbert Trendell's *Dress and Insignia Worn at His Majesty's Court*, are discussed below.[36] As has been pointed out in their classic studies by David Cannadine and Bernard Cohn, the India of the Raj was stratified and classified from top to bottom.[37] At the top the viceroy represented the empress or emperor through pomp and ceremony. By Lord Curzon's time, the viceroy no longer had a state elephant, so that he had to borrow one in 1903 for the Imperial Durbar described in chapter IX. He did, however, have a band, state carriages, and two steam

PERFORMING EMPERORSHIP 79

launches which could take him up the Hooghly, as the Ganges is called in Bengal, to his country estate at Barrackpore.

Coronation Robes

When Bonaparte was crowned in 1804 as Napoleon I, slightly less than twelve years after the French had instituted a republic after executing their king on 21 January 1793, a very special costume was needed and Jean-Baptiste Isabey (1767–1855) was the man to design it. As can be seen in Figure 1, the coronation robes consisted, first of all, of an ankle-length tunic in ivory satin fringed with gold and embroidered with gold thread, worn with white satin shoes, also embroidered in gold. The tunic almost vanished beneath an enormous crimson velvet cloak with a long train. This came down to Napoleon's feet in front and extended behind him for at least a metre, making it at least 4.5 metres long. It was edged and lined with ermine, which made it very bulky, and was embroidered in gold and silver thread with foliage, bees, and the letter N. Ermine covered Napoleon's breast almost to his waist in a tippet, a kind of bib, and over this he wore the chain and the Great Eagle of the Legion of Honour. A corner of the cloak ending in a gold tassel hung over his right arm, at his neck was a ruff and jabot of fine lace, white satin gloves covered his hands and he wore a wreath of gold oak and laurel leaves on his head. While the wreath gave Napoleon the appearance of a Roman emperor, the voluminous embroidered velvet cloak lined with ermine, the lace collar and jabot, and the chain and decoration over the ermine collar were reminiscent of Louis XVI's costume at his coronation in Reims in 1775. As a man of the eighteenth century, Louis had worn a powdered wig, knee breeches, and silk stockings, but otherwise the resemblance is striking.

This ankle-length tunic and velvet cloak constituted Napoleon's *grand costume*. Isabey also designed a *petit costume* for him, shown in Figure 15, which consisted of an embroidered knee-length tunic with a wide silk sash round the waist, a short velvet cloak over the right shoulder, heavily embroidered with gold, silver bees, and Ns, a plumed hat, and a sword with the Regent diamond in the hilt. With this he wore white silk stockings, shoes, and gloves. By 1811, Napoleon had three velvet and two silk *petits costumes* in various colours, including a green version for his coronation as King of Italy. He wore these *petits costumes* at banquets, receptions, and for his own wedding to Marie Louise, Archduchess of Austria, in 1810. When he returned from the island of Elba in 1814 for what is known as 'the Hundred Days', Mansel points out that he 'insisted on wearing his *petit costume* at the proclamation of the new constitution on 1 June instead of the uniform of the Garde nationale de Paris'.[38]

In light of the contrast between Napoleon and Franz I of Austria discussed in chapter I, we might ask what imperial costume Franz wore when he proclaimed

Figure 15 Napoleon I in his *petit costume*, 1810. Engraving after a painting by Jean-Baptiste Isabey. Napoleonic Museum, Île d'Aix. Photo © Josse/Bridgeman Images

himself emperor of Austria in 1804. The answer, for the next twenty-six years, is none. At the coronations of his third and fourth wives as queens of Hungary, he wore the customary cloak, red tunic, and trousers of the kings of Hungary and the crown of St Stephen. He had never needed robes as emperor of Austria, for he was never crowned as such. In 1804 he had simply proclaimed himself emperor of Austria, in what Brigitte Mazohl calls an autocratic *coup d'état*.[39] When a splendid portrait was needed, he had himself painted, for instance by Johann Baptist Hoechle in 1811, in the robes of the Order of Leopold, which he founded in 1808 in honour of his father, the emperor Leopold II. Alternatively, he had himself depicted in the red velvet robes of the Golden Fleece, as in the portraits by Giuseppe Tominz (1821) and Johann Baptist Lampi the Elder (1825). In these he is shown pointing to the Rudolfine crown which had been commissioned by his forebear Rudolf II, who reigned as Holy Roman Emperor from 1576 to 1612. The crown is next to him on a table and, by drawing the viewer's attention to it, he indicates his descent from centuries of Habsburgs elected and anointed as emperors, thereby conveying his own status and lineage.

In 1830, he was already sixty-two years of age and conscious that he must officially designate his eldest son Ferdinand (1793–1875) as his successor, even though Ferdinand was not capable of governing alone, being mentally impaired and epileptic. In the days of the Holy Roman Empire, choosing Ferdinand as his successor would have meant having him elected and crowned 'king of the Romans'. Franz chose instead the expedient of having him crowned 'the junior king' of Hungary in Pressburg (Bratislava) in 1830. This served a dual purpose, for Austrian hegemony over Hungary was threatened. Franz himself was 'the senior king', having been crowned in Buda in 1792. For Ferdinand's coronation Franz at last needed robes as emperor of Austria, so he commissioned Philipp von Stubenrauch (1784–1848), the leading theatre designer of the day, to produce the design for the cloak that was mentioned at the very beginning of this book. Franz's cloak, though a beautiful garment of red velvet, is far more modest than Napoleon's imperial cloak. For one thing, at only 176 cm in length, it is far shorter and is open down the front, unlike Napoleon's. It is also less bulky, for though it is edged with ermine, it is lined with silk. It is embroidered all over in gold by the master embroiderer Johann Fritz with double eagles wearing the Rudolfine crown and holding the sword and the imperial orb in their claws. On the front of the cloak, the eagles are holding the red, white, and red shield which is the emblem of Austria. The cloak has a border of acorns and oak and laurel leaves, again embroidered in gold.[40] Instead of Napoleon's thick tippet of ermine, Franz wore a wide ermine cape over his shoulders, open at the front and under the cloak an ivory satin tunic embroidered in gold and stopping some fifteen centimetres above the knee. With this he wore white silk stockings, shoes, and gloves, and round his shoulders the chains of the four so-called 'Hausorden' of the House of Habsburg, which included that of the Golden Fleece. It was in this costume that Franz finally had himself portrayed by Friedrich von Amerling as emperor of Austria (Figure 16), an image that was then widely distributed to his subjects in the form of an engraving (Figure 22). To put the dimensions of Napoleon's and Franz's imperial cloaks into perspective, the robe of state or parliament robe of Elizabeth II, the present Queen of the United Kingdom of Great Britain and Northern Ireland, is a velvet cloak 4.5 metres in length and the robe of estate, the actual coronation cloak of the British monarchs, is 6.5 metres in length![41]

Franz I's robes as emperor of Austria were never used for an imperial coronation. Ferdinand I, king of Hungary since 1830, was crowned king of Bohemia in Prague in 1836 with the traditional robes and the crown of King Wenceslas ('die Wenzelskrone'), but the services of Philipp von Stubenrauch were needed again, when it was decided that Ferdinand should also be crowned king of Lombardy-Venetia in Milan in 1838. Lombardy-Venetia was a kingdom created at the Congress of Vienna in 1815 and given to Austria as part of her crown lands but lost after the war with France in 1859–60. For this coronation, Stubenrauch designed a richly embroidered ivory silk tunic reaching to just above the knee and a dark blue velvet

Figure 16 Friedrich von Amerling, *Franz I, emperor of Austria, in his imperial robes.* 1832. Oil on canvas. Kunsthistorisches Museum, Vienna. Photo © Luisa Ricciarini/ Bridgeman Images

cloak also covered in gold embroidery.[42] This was the last time that the Iron Crown of Lombardy, now kept in Monza, was used at a coronation.

Ferdinand was forced to abdicate as emperor of Austria as a consequence of the popular uprising of 1848 which demanded a constitution and the extension of the franchise. This brought his nephew Franz Joseph (1830–1916) onto the throne at the age of eighteen and, though a coronation as emperor of Austria was planned in 1854, it never took place. Franz Joseph's first and only coronation came almost twenty years into his reign when he was crowned king of Hungary in Buda in 1867, inaugurating the dual monarchy of Austria-Hungary and thus publicly recognizing his Hungarian subjects' constitution and parliament.[43] On this occasion he wore the distinctive Hungarian coronation robes and the crown of St Stephen and was invested with the insignia of sceptre, sword, and orb. After his anointing and coronation in the court chapel to the sounds of Liszt's Coronation Mass, which was followed by the empress's anointing and coronation, the emperor rode to the garrison church where he inducted some two dozen notables into the Order of the Golden Spur. He then swore an oath to respect the

Hungarian constitution and rode out to the coronation mound, constructed from earth brought from all the provinces of the kingdom. As ceremonial dictated, he galloped up to the top of the mound where he struck out with his sword to the four points of the compass to indicate that he would defend all parts of the kingdom. The Hungarian magnates appeared in all the glory of their traditional costumes. Franz Joseph's grandnephew Karl (1887–1922) was the last Austrian emperor, the last king of Bohemia, and the last king of Hungary. He was crowned Karl IV of Hungary on 30 December 1916 in a last-ditch attempt to save at least one of the kingdoms for the Habsburgs.

From the various depictions of Agustín, the first emperor of Mexico, all of them difficult to regard as realistic portraits of the man and equally difficult to attribute to named artists, it appears that, at his coronation, he wore a knee-length long-sleeved gathered tunic with lace ruffles at the wrists and a lace jabot at his neck, under a red embroidered and fringed cloak, possibly of velvet, with an ermine collar (see Figure 12). The embroidery on the cloak depicts eagles and what appear to be crossbows with quivers. He is holding a marshal's baton. In at least one depiction he is wearing a bright blue cloth sash, but other paintings show him with a decorative leather belt. If the paintings are accurate, he had a hooped imperial crown set with large pearls. Maximilian, the second Mexican emperor, who was in power from 1864 to 1867, had designs ready for his imperial mantle as well as for his throne before he landed in Mexico, but he was never crowned, and so they remain melancholy reminders of the hope with which the thirty-one-year old Austrian archduke set out for his new territory.

The House of Braganza arrived in Brazil from Portugal, so the new emperor Pedro I, previously the Crown Prince of Portugal, faced the challenge of creating coronation robes that would not simply duplicate those of the kings of Portugal. Jean-Baptiste Debret's portrait of João VI in the Museu Nacional de Belas Artes in Rio de Janeiro dating to 1817 demonstrates that his coronation robes conformed to a European convention: a billowing red velvet cloak lined with gold-embroidered white silk fastened at the neck, a tunic covered with decorations, a plumed hat clamped under the arm, white knee breeches, and white silk stockings. He had succeeded to the Portuguese crown on the death of his mother while still in Brazil, and it was only after he sailed for Portugal in 1821, that his son Pedro, then the Crown Prince of Portugal, broke away from the motherland and named himself emperor of Brazil. As we saw in chapter II (Figure 9), Pedro I created a different costume for his coronation, combining military uniform and riding boots with spurs with a green velvet cloak modelled on the ponchos worn by the indigenous Brazilians. Over that again was a wide collar of orange toucan feathers.[44] D. Pedro had a new crown made and in his right hand he held the immensely long imperial sceptre—some two metres in length—surmounted by the Braganza emblem of a wyvern sejant.[45] This was an imperial costume for an emperor in the tropics.

Pedro I's long sceptre is reminiscent of Napoleon's and was retained by his son, but, instead of his father's military tunic and boots, Pedro wore a costume resembling that of his grandfather Franz I of Austria: an ivory satin tunic embroidered in gold stopping some centimetres above the knee. As he got older and reached his full height of two metres, it stopped halfway up his thigh. Reminiscent of Napoleon's costume is the wide sash and a lace ruff and jabot. Like his grandfather he wore white silk stockings, white embroidered silk slippers, and white gloves. Over his satin tunic he wore the green velvet cloak and orange feather collar that his father had worn. D. Pedro, a very tall man, must have presented a striking picture in this costume when he wore it each year at the opening and closing of the legislative assembly and on other gala occasions such as his birthday, the adoption of the constitution, and the proclamation of independence.[46] As time went on, he only wore it once a year at the opening of the assembly when he gave the speech from the throne.

At his coronation as king of Prussia in Königsberg (nowadays Kaliningrad) in 1861—only the second coronation of a Prussian king after that of Friedrich I, the first king in Prussia, in 1701—, Wilhelm I wore the Prussian crown made for Friedrich I and a red velvet gold-embroidered mantle lined with ermine, but, as befitted his self-understanding as soldier, under the mantle he wore military uniform. His son Friedrich III reigned for only ninety-nine days in 1888 and was gravely ill throughout this time and often away from Potsdam and Berlin, seeking cures of various kinds for his throat cancer. His son Wilhelm II planned a coronation in 1889 as king of Prussia and even had a new crown made for it, the so-called Hohenzollern crown, but this never took place. The imperial crown of the German Empire only existed as an image, not as an actual object.[47] Instead, Wilhelm II was acclaimed as German emperor at the formal opening of the Reichstag in the White Hall of the Berlin Palace on 25 June 1888, wearing the floor-length crimson cloak of the Order of the Black Eagle and a helmet with white plumes. The Order of the Black Eagle had been instituted by Friedrich I, king in Prussia, on the occasion of his coronation in 1701, so Wilhelm II is making a link with the very first Prussian coronation. In addition, since there were no imperial German insignia, it was the Prussian crown jewels that were borne before him into the White Hall. Anton von Werner painted the annual opening of the Reichstag five years later in 1893 and showed Wilhelm not only wearing the red cloak of the Order of the Black Eagle again but this time the distinctive helmet of the Household Guards surmounted with its golden eagle which became his trademark.

Court Dress and Military Uniform

Napoleon's lavish coronation costumes must be seen in the general context of dress at his court. Bonaparte had realized, even before he became Napoleon, that dress was a key tool with which to control those who came into contact with him. Philip Mansel explains that:

> Dress revealed Bonaparte's monarchical ambitions before the proclamation of the Empire in May 1804. Among the early decrees of the consulate was one creating, on 9 December 1799, heavily embroidered official uniforms for the consuls and ministers, followed later that month by uniforms for members of the legislature and the Conseil d'État, in May 1800 by prefects and senators, and in May 1801 by members of the Institut and most remaining public officials.[48]

By 1801 it was already *de rigueur* for everyone attending Bonaparte's receptions to wear either a military or other uniform, if they were entitled to one, or to appear in late eighteenth-century court dress, the so-called *habit habillé*, a costume that had been phased out by now at other European courts. The diplomat André-François Miot, comte de Melito (1762–1841), returned to Paris in 1802 after a two-year absence and commented on the changes in his memoirs:

> The monarchical manners which had begun to manifest themselves at the moment of my departure from Paris had extended their sway everywhere and the little that remained when I left the capital of the austere habits of the Republic and the Revolution had disappeared completely. Brilliant liveries, sumptuous garments similar to those in use during the reign of Louis XV had taken over from the military fashions which, during the course of the Revolution, had influenced civic costumes. No more boots, no more pantaloons, no more sabres, no more cockades: they were replaced by silk stockings, buckled shoes, dress swords, hats under the arm. This had not all become perfectly established, however; the gaucherie of some, unaccustomed to court fashions, the irregularity in others of certain elements of their dress which embodied traces of the costume they had just relinquished, presented a pretty bizarre sight.[49]

Even the First Consul himself got it wrong, reports Miot, wearing a black cravat with an otherwise superb coat of purple velvet edged with gold and wearing white silk stockings. Note how, in the quotation above, Miot characterizes the court costume Bonaparte had reintroduced as that of the reign of Louis Quinze, who had been dead for thirty years, not that of the more recently executed Louis XVI. As time went on, this introduction of colour and display was extended to those who held court office. Jean-Baptiste Isabey created uniforms for each of the departments in the Emperor's household: 'Scarlet for the *grand maréchal du palais*; crimson for the *grand chambellan*; light blue for the *grand écuyer*; green for the hunt; violet for the *grand maître des cérémonies*.'[50] Holders of the important court offices had to order and pay for their costumes themselves. The army too were given richly embroidered uniforms, some of which can be admired today in the Musée de l'Armée at Les Invalides in Paris.

Napoleon himself was a soldier almost constantly on campaign during his ten-year imperial reign and so he wore military uniform day to day. His portraits, for instance, the depiction of him by Jacques-Louis David standing by his desk in his study (Figure 25), show him in the blue and white uniform of a colonel in the Grenadier Foot Guards, the same uniform that Paul Delaroche (1797–1856) painted the defeated Napoleon wearing at Fontainebleau in 1814. Another uniform that he commonly wore was the dark green and white uniform of the Imperial Horse Guards. Again, in contrast to Napoleon, though Franz I of Austria wore the dress uniform of an Austrian field marshal on formal occasions, he was often to be seen, like many of his subjects, wearing a black frock coat (see Figure 6). Several of the myths about 'the Good Emperor Franz' concern him doing a good deed to someone who does not recognize the emperor because of his ordinary clothing—following the coffin of a poor man who had no other mourners or rowing someone across the lake at the Franzensburg, for instance.[51]

However, the Viennese court, like the Paris court, also began in the first decade of the nineteenth century to introduce uniforms for three important groups of men: officials in the various government departments, holders of the honorary court offices such as Lord Chamberlain, Lord High Steward, Privy Counsellor, etc., and officials in the court bureaucracy.[52] After a meeting to regulate official dress was held in Vienna on 2 March 1812, the details of the various uniforms for state officials were finally agreed by the emperor on 25 April 1814 and published in a handy booklet.[53] The dress for high court officers was laid down on 1 July 1814 and that for court bureaucrats on 11 September 1814. Dark green was the basic colour of the coats of the state bureaucrats with facings of different colours, according to which department they were attached to. Courtiers and court bureaucrats wore a colour described as 'stahlgrün' (literally steel green), a green so dark as to appear almost black.[54] In the Kaiserliche Wagenburg (the Imperial Coach House) in Vienna we can still admire the dark green tailcoat of a Privy Counsellor richly embroidered with gold oak leaves and laurels on the chest, collar, and cuffs, as stipulated in 1814. Here, too, we can see how the uniforms of officials in the imperial bureaucracy differed from those in the government ministries. Each uniform indicated the grade a particular official had reached in the civil service, differentiated by the width of the embroidery on collar and cuffs and on whether it was of gold or silver. Holders of court office, ambassadors, and other diplomats each had a dress uniform ('Gala-Uniform'), a levée uniform ('Staats-Uniform'), and an everyday or field uniform ('Campagne-Uniform'). The field uniform or levée uniform of a more senior diplomat was the dress uniform of the next lowest in rank. Military uniform trumped court uniform. Kugler and Haupt point out that a cavalry general who had been appointed to the office of Master of the Emperor's Horse continued to wear his general's uniform with his key of office and did not have a court uniform made for him.[55] In a move similar to that of Austria, Prussia also introduced uniforms for various state servants on 14 February 1804.[56]

Franz Joseph identified much more strongly with the military than had his grandfather Franz I, and all his biographers emphasize the role that military training played in his education, both practical and theoretical. This suited him very well, for he showed great enthusiasm for all things military from an early age and saw the army as an essential pillar of the dynasty. This belief was greatly strengthened by the events of 1848 when the imperial family was forced to flee Vienna and take refuge in the bishop's palace in Olmütz in Moravia for six months. Franz Joseph showed his devotion to the army by virtually always wearing military uniform, either the blue coat of the everyday uniform of an Austrian field marshal or, on formal occasions, the dress uniform with its white coat and red trousers, as in Figure 26. The only real exception to this, apart from some photographs of him in 1867 on a visit to France wearing civilian clothing, was the Austrian hunting costume he wore when engaged in one of his favourite leisure pursuits. Other members of the court entitled to wear military uniform then began to do so, though all the civil uniforms introduced in the early part of the nineteenth century remained in use in Vienna until 1918. In 1849, Franz Joseph also introduced a standard uniform for all government, as opposed to court, functionaries, a dark green coat with red piping and red velvet collar and cuffs embellished with gold embroidery. What it meant to have to wear the uniforms of the period is vividly related by Prince Erwein von Lobkowicz (1887–1965), a young guards officer at the time of Franz Joseph's death. He relates how long it took to don dress uniform with all the complicated tying of gold braid, how difficult it was for a tall man to sit down to dinner wearing a sword and high riding boots, how intricate were the details of each different costume needed on a range of different occasions, including mourning, and he even spares a thought for the servants who had to maintain this clothing.[57]

As the nineteenth century continued, monarchs made their function as commanders-in-chief of the armed forces visible by wearing military uniform. After the Franco-Prussian War in 1870–71 Wilhelm I was invited by the German princes to accept the title of German emperor—he himself wanted to be called emperor of Germany—and was acclaimed in the Hall of Mirrors at Versailles on 18 January 1871, the 170th anniversary of the coronation of Friedrich I as King in Prussia. The various versions of Anton von Werner's famous painting show how Wilhelm, like everyone else on that occasion, including the German and Prussian Chancellor Otto von Bismarck, wore military uniform. Wilhelm I's son, Crown Prince Friedrich Wilhelm, later briefly Emperor Friedrich III, was a decorated army officer who had served in the three so-called Wars of Unification in 1864, 1866, and 1870–71 respectively, so it was only natural that he should wear uniform on a day-to-day basis.

His son and successor Wilhelm II did not have his father's battle honours but possessed a large collection of uniforms and was known for frequently changing them to suit the occasion, rather like theatrical costumes. He even had a wardrobe 'fitted with wheels that could be rolled around the palace to accommodate his frequent, impromptu uniform changes'.[58] The novel *Der Untertan* by Heinrich Mann (1871–1950), the brother of Thomas Mann, whose title has been variously translated into English as *The Patrioteer*, *The Loyal Subject*, and *Man of Straw*, satirizes the unthinking obedience, moral bankruptcy, and hypocrisy of the reign of Wilhelm II. In it the protagonist Diederich Hessling, who is on his honeymoon, follows the Kaiser on a state visit to Rome. Diederich waits outside the Quirinal Palace to cheer the Kaiser each time he appears and to follow him to his destination in order to cheer him again. At the end of the day, when the emperor's car comes to a halt for his last engagement, Diederich 'saw the seventh uniform getting out'.[59] It was not only Heinrich Mann who laughed at this love of uniform, for the eagle helmet and Wilhelm's characteristic upturned waxed moustache were a gift to caricaturists everywhere.[60] Eva Giloi sees Wilhelm II's obsession with uniforms as 'a proxy for military victory', an area in which he could not compete with his father and grandfather, who really were military heroes.[61] He took some forty different uniforms with him into exile in the Netherlands in 1918 and had magnificent portraits of himself painted in some of them, years after he had been forced to abdicate as emperor and supreme commander of the armed forces.[62]

Maximilian, accustomed to court and military uniform from his upbringing in Vienna and his time as governor of Lombardy-Venetia, came to Mexico already prepared with designs for the uniforms for court officers and for the palace guard in Mexico City.[63] The guards' helmets of gilded nickel, surmounted by the Mexican eagle standing on a prickly pear with a snake in his beak, can be seen today in the Court Furniture Depository (the Hofmobiliendepot) in Vienna, and the watercolour sketches for their uniforms are preserved in the Bildarchiv of the Austrian National Museum.[64] These sketches show that the guardsmen wore brilliant red coats decorated with gold embroidery, tight white trousers, and gleaming black riding boots.

Neither Maximilian nor Napoleon III were crowned, but both had state portraits painted in which they wore military uniform and had an imperial cloak of velvet lined with ermine depending from their shoulders, while they stood next to the imperial insignia. These portraits are discussed in chapter IV. Napoleon III, however, allowed himself to be photographed in civilian clothes, and this image circulated widely as a *carte de visite*, also discussed later. As recorded in photographs, Maximilian liked to wear Mexican dress, especially when he was on one of his six journeys away from the capital.[65] The Prussian ambassador, Baron von Magnus, writing to Bismarck in Berlin, found this ridiculous and counterproductive:

And when the emperor is in the countryside and, in order to flatter the people, is riding a mule in Mexican costume or if he appears with a team of mules with bells on their harness, the people call him mockingly 'pulquero', because the sellers of 'pulque', the national drink, usually have bells on the harness of their mules.[66]

Maximilian, it seems, could not get it right. He was criticized if he demanded too much courtly magnificence and laughed at if he did not demand enough.

Dress in India

Britain fully followed the trend for regulating court dress in all circumstances, taking into account the particular challenges arising from clothing imperial officers in tropical climates. In Herbert Trendell's *Dress and Insignia Worn at His Majesty's Court* issued in 1921, two sections set out the dress code for 'Officers of the Government of India'.[67] The various costumes are described in minute detail and graded according to the importance of the wearer. The governors of Madras, Bombay, and Bengal constitute the first class, so their uniforms are described first, divided into full and levée dress. Uniforms of the second class are for the governors of the United Provinces of Agra and Oudh, Punjab, Bihar, and Orissa and the Lieutenant Governor of Burma. The handbook goes on to list a further seventy-five categories of other functionaries who are entitled, indeed expected, to wear third-class full and levée dress. No fourth class is given, but there are ten categories of person who are to wear fifth-class full and levée dress. Also described is civil uniform, divided into the categories of undress (morning), mess dress, hot weather uniform, and hot weather dress uniform. Undress is also specified for classes 1, 2, and 3, and other uniforms are detailed for so-called mounted duties. There is a section devoted to the special uniform to be worn by viceregal staff—a blue evening dress coat with a black velvet collar, the Star of India, a white dress waistcoat and black trousers. The number and position of the buttons with their royal cypher and imperial crown on the front and back of the coat are described.[68]

Trendell also stipulates the 'alternative official dress for Indian gentlemen who may become Members of Councils and Ministers, and who do not desire to wear civil uniform'. This consists of a turban ('a pugree'), a long Indian men's coat buttoned up to the neck and 'falling loose to the knees', worn with white trousers or what are called white pyjamas. As with all the other uniforms, the colour, fabric, lining, velvet collar and cuffs, buttons, and any embroidery are set out in detail and the uniforms are divided into first, second, and third class. Black silk socks are expected to be worn with black patent leather shoes and a 'gilt buckle, rose, shamrock, and thistle pattern'.[69] According to the Government of India Act, passed in 1919, Indians could now become members of provincial councils and of the bicameral Imperial Legislative Council, but their British overlords are nonetheless still telling them how to dress!

The same 'Indian gentlemen' are invited by Trendell to wear their ceremonial national dress instead of uniform on special occasions, and here we see clothing used for purposes of control.[70] Two examples of special occasions were Queen Victoria's Golden Jubilee in London and the Delhi Durbars. The British Raj encouraged and expected Indian princes to modernize in their own territories and to adopt British notions of law, order, education, technology, and hygiene. They were at the same time supposed to look exotic and Indian. Victoria's Golden Jubilee was celebrated in London in June 1887 and eleven Indian chiefs and nobles attended the celebrations. Miles Taylor relates how, towards the end of April, only three months before the Jubilee, the queen indicated that she wished all the Indian visitors to wear native costume in her presence. This created a problem for some of them who were already in London and who were so westernized that they never wore Indian dress anyway. Naturally, they had not brought all their jewels and other exotic accoutrements with them. 'Nonetheless', writes Taylor, [Lord] 'Dufferin ensured that new wardrobes of "oriental costume" were organised in time.'[71] The queen also expected Indian princes to wear their native dress when they came to visit her in Osborne on the Isle of Wight or in Windsor Castle.

The durbars were designed to be pageants of Indian exoticism and the princes therefore were instructed how to dress. A particularly telling incident relates to one of the great princes, Sir Sayajirao III, the Gaekwad of Baroda (1863–1939), second highest in rank among the Indian chiefs.[72] He became the maharaja in 1875 and attended the 1877 durbar as a fourteen-year-old. The official photograph taken at that time shows him wearing a velvet jacket with gold embroidery and silk trousers, a tasselled turban decorated with a large jewelled badge, a jewelled collar, earrings, and bracelets, and holding an immensely long sabre. He took part again in the 1903 durbar, this time as a man of forty, and was photographed sitting, wearing a simpler costume, a long, white, padded silk coat with embroidery at neck, sleeves, and hem. He wore a simple head covering, a necklace of huge pearls and the Star of India, and held a long silver-headed cane. At the 1911 durbar, now a man of almost fifty, the Gaekwar had simplified his costume yet again and appeared before George V and Queen Mary in a long white linen coat over white trousers. He wore a, by Indian standards, simple pearl necklace and the Star of India and carried a walking stick. After he had bowed once to the king-emperor and the queen-empress, not twice like the Nizam of Hyderabad, he moved away sideways, as he was supposed to do, and then turned his back on the royal couple and trotted off down the steps. Newsreel films, shown in Britain and still accessible today, illustrate the difference between his bow to the king and the obeisances of other Indian princes.[73] The Gaekwar was accused in the English-language press in India and in England of a calculated insult, and, though his granddaughter Gayatri Devi, the Maharani of Jaipur, claims in her autobiography that her grandfather Sir Sayajirao had been unable to attend the dress rehearsal and was unaware of the correct protocol, she is alone in believing this.[74] The consensus is that his behaviour was an act of resistance to the control of his appearance and the management of his image forced on him by the British. In her analysis of how portraiture, photography, and dress were used as an instrument of control by the Raj, Julie Codell quotes Viceroy Hardinge's reprimand to the Gaekwar, 'for removing his jewellery and changing into "the ordinary white linen everyday dress of a Mahratta with only a walking stick in his hand"'.[75] Cohn comments that the walking stick, 'an accouterment of the white sahibs, civilian and military', gave particular offence in the hand of an Indian.[76] In other ways too, the Gaekwar was too independent for British tastes, introducing educational and technological reforms and supporting Indian nationalism.

Whichever territory we examine, we see what are, to a modern eye, maniacally detailed instructions about what to wear in order to enforce a hierarchy and control the wearer. At the same time, dress makes the hierarchy visible, in the same way that the system of gun salutes for Indian princes, discussed below, made hierarchical distinctions audible. This obsession with ranking all their members and making that rank clear to all those in the know was a central element of all nineteenth-century courts.

Pedro II—the Exception

The exception to all the gold braid, epaulettes, swords, spurs, and gleaming jackboots that other emperors were wearing was Pedro II of Brazil. When he first came to the throne in 1841 as a very young man, he wore the formal dress of a senior European courtier, which was the alternative to military uniform, that is, a heavily embroidered close-fitting jacket with a high collar. From the 1860s, however, he was often, and from the 1870s invariably, dressed in a black double-breasted coat.[77] On one of his protracted journeys, he visited the imperial and Prussian court of Berlin in April 1877. Crown Princess Victoria reports to her mother Queen Victoria that he and his wife 'made a very good impression, except that everyone at Court (gentlemen and ladies) were horrified at the Emperor's persistently appearing at the Court soirées with a black cravat and without any orders, and all his gentlemen with black cravats'.[78] He had not changed his habits by the time he arrived at Windsor at the court of the queen-empress and caused just as much upset there. Queen Victoria's comment to her daughter on 2 July 1877 was: 'But to come to the State Ball and Concert in a frock coat—with a black cravat and boots—is really quite incomprehensible and shocked people here very much.'[79] Pedro II clearly did not feel out of place at a splendid event such as a state ball at which every other man present was wearing dress uniform, either military or court, and all their decorations!

Medals, Honours, and Decorations

That honours, decorations, and medals were a *sine qua non* of court costume for anyone who was entitled to wear them can be seen in any portrait or photograph of a courtier or aristocrat during the nineteenth and early twentieth centuries. On formal occasions, important figures are often covered in medals, chains, and insignia. These decorations originally denoted membership in an order of chivalry and were religious in nature. However, from the late Middle Ages on these orders had become more secular, with their own statutes and rules and a Grand Master whom they had to obey. Membership of such an order was denoted by special clothing and insignia and, since in a monarchy the Grand Master was always the sovereign, members of the order were bound closely to him by an oath of loyalty. The British Order of the Garter, founded in 1348, is one example of such an ancient order still in existence. Apart from the monarch and the Prince of Wales, it can only have twenty-four full members at any one time, though it is allowed to name additional so-called 'supernumerary members', usually other members of the royal family or foreign dignitaries. The Order of the Golden Fleece, of which today there is a Spanish and an Austrian branch, was founded in 1430 and is similarly limited in the number of its members. The Austrian branch remains close to its founding principles, for it is still dedicated to protecting the Catholic Church and its members have to be Catholics and high aristocrats, while the Spanish branch is now an order of merit and can admit anyone of any faith or rank. As well as the Golden Fleece, which all Austrian emperors, archdukes, and other high Austrian aristocrats are portrayed wearing, there were another three so-called Austrian 'Hausorden' or family orders: the Order of St Stephen, founded in the eighteenth century by Maria Theresia, the Order of Leopold, founded by Franz I in 1808, and the Order of the Iron Crown, founded by Napoleon in 1805 at his Italian coronation in Milan but revived in 1816 by Franz I, since Austria now ruled Lombardy-Venetia.

Apart from the ancient orders of chivalry, most other orders in the period we are discussing were orders of merit, that is, the decoration was conferred as a reward for outstanding service. Napoleon created the first such order, the Legion of Honour, still important in France today. Napoleon—or Bonaparte, as he still was—proposed the Legion to his colleagues on the Council of State in 1802 when he was First Consul, explaining what he thought the point of such a decoration was. He wanted, he said, some way to acknowledge bravery on the battlefield and long military service but also learning, artistic achievement, and service to the state, and he wanted it to be open to all in the spirit of equality of the French

Revolution. He had difficulty getting the idea accepted, however, and the Tribune only passed the necessary legislation by fifty-six votes to thirty-eight and the Legislature by 166 votes to 110. In the Council of State he was opposed by Counsellor Berlier who said that such toys and ribbons should be reserved for monarchies and were unworthy of a Republic such as France had become. Napoleon replied with characteristic pragmatic cynicism, using the word 'hochets', literally, rattles or toys:

> The Romans had patricians, knights, citizens and slaves. For each thing they had a different costume, different customs. They observed all sorts of distinctions, names which made reference to past service, mural crowns, the triumph! I challenge anyone to show me an ancient or modern republic which has not had distinctions. These are called children's toys! Well, it's by means of toys that people are led.[80]

After he became emperor, in a decree issued on 30 January 1805, Napoleon made the Legion of Honour more regal by instituting a grand decoration. This decoration, a cross on a large sash and a silver star with an eagle, the Napoleonic symbol par excellence, became known as the *Grand aigle* (Great Eagle), and later in 1814 as the *Grand cordon* (Great Sash). Award of the Legion of Honour conferred the right to the title 'Knight of the Empire' (Chevalier de l'Empire), a title which was made hereditary after three generations of grantees, thereby turning the order of merit into something much more like an order of knighthood on the royal pattern. This also illustrates the link between honours and titles.

Prussia's highest honour was membership in the Order of the Black Eagle, founded by Friedrich III, Elector of Brandenburg, in 1701 at the time of his coronation as Friedrich I, King in Prussia. During the Napoleonic Wars, in 1813, Friedrich Wilhelm III, King of Prussia, founded a Prussian military order of merit, the Order of the Iron Cross. This was refounded in 1870 at the time of the Franco-Prussian War by Wilhelm I and again by his grandson Wilhelm II in 1914, in both cases acting not as German emperors but as kings of Prussia. Wilhelm II awarded so many Iron Crosses during World War I, however, that it became a German and not merely a Prussian order.

Honours were also an important feature of the Brazilian emperors' relations with their subjects. When the Portuguese royal family moved to Brazil, it brought the Noble Corporation of the Kings at Arms from Portugal with it and set it up in Brazil on 8 May 1810. Its task was to regulate such matters as coats of arms. Though noble titles were never hereditary in Brazil, Moritz Schwarcz explains how individuals were prepared to pay the quite considerable cost of acquiring letters patent and armorial bearings from the kings-at-arms. João VI, King of Portugal and Brazil, conferred 254 titles during his four-year reign, while during the imperial period, that is, the reigns of Pedro I and Pedro II, 'the total number of titles bestowed reached 1,439'.[81] On the day of his coronation, for instance, Pedro I conferred on Antônio Joaquim Pires de Carvalho e Albuquerque, who had fought for Brazilian independence in Bahia, the title of Baron of Torre de Garcia d'Avila.[82] He also ennobled twenty-five of his advisers and associates on his birthday in October 1825, in recognition of the fact that Portugal had now recognized Brazil's independence. In the course of his nine-year reign, he ennobled a total of 119 men.[83] Pedro II had an ambivalent attitude toward titles and honours, since he disapproved of any system of patronage and preferred to distribute honours in ones and twos throughout the year, rather than having a Birthday Honours List such as is still usual in Britain today. During the course of his long reign he bestowed in total about a thousand titles of nobility, many of which consisted of the title of baron without *grandeza*: that is, the holders were on the lowest rung of the nobility and had no right to display a coat of arms or to keep their heads covered in the presence of the emperor.

Orders of knighthood were divided into ranks or classes, and the higher the class into which someone was admitted, the more likely it was that he would be allowed to put a title such as 'Sir' or Excellency or 'Freiherr' (Baron) before his name. There were three ancient Portuguese orders of knighthood: the Orders of Christ, of Santiago, and of São Bento of Aviz and, even after Brazil's independence from Portugal, Pedro I continued to admit favoured persons into these three orders. In addition, on 1 December 1822 he created the first Brazilian order, the Imperial Order of the (Southern) Cross in honour of his coronation and, in 1829 on the occasion of his second marriage to Amélie von Leuchtenberg (1612–73), the Imperial Order of the Rose, whose white star set in a garland of roses was designed by Jean-Baptiste Debret.

A useful comparator with Brazil is the Austro-Hungarian monarchy. Here too there was a huge expansion in the number of honours distributed in the later nineteenth century and William Godsey comments that

> of the time spent at his desk, the emperor-king Francis Joseph (r.1848–1916) devoted a good deal of it to signing off on titles of nobility, orders of knighthood for public service (the Order of Saint Stephen, the Leopold Order, the Order of the Iron Crown, and the Francis Joseph Order), and other awards and distinctions at the sovereign's disposal.[84]

Many of these were at the recipients' request, writes Godsey, who were thereby 'buying into as much as being co-opted into a modern Habsburg social pyramid based on merit as well as on birth and status'.

Both the emperors of Mexico invented orders of knighthood. Just as Agustín I used the figure of the Virgin Mary of Guadalupe to legitimize his own reign at a critical juncture in December 1822, he had already used her in February 1822, even before he had been declared emperor and months before his coronation, when he created an order of knighthood. He named this order the National, later Imperial, Order of Our Lady of Guadalupe.[85] The medal of the order has an enamel plaque of the Virgin in the centre, surrounded by the motto 'independencia religion union', referring to the Three Guarantees which were the watchword of Mexican independence. This in turn is placed in the centre of a so-called 'cross pattée', that is, a cross whose arms widen at the outermost edge, and is surrounded by a golden wreath. The whole medal hangs from the beak of the Mexican eagle standing on a prickly pear and holding a snake in its mouth, thus combining the religious and the political.

The Order of Guadalupe was re-established by President Santa Anna in 1853, abolished two years later in 1855 and established anew by the Regency on 30 June 1863. The Mexican deputation which came to Miramar in April 1864 on the fateful visit during which Maximilian committed himself to becoming their emperor clearly brought a quantity of the sashes and medals of the Order of the Virgin of Guadalupe with them. For, as the *Advenimiento* relates, on that occasion Maximilian awarded Gutierrez de Estrada the Grand Cross of the order and created seven other members of the deputation either 'comendadores' or 'caballeros'. He took a stock with him on his journey to Mexico and, on his progress from the port to the capital, he made the most prominent citizens of Córdoba, Orizaba, and Puebla members of the order, as well as the administrator of the hacienda he visited and the French generals Brincourt and De Maussion. When he appeared in the cathedral in Mexico City for the Te Deum, he himself was not only wearing the uniform of a Mexican general but the sash and order of the Grand Master of the Order of Guadalupe which he also wore on other official occasions. The Mexican deputation must therefore have brought enough of the relevant insignia to Miramar.

On 1 January 1865, as announced in the first number of the *Diario del Imperio*, the official newspaper of the new empire, Maximilian created two new orders, the Imperial Order of the Mexican Eagle and the Imperial Order of St Charles.[86] The Order of the Mexican Eagle was the most important decoration of the Second Empire, its holders taking precedence over holders of the Order of Guadalupe. It was awarded to such important foreign monarchs as Napoleon III, Franz Joseph of Austria, Alexander II of Russia, Leopold I of Belgium, Victor Emanuel II of Italy, and Charles XV, King of Sweden and Norway.[87] On 10 April 1865, the first anniversary of Maximilian's acceptance of the crown of Mexico, he inaugurated the Imperial Order of St Charles specifically for women. It was called after Carlota's patron saint, St Charles Borromeo, and was designed to reward charitable or other service to the community. The empresses of France, Austria, and Brazil were awarded this honour, together with a number of European queens and princesses. Each of the three orders—Mexican Eagle, Guadalupe, and St Charles—was graded with the holders of the Grand Cross at the apex above a series of various lower ranks. Maximilian also instituted medals for military, civic, scientific, and artistic merit and, for instance, distributed decorations and the gold Medal of Military Merit on Independence Day in 1865.

Monarchs used the elaborate system of orders, titles, medals, and, in the case of those inhabiting the higher ranks, elaborate costumes to be worn on certain occasions as an important instrument in the regulation of the hierarchy not just of the court but of the army and of the government too. Decorations did not just reward good service or bravery but made them visible. They showed that the individual thus honoured stood high in the monarch's regard.

This system of organizing a court society according to hierarchical principles determined by the monarch can be seen particularly clearly in the Indian Empire, though importing a European system caused various difficulties there unforeseen by the British. Victoria first became queen of India in 1858 after the Uprising of 1857 and shortly thereafter the then British prime minister Lord Palmerston (Henry John Temple, Viscount Palmerston, 1784–1865) suggested to her that 'an Indian order of knighthood be established as a means of rewarding and strengthening the personal bonds of loyalty between Queen Victoria and the loyal Indian princes'.[88] These Indian princes were crucially important for stable government in India. While Victoria, through her Viceroy and other functionaries, ruled two thirds of India, the other third was governed by between 500 and 600 princes ruling their own states, who were supposed to keep order within their own territories, under the tutelage of the British, and collect taxes. In David Cannadine's words, 'these rajas and majarajas, nawabs and nizams [...] after 1857 were no longer reviled as alien and corrupt [by the British], but acclaimed as familiar and traditional.'[89] The British saw in these princes the equivalent of the British dukes, marquesses, and earls who had inherited their titles and lands and wealth down the centuries and helped to govern Britain by sitting in the House of Lords and sometimes holding ministerial positions.

Nothing happened until eighteen months later, when the queen recommended the idea of an order of knighthood for India to Lord Canning, the first Viceroy of India, whereupon another nine months passed without any progress being made. At first the idea was to award membership of the order only to Indians, but it was soon realized that there would be no kudos for an Indian prince in joining an order that did not include any Europeans. The next problem was what to call the order. As related by Miles Taylor, Prince Albert energetically promoted the project and suggested that the order should be called 'the Eastern or Morning Star', for, as he explained to Sir Charles Wood, the Secretary of State for India, the Magi came from the East, the light of the world came from the East, and India was in the East.[90] He also set about drafting a list of Latin mottoes, his final choice being 'lux caeli dux noster' (heaven's light our guide). Fortunately, Wood and Lord Canning were able to convince him that, for an Indian, India is not in the East but in the West; and that Latin mottoes may be fine for British orders such as the Order of the Garter but not 'for Princes whose ancestors were sitting on their

thrones four or five centuries before the Garter... [was] dreamt of'.[91] Canning
also made the point that 'Indians do not think of... themselves as Orientals.' So
many other names for the order were proposed that Albert, exasperated, wrote to
Wood that it should be called the 'golden impossibility', since agreement seemed
impossible. The new order was finally announced on 25 June 1861 as 'The Most
Exalted Order of the Star of India'.[92]

On 1 November 1861, Queen Victoria inaugurated the new order in two
ceremonies that took place simultaneously in London and in Allahabad. At the
ceremony in London she clothed her husband Prince Albert, their son the Prince
of Wales, and Duleep Singh, the deposed and dispossessed Sikh prince who had
been brought to England at the age of eight and adopted by the queen, in a long
light blue satin mantle lined with white silk and covering the body. This mantle
was fastened with a white silk cord decorated with blue and silver tassels and, on
the left side, over the heart, were embroidered the rays of the sun with the motto
'Heaven's light our guide' surrounding a star. Around their necks she hung a gold
collar decorated with palm fronds and lotuses on either side of a crown. Hanging
from the crown was a star and from the star hung a portrait of the queen herself,
made to look rather Indian. There was also a badge, a kind of brooch. At the
ceremony in Allahabad Lord Canning clothed the Maharajas of Gwalior, of Indore
and Patiala, and of Kashmir and the Begum of Bhopal in the long pale blue mantle
and hung the collar with its star and portrait of Queen Victoria round their necks
(Figure 17). The Nizam of Hyderabad, the Gaekwar of Baroda, and the Nawab of
Rampur were also entitled to receive these British honours but chose to do so in
their own territories. The Star of India was primarily being used to reward five
Hindu princes and three Muslim rulers who had been loyal to Britain during the
rebellion and its aftermath. To the British mind, to receive membership in the
Order of the Star of India was a great honour that Indian princes should be
grateful to receive, but their Eurocentric viewpoint failed to grasp what the receipt
of clothing meant in India.

Accepting clothing meant accepting the authority of the giver and confirming
the recipient's subordinate position, just as, in Europe in the sixteenth and
seventeenth centuries, the followers or servants of a prince or high aristocrat
wore his livery as a sign of their loyalty. Bernard Cohn points to the tradition of a
Muslim ruler accepting *nazr* (gold coins) from a subordinate and presenting him
with a *khilat*, a robe or set of clothes in return.[93] The Nizam of Hyderabad,
therefore, declined to be honoured with a knighthood and membership of the
Order of the Star of India, because he was being asked to wear the mantle and the
jewelled insignia. Through his prime minister Salar Jung he pointed out to
Canning that the 'people of this country have a particular antipathy to wearing
costumes different from their own' and if the robe were made out of velvet or silk
it would be in contravention of Muslim law. Nor could the Nizam wear the
pendant with the portrait of the queen because 'Muslims were "prohibited from

Figure 17 William 'Crimea' Simpson, The Begum of Bhopal at the first investiture of the Star of India in 1861. Chromolithograph. Private Collection The Stapleton Collection/Bridgeman Images

wearing the likeness of any created being on their person".'[94] The Nizam, therefore, did not go to Allahabad to be invested with the order and, when the patent arrived in Hyderabad with the cloak and the insignia, it is recorded that he 'made proper reverence' to these objects but did not put on the cloak. Another difficulty was that the Indian recipients expected to be able to keep the cloak in their treasury and bring it out to show at certain times, but the British wanted it back on the death of the recipient, a deeply offensive notion, to show that the knighthood was not hereditary.

Twenty years later, in 1876, Queen Victoria was proclaimed empress of India and instituted two more orders of chivalry. The first was the Most Eminent Order of the Indian Empire, divided in 1887 into three ranks of Knight Grand Commander, Knight Commander, and Companion. The mantle, worn only by Knights Grand Commanders, was of dark blue satin lined with white silk with a representation of a star on the left shoulder. The collar, also worn only by Knights Grand Commanders, was made of gold and composed of alternating golden elephants, Indian roses, and peacocks. The queen also instituted an order specifically for women, the Imperial Order of the Crown of India.[95] These new Indian decorations were to reward the high British officials ruling India—the so-called proconsular elite—but also the Indian princely elite. They, and their respective civil servants, were all to be tied into the same system and ranked. An important prince could expect to be made a knight grand commander of the Order of the Star of India just as his father had been and just as British viceroys and governors were. The spouses of British proconsuls and Indian princes were then included in the Order of the Crown of India. Career civil servants could expect to be given a decoration once they had reached a certain rank in the service or in the army, just as, in modern-day Britain, they still can. The two elite groups of British officials and Indians were, therefore, entitled—and were expected—to wear the mantle and collar of one of the Indian orders on formal occasions and on other occasions to wear just the medal or the ribbon. The initiated in either group would of course recognize which rank the other belonged to.

Cannadine's conclusion is that the British came to India, as to other colonies and conquered territories, bringing with them the rigidly hierarchical concept of society that they knew from home, which they then applied to India. In their partial understanding of the caste system, it mirrored in many ways the stratified society they were accustomed to in Britain.[96] The graded system of honours and decorations was a way to distinguish further the upper levels of this stratified society and make them compete in their loyalty and service to the crown. No matter how friendly Queen Victoria was to Indian princes when they came to visit her in Osborne on the Isle of Wight or in Windsor Castle—and she always welcomed them, provided that they remained exotic exhibits by wearing their most colourful Indian dress—, it took a long time for Indians to be allowed a measure of self-government. Honours, like court costume, were a means of exerting control. Whether it is true or not to say, as Napoleon did, that 'it's by means of children's toys that people are led', the rulers who distributed them certainly intended them to function in that way.

Notes

1. Mann, *Königliche Hoheit*.
2. Mann, *Königliche Hoheit*, p. 175.
3. Moritz Schwarcz, 'The banana emperor', pp. 315–16.
4. Mansel, *The Eagle in Splendour*, p. 37.
5. Winkelhofer, *Der Alltag des Kaisers*, p. 104.
6. Fugger, *Im Glanze*, pp. 82–8.
7. Winkelhofer, *Der Alltag des Kaisers*, p. 105.
8. Hamann, 'Der Wiener Hof'; Lobkowicz, *Erinnerungen*.
9. Spitzemberg, *Das Tagebuch*, 'Einleitung', p. 16.
10. Broers, *Napoleon*, I, p. 140.
11. Dwyer, *Napoleon, The Path to Power*, pp. 298–300.
12. Dwyer, *Citizen Emperor*, pp. 107–8.
13. *Étiquette du Palais Impérial*.

14. Trabouillet, *L'État de la France*.
15. Barman, *Citizen Emperor*, pp. 78–9.
16. Quoted from Barman, *Citizen Emperor*, p. 79.
17. Barman, *Citizen Emperor*, p. 79.
18. Pani, 'El proyecto', p. 438.
19. Pani, 'El proyecto', p. 428.
20. Pani, 'El proyecto', p. 429.
21. *Reglamento para el Servicio*.
22. Pani, 'El proyecto', p. 436.
23. Corti, *Maximiliano y Carlota*, pp. 39–43.
24. Stillfried-Alcántara, *Ceremonial-Buch*, p. 1.
25. Curzon, *British Government in India*, vol. 1, p. 202.
26. Bradley, *Lady Curzon's India*, p. 20.
27. Curzon, *British Government in India*, vol. 1, p. 102.
28. Curzon, *British Government in India*, vol. 1, p. 233.
29. Curzon, *British Government in India*, vol. 1, pp. 235–6.
30. Curzon, *British Government in India*, vol. 1, p. 104.
31. Curzon, *British Government in India*, vol. 1, p. 237.
32. Bradley, *Lady Curzon's India*, p. 22.
33. Curzon, *British Government in India*, vol. 1, pp. 238–9.
34. Lethbridge, *The Golden Book of India*, p. viii.
35. *Warrant of Precedence for India*.
36. Trendell, *Dress and Insignia*, pp. 48–9 and pp. 169–84.
37. Cannadine, *Ornamentalism*; Cohn, 'Representing Authority'.
38. Mansel, *The Court of France*, p. 115.
39. Mazohl, 'Gewinner und Verlierer', p. 54.
40. Haag, *Meisterwerke*, p. 172.
41. See Textile Research Centre, Leiden: https://trc-leiden.nl/trc-needles/individual-textiles-and-textile-types/secular-ceremonies-and-rituals/robe-of-estate-uk
42. Haag, *Meisterwerke*, p. 174.
43. Vocelka and Vocelka, *Franz Joseph I*, pp. 195–207.
44. Debret, writing at the time, says that they were toucan feathers, but Moritz Schwarcz (*The Emperor's Beard*, p. 53), describes them as the feathers of the indigenous bird known as the cock of the rock and says that toucan feathers were substituted in the 1860s.
45. A wyvern is winged, has only two legs, and a coiled serpent's tail. 'Sejant' means that it is erect and resting on its haunches.
46. Moritz Schwarcz, *The Emperor's Beard*, p. 62.
47. Stickler, '"Erneuerung der Deutschen Kaiserwürde?"', p. 334.
48. Mansel, *Dressed to Rule*, pp. 79–80.
49. Miot de Mélito, *Mémoires*, p. 43.
50. Mansel, *Dressed to Rule*, p. 83.
51. Telesko, *Geschichtsraum Österreich*, pp. 164–5.
52. Kugler and Haupt, *Uniform und Mode am Kaiserhof*.
53. *Vorschrift für die [...] bewilligte Uniform*.
54. https://www.kaiserliche-wagenburg.at/besuchen/sammlungen/monturdepot/ausgesuchte-meisterwerke/

55. Kugler and Haupt, *Nach Rang und Stand*, p. 52.

56. *Bildliche Darstellung.*

57. Lobkowicz, *Erinnerungen.*

58. Giloi, *Monarchy, Myth, and Material Culture*, p. 269.

59. Mann, *Der Untertan*, p. 282.

60. http://www.delaszlocatalogueraisonne.com/catalogue/works-in-public-collections/german-emperor-wilhelm-ii-king-of-prussia-4952

61. Giloi, *Monarchy, Myth*, p. 337.

62. Verroen, *Huis Doorn*, p. 6.

63. Barta, Ott-Wodni, and Skrabanek, *Repräsentation und (Ohn)Macht*, p. 91.

64. Barta (ed.), *Maximilian von Mexiko*, p. 175.

65. Ratz and Gómez Tepexicuapan, *Ein Kaiser Unterwegs.*

66. Quoted from Pruonto, *Das mexikanische Kaiserreich*, p. 59. 'Pulque' is an alcoholic drink made from the fermented sap of the agave plant.

67. Trendell, *Dress and Insignia*, pp. 48–9, and pp. 169–84.

68. Trendell, *Dress and Insignia*, p. 184.

69. Trendell, *Dress and Insignia*, p. 48.

70. Trendell, *Dress and Insignia*, p. 49.

71. Taylor, *Empress*, p. 235.

72. Codell, 'Photographic Interventions'.

73. https://www.youtube.com/watch?v=5_kKAfRxPPs

74. Devi, *A Princess Remembers*, pp. 21–2.

75. Codell, 'Photographic Interventions', p. 113.

76. Cohn, *Colonialism*, p. 129.

77. Moritz Schwarcz, *The Emperor's Beard*, p. 254.

78. Fulford, *Darling Child*, p. 249.

79. Barman, *Citizen Emperor*, p. 282.

80. Lavisse and Sagnac, *Histoire de France*, vol. III, p.161.

81. Moritz Schwarcz, *The Emperor's Beard*, p. 119.

82. Barman, *Brazil*, p. 102.

83. Moritz Schwarcz, *The Emperor's Beard*, p. 119.

84. Godsey, 'A Noblewoman's Changing Perspective', p. 40.

85. *Constituciones.*

86. A digitized version of the *Diario* is available on the CD accompanying Hernández Sáenz, *Espejismo y realidad.*

87. Hernández Sáenz, *Espejismo y realidad*, pp. 52–3.

88. Taylor, *Empress*, p. 83.

89. Cannadine, *Ornamentalism*, p. 44.

90. Taylor, *Empress*, p. 83.

91. Taylor, *Empress*, p. 84.

92. *The London Gazette*, 25 June 1861, p. 2622.

93. Cohn, *Colonialism*, p. 114.

94. Cohn, *Colonialism*, p. 120.

95. Cannadine, *Ornamentalism*, p. 88.

96. Cannadine, *Ornamentalism*, p. 42.

IV

Being an Imperial Consort

Within the structure of an imperial court, the empress played a key role, but one which was a challenge to negotiate for the twenty women who played it between 1804 and 1947.[1] They had to fulfil a biological imperative whose success was out of their hands while conforming to expectations of how they should act that often ran counter to their own individuality. As I have written elsewhere, the consort 'was assigned a role in a political and dynastic drama whose script had been written by others'.[2] In the latter part of the nineteenth century and the first half of the twentieth, they were also playing this role at a time when the place of women in society was more and more up for debate, while at the same time they themselves were subject to increasing exposure in the developing mass media. The aim of this section is not to discuss each of these women individually—that would need a separate book, which they deserve—but to show by means of some examples how their role was defined, how it evolved, and what individual empresses achieved in spite of the limitations imposed on them.

Motherhood

As with any consort in any century, providing her husband with an heir was the empress's most important task. In all the territories discussed in this book, apart from Britain, the heir had to be male and only some of the empresses gave birth to sons. Napoleon I divorced his first wife Joséphine de Beauharnais (1763–1814) because, though she was already a mother of grown-up children, she was too old to bear him a son. In 1810 he then took as his second wife the Austrian Archduchess Marie Louise (1791–1847), who was young enough to be his daughter, and a year later she gave birth to a son, Napoléon Joseph Charles Bonaparte (1811–32). His father had him baptized in the cathedral of Notre-Dame in Paris, called him the Prince Imperial and an 'enfant de France' (a royal child), and gave him the title of King of Rome, an allusion to the designated successors of the Holy Roman Emperors who were elected as Roman Kings while their fathers were still alive. Marie Louise's mother, Maria Theresia of Bourbon-Naples (1772–1807), had been the first empress of Austria and was Franz I's second wife and his double first cousin. She gave birth to his heir Ferdinand I in 1793. Another of her daughters, Leopoldine, Archduchess of Austria (1797–1826), was the first wife of Pedro I of Brazil and the mother of his heir, Pedro II. Eugénie de Montijo,

Projecting Imperial Power: New Nineteenth-Century Emperors and the Public Sphere. Helen Watanabe-O'Kelly, Oxford University Press (2021). © Helen Watanabe-O'Kelly. DOI: 10.1093/oso/9780198802471.003.0005

Countess of Teba, wife of Napoleon III (1826–1920), gave birth to a son, Napoléon François Charles Joseph Bonaparte, who was given the title Prince Imperial (1856–79). Just as his uncle had done, Napoleon III had his son christened in Notre-Dame and again called him an 'enfant de France'. The Pope and the Queen of Sweden, represented by proxies, were the godparents.[3] Victoria, Princess Royal (1840–1901), consort of Crown Prince Friedrich Wilhelm, later Friedrich III, German Emperor and King of Prussia, bore him four sons and four daughters. All the daughters and two of the sons lived to adulthood, including the heir Emperor Wilhelm II.

These may look like successful performances of the empress's biological role, but the cost was often very high for the women concerned. Maria Theresia of Bourbon-Naples bore twelve children in seventeen years, of whom five died either in childhood or, like her last child, at birth. She herself did not survive this birth and was dead at the age of thirty-five. Two of her children were mentally disabled: the heir Ferdinand I, who succeeded his father as emperor of Austria in 1835 but had to abdicate in 1848, and her second last child Maria Anna (1804–58). Leopoldine of Brazil gave birth to seven children in seven years, three of whom died either at birth or in childhood. She herself died before her thirtieth birthday, miscarrying her eighth child. After miscarrying her first pregnancy a few months after her marriage in January 1853, Empress Eugénie had such a long and difficult labour in 1856 that she could not have any more children. The importance of giving birth not just to the heir but also to 'a spare' is illustrated by the fact that neither the son of Napoleon I nor of Napoleon III lived to succeed his father. The first Prince Imperial died of tuberculosis at the age of twenty-one in 1832, the second was killed in 1879 at the age of twenty-two, fighting for the British in the Anglo-Zulu War. Crown Princess Victoria's labour when she gave birth to the future Wilhelm II was so prolonged and severe that medical intervention was required, and Wilhelm suffered severe damage to his left hand and side which left him disabled for life. This traumatic birth and her disappointment at his disability led to a permanently disturbed relationship between son and mother which deteriorated steadily, so that by the time of Wilhelm II's accession, he was openly inimical towards her. Two of Victoria's other sons died as children—Sigismund at the age of twenty-one months of meningitis and Waldemar at the age of eleven of diphtheria.

There were also expectations that an empress should fulfil the emotional demands of motherhood. This did not always come easy to these women of high birth, any more than to ordinary women. Elisabeth, duchess in Bavaria, empress of Austria (1837–98), is an example. She married her cousin Emperor Franz Joseph in 1854 when she was only sixteen and had difficulty adapting to the excessively rigid ceremonial of the Viennese court and the demands of her new role, for which she was not prepared. Only two weeks after her wedding she wrote a poem of which the second stanza runs:

Ich bin erwacht in einem Kerker,
Und Fesseln sind an meiner Hand.
Und meine Sehnsucht immer stärker—
Und Freiheit! Du mir abgewandt![4]

A year after the wedding, she gave birth to a daughter called Sophie, and after another year to a second daughter named Gisela. In 1857 the imperial couple took these two young children with them on a trip to Hungary where both became ill and, though Gisela recovered, Sophie died. In 1858 Elisabeth's son Rudolf was born. Whether it was because of Sophie's death or because of the rigours of three pregnancies in four years, Elisabeth distanced herself from Gisela from then on and had a troubled relationship with her son, while she lavished an almost suffocating care on her youngest Marie Valerie, who was born ten years later.[5] Elisabeth suffered from various illnesses for the rest of her life which have often been described as psychosomatic. What is clear is that she was an unhappy woman and that this had a major impact on her relationship with her children with whom, apart from one Habsburg family photograph dating to 1859, she was never photographed.[6]

Several empresses did not give birth to a male heir who lived long enough to succeed their fathers. Both sons of Teresa Cristina of the Two Sicilies (1822–89), consort of Pedro II of Brazil, died before the age of two, though the couple had two daughters who lived to adulthood. Other empresses did not bear children at all. In the case of Maria Ludovica Beatrix of Austria-Este (1787–1816) and Caroline Auguste of Bavaria (1792–1873), the third and fourth wives of Franz I respectively, this was not important, since Franz already had two living sons by his second wife. Maria Anna of Savoy (1803–84) was married to one of these sons, Emperor Ferdinand I, for forty-four years, but he was not capable of fathering a child and it is not clear that he was even able to consummate the marriage. Charlotte of Belgium (1840–1927), empress of Mexico, did not bear any children before her husband was shot in 1867. It can be seen from this that a successful performance as mother and even more as the mother of a male heir depended on luck.

Beauty and Fashion

Alongside the expectation that an empress would be frequently pregnant as a sign of her husband's masculinity and the continuity of the dynasty, she was required to add lustre to her husband and his court by her beauty and her magnificent dress and jewels. This was considered all the more important in a period when an emperor's dress became standardized as military uniform. It was, of course, a cliché to say how beautiful an empress was. For instance, in the account of

Maximilian and Carlota's progress from their first landing in Mexico to their arrival in Mexico City, Carlota's beauty was constantly commented on, a typical comment being that she 'had in her beautiful face the sweetness of the angels'.[7] The empress who best fulfilled the brief to appear on important occasions splendidly and appropriately dressed, to lead fashion, and to be acknowledged as a beauty was Empress Eugénie. She epitomized charm, grace, and glamour, something that is well captured by her favourite painter Franz Xaver Winterhalter (1805–73) in the portraits discussed in the next chapter. She was famous for her patronage of the couturier Charles Frederick Worth (1825–95) and knew that her position demanded that she encourage French fashion, once the emperor had pointed out to her how important it was for the economics of the silk industry that she wear Lyons silks, even when the patterns were not to her taste. These gowns she called her 'robes politiques'.[8] She was often criticized, as queens and other prominent women always have been, for devoting too much attention to her clothes, but her friend Princess Pauline von Metternich, the wife of the Austrian ambassador to the French court, relates in her memoirs how Eugénie's everyday garb was simple and practical, allowing freedom of movement for the vigorous walking and climbing that she enjoyed so much.[9]

Elisabeth of Austria also became known for her beauty. She was famous for her coronet of thick dark hair which, when loose, came down to her heels and whose voluminous mass we can judge for ourselves in the two so-called 'intimate portraits' of her with her hair loose painted by Winterhalter in 1864 and 1865 respectively which hung in her husband's private apartment. Her conflicted relationship with her husband and family and her aversion to the rigidity of Viennese court life were mirrored in an equally conflicted attitude to her own body which involved a complicated beauty, exercise, and diet routine. She never let herself be photographed after 1868 when she was thirty-two, so that the only images of her are as a young woman (Figure 18).[10] After the suicide of her only son Rudolf at Mayerling in January 1889, she always wore black.

So important was an empress's appearance considered to be that Wilhelm II policed the dress of his wife Auguste Viktoria, duchess of Schleswig-Holstein-Sonderburg-Augustenburg (1858–1921). It is recorded in several sources that he bought her extravagant hats and dresses, designed her jewellery, and wanted her to equal, if not outshine, foreign royalty.[11] He also checked that she did not put on too much weight (this, though she was the mother of seven children!). Once an empress's appearance became known to all, thanks to the new media of the daguerreotype and the photograph, it was public property and could be commented on and criticized. Media exposure also enabled myths to be more easily constructed around these women, as happened to Elisabeth of Austria.

A perceived lack of beauty could result in an empress being written off as stupid and uncultured. Teresa Cristina of the Two Sicilies, empress of Brazil, was short and dumpy and walked with a limp and, on her arrival in Brazil in 1843, Pedro II's

Figure 18 Hans Bitterlich, Statue of Elisabeth, empress of Austria, in the Volksgarten in Vienna. 1907. Marble. Photo © Ekkehard Henschke

first instinct was to reject her as his bride.[12] In her middle years and perhaps as a result of her pregnancies, she did not improve in terms of beauty. Photographs show, however, that, once beyond the menopause and once fashions had changed to become more flattering to her, in her fifties and sixties she presented a pleasing appearance, radiating the serenity and goodness that struck Crown Princess Victoria of Prussia who wrote in a letter to her mother Queen Victoria: 'The Empress is really almost the kindest soul I ever saw.'[13] Aniello Ângelo Avella makes the valid point that historians often interpret physical defects as meaning cultural mediocrity and demonstrates that Teresa Cristina, often called 'the Silent Empress', was active in two cultural spheres: music and archaeology. She promoted archaeological excavation on two properties she inherited to the north of Rome.[14] She personally wrote to her brother Ferdinando II, king of the Two Sicilies, asking for archaeological objects from Pompeii and Herculanum to be sent to Brazil so that a considerable collection was amassed, and in exchange she sent him interesting Brazilian objects.[15] In the musical field, she was a good singer and an important patron of Italian opera in Rio de Janeiro.

Charitable Activities—Education and Health

After motherhood and a pleasing outward appearance, the next duty of an empress, as Mother of the Nation, consisted of engaging in good works. The minimum that was expected of her was to show that she cared for her subjects and was informed about social problems, that she was prepared to visit institutions on special occasions, and that she used her patronage to enable funds to be raised. This understanding of the involvement of a great lady in charitable activities did not differ greatly from that of royal and noble women down the centuries and was seen as part of their Christian faith and sense of duty. Caroline Auguste of Bavaria, Franz I's fourth and last wife, fulfilled these expectations when she gave practical help—food and clothing—to those affected by the catastrophic floods in Vienna in February and March 1830, and again in 1831 when there was a cholera epidemic.[16] After her return in 1862 from almost two years absence from Vienna, Elisabeth of Austria made a concerted effort to carry out the duties expected of her, including numerous visits to educational establishments, orphanages, workhouses, and psychiatric hospitals.[17] She was even depicted at this period as the comforter of the sick and protector of the poor, modelled on the Virgin Mary and St Elisabeth of Thuringia.[18] She did not, or perhaps could not, sustain this effort.

What is striking, however, is the extent to which other empresses during the second half of the nineteenth century developed a different kind of more formal and organized charitable activity, whose purpose was to find long-term solutions for social problems. Like other noble ladies seeking an outlet for their intelligence, organizational ability, and drive, they had to operate within the spheres of charitable activity that were limited by contemporary gender roles. This meant that they focused on aid for mothers and orphans, on the education of young women, and on the medical sphere, though they could, like Crown Princess Victoria of Prussia, also be practitioners, patrons, and collectors of fine and applied art. Nonetheless, independently of their husbands, outside the confines of the court and in collaboration with professionals and members of the middle class—architects, doctors, nurses, teachers, educational reformers—these empresses found an outlet for their energy in founding organizations and institutions, some of which are still active today.[19]

The three Prussian empresses are impressive examples of the organizational drive just mentioned. They were, for instance, active in providing care for the war-wounded. Augusta of Sachsen-Weimar-Eisenach (1811–1890), queen of Prussia and first German empress, was a pacifist who was not happy about the Prussian strategy of going to war against other European territories in order to bring about German unification under its leadership. This led to three wars in 1864, 1866, and 1870/1 against Denmark, Austria, and France respectively. In 1866 after the Austrian War of Unification, Queen Augusta, as she then still was, founded the so-called 'Vaterländischer Frauenverein' (Patriotic Women's Organization) to care for the war-wounded of any nation. In doing so, she presented a contrasting picture of non-partisan care to the militaristic image of Prussia. She consulted Florence Nightingale in England to learn more about nursing wounded soldiers and she made the acquaintance of Henri Dunant, the founder of the Red Cross. Augusta's 'Vaterländischer Verein' became the forerunner of the German Red Cross and it was she who organized the first international conference of the Red Cross in Berlin in 1869.[20] That she identified herself with the Red Cross and its aims can be seen in the Red Cross badge she wears prominently on her breast on many of her portraits. After the death of the famous surgeon Bernhard von Langenbeck (1810–87), who was not only the Director of Surgery at the Charité Hospital in Berlin from 1848 onwards but took part in all the Prussian wars as a military doctor, Augusta wrote to Minister of State von Gossler to demand that the Surgical Society, founded by Langenbeck, get a premises of its own to be named after him. A piece of land was donated by the government and Augusta gave a considerable sum towards the building costs. The Langenbeck-Virchow House, as it is now called, still exists, though on a different site, and, after a chequered history in the GDR, is again the premises of the German Surgical Society and of the Berlin Medical Society, co-founded by Langenbeck and another famous doctor, Rudolf Virchow (1821–1902). A bust of Augusta, again with the badge of the Red Cross prominent on her breast, adorns the foyer (Figure 19).[21]

Her English daughter-in-law Crown Princess Victoria was extremely active in two fields: medicine and education. In 1866 she turned rooms in Schloss Erdmannsdorf in Silesia into a hospital for those wounded in the Prussian war with Austria. In 1869 she took part in 'the Congress of Geneva', as she calls it in a letter to her mother Queen Victoria, that is, the Red Cross conference just mentioned, and she too made great efforts on behalf of wounded soldiers during the Franco-Prussian War. Her husband notes in his diary that at first 'all her endeavours and offers of help in the matter of tending the sick were contemptuously rejected—presumably on account of the anti-British feeling.'[22] However, in early autumn 1870 she moved to the castle at Bad Homburg vor der Höhe, near her sister Alice, who in 1862 had married Ludwig IV, Grand Duke of Hesse and was living in the Hessian capital Darmstadt.[23] Alice was deeply involved in the improvement of hospitals and nursing care in Darmstadt and together the two sisters visited several military hospitals, for instance in Mainz, Bingen, and Wiesbaden. Advised by her own doctor and by Miss L. Lee, a nurse trained by Florence Nightingale, Victoria commissioned the architect Louis Jacobi (1836–1910) to build a model military hospital in the courtyard of the old barracks at Bad Homburg.[24] Here, 1,700 wounded German and French soldiers, including zouaves from North Africa, were treated. She had an intensely practical interest in everything to do with modern medicine: hygienic conditions, the provision of clean water, the improvement of sewage treatment, the nutrition of babies, and she

Figure 19 Bust of Empress Augusta by Theodor Litke after a model by Bernhard Roemer. 1892. Marble. Collection of the Humboldt University, Berlin, Charité. Photo © Ekkehard Henschke

even tried to get the Prussian government to found a Ministry of Health.[25] She also did all in her power to promote the professional training of nurses and supported the 'Verein für häusliche Gesundheitspflege' (Society for Nursing in the Home), an organization to train nurses outside of religious orders. They became known as 'Victoriaschwestern' (Victoria nurses) and the first five were qualified in 1885.

But this was only one of her initiatives to improve training and education for women.[26] In 1865 Dr Wilhelm Adolf Lette had seen colleges for women in England and on his return founded a society called 'Verein zur Förderung der Erwerbsfähigkeit des weiblichen Geschlechts' (Society for the Promotion of Gainful Employment for the Female Sex) based on the British 'Society for the Promoting of Employment for Women'. The society was, not surprisingly, usually known by the much snappier title of the 'Letteverein'. In 1866, with support and donations from Victoria, it opened the Lettehaus in Berlin, which provided lectures for women, had an employment agency, and held bazaars of handicrafts. In 1869 a residence for foreign teachers called the Victoria-Stift was opened and in 1872 a secretarial and training school for girls. In 1873, these organizations were able to move into a new building, supported by large donations from the princess. On 25 September 1875, Victoria wrote to her mother about a visit she paid to the Lettehaus, an institution, as she reminded her mother, that she helped to found: 'The pupils gain their living in different professions, bookkeeping—as clerks in telegraph offices and insurance offices.'[27] There was also a dressmaking and sewing school and Victoria reports that they have trained 600 pupils in total. The Lettehaus still exists as a technical and art college, which today admits students of both sexes.

Another initiative was the founding in 1868 of what came to be called the Victoria-Lyceum, a college for women, the idea for which came from the Scottish educationist Georgina Archer (1827–82), who had lived and worked in Berlin since the mid-1850s.[28] Archer realized that, after they left school, women had no opportunity for further education, so she proposed to the Crown Princess the establishment of lecture courses for women given by university professors. James Albisetti writes that 'similar ideas reached Victoria at this time from her country-woman Josephine Butler, the president of the North of England Council for the Promotion of the Higher Education of Women.'[29] The first lectures were on French and German literature and history of art. In 1869, courses on music, English literature, physics, and geology were added and, later on, chemistry, botany, philosophy, and pedagogy. From 1873 on, the lectures took place in the afternoons, so that teachers could attend. In this way, the Lyceum contributed to the higher education of female teachers. By its ninth year, more than nine hundred women were attending the Lyceum. Victoria worked closely with two other pioneers of women's education: Helene Lange (1848–1930), from 1902 president of the Allgemeiner Deutscher Frauenverein, and with Henriette Schrader-Breymann (1827–99).[30] Schrader-Breymann founded the Pestalozzi-Fröbel House in Berlin which also still exists today. Schrader-Breymann and Lange both report in their memoirs that the Crown Princess dreamed of a comprehensive educational college where women could study any subject they wanted from practical housekeeping skills to university subjects. She also supported the founding of a Catholic school of domestic science for girls in 1896 in Bad Homburg[31] and yet another of her projects was the founding of public libraries.

It was Victoria's daughter-in-law Auguste Viktoria, a woman with whom she had little sympathy, who was able to advance the cause of women's education further after Victoria's death. In 1905, Auguste Viktoria convened a conference, in which Helene Lange participated, to discuss how to reform schooling for girls, and in 1908 a law was passed in Prussia establishing High Schools for Girls, which enabled them to take the 'Abitur', the examination that qualified them to attend University.[32] In her involvement in this important reform, the teacher and educational reformer Marie Martin (1856–1926) was the link between Auguste Viktoria and such important figures as the theologian Adolf von Harnack (1851–1930), who was also on the side of reform.

Auguste Viktoria was also active in the medical field and was the patron of a children's hospital and of a home for fallen women. During World War I, while her husband's standing constantly fell, her care for the war-wounded ensured that hers rose. Popular depictions of her comforting a wounded soldier or putting her arms around hungry and ragged children show her prominently wearing a large cross to highlight the fact that she was acting out of an impulse of Christian charity.[33] These activities ensured that, when her coffin was brought back from exile in the Netherlands to Potsdam in 1921, thousands came out onto the streets to mourn her death. She was also, of course, known to her subjects for promoting the construction of large numbers of new churches in Greater Berlin and through-out Germany, as discussed in detail in Chapter VI.

Alexandra of Denmark (1844–1925), consort of Edward VII, King of Great Britain and Ireland and Emperor of India, was equally involved with medical charities. During the Second Boer War in 1902, Queen Alexandra's Imperial Military Nursing Service was founded under Royal Warrant, with the queen-empress as its president from then until her death in 1925. Queen Alexandra's Naval Nursing Service (QAIMNS) was founded in the same year and the empress presided over it also for the same length of time. These two organizations still exist and are part of the army and navy respectively, though the name of the first of them has changed with the times. In 1949, QAIMNS dropped the words 'imperial' and 'military' from its title and became instead Queen Alexandra's Royal Army Nursing Corps.

Another empress who made a permanent contribution to ameliorating the social problems of her day was Empress Eugénie of the French. When the City of Paris voted to give her a diamond necklace worth 600,000 francs as a marriage gift in 1853, she asked that the money be used instead for charitable purposes. It went towards constructing a school for poor girls which would give them literacy and professional training, so that they could earn their living independently when they left. It was opened in 1856, the year of her son's birth, so Eugénie decided to call the school the Maison Eugène Napoléon after her son. Alison McQueen has shown how the empress was involved at every stage of the planning, from finding the site to putting her stamp on the architecture, from increasing the funding to planning the facilities and choosing the staff.[34] The architect chosen was Jacques-Ignace Hittorff (1792–1867), an established architect of German origin working on many projects all over Paris between 1861 and 1866, among them the rebuild-ing of the Gare du Nord. He initially thought that he was designing quite a modest structure, possibly reusing an existing building. Eugénie was having none of this, wanted her school to educate and house 300 girls, and rejected the first three sites he proposed, finding her own in the Faubourg St Antoine near the place de la Nation, where the Maison Eugène Napoléon is still to be found.[35] Hittorff came up with a two-storey design in the shape of a pendant necklace, so that the school was popularly known as the 'Maison du Collier' (House of the Necklace). It had central heating, fresh water, good washing facilities for the girls, and even a mechanical washing machine in the laundry. It also had gardens in each of the courtyards, an infirmary, and a pharmacy. Eugènie wanted everything to be of the best quality, and the Maison ultimately cost 1,607,000 francs, three times the original gift from the city of Paris. Eugénie decreed that two statues which were originally supposed to represent Saint Louis and Saint Eugénie should depict instead Saint Napoléon and Saint Eugène. She considered a large chapel essential and played a major part in the design of the wall painting on the hemicycle above the altar. This was executed by Félix-Joseph Barrias (1822–1907) and depicts Eugénie kneeling in her white wedding dress in front of the altar, on which we see a representation of the Maison. She is dedicating it to the Virgin, Saint Catherine, and Saint Vincent de Paul, who are depicted in the upper half of the painting. On the Virgin's left next to the altar are the girls who hope to be saved by being admitted to the Maison and, on the other side, those who have already been redeemed by it. The Sisters of St Vincent de Paul, who were the teachers, are also depicted. Eugénie retained control over admissions and over who was appointed chaplain, doctor, and organist and she continued to support the institution financially to the tune of 150,000 francs annually until her husband was forced to abdicate in 1870 and she had to leave France.

This was not the sum of her involvement in charity work. Money collected to celebrate the birth of her son helped to build an orphanage called the Orphelinat du Prince Impérial. She also supported crèches for older children and lent her name as patron to a number of other charities. She was also famous for her visits to cholera sufferers in hospitals in Paris in 1865 and in Amiens in 1866, at a time when the risk of infection was very real. Matthew Truesdell describes the enthusiastic reaction to the Amiens visit: 'Medals were struck, poems were written, and Amiens named a city square and one of the hospital wards Eugénie had visited in her honor.'[36] Eugénie was credited with heroism, courage, and humanity.

Like Crown Princess Victoria, she also supported higher education for women. There was an outcry when the great educational reformer Victor Duruy (1811–94), who was appointed Minister of Education in 1863, instituted a lecture course for women at the Sorbonne. Even the pope condemned it as spreading impious ideas which would destroy the social order. Eugénie ignored these strictures and sent her two nieces to hear the lectures, accompanied by their governess.[37] During her regency in 1865 she seized the opportunity to award the Légion d'Honneur to the painter Rosa Bonheur (1822–99), the first woman painter to be so honoured, an unconventional woman who refused to be limited by contemporary gender notions, who dressed as a man and lived with a female companion.[38] The empress went herself to the Château de By, the estate that Bonheur had been able to acquire with the proceeds of her painting and where she had her studio, to present her with the honour, saying: 'I am happy to be the godmother of the first woman artist to receive this high distinction.'[39]

Figure 20 Empress Eugénie presiding at a Council of Ministers at the Élysée Palace, Paris. *Illustrated London News*, 11 June 1859. Coloured engraving. Private Collection Stefano Bianchetti/Bridgeman Images

Queen Victoria was in a different position as empress regnant rather than empress consort and because she was of necessity dependent on others to carry out any charitable involvement on her behalf in distant India. Famine relief, women's health, and women's education were three of the causes that she supported. The perception of a caring empress was not only important for her image but unlocked contributions from other donors. Queen Victoria's contribution in 1874 of 10,000 rupees (around £1,000) to a famine relief fund for Bihar meant that £131,000 was donated in India and £146,000 in Britain with the Government of India matching this combined sum.[40] Miles Taylor describes how 'catastrophic hunger and death returned to India' in 1876–78, in 1896, and in 1899–1900, and how inadequate the official response was, but how quite small donations from the queen towards the various relief funds were portrayed in India as the Mother of India caring for her people in their hour of need. She became associated with schools and colleges for girls first through Mary Carpenter, whom she had met in 1868, and then through her daughter-in-law Louise, Duchess of Connaught, who lived in India when her husband was commander-in-chief of the Bombay army and who became interested in female education there.[41] Queen Victoria also gave her blessing to the founding of hospitals for women and the improvement of medical care for pregnant women. Miles Taylor explains how the 'National Association for Supplying Female Medical Aid to the Women of India', better known as the Countess of Dufferin Fund, founded in 1885,—Lady Dufferin was Vicereine from 1884 to 1888—'was the single largest project of philanthropy outside Britain to which the queen's name was attached in her lifetime'.[42] Because of the queen's patronage, Lady Dufferin (1843–1936) was able to use the Golden Jubilee of 1887 for fundraising purposes. The Fund was resolutely non-sectarian, refused to employ missionaries, and was insistent that much of the substantial funds raised should go towards training Indian medical personnel. Lady Dufferin's successors as vicereine ensured that the Fund continued to flourish, so that by 1896 seventy hospitals had been established and around three million women treated. That the queen's name was associated with this endeavour ensured that she was known as a compassionate monarch and became more and more identified with Mother India and with the goddess Lakshmi up to her death in 1901.

Political Involvement

Politics was one area that empresses, like other consorts, had to negotiate with great care, since they were only rarely allowed to be involved at all. Nonetheless, some of them were able to use their influence on their husbands behind the scenes and others could use their own political capital.

An example of the latter is the triumphal entry of Ana María de Huarte y Muñiz (1786–1861), wife of Agustín de Iturbide, into the town of Valladolid in the province of Yucatán on 21 August 1821. This was his and her home town, where she was the daughter of one of its most important citizens. Indeed, she was superior to her husband both financially and socially.[43] Her entry took place at a key moment before the Treaty of Córdoba, confirming Mexican Independence, was signed and it closely resembled a royal entry, in which her social capital surely supported his future political advancement.[44] Thousands of people lined the streets leading from the entrance of the city to the Plaza de la Constitución, a route designated the Royal Road ('la llamada calle real'). The houses along this triumphal way were hung with cloths and tapestries, the streets were strewn with flowers, and there were triumphal arches decorated with emblems. As Ana Huarte, the wife of 'the Immortal Mexican Hero', as the title of the published account has it, moved through the city in a triumphal car, young ladies rained down flowers from the balconies. The triumphal car was sky blue outside and adorned with garlands. A laurel wreath entwined with a palm and an olive branch were painted on the front of the carriage, while on the back was an emblem of an arm coming out of a cloud holding a sword cutting some chains. Below that was an eight-line stanza saluting the return of a native daughter to the city. The interior of the carriage was upholstered in red damask and velvet with fringes and other decorations in gold. Surmounting this was a kind of throne, on which Ana sat. She was met first by her relatives and her father and then drawn through the city to the cathedral for a thanksgiving mass for her safe arrival. She was accompanied by the military, cannon were fired, and music played. At her father's house she received the ladies of the town, followed by a banquet and a concert.

Leopoldine of Brazil

Several consorts played an important role at key moments in the political development of their territories, among them Leopoldine of Brazil, Elisabeth of Austria, Carlota of Mexico, and Eugénie of the French. When Leopoldine, Archduchess of Austria, arrived in Brazil in 1817, already married by proxy to Crown Prince Pedro, her father-in-law João VI was king of both Brazil and Portugal, having succeeded his mother the year before. However, under pressure from the Portuguese Cortes, he sailed for Portugal in 1821 to ascend the throne there, leaving his son as regent in Brazil. As explained in chapter II, the Cortes then tried to reduce Brazil to the status of a powerless decentralized colony ruled from the Mother Land and furthermore decided that D. Pedro should give up his regency and return to Portugal. On 9 January 1822, in response to a petition signed by some 8,000 people, D. Pedro agreed to stay in Brazil and Portuguese troops were driven out of Rio. If Pedro had accepted the orders of the Cortes, he and his family would have returned to Europe and Leopoldine would not only have returned to a more health-giving climate but might have been able to see her beloved father and sister again. However, her sense of duty led her to identify with her adopted country and to sacrifice her own wishes. On 6 June 1822 she asked to have texts sent to her from Vienna, including a description of the governance of the North American free states. This study of political systems was not something that her uneducated and thoughtless husband would have thought of undertaking. She came to the conclusion, in a letter to her sister Marie Louise on 1 August 1822, that: 'Brazil is too large, powerful and, knowing its political strength, incapable of being the colony of the little mother country.'[45] As Oberacker shows, her letters at this time make plain that by now she had realized that the only solution for Brazil was not absolutist rule but a constitutional monarchy. In August 1822, D. Pedro set off for the south of Brazil to quell an insurrection there and made Leopoldine his regent with full powers in a decree dated 13 August 1822.[46] She worked closely with José Bonifacio de Andrada y Silva (1763–1838), the de facto Prime Minister, gave audiences as her husband's deputy, and fulfilled the public duties of the ruler. The Portuguese Cortes continued to deny self-government to Brazil, removed the regency powers that his father had given D. Pedro, and demanded that he return to Portugal within two months. The Cortes had already sent a fleet with 7,300 men to bring Brazil to heel. On 2 September, Leopoldine presided over the Council of

State in the Boa Vista Palace, at which it was decided to proclaim Brazil's independence from Portugal, that is, if D. Pedro was prepared to agree. This meant his renouncing any possibility of becoming king of Portugal. José Bonifacio and Leopoldine both wrote to D. Pedro to declare Brazilian independence. Their letters reached him on 7 September 1822 on the banks of the Ipiranga, a small river near São Paolo. Having read the letters, he uttered the famous 'Grito de Ipiranga' or 'Cry of Ipiranga', which ended with the rallying cry 'Independence or Death'. Since his father was king of Portugal, Pedro decided to take the title of 'constitutional emperor' of Brazil. Leopoldine did her best to influence her own father, the Austrian emperor, begging him on 6 April 1823 to recognize the new independent territory of Brazil.[47]

It was on his trip to São Paolo in September 1822 that D. Pedro made the acquaintance of, and became infatuated with, a married woman by the name of Dona Domitila de Castro de Canto e Melo (1797–1867). He brought her to Rio, ennobled her, her family, and the three daughters she bore him, forced Leopoldine to accept her as a lady-in-waiting, and showered her with jewels and gifts. This humiliation made the last four years of Leopoldine's life miserable, though she gave birth to the longed-for son and heir on 2 December 1825, having already buried two princes as babies. Leopoldine died a year later on 11 December 1826 of a miscarriage. Valdirene do Carmo Ambile and Luiz Roberto Fontes have con-clusively shown, on the basis of a CT scan of her skeleton, that her death was not due to her husband's physical ill treatment, as rumoured at the time, but to a miscarriage, which of course his treatment of her may have brought on.[48]

Elisabeth of Austria

As we saw above, Empress Elisabeth had a very ambivalent attitude towards both her public and private role. She did not find the extreme rigidity of the court and the aloofness required of an empress any easier during the forty-four years of her marriage but on the contrary less and less tolerable.[49] She did, however, play an important part in one area of politics when her advocacy helped to achieve a solution to Austria's conflict with Hungary. The Hungarian revolution of 1849 had been brutally quelled with the help of Russian troops, but the desire of the Hungarians for a constitution and for self-government remained strong. In 1864 it became clear to Franz Joseph, influenced by his wife, whose sympathies were firmly on the side of the Hungarians, that he needed to reach a compromise with them. It is thought that, even before her marriage, she was influenced in favour of Hungary and its culture by her Hungarian tutor, Count Johann Mailáth von Szélhely, an influence that was confirmed when she and Franz Joseph visited Hungary in 1857. In 1863 she began to learn the Hungarian language systemat-ically and, as part of her studies, to read Hungarian newspapers, thus informing herself about current affairs from the Hungarian point of view. According to Alice Freifeld, she apologized for the execution of the thirteen Hungarian revolutionaries known as the Arad Martyrs who were shot in 1849 and she went on a pilgrimage 'to pray for reconciliation with Hungary'.[50] Through Ida von Ferenczy (1839–1928), who taught her Hungarian conversation from 1864 and became a close friend, she also developed contacts to the leading liberal Hungarian politicians of the day such as Ferenc Deák (1803–1876) and on 8 January 1866 she became acquainted with the charismatic Gyula Count Andrássy (1823–1890). Elisabeth put ceaseless pressure on her husband to respect the wishes of the Hungarians and played an important role as unofficial go-between in the negotiations.[51] All this was regarded as very controversial in Vienna, especially when the imperial couple went to Hungary for six weeks at the end of January 1866 and she addressed the Hungarian parliament in flawless Magyar. In July 1866, Elisabeth moved for safety to Buda with her children during the war with Prussia and she was received by cheering crowds on her arrival.

In January 1866, Lajos Kossuth, in exile in Italy, called for the overthrow of the monarchy and here Elisabeth played a critical role, mediating between Andrássy in Budapest and Franz Joseph in Vienna and convincing Franz Joseph that Andrássy was prepared to save the monarchy if a compromise could be agreed. In February 1867, Count Andrássy, who had led the Revolution against Austria in 1848 and had only escaped hanging by fleeing to Paris and then to London, was appointed prime minister of Hungary, while Count Ferdinand von Beust (1809–1886) was named prime minister of Austria. Beust, Andrássy, and Franz Joseph were able to arrive at what is known as the 'Ausgleich', the compromise in which Franz Joseph, as king of Hungary, recognized the right of the Hungarian nation to function as a separate polity linked to Austria in the so-called 'dual monarchy' of Austro-Hungary. He could only be accepted as king, however, if he were crowned with the sacred crown of St Stephen according to the ancient ritual, invested with the sceptre, sword, and orb, clothed in the coronation mantle and anointed.[52] He would then have to swear an oath to respect the constitution of the country, followed by a ride in full regalia up a hill composed of earth taken from all the districts of the kingdom. Here he would have to slash with his sword towards each of the four points of the compass to express his will to defend the kingdom. Franz Joseph accepted the necessity of a coronation—his first and only coronation—and it took place in June 1867, not in Pressburg (Bratislava) but in Budapest. The ceremony and the accompanying celebrations were on a magnificent scale and constituted one of the high points of Franz Joseph's reign. The actual coronation took place to the strains of Liszt's Coronation Mass and, immediately after her husband was crowned and anointed, Elisabeth too was anointed and touched with the crown on her right shoulder, the first time that a Hungarian queen was crowned in the same ceremony as her husband. She had achieved her wish that her husband should remain king of Hungary and that the two lands remain united. There was clearly also a rapprochement with her husband, for a year later their fourth child Marie Valerie was born, whom Elisabeth brought up to speak Hungarian as her first language.

The Hungarians presented Elisabeth with the estate of Gödöllö and in 1869 she spent no fewer than 130 days there and in Budapest.[53] When Ferenc Deák died in 1876, she publicly knelt before his coffin, an image that became known to all Hungarians through a famous lithograph by Mihály Zichy.[54] Elisabeth, however, was more and more in flight from her duties as empress, so the Hungarians hardly saw her after that, though she did briefly attend the 1896 celebrations for the Hungarian Millennium. On her assassination in 1898, there was a huge outpouring of grief in Austria and in Hungary. Monuments to her were erected in many of the places she visited, the most famous being the white marble seated figure with her hands folded in her lap by Hans Bitterlich (1860–1949) in the Volksgarten in Vienna, unveiled in 1907 (Figure 18). Raised on a plinth with a marble pergola behind her and a tall pillar topped with an urn on each side, the serene and youthful figure, simply dressed, looks down onto a pool with two jets of water. An open book is at her side, two dogs lie at the foot of the plinth. The whole is placed in a tranquil garden of flower beds, pools, lawns, and trees in an ensemble designed by Friedrich Ohmann (1858–1927).

Eugénie and Carlota

Several emperors gave their consorts actual political authority by making them regents when they themselves had to be away from the seat of government. We saw this already with the regency of Leopoldine of Brazil during a key period for Brazilian independence in 1822. Maximilian of Mexico made his consort Carlota regent when he was absent on two journeys around parts of Mexico from 4 August to 30 October 1864 and from 18 April to 24 June 1865.[55] That Carlota was fully au fait with the international political context and its implications for her husband's regime and with the military situation is clear from her correspondence with Empress Eugénie discussed below. Carlota left for Europe on 8 July 1866 to try to raise military and financial support for her husband's Mexican Empire from Napoleon III and Pope Pius IX and never saw Maximilian again. In both endeavours she was unsuccessful, and the strain caused her to lose her reason, becoming overwhelmed with the paranoid delusion that everyone wanted to poison her.

Empress Eugénie was named regent by Napoleon III on three occasions when he was abroad. The first was during the war with Italy in 1859, depicted in Figure 20, the second was during his trip to Algeria in May and June 1865, and the third during the Franco-Prussian War in 1870–71. The official account of the emperor's journey to Algeria announces in its title that it also contains an account of the empress's regency.[56] During the emperor's absence she was given the authority to preside over the council of ministers and the privy council but not to initiate or pass new laws (Figure 20). According to the account, she prorogued the legislative council, received the new Turkish ambassador, and solved a whole series of problems, from difficulties with ancient titles of nobility to strikes with 'that mixture of tact, sweetness and firmness which are characteristic of her'.[57] She was made regent for the third time during the Franco-Prussian War in 1870–71, which left her trying to hold the government together in Paris at a particularly difficult time, when the French army was losing battle after battle and insurgency was growing at home. The prime minister Émile Ollivier (1825–1913) was forced from office, whereupon Eugénie appointed General Charles Cousin-Montauban, Comte de Palikao (1796–1878), to take his place. Napoleon, very ill and knowing that he was of no use to the army on the battlefield, wanted to return to the capital, but both Palikao and Eugénie urged him to stay. After the defeat at the Battle of Sedan on 2 September and his capitulation, Eugénie is reported to have said: 'A Napoleon does not capitulate. Why did he not get himself killed? He has not realised that he has dishonoured himself.'[58] Crown Princess Victoria of Prussia, writing to Queen Victoria, says: 'I wonder if it is true that she [Eugénie] pushed her husband into the war as much as she could and said "celle-ci c'est ma guerre". I hardly believe it—still it is related on very good authority.'[59] Eugénie denied that she influenced her husband, writing to her husband's cousin Prince Napoleon: 'I have never been and will probably never be a political woman, that is an amphibious being with whom I have no sympathy. There are no influences (which the emperor would anyway not tolerate).'[60]

Whether she said this because it was the kind of thing a woman was expected to say or not, she was certainly au fait with all the serious matters relating to the government of the day. This is evidenced by the remarkable correspondence in French between herself and Carlota of Mexico, which was at its most intense in the years 1864 and 1865, with twenty-four letters from Eugénie and nineteen from Carlota in those two years.[61] They were writing to each other at the same time as their husbands were also engaged in frequent correspondence, and both empresses show great political awareness and knowledge. Some of Carlota's letters run to two and a half or three thousand words and she was clearly using her correspondence with Eugénie to try to influence Napoleon III's decisions. She frequently included documents in her letters such as decrees and press reports which she wanted him to see. Her first letter from Mexico is dated 18 June 1864 and she begins full of optimism, praising the French officers and the intelligent and literate indigenous Mexicans and describing for Eugénie their first court ball and the castle of Chapultepec with its beautiful view. Eugénie counsels the iron fist in the velvet glove in her first response on 30 July 1864. Carlota comes back again and again to the military problems of Mexico, saying for instance on 10 September and 27 December 1864, 26 January, 3 February, and 14 April 1865 that more

French troops are needed. Eugénie firmly rejects this suggestion in her letter of 31 May 1865, expressing herself with brutal clarity:

> In the present circumstances there is no reason to increase the army of occupation. It is impossible to occupy the whole of Mexico and the troops are sufficient to ensure peace in one part of the country and to guarantee the honour of our flag.[62]

Another topic between the empresses is the financial problems of the Mexican Empire and the difficulty of obtaining loans from European investors, first expressed by Eugénie in an undated latter of 1864 at the very moment that Carlota and her husband have arrived in Mexico. On 16 November 1864, she comes back to this topic again: 'the big question is the financial one. From one moment to the next you will be obliged to take out a new loan which will probably be paid in part in Europe.'[63] The third most frequent topic is the attitude of the church towards the law promulgated by Benito Juárez in 1859 which nationalized church wealth and which the royalists and conservatives had expected Maximilian to annul.[64] The church had owned more than 50 per cent of the territory of Mexico, and returning this land to ecclesiastical ownership was impossible. Neither did Maximilian revoke laws guaranteeing freedom of worship, shutting down the monasteries, and allowing secular marriage. Carlota agreed with his stance, as she makes clear in a letter to Eugénie on 8 December 1864. The pope, speaking through his Apostolic Nuncios, first Pierre-François Damas and then Monseigneur Francesco Meglia, insisted on having Catholicism declared the sole state religion. In the same letter Carlota also rejects this, saying that it is not simply a question of reviving a dormant religion, as Napoleon I did in France during his first consulate. In Mexico it would mean grafting a nineteenth-century understanding of the faith onto the decaying remains of the faith of the sixteenth century, especially as Catholicism in Mexico has become mixed with indigenous religions. Many Mexicans tend towards Protestantism, she writes, as being both easier for the individual to comply with and less costly in terms of paying for the sacraments.[65] Her last letter to Eugénie is the short note dated 13 August 1866 from the Grand Hotel in Paris in which she asks for a meeting on the following day, her second with the empress and first with the emperor, neither of which brought her the financial and military support that she knew her husband needed in Mexico.

The Prussian Empresses

The young Jules Laforgue (1860–87) took up a post as Empress Augusta's Reader in French at the end of 1881, when the empress, consort of Wilhelm I, was already seventy years old and in a wheelchair as the result of a bad fall. He provides an acute portrait of an intelligent, well-read but difficult woman who spoke perfect accent-less French at all times and whose sympathies lay strongly with Catholicism and Catholics.[66] This stemmed partly from her love of France but was also due to the eight years she and her husband had spent in Koblenz in the Catholic Rhineland from 1849 when Wilhelm was governor general there. She blossomed in the more liberal climate there, won over the local notables with her open friendly hospitality and found a role in charitable activities, unlike in Berlin where she always had to take second place behind her mother-in-law.[67] She disapproved of the draconian anti-Catholic laws being promoted by Bismarck, as her daughter-in-law Crown Princess Victoria relates to her own mother in a letter of 12 April 1875. Victoria comments: 'The poor Empress's heart and soul as it were is wrapped up in the Catholic institutions of the Rhine.'[68] Augusta was also a pacifist, something that she expressed in her correspondence with other European courts, and her constant efforts to influence her husband in this regard also made her Bismarck's enemy and led him to stir up the press against her.[69]

Crown Princess Victoria herself was subject to even more suspicion from Bismarck and the Prussian court. Empresses of foreign origin always had their nationality thrown in their faces in difficult times, especially if they could be accused of working to further the interests of their natal territory and not their marital one. This was true of Anne of Austria in seventeenth-century France and of Marie-Antoinette in eighteenth-century France, and it was true of Victoria in nineteenth-century Prussia. She had been brought up by her mother Queen Victoria and her father Albert of Saxe-Coburg-Gotha to believe in democracy, parliamentary government, and liberal laws. Her parents hoped that she would able to introduce these values into her new territory after her marriage. Up to his death in 1861 Prince Albert, who had also been a father figure to Victoria's husband Friedrich Wilhelm, Crown Prince of Prussia, trained his daughter— first in person and then in hundreds of letters—to influence her husband to espouse liberal values, something his mother Augusta also hoped for.[70] That was Victoria's tragedy, writes Frank Lorenz Müller. Because she made it obvious that her identity was British and not Prussian and because she was seen to dominate her husband, she sabotaged her own hopes and plans.[71]

On 2 February 1867, while her hopes for her role in her new homeland were still high, she wrote a long statement to her mother about what those were. It is worth quoting, first, as a manifesto from a princess whose field of action was so much more restricted not only than that of a prince but than that of her own mother who was a reigning queen and empress; second, in the light of the failure of her husband and herself to influence Prussian and German politics as they had hoped; and, third, as a corrective to the assassination of her character that was carried out by the press during her time in Berlin and subsequently by historians:

You are quite mistaken if you think I like politics. I should prefer never to hear a single word about them. But I feel a deep interest in the cause of liberty and progress [...] I love Germany. I glory in national feeling and I am ambitious for her greatness, unity and happiness. I am anxious that Fritz's endeavours to promote this end may some day be crowned with success, and that dear England may sometime or other look upon us as fit to share her position in the world—not only by the force of our arms and the military talents of our nation but by the development of our freedom and our progress in civilisation. I do not know whether this is being fond of politics. It is more a feeling of the heart than of the head, and consequently a woman's *point de vue*. All interests me that can lead to this result—every branch of science, art and industry, and I should like to help to push on and give all I possess to make the condition of my fellow creatures (more especially my countrymen) better in every way, to raise them each individually. You see with me the desire is not to meddle with or to direct things which are not my business—I am far too lazy for that—but to try and add my little might to all great and good purposes gives me pleasure, and not for the effect it may produce for myself but for the inward satisfaction it causes. I think this is a part all women may take in politics and the one they are most fit for.[72]

In spite of what she says above, she came back again and again in her letters to her mother to the topic of Britain's superiority to Prussia. On 6 July 1873, for instance, she wrote: 'England is the only country at present which devotes all its energies to the cause of "culture" and real civilisation';[73] or on 11 December 1880: 'I hold the British Constitution to be the best and most useful and blessed form of government in the world.'[74] These are two typical statements and must be set against her disapproval of, even revulsion at, the way politics had developed in Prussia during the twenty years she had known it. On 24 May 1880 she wrote to her mother:

I am shocked at the state of politics here. Bismarck plays the very D with everyone, and everyone takes it as a matter of course. Their apathy and servility and want of independence and dignity is grievous and shows how the German character has deteriorated through the inordinate vanity this man has instilled into people blinding them to better and higher feelings and aspirations. A more unwholesome and unsatisfactory state of things cannot be imagined. Where is public opinion? Where is an honest and energetic opposition to counterbalance a power so unlimited and so much abused. Despotism is rampant and the public seem utterly blind and to have lost all political instinct (if ever they had much). [...] A huge and perfect army and a statesman whom none can trust or believe—but everyone fears—do not in my opinion constitute the beatitude but everyone here seems to think the present state of Imperial and Prussian Germany the envy, dread and admiration of the world. They feel so very big, and their talk is so very tall that it is very trying to others who had dreamed of a better future, of a free and pacific Germany with a wise and enlightened government. Dreams of this kind will not come true, I fear.[75]

She was biased in favour of her homeland, certainly, but many historians nowadays would agree with her analysis. Her dreams never came true because eight years later her beloved husband was dead, and her son, Wilhelm II, took Germany on a very different course into a world war that, fortunately, she did not live to see.

At the time of Wilhelm II's marriage in 1881, Crown Princess Victoria had high hopes that Auguste Viktoria would exercise a softening and civilizing influence on her husband with beneficial effects on his rule as Kaiser. Victoria's assessment of her daughter-in-law's character turned out to be very wide of the mark. John Röhl characterizes her as 'empty-headed, small-minded, xenophobically German and piously orthodox'. He goes on: 'She disliked all rationalists, found all atheists repugnant, and sensed a malicious enemy in each Catholic. She believed in the literal truth of every sentence in the Bible', and he cites Bernhard von Bülow as evidence of her dislike and mistrust of foreigners.[76] Harry Graf Kessler recounts in his diaries that she was so out of touch with contemporary society by the end of the reign that 'it was difficult to make her understand that Social Democrats did not eat small children.'[77] This meant that her influence on her husband intensified, rather than counteracted, his own most dangerous qualities.

Widows

Given the fact that Wilhelm II and Karl I had to relinquish their imperial thrones in 1918 and that from 1947 George VI was no longer Emperor of India, one might think that the imperial courts and their ceremonial necessarily came to an end everywhere at that time. However, many empresses long outlived their husband and, until their deaths, the imperial regimes they had been such an important part of were not quite forgotten. Ana María de Huarte y Muñiz lived on after her husband's death for thirty-seven years in exile in the United States and died in Philadelphia in 1861. Amélie of Leuchtenberg (1812–73), the second wife of Pedro I of Brazil (1798–1834), outlived him by thirty-nine years, residing mostly in Portugal. Since her husband had abdicated as emperor of Brazil and king of Portugal, she had to fight for recognition for herself and her only child Maria Amélia (1831–53) from her husband's dynasty, the Braganzas. Caroline Auguste of Bavaria, the fourth and last wife of Franz I of Austria, outlived her husband by thirty-eight years, dying in 1873. Marie Louise of Austria outlived Napoleon I by twenty-six years, was given the title of Duchess of Parma, Piacenza and Guastalla, married twice more, and was widowed a second time. Empress Eugénie spent the last fifty years of her life in England, forty-seven of them as a widow. Charlotte of

Belgium (1840–1927), better known as Carlota of Mexico, the consort of Maximilian I of Mexico, became mentally ill in the summer of 1866 after her failed attempt to rescue the Mexican Empire and lived for a further sixty years first at their castle at Miramar, near Trieste, and then in Belgium.

Zita, princess of Bourbon-Parma (1892–1989), was the last empress of Austria and queen of Hungary, consort of Karl I of Austria and IV of Hungary (1887–1922). She bore him eight children during their eleven years of their marriage and is credited with exerting a strong influence on her husband during the difficult days of World War I when he succeeded the aged Franz Joseph on 21 November 1916 as emperor and had himself crowned king of Hungary on 30 December of that year, only five weeks later. She was closely involved in a secret plan to enable Austria to make a separate peace with France in 1917, using as a go-between her brother Sixtus of Bourbon-Parma (1886–1934). When the plan failed and became known, Austria's German allies castigated Karl as a traitor and criticized him for apparently acting under the influence of his wife, whose Italian heritage was used as a stick with which to beat her.

Zita was widowed in 1922 and lived the life of an exile for the next sixty-seven years, dying at the age of ninety-six in 1989 in Switzerland. Her body was embalmed so that it could be brought to Vienna for her to lie in state in the Cathedral of St Stephen. After the Papal Requiem Mass was sung there, her coffin was placed on the same black carved royal hearse pulled by six black horses that had been used for the funerals of Archduke Rudolf in 1889, of Empress Elisabeth in 1898, and of Franz Joseph in 1916. It was drawn through the streets of Vienna accompanied by 200 members of the Habsburg dynasty in a procession 1.3 kilometres long. Forty thousand bystanders lined the route. The coffin was then formally interred in the Imperial Burial Vault of the Habsburgs (the Kapuzinergruft) in the Capuchin Church in Vienna, according to the funeral ceremonial of the Habsburgs. The whole event was transmitted on television and can still be seen on YouTube. Only when her eldest son, Otto von Habsburg (1912–2011), who under other circumstances might have succeeded as emperor of Austria, king of Hungary, and king of Bohemia, died in 2011 at the age of ninety-eight and had a similarly grand funeral, can we say that the imperial court had finally come to an end.

Notes

1. Not counted are Ernestine Wilhelmine of Württemberg (1767–90), first wife of Franz II, Holy Roman Emperor, who died in childbirth before he created himself Emperor of Austria, and Hermine von Schönaich-Carolath (1887–1947), whom the German Emperor Wilhelm II married after his abdication.
2. Watanabe-O'Kelly, 'The consort', p. 37.

3. Smith, *Napoleon III*, pp. 36–38.

4. 'I have awoken in a prison and there are fetters on my hands and my longing grows ever stronger, while freedom—you have turned away from me!' The original is quoted from Vocelka and Vocelka, *Franz Joseph*, p. 132.

5. Vocelka and Vocelka, *Sisi*, pp. 75–7.

6. Praschl-Bichler, *Familienalbum*, p. 9.

7. *Advenimiento*, p. 273.

8. Viney, 'empress Eugénie', pp. 185–6.

9. Metternich, *My Years*, p. 103.

10. Vocelka and Vocelka, *Sisi*, p. 75.

11. Peers, 'The Emperor of signs?', p. 51.

12. Barman, *Citizen Emperor*, p. 97–8.

13. Fulford, *Darling Child*, p. 249.

14. Avella, 'Teresa Cristina', n. pag.; Avella, *Teresa Cristina de Bourbon*.

15. The exchange of letters is quoted in the original Italian in Avella, 'Teresa Cristina' and in Portuguese in Avella, *Teresa Cristina*, p. 115.

16. Telesko, *Geschichtsraum Österreich*, p. 189.

17. Vocelka and Vocelka, *Sisi*, p. 47.

18. Telesko, *Geschichtsraum Österreich*, p. 228.

19. Eichler, 'Victoria als Malerin'.

20. Wagner-Gyora, 'Beruf Kaiserin', pp. 348–9.

21. See *Frauensache*, p. 207.

22. Fulford, *Your Dear Letter*, p. 286.

23. Franz, 'Victorias Schwester in Darmstadt'.

24. Dölemeyer, 'Victoria in Kronberg'.

25. Dölemeyer, 'Victoria in Kronberg', p. 127.

26. Göttert, 'Victoria und die deutsche Frauenbewegung'.

27. Fulford, *Darling Child*, p. 194.

28. Göttert, 'Victoria und die deutsche Frauenbewegung', p. 98.

29. Albisetti, *Schooling*, pp. 117–19.

30. Lange destroyed her correspondence with Victoria after the empress's death in 1901 for fear of reprisals from Victoria's son, Wilhelm II. See Gyora-Wagner, 'Beruf Kaiserin', p. 358, fn. 52.

31. Dölemeyer, 'Victoria in Kronberg', p. 117.

32. Wagner-Gyora, 'Beruf Kaiserin', p. 365.

33. *Frauensache*, p. 208.

34. McQueen, 'Women and Social Innovation'; Truesdell, *Spectacular Politics*, pp. 126–7.

35. http://fondation-eugenenapoleon.org/

36. Truesdell, *Spectacular Politics*, p. 132.

37. Milza, *Napoleon III*, pp. 337–8.

38. Saint-Félix, *Le Voyage de S.M. l'Empereur*, p. 214.

39. https://www.legiondhonneur.fr/fr/decores/rosa-bonheur/133

40. Taylor, *Empress*, pp. 127–30.

41. Taylor, *Empress*, pp. 203–4.

42. Taylor, *Empress*, p. 205.

43. Navarro Méndez, 'La mujér del emperador, p. 18.
44. *Entrada pública en Valladolid.*
45. Kann, *D. Leopoldina*, p. 402.
46. Oberacker, *Leopoldina*, pp. 337–8 and in general pp. 328–55.
47. Kann (ed.), *D. Leopoldina*, pp. 417–18.
48. Ambile and Fontes, 'O que pode ter matado'.
49. Hamann, 'Der Wiener Hof'.
50. Freifeld, 'Empress Elisabeth', p. 147.
51. Vocelka and Vocekla, *Sisi*, pp. 52–61.
52. Beke-Martos, 'After 1848'.
53. Freifeld, 'Empress Elisabeth', p. 151.
54. Freifeld, 'Empress Elisabeth', p. 152.
55. Ratz and Gómez Tepexicuapan, *Los Viajes.*
56. Saint-Félix, *Le Voyage de S.M. l'Empereur*, pp. 209–14. Includes a portrait.
57. Saint-Félix, *Le Voyage de S.M. l'Empereur*, p. 213.
58. Quoted from Price, *The French Second Empire*, p. 452.
59. Fulford, *Your Dear Letter*, p. 311.
60. Quoted from Milza, *Napoleon III*, p. 339.
61. Corti, *Maximiliano y Carlota*, pp. 601–81.
62. Corti, *Maximiliano y Carlota*, p. 662.
63. Corti, *Maximiliano y Carlota*, p. 634.
64. Pruonto, *Das mexikanische Kaiserreich*, pp. 144–50.
65. Corti, *Maximiliano y Carlota*, pp. 636–7.
66. Laforgue, *Berlin*, p. 42.
67. Fischer, *Wilhelm I.*, p. 121.
68. Fulford, *Darling Child*, p. 177.
69. Wagner-Gyora, 'Beruf Kaiserin', pp. 347–8.
70. For Albert's influence on Friedrich Wilhelm see Müller, *Our Fritz*, pp. 66–70.
71. Müller, '"Frauenpolitik"'.
72. Fulford, *Your Dear Letter*, p. 119.
73. Fulford, *Darling Child*, p. 101.
74. Fulford, *Beloved Mama*, p. 94.
75. Fulford, *Beloved Mama*, pp. 79–80
76. Röhl, *Young Wilhelm*, p. 365. This vicious characterization is vigorously contradicted by Peers, 'The Emperor of signs?', p. 50.
77. Kessler, *Tagebuch*, vol. 6, p. 714.

V

Seeing the Emperor

Diederich was alone when he rushed out onto the bridle path towards
the emperor who was also alone [...] the emperor, looking down
from his horse, flashed his eyes at him, Diederich tore off his hat, his
mouth stayed wide open, but the shout did not come. Because he had
stopped too suddenly, he slipped and sat down hard in a puddle, his
legs in the air, sprayed all over with dirty water. Then the emperor
laughed. This man was a monarchist, a faithful subject!

Heinrich Mann, *Der Untertan*[1]

The Emperor in Person

The novel *Der Untertan* by Heinrich Mann (1871–1950) was mentioned in
chapter III in connection with Wilhelm II's love for changing into different
uniforms in the course of a day. The passage above describes the moment when
the loyal subject Diederich Hessling sees and is seen by his emperor, whose
flashing eyes and waxed moustache he tries to imitate. Seeing and being seen is
the glue that cements the relationship between ruler and ruled. The Golden Bull of
1356, for instance, the document which codified the ceremonial for the coronation
and anointing of a Holy Roman Emperor, specifies that, after exiting from the
cathedral, the newly crowned and anointed emperor, wearing the imperial crown
and insignia, shall appear before the people. This took place for the last time in
1792 in Frankfurt at the coronation of Franz II/I. As we saw in chapter I, on 5
December 1804 shortly after his coronation as emperor, Napoleon, wearing his
coronation robes, crowned with his golden wreath and holding the sceptre,
appeared before his army to bestow on each regiment its own eagle standard.
Again, dressed in his imperial robes, he received all the various groups that
exercised authority in the state over the course of the succeeding three days.
This included 7,000 representatives of the army and the navy, of the national
guard, and of the guards of honour. After his coronation in 1841, the young Pedro
II of Brazil showed himself to the people in his imperial regalia from a sixty-
three-metre-long veranda constructed along the west side of the Palace Square in
Rio de Janeiro. The fact that the emperor in person, the anointed ruler, is
physically present gives such ceremonial appearances an immense auratic power.

Projecting Imperial Power: New Nineteenth-Century Emperors and the Public Sphere. Helen Watanabe-O'Kelly,
Oxford University Press (2021). © Helen Watanabe-O'Kelly. DOI: 10.1093/oso/9780198802471.003.0006

That the ruler should present him or herself to the public gaze became even more important in an era when subjects began to call for political representation and did so more and more as the nineteenth century progressed. From now on, emperors, like all rulers, had to be on show, both those whose legitimacy was not in question and those whose rule was not yet fully established. In 1864, for instance, Maximilian of Mexico and his consort used their slow progress from the coast to Mexico City to show themselves to, and to see, their new subjects in each of the towns they visited, before processing down the hill from the shrine of the Virgin of Guadalupe on the outskirts of Mexico City to the cathedral at its heart through streets lined with people.[2] When the façade of Buckingham Palace was reconstructed in 1913 as part of the redesign of the Mall and after the erection of the Victoria Memorial in front of Buckingham Palace, King-Emperor George V insisted that the central balcony of the palace should remain open, so that he and other members of the royal family could show themselves to the people on important occasions and also see their subjects filling the Mall all the way up to Admiralty Arch. As Tori Smith points out, 'the palace balcony became the stage on which the King and Queen appeared at moments of national crisis and cerebration' and it has remained so ever since.[3] Bernard Cohn points out how important it is for Indians

> to see and be seen, to be in the sight of, to have the glance of, not only their deities, but persons of power. The concept of darshan, to see and be seen, includes going to a temple, visiting a holy man or guru, or waiting for a glimpse of a movie star or the prime minister.[4]

We might add seeing or being seen by an empress or emperor.

Another example of the ruler's appearance before his subjects was traditionally the solemn entry into a city in his or her realm. At the city gates, the early modern ruler was formally greeted by members of the city council and presented with the keys to the city, which he returned. Through this meeting, ruler and citizens entered into a relationship of mutual obligation, whereupon the ruler processed to the principal church to celebrate a Te Deum along streets lined with the citizens. The nineteenth-century version of this is the royal or imperial visit. The *Northern Star*'s editorial of 3 December 1843 on Queen Victoria's visit to Nottingham daringly demanded that the Queen should see something more from her carriage 'than the blind that shuts out poverty from Royal Inspection . . . while she travels at our expense, we require to see and be seen. To see, in order that we may have the worth of our money—and to be seen in order that her Majesty may know from whence her Exchequer is filled'.[5] In similar vein, a Berlin newspaper complained in 1906 that Wilhelm II, on a visit to the Rhineland, had neither seen a line of veterans and nor been seen by them:

The grenadiers wanted to see their emperor, a glance from his beloved eye would have done them good; they wanted to feel that his eye was still there for them so that they might draw courage for their hard struggle for existence and in order to activate patriotic feeling![6]

Queen Victoria sixty years before is being asked to see the poverty of her people and give them a show to look at, for they are funding her through their taxes. Wilhelm II is being asked to show his subjects by his gaze that he cares for them and thereby gives them courage. In both cases, being seen is as important as seeing.

Having been constantly in the public eye from her marriage to Prince Albert in 1840 until his death in 1861, visiting parts of her kingdom, opening buildings, and engaging in charitable activities in what Plunkett calls 'civic publicness',[7] there was a crisis in Queen Victoria's reign when she withdrew from London to the Isle of Wight in 1861 to mourn her husband and was not seen in London for five years. Indeed, for eleven years up to 1872, she rarely emerged from seclusion, which contributed to a growing republican movement. It is dangerous for a monarch not to be seen by the people at regular intervals. Pedro II of Brazil might arguably have been able to retain his crown, if he had not spent years at a time abroad on trips funded by his subjects—ten months from 25 May 1871, eighteen months from 26 March 1876, and fourteen months from 30 June 1887.[8] Wilhelm II usually spent more than half the year away from both Potsdam and Berlin and people joked that his signature 'Wilhelm I.R.' (meaning 'Wilhelm imperator et rex') stood for 'Wilhelm immer reisefertig', that is, 'Wilhelm with his bags always packed'.[9] If the ruler is physically absent, he or she can neither see nor be seen.

The power of the royal gaze and the power to gaze at the monarch in a less formal way is illustrated by the myth that grew up around Wilhelm I, first German emperor, and his daily appearance in the 1870s and 1880s at what came to be known as 'the historic corner window'. This was the window of his study and, whenever he was in residence, he appeared there every day at noon to observe the changing of the guard.[10] To understand how visible he was, it is necessary to know that since 1829 he had lived in what became known as 'Emperor Wilhelm's Palace' at the bottom of the boulevard called Unter den Linden. He never moved into the much grander Royal Palace nearby—neither after his coronation as king of Prussia in 1861 nor after 1871 when he was named German emperor. Emperor Wilhelm's Palace fronted directly onto the street, so there was no barrier between his windows and the public, a risky situation, one might think, for a ruler who in June 1878 survived his third assassination attempt. Baedeker's guidebook to Berlin, both the German and the English editions, informed out-of-town tourists that the apartment in 'the Emperor William's Palace' on the ground floor near the Opera House was his and explained how the visitor could tell if the emperor was in residence.[11] It also became known which was his study window. That he had been there since six o'clock in the morning, as one popular periodical explained to its readers, was interpreted as a sign of his constant toil on behalf of his subjects.[12] That his subjects could see him and that he could see them created a bond between them that had nothing to do with actual acquaintance. A celebratory publication which appeared nine years after his death, entitled *Wilhelm der Große*, devoted no fewer than six out of 112 pages to his appearance at this window.[13] It included three engravings of the Kaiser seen at the window from outside wearing, respectively, his spiked helmet and uniform, with his grandson, the future Wihelm II, and looking out over the heads of the guardsmen, as well as a fold-out folio engraving depicting the Kaiser inside his study, holding a document and gazing out. Did the emperor like to have the public crowding round him wherever he was? asks the author of *Wilhelm der Große*, to which he provides his own answer: 'Of course! This honest affection from an entire great people was balm to his loving noble heart.'[14]

A fictitious relationship between emperor and subjects is being constructed and fictitious emotions imputed to both parties, but this is clearly part of the sentimental myth that built up around Wilhelm I after 1871 that Eva Giloi explores in such convincing detail.[15] With this example we have moved from seeing the emperor to the representation of that seeing, and with this we come to the fundamental question of the emperor as image.

The Emperor as Image

Most people never had the chance to see the emperor in the flesh, which is why images were so important. The manner in which these images were produced, controlled, disseminated, and received underwent huge changes over the course of the nineteenth century. How they were constituted depended on who commissioned them—the emperor or imperial household on the one hand, the press, whether benevolent or not, on the other—and what medium was being used. Formal portraits in oils, photographs, and film all follow different laws. The image of the emperor had not only to be disseminated widely, but the public, which is what 'the people' gradually came to be called over the course of the nineteenth century, had to assent to the message that the image was presenting.[16] 'Politics requires images, it gives rise to images; but it can also follow where images may lead', writes Horst Bredekamp.[17]

Beyond the more banal function of showing the people what he or she looked like, depictions of the monarch often stood in for the real person in what Horst Bredekamp calls 'a substitutive image act'.[18] In chapter II we saw how images of Agustín I, emperor of Mexico, were pulled through the streets of Guadalajara and Mexico City in 1822; and Benner describes the occasion on 27 January 1907 when the theologian Adolf von Harnack gave a speech on Wilhelm II's birthday, a public holiday. Harnack stood in front of Wilhelm's portrait in the university in Berlin—the icon of the Kaiser, Benner calls the portrait—and in his speech not only addressed the portrait as a substitute for the emperor but called up the vision of an emperor—what Benner calls the 'Kaiserimago'—in the hearts of his listeners and which, he said, Wilhelm was filling with new life.[19] For Harnack, the 'Urbild', the originary image, in people's hearts enabled the audience to revere the painted image which was an avatar of the man himself. Using a portrait as a substitute for the ruler was even more important in the case of Victoria, empress of India, who never set foot in the vast country she ruled over. We see this in Figure 13 depicting the Imperial Durbar of 1877, where the viceroy Lord Lytton is seated beneath a large full-length portrait of the empress, indicating that she is the one who is conferring honours and decorations on the Indian princes appearing before her and that he, the viceroy, is merely her instrument. Miles Taylor describes how, on the occasion of her Golden Jubilee in 1887,

> depicted in a transparency, or in a photograph, or by a reproduction of a portrait, Queen Victoria was carried aloft on elephants, or inside carriages or palanquins, in the processions leading to the durbar, and then placed on a dais, or inside an improvised *pandal* marquee or on a throne during the ceremony itself. Local Indian officials addressed her image, sometimes paid homage with a bow or salute, or prostrated themselves before her.[20]

Ten years later at her Diamond Jubilee, he relates how the queen's portrait or photograph was drawn around several Indian towns in a procession or was saluted or done obeisance to as if the image was the woman.[21]

Some imperial images, such as that on the coinage, were wholly in the control of the authorities. It is striking to see how soon after assuming power a ruler put his head on coins and how useful coins were as a medium to promote the imperial idea. In 1803, a year after he became First Consul, Napoleon I's profile was already on the French coinage. From 1807, that profile was crowned with a laurel wreath, making the point that he was now an emperor, a victorious *imperator*. Coinage during the reign of Napoleon III underwent a similar mutation. The first coinage minted in 1853 bore Napoleon III's profile, while from 1862 the same profile wore a laurel wreath, again signalling that Napoleon was a victorious army commander. In Mexico the *peso* took over from the *real* in 1863, and when Maximilian, archduke of Austria, the new emperor of Mexico, arrived in 1864, he was the first to have coins minted with the denomination *peso* on them. He placed his profile on the obverse under the words 'Maximiliano Emperador' and on the other side, the reverse, the imperial Mexican arms and the words 'Imperio Mexicano'.

Postage stamps were another ubiquitous medium in daily use which made the ruler's image known to his or her subjects. The world's first postage stamp, the Penny Black of 1841, showed the young Queen Victoria in profile wearing a coronet with her hair pulled up into a knot at the back, an image that continued to be used until her death in 1901. The depiction on the stamp did not resemble her actual profile even when she was young and corresponded not at all to her appearance as an old woman. A very similar image of Victoria was used on postage stamps in India, sometimes with the nose slightly elongated and at others with the whole profile Indianized—that is, with the eyes made bigger and the jaw heavier.[22] It was not until the 1880s that Indian stamps showed Queen Victoria as an old woman, wearing her small imperial crown over her widow's cap and lace veil.

Napoleon III had himself depicted on two sets of stamps in 1853 and 1862 respectively, again, as on the coinage, at first in profile and then with the addition of a laurel wreath in 1862. Franz Joseph of Austria, the first Austrian ruler to be depicted on stamps, was also shown in profile wearing a laurel wreath from 1867, in a stylized but reasonably realistic manner. If the point of having the ruler's portrait on postage stamps was so that his people should get to know him, Pedro II of Brazil comes off best, being depicted between 1866 and 1884 most often realistically and in full face. There were some portraits of him in profile, but he was never distanced from the viewer by wearing a coronet like Victoria or a laurel wreath like Napoleon III and Franz Joseph.

The Imperial State Portrait

Official portraits in oils, commissioned by the emperor or empress themselves, were another area that could be controlled by the sitter. The state portrait of the newly crowned or inaugurated monarch is a *sine qua non* of imperial, as of royal, image-making. Napoleon I had himself painted in his coronation robes by no fewer than four official painters: Anne-Louis Girodet de Roucy Trioson (1767–1824), François Gérard (1770–1837), Robert Lefèvre (1755–1830), and Jacques-Louis David (1748–1825). The latter had already done sterling service in 1801 in creating the stirring depiction of a heroic Napoleon on a rearing horse crossing the Alps, but, of the coronation portraits, Napoleon clearly liked Gérard's the best (see Figure 1). He 'gave copies of it, in preference to any other, to relations, allies, courtiers and every French mission abroad, both diplomatic and consular'.[23] It shows him standing in front of his throne with its large golden N on the back, wearing the golden laurel wreath in which he entered Notre-Dame for his coronation and holding the staff of Charlemagne in his right hand. The orb and the *main de justice* are lying next to him on green velvet cushions, while his sumptuous cloak of gold-embroidered red velvet lined with ermine hangs from his shoulders and billows across the carpet studded with bees at his feet. Under the cloak he is wearing a long robe of white satin embroidered in gold.

The depictions by the four aforementioned official painters are conventional, showing the emperor standing. Conventional is not a term that can be applied to *Napoleon on his Imperial Throne* by the young Jean-Auguste-Dominique Ingres (1780–1867) (Figure 21). This was not commissioned at all but was painted by Ingres for presentation at the Salon in 1806. By exaggerating the various iconographic elements, it reveals Napoleonic image-making with almost grotesque clarity. It shows, not the man, but the emperor, seated, a strange pale-faced effigy whose body can scarcely be discerned under the weight of the drapery and who is surrounded with imperial symbols.[24] Our eyes are drawn to the top of the canvas towards the figure of Charlemagne on top of the sceptre the emperor is holding in an unrealistically long right arm and then down to the bottom of the canvas to the enormous eagle on the carpet at his feet. Ingres inflated the arc on the back of the throne to three times its actual size so that it appears to be a golden halo round the emperor's head. This arc is echoed by the semi-circle of the ermine collar and the chain of the Legion of Honour, the order of merit instituted by Napoleon in 1802. The rich red velvet of the robe is covered in golden bees, the

Figure 21 Jean-Auguste-Dominique Ingres, *Napoleon I in his coronation robes*. Oil on canvas. Musée de l'Armée, Paris. Photo © Josse/Bridgeman Images

hand of justice, the sword at the emperor's left side and the scales on the carpet depict Napoleon as dispenser of royal justice, the big N embroidered on the cloak and the globes on the throne refer to Napoleonic ambition. This is imperial symbolism laid on with a trowel.

We saw in the Introduction how it took until 1830 for Franz I of Austria to acquire the robes of an emperor of Austria. In 1832 he finally had himself painted as emperor by Friedrich von Amerling (1803–87) wearing the cloak designed by Philip von Stubenrauch described there (see Figure 16). In this famous portrait he is seated on a throne covered with a golden cloth, wearing the Rudolfine crown, and holding the sceptre in his right hand with the sword at his side. He wears the collars and orders of the four Habsburg so-called 'Hausorden' of which he was Grand Master: the Orders of the Golden Fleece, of St Stephan, of the Iron Cross, and the Leopoldorden, and his gleaming white silk hose are mirrored in the satin lining of the cloak. Out of all this magnificence the thin melancholy face of the sixty-four-year old emperor gazes out. This expression was interpreted by contemporaries as the emperor's empathetic response to the fate of his subjects and of the many nations he ruled over.[25] He died three years later in 1835, but this image of the first Austrian emperor in his imperial robes was projected in large numbers to the late emperor's subjects by means of a widely distributed lithograph by Thomas Driendl created in 1836, which shows the imperial family grouped around it (Figure 22). The image of the seated emperor in its huge frame, far larger than any of the other fourteen figures depicted, dominates the composition and the dead man completely outranks his son and successor Ferdinand, who is shown drooping in the foreground supported on his wife's arm with his hydrocephalic head and vacant expression very noticeable.

The point of an imperial portrait is to overwhelm the viewer with the regal or imperial status of their subject, and the more recently this subject had achieved imperial dignity, the more important it is to convey the imperial message. Franz Xaver Winterhalter (1805–73), having been the favoured painter of Louis-Philippe, King of France (1773–1850), and Queen Victoria, was invited to Paris in 1853 to paint the newly elected Emperor Napoleon III and his consort Empress Eugénie. Napoleon III had been proclaimed Emperor of the French on 2 December 1852—the anniversary of the coronation of Napoleon I, of the Battle of Austerlitz, and of his own *coup d'état* of 1851—and Winterhalter's famous portraits were finished in December 1853 at a cost of 24,000 francs.[26] In the words of Paul Perrin, they have no other purpose 'but to legitimate the presence on the imperial throne of a man and of a woman who were not destined to occupy that place'.[27] The portrait of Napoleon III fills this brief perfectly (Figure 23). Everything about the figure in the painting denotes regal control from his waxed moustache to his skin-tight pantaloons and gleaming boots: his shoulders are pulled back, his waist is cinched in, his right hand grips the *main de justice*, his left rests on his sword, his gaze is turned inwards, as though considering great

Figure 22 Thomas Driendl, lithograph after a drawing by Johann Ender, The Imperial Family is grouped around Amerling's Portrait of Franz I after his death, c. 1836. Wikimedia Commons

matters. His costume consists of a marshal's uniform worn with the sash and collar of the Grand Master of the Légion d'Honneur. The figure is framed by imperial trappings—the cloak lined with ermine, the crown, sceptre, and throne— and by the background of red and gold: the huge red curtain, the red velvet-covered table, and the red carpet. Through the window the Tuileries Palace is visible. Ormond and Blackett-Ord complain of this portrait that 'Winterhalter is content with the superficial trappings of power. The man himself is blandly impersonal', but that is precisely the point.[28] This is not a portrait of an individual, into whose personality the viewer gains an insight, but a depiction of Napoleon-as-Emperor. This portrait and its companion piece depicting the empress fulfilled their purpose, for, as Ormond and Blackett-Ord point out, they were so popular that special forms had to be printed to request copies of them for prefectures, consulates, and embassies, and 'the portraits were engraved, transferred to Sèvres porcelain, woven into tapestry, made into miniatures, interpreted in sculpture, to become universal talismans of the Second Empire.'[29]

Figure 23 Franz Xaver Winterhalter, *Portrait of Napoleon III, emperor of the French*, c.1852. Oil on canvas. Museo Napoleonico, Rome, G. Dagli Orti/De Agostini Picture Library/Bridgeman Images

Winterhalter used the identical *mise-en-scène* for a portrait of Wilhelm I painted in 1861, the year he was crowned King of Prussia. In this coronation portrait, Winterhalter has painted a manly figure wearing his dress uniform with carefully rendered medals and decorations, resting his marshal's baton vertically on the table next to him. The crown and sceptre on a cushion next to him, the ermine-lined cloak spilling down from the table to the floor, the Prussian eagle on the cloth covering the table, and the red gold-fringed curtain with a coat of arms behind the king half covering a massive column indicate his regal status. Beyond the column we see the balustrade of what might be a terrace and beyond that again the countryside. The original of this portrait was lost in World War II, so that it is known today only from a copy.

So successful was this iconographical model that Albert Gräfle (1807–89) based his imperial portrait of Maximilian of Mexico in Chapultepec Castle in Mexico City on it (Figure 24). Gräfle was Winterhalter's pupil and assistant in Paris between 1839 and 1848 and clearly learned a great deal from his master. He painted Maximilian in 1865 wearing military uniform, the same uniform that he

Figure 24 Albert Gräfle, *Maximilian I, emperor of Mexico*. Oil on canvas. Museo Nacional de Historia, Castillo de Chapultepec, Mexico City. Mondadori Portfolio/ Bridgeman Images

had designed for his military cabinet, it seems, of which depictions are preserved in the picture archive of the Austrian National Library.[30] The viewpoint is low, so that the emperor appears tall and manly. As in the case of Napoleon III, a voluminous imperial cloak covers his shoulders and cascades down behind him. It is made of red velvet embroidered with the Mexican eagle and lined throughout with ermine. At his neck hangs the Golden Fleece, of which order he was automatically a member as Archduke of Austria and younger brother of the Austrian emperor, and round his shoulders over the ermine collar we see the chain of the Grand Master of the Order of the Virgin of Guadalupe. The imperial insignia are next to him on a table, behind him is a red velvet throne, a large column, and a red curtain with a gold fringe. To his left a window reveals a blue sky with small clouds. Gräfle also painted a companion portrait of Carlota, based on Winterhalter's portrait of Eugénie.

Clearly based on Winterhalter and Gräfle and using the same iconography yet again is a posthumous painting of Agustín, the first Mexican emperor, by Petronilo Monroy (1836–82) dating to 1865. This was one of the portraits of the heroes of Mexican independence commissioned by Maximilian for his Galería de Iturbide in the Palacio Real in Mexico City, and Monroy has painted Agustín as though he were a man of the 1860s and not of the 1820s.[31] He is shown in full dress military uniform and boots with the usual attributes: sash and decoration, imperial cloak, crown and sceptre on a side table, red curtain and throne behind him. His left hand rests on his sabre, his right on a document, presumably the constitution.

Pedro II of Brazil (1825–91) came to the throne very young and reigned for almost sixty years, so that his image evolved considerably over the decades. He was crowned in 1841 at the age of only sixteen and, as Lilia Moritz Schwarcz points out, remained shut up in the palace for some years, continuing his education and remaining invisible in person to his subjects.[32] Images were therefore all the more important. The earliest of them show a beardless youth in the court dress of his father's reign—that is, in a heavily embroidered short jacket with a high collar—and wearing a diffident expression. Moritz Schwarcz comments on how many virtually identical portraits of Pedro there were, with only a small detail changed each time. 'Dom Pedro's face is "spread around". Only in this way does it become real', she writes.[33] As a mature man, D. Pedro was almost six feet in height with the impressive beard which he wore for the rest of his life, covering the protruding Habsburg chin he had inherited from his mother. The contribution the right image can make to the projection of imperial dignity can be seen by comparing François-Auguste Biard's portrait of D. Pedro, painted in Rio in 1858 and included as a woodcut in his book *Deux Années au Brésil*, and Pedro Américo de Figueiredo e Melo's painting of 1872. Biard shows a tall, rather diffident man whose hesitant expression and somewhat limp stance do not convey imperial authority in spite of the robes he is wearing. By contrast, Américo de Figueiredo e Melo's portrait presents a strong mature confident man with a full red beard at the opening of parliament (Figure 10). He wears not only the imperial robes but his crown, and the portrait conveys what a commanding figure he represented. This is augmented by the fact that behind him we see key members of his court attending the ceremony, as well as his wife, his daughter and his son-in-law in the balcony above them.

This is a very unusual depiction of Pedro II, however. Like his grandfather Franz I, as an adult he usually—and after 1870 invariably—dressed in a black frock coat, in which costume he was photographed on innumerable occasions.[34] Even when Pedro was portrayed by Victor Meirelles de Lima (1832–1903) in 1864 in an admiral's uniform and wearing the sash of the Grand Cross of the Order of the Cross, the image is not of a military man but of a scholar and thinker. He holds his hat in his left hand and rests his right hand on his hip, but he is standing indoors in an elegant salon in front of a table on which are two globes and three books. Next to him are not his imperial insignia but a bust of an eighteenth-century philosopher. Pedro was in many ways an exception to other contemporary emperors and saw himself differently to them, and his portraits show this.

The Emperor as Servant of the People

Three emperors—Napoleon I, Franz I, and Pedro II—were also portrayed at their desks. In the case of the first two, the aim is to portray them as the servants of their people, working tirelessly in their studies. Jacques-Louis David famously depicted Napoleon I in his study in the Tuileries in 1812 (Figure 25). The clock on the wall reads four o'clock and the candles have almost burned down, indicating that this is four in the morning and that Napoleon has been up all night working. We can read the word 'Code' on one of the documents on the table, indicating that this is the Code Napoléon, his famous set of laws, and lying around are other papers and a quill pen. Napoleon's eyes are tired and he is rather dishevelled. The viewer is not allowed to forget that he is a soldier, however, for he wears the uniform of a

Figure 25 Jacques-Louis David, *Napoleon I in his Study at the Tuileries*. 1812. Oil on canvas. Private Collection Samuel H. Kress Collection/Bridgeman Images

colonel of the Imperial Guard Foot Grenadiers and his sword is resting on the chair and, as always, he wears his Légion d'Honneur and the Order of the Iron Crown.

The same subject matter is portrayed with tellingly different details by Johann Stephan Decker in his portrayal of Franz I in his study in the Hofburg in Vienna in 1826, as shown in Figure 6. Franz wears not a military uniform but a black frock coat. There is none of the elaborate furniture or gold-embroidered upholstery of David's painting. Franz simply sits at his desk at midday, perusing one document with a pile of others in front of him and yet more on a second higher desk nearby. The furniture, apart from a couple of chairs and the two desks, consists of large closed cupboards, doubtless containing other documents. In a Biedermeier touch, the emperor's only companion is a canary in a cage by the window. We have already discussed the myths that grew up around Wilhelm I at the corner window of his study in his palace in Berlin where, so his subjects were told, he had been constantly working since early that morning. Pedro II of Brazil, on the other hand, who was very often portrayed at a desk, usually has his finger in a book and is sitting in front of a pile of other books. The impression given here is of a scholar following his learned hobbies, rather than of a monarch tirelessly governing on behalf of his people.

The Emperor in Uniform

Unlike Napoleon III, Agustín, and Maximilian of Mexico, the four Habsburg and three Hohenzollern emperors came to the throne through dynastic succession and were, in addition to being emperors, monarchs of other territories: the Habsburgs were archdukes of Austria, kings of Bohemia and Hungary, and the Hohenzollerns kings of Prussia. This gave them a legitimacy and a sense of their own importance that predated their imperial dignity. Indeed, Wilhelm I rated his status as king of Prussia far more highly than he did his role as the first German emperor. For all of them, the army was a central pillar of their power and they therefore usually dressed in military uniform.

Franz Joseph succeeded to the throne in 1848 after his uncle's abdication and after the uprising which caused him and his family to take refuge in Olmütz for six months had been quelled, so he felt indebted to the army for saving the monarchy. He surrounded himself with military advisers and made military discipline 'part of the ceremony that regulated all aspects of his public life'.[35] He virtually always wore military uniform, even at such important religious ceremonies as the Washing of the Feet on Maundy Thursday and at the Corpus Christi procession (Figure 26). He, too, was portrayed by Winterhalter, but this portrait, dating to 1864, provides an instructive contrast to that of Napoleon III, for there is no imperial *mise-en-scène* here.[36] Franz Joseph, who by this point had been on the

Figure 26 Franz Xaver Winterhalter, *Franz Joseph I, emperor of Austria, wearing the dress uniform of an Austrian Field Marshal with the Great Star of the Military Order of Maria Theresia.* 1864. Oil on canvas. Kunsthistorisches Museum, Vienna/Bridgeman Images

throne since 1848, wears the full-dress uniform of an Austrian field marshal with the Great Cross of the Military Order of Maria Theresia. His left hand is on his sword, at his neck is the Order of the Golden Fleece, and he wears the three other Austrian royal orders, the so-called 'Hausorden'. His tall straight figure is mirrored by the pillar on either side of him and is silhouetted against a cloudy landscape which opens up behind him. The red lining of his cloak, tossed onto a red chair, mirrors the vivid red of his trousers. There is no crown, sceptre, or imperial cloak. Julius Victor Berger depicted Franz Joseph in 1879 for the Supreme Court wearing the imperial robes of his grandfather, holding a sceptre with the Rudolfine crown next to him on a cushion, and Eduard von Engerth did so in 1861 in the robes of the Order of the Golden Fleece, this time next to the Bohemian crown jewels; and he was of course portrayed in royal Hungarian robes after his coronation as King of Hungary in 1867, but it was as a soldier, as supreme commander of the armed forces, that he was most frequently depicted during his almost seventy-year reign. This remained the case right up until his death at the age of eighty-six. In 1907, for instance, Philip de László (1869–1937), who had already painted him in uniform twice before, painted him yet again in the red full-dress uniform of a field marshal of the Hungarian cavalry.[37]

The Hohenzollerns Wilhelm I, his son Crown Prince Friedrich Wilhelm, later Emperor Friedrich III (1831–88), and Friedrich's son Wilhelm II identified themselves even more strongly with the military and it was only logical that their portraits should depict them as field marshals and generals, magnificent and manly. Wilhelm I became emperor of a unified Germany by successfully waging three wars. This success gave the army 'a nimbus of glory', so that 'the military wove itself more deeply into the fabric of everyday life after 1871.'[38] Wilhelm I's son and heir Friedrich Wilhelm saw distinguished service as an officer in all three wars. Frank Lorenz Müller describes how carefully Friedrich Wilhelm, a fine figure of a man with a magnificent reddish beard and moustache, curated his image and how often he was portrayed in uniform, for instance, by Reinhold Begas in 1867, by Heinrich von Angeli and Franz von Lenbach in 1874, by Gottlieb Biermann and Minna Pfüller in 1888. The most important of the painters Friedrich Wilhelm patronized was Anton von Werner (1853–1915) who became *the* Prussian image-maker. Werner painted, for instance, several versions of the proclamation of the German Empire in the Salle des Glaces in Versailles in January 1871. Each of the three versions, produced in 1877, 1880, and 1885 respectively, shows the uniformed Crown Prince at his father's side, and each version became more and more celebratory of the main actors and less faithful to the actual, rather perfunctory event.[39] In 1897, nine years after Friedrich III's death, Werner completed 'Kaiser Friedrich als Kronprinz auf dem Hofball 1878' (Emperor Friedrich as Crown Prince at the Court Ball in 1878). It shows the tall handsome figure in the centre of the painting wearing a gleaming white cuirassier uniform and surrounded by intellectual, artistic, and political luminaries of the period. This is the official portrait as myth-making after Friedrich's death from throat cancer at the age of fifty-seven.

If Friedrich III had been a successful army commander in his younger days, his son Wilhelm II (1859–1941) was not. He came to the throne in 1888, the 'Year of the Three Emperors', on the deaths of both his grandfather and father, and had a crown made for a planned coronation in 1889 that never took place. He was a supreme publicist who used public events of all kinds to place himself centre stage, usually as a military or naval commander, and who employed the growing mass media to disseminate news and images of these appearances. Though he had a withered left arm, he loved everything to do with both the army and the navy. John C.G. Röhl comments that 'the young heir to the throne threw himself heart and soul into the Prussian-nationalistic and militaristic atmosphere of this new world.'[40]

Wilhelm constantly had himself painted in uniform during his reign, as might be expected. More surprising is that, after his abdication and during his twenty-three-year exile in Huis Doorn, the small manor house in the Netherlands that he inhabited from 1918 until his death in 1941, he continued to do so. The dining room at Huis Doorn is dominated by two of these huge portraits, painted on the occasion of his seventieth birthday in 1929 by Alfred Schwarz (1867–1951). Schwarz was one of the imperial family's favourite painters, and Schwarz's well-known portrait of Empress Auguste Viktoria, who died in 1921, hangs in the same room. Schwarz had already depicted Wilhelm during his reign in a whole series of different military uniforms and in the robes of a Doctor of Civil Laws, an honorary degree conferred on him by Oxford University in 1907. In 1929, in addition to the two uniform portraits just mentioned, Schwarz painted a third portrait of the ex-Kaiser, this time in the uniform of the Leib-Garde-Husaren regiment. He is shown impressively outlined against a black pillar. His black tunic is swathed in gold lace, and from the Iron Cross to his gleaming black boots and from the black scabbard on which his left hand rests to the shako in his right, he is every inch a Prussian officer. This and the other two uniform portraits by Schwarz are state portraits of an ex-emperor who no longer has a state. Eleven years after the end of World War I, in which 1.8 million German soldiers died, and eleven years after his own forced abdication, this elderly man is still projecting himself as a military commander, as the epitome of Prussian militarism. Wilhelm II had always believed his own propaganda, though, according to Benjamin Hasselhorn, he spent these years neither embittered nor plotting his return.[41]

Possessing the Emperor's Image

Representative portraits in oils of every royal figure continued to be produced throughout the period and sometimes, as we saw above, copies were made and distributed to ministries, embassies, and town halls. Formal portraits of monarchs in oils are still produced today for just such official purposes. Oil paintings were also often disseminated in the form of woodcuts or of copper and steel engravings. The nineteenth century saw a revolution in image-making, however, only comparable to the digital developments of our own day. In the 1830s a number of inventors, working independently of each other, invented early forms of what today is called photography. Louis-Jacques Daguerre (1787–1851) unveiled his invention of the daguerreotype in 1839, which the French government bought and presented to the world for free. This enabled one permanent image to be made on a copper plate. Simultaneously Henry Fox Talbot (1800–77) was working on a different technique in Britain, which he also unveiled in 1839. Earlier than either of them was Antoine Hércules Romuald Florence (1804–79) who invented what he was the first to call 'photographie' in Brazil in 1834. Techniques to enable images to be captured from reality were constantly improved and refined throughout the nineteenth century: in 1848 Frederick Scott Archer invented the wet collodion process which enabled images to be printed on paper; in 1871, Richard Maddox pioneered the use of gelatin instead of glass plates; in 1887, Eastman introduced celluloid-based film; in 1888, Kodak brought out the first camera that amateurs could easily use. In 1854, André-Adolphe-Eugène Disdéri (1819–89) invented the so-called *carte de visite*—a small photograph measuring 54 mm by 89 mm pasted onto thicker card—and patented a method of taking eight separate negatives on a single plate, which made the process much cheaper.

Monarchs immediately showed interest in this new medium. In August 1839, the same month that the French government had made Daguerre's invention public, Friedrich Wilhelm III, King of Prussia, had it demonstrated to him in Charlottenburg Palace. His successor, Friedrich Wilhelm IV, created a studio for Hermann Biow, a daguerreotypist from Hamburg, in the palace.[42] Pedro II of Brazil was another early adopter. According to Moritz Schwarcz, he acquired daguerreotype equipment before it was commercially available in Brazil and took photographs himself as soon as this became possible.[43] Queen Victoria and her husband Prince Albert of Saxe-Coburg-Gotha were also in the vanguard and promoted the new medium enthusiastically. They became patrons of the Photographic Society (later the Royal Photographic Society) in 1853. There were court photographers in Berlin in 1857. When Disdéri published photographs of royalty as *cartes de visite*, the format took off and people began to collect them and put them into albums. During the first months of the invention, 270,000 images of the British royal family were apparently sold[44] and Napoleon III's image was another strong seller. When the photographer John Edwin Mayall put an album of fourteen *cartes de visite* of the British royal family on the market in 1860, wholesalers ordered 60,000 copies within a few days and about 400 million *cartes de visite* were sold in England alone during the 1860s.[45]

Photographs, in whatever format, brought emperors and monarchs much closer to their subjects, for the photograph purported to be a realistic representation of its subject, though it was, of course, often retouched, composed of a collage, or hand coloured. In some cases, a photograph revealed a monarch's actual appearance for the first time. Queen Victoria's millions of Indian subjects finally got a realistic idea of what she looked like when thousands of *cartes de visite* of her image as an old lady dressed in black, wearing some very fine lace and her small imperial crown, were distributed on the occasion of her Golden Jubilee in 1887. The downside of this new closeness was that the auratic power conveyed by a state portrait was missing. An individual could own a photograph of her ruler, pore over it, frame it, and put it on the wall of her living room or into an album next to an image of her husband or herself. Photographs often showed an emperor or empress in less godlike poses and in more quotidian settings than in the elaborate environments of the state portrait. Disdéri's *carte de visite* of Napoleon III shows him in day clothes, standing next to an ordinary armchair and in front of a table. Hermann Biow's daguerreotype of King Friedrich Wilhelm IV, reproduced in Pohl, shows an unprepossessing man in front of a rumpled curtain wearing a uniform jacket whose sleeves are visibly too long, as though he were wearing a cast-off.[46] Crown Prince Friedrich Wilhelm of Prussia, the future Emperor Friedrich III, often had himself photographed with his wife and children, thus promoting the image of a happy family life, or wearing ordinary clothes such as hunting costume, revealing his bare knees.[47] Such images certainly brought royal and imperial figures much closer to bourgeois society, but they also aroused the expectation that these persons should conform to bourgeois morals and norms. In addition, once the Kodak camera enabled ordinary citizens to take snapshots, royal and imperial persons lost control over their own image.

The writer Jules Laforgue (1860–87), who came to Berlin at the end of 1881 to take up a post as Empress Augusta's Reader in French, confirms the ubiquity of images of the imperial family. According to his account, 'the busts of the emperor and of the crown prince can be found in all the restaurants in Berlin, in all the bistros, in all the open-air booths which sell mineral water' and furthermore that all along Unter den Linden, photographs of the royal family were advertised:

> here the Crown Prince's family skating with ladies of honour and an aide-de-camp; there a group of huntsmen in the snow: the Crown Prince with his pipe in his mouth, Prince Wilhelm, Minister Puttkamer, the Russian ambassador Count Shuvalov...; again, the young princesses, daughters of the imperial prince, wearing historic costumes...[48]

This means that these images could be purchased, just as the busts could.

If Wilhelm II had himself painted frequently, he virtually never did anything or went anywhere without at least one photographer in attendance. 'He was the first

German monarch to live and work in close proximity—one might even say symbiosis—with photographers and cameramen', writes Clark.[49] During his reign there were some 120 photographers in Germany who were authorized to put 'By Royal Appointment' ('Hofphotographen') on their letterhead.[50] Martin Kohlrausch cites the Berlin photographer who advertised pictures of the emperor in 267 heroic poses, 'all different'.[51] Wilhelm's image was sold and marketed in all kinds of formats and he was known for striking a pose whenever he knew that a photographer was near. This is brilliantly captured by Le Petit Journal, at this point France's biggest daily with a circulation of two million (Figure 27). The caricaturist mocks the way Wilhelm, instantly recognizable from his flashing eyes, his upturned moustache, and his military uniform, turned his journey to the Holy Land in 1898, discussed in chapter VI, into a media event. Not only is a painter busily painting a portrait in the left foreground but there are seventeen cameras trained on the Kaiser in the right foreground and in the middle of the caricature. If we look closely, we can count a further twenty-four cameras in the background, one on every single vantage point. Le Petit Journal is also mocking Wilhelm's utterance in the Church of the Redeemer in Jerusalem when he said: 'From Jerusalem came the light, the blessed light, in whose radiance our German people has become great and glorious.' The extraordinary collection of 12,000 photographs in Huis Doorn, which have only been investigated relatively recently, document Wilhelm's obsession with his own image.[52] Portraits of himself constitute the largest group of images both from the period of his reign and during his exile. Though he took a photographer with him on his steam yacht the 'Hohenzollern' on his yearly Scandinavian cruise which was supposed to be a holiday, most of the photographs that he commissioned show him in uniform maintaining an erect military pose and gazing off into the middle distance, in other words, very similar to the formal portraits in oils. In 1902, for instance, T.H. Voigt, one of the Kaiser's favourite photographers, took a series of portrait photographs of him wearing, respectively, the uniforms of the Austrian Hussar Regiment, of the Order of St John, of which he was Grand Master, of the Hungarian Hussar Regiment, as Captain General of the Spanish Army, and as Admiral of the German Imperial Navy.[53] The swift growth of the illustrated press also made sure that pictures of the emperor were very widely distributed. During Wilhelm's reign there were some thirty-five illustrated magazines in Germany. In 1889, the Leipziger Illustrierte Zeitung had a circulation of 20,000, by 1915, this had grown to 35,000. By 1915, the Berliner Illustrirte Zeitung, founded in 1892, had a circulation of an astonishing 800,000.[54] Everyone knew what the Kaiser looked like and where he had been. Again, as with the ubiquity of his image, this was a double-edged sword, for it aroused expectations of a connection with Wilhelm which, as we saw above when he ignored the veterans, were not necessarily fulfilled; and it also reminded his subjects how often he was away from both Berlin and Potsdam.

Figure 27 Auguste Roubille, *Wilhelm II* from his series of 13 caricatures of political figures around 1900. The title 'Musée de Sires' (museum of monarchs) is a pun on 'Musée de Cires', meaning waxwork museum. Colour lithograph. Bibliothèque des Arts Décoratifs, Paris. Archives Charmet/Bridgeman Images

Photographs of members of the Prussian imperial family, as of other royal families of the day, became cult objects and were given as prized gifts to selected persons. The recipients of these gifts were graded according to their status and the photograph they received accorded with that status. They might receive a photograph in a valuable silver frame or in a simple one, it might be signed by the Kaiser or not, it could be large or small. These photographs were not simply 'given' to the recipient, they were 'presented' ('verliehen'), and they continued to be presented in large numbers during the emperor's twenty-three-year exile in the Netherlands. On the occasion of his seventieth birthday, he not only had himself painted numerous times, as mentioned above, but he also had himself photographed, again in uniform and wearing the Iron Cross. Three hundred and sixteen officials and workers looking after the Hohenzollern fortune were presented with such an official portrait photograph, graded in the way just described.[55] During his exile, he also began to colour the photographs himself. He used photographs to keep his memory alive in Germany among faithful monarchists, hoping for the restoration of his heir to the imperial and Prussian throne. When the Nazis came to power, they forbade the distribution of imperial portraits in 1939.[56] However, it is on record that, in 1942, 6,433 photographs of Wilhelm were sent to Germany, prints of thirty-one different images. Among them were no fewer than 3,000 prints of one of the images.[57]

Eva Giloi provides a subtle and detailed analysis of Wilhelm II's practice in relation to own image and comes to the conclusion that

Wilhelm II's resentment of the 1907 copyright law and of his status as a public man; his stinginess in distributing royal photographs, using them to mark social distance, not populism; his coy lack of support for patriotic memorabilia producers and his reliance on others to distribute his image: all temper the Kaiser's reputation as a media monarch attuned to the 'professional publicity techniques' of twentieth-century marketing.[58]

The 1907 copyright law stated that only the photographer had the rights to an image of someone who could be regarded as a public figure.

Film was another medium that Wilhelm adopted enthusiastically from 1908 on. He had events such as parades, official openings, and state visits filmed and distributed and, once World War I began, this included his visits to the front. He 'used modern media technology as a means to reinvigorate a premodern, regal aura'.[59] The Jewish writer Stefan Zweig, in the memoirs he composed between 1939 and 1941 just before he took his own life in exile in Petrópolis in Brazil, describes seeing one of these newsreels in Tours in France in the spring of 1914.[60] The film showed Wilhelm II visiting the aged Franz Joseph in Vienna. Zweig records his shock at hearing the extremely hostile reaction of the French cinema-goers to the German emperor, realizing at that moment the extent to which hatred of the Germans had been engrained in ordinary French people through propaganda. Photographs, published in the illustrated press, and films shown in every cinema in the developed world, made monarchs and their doings ubiquitous and visible in a way that would have been unthinkable half a century before—and because they were visible, they could also be mocked and criticized. A monarch could promote his own image or not, but he could not control how that image was received. This was also true of one further medium in which emperors were constantly portrayed: statuary. This is discussed in the last chapter.

Notes

1. Mann, *Der Untertan*. The novel was completed in 1914 but not published in German until 1918.
2. *Advenimiento;* Pani, 'El proyecto'.
3. Smith,'A grand work', p. 36.
4. Cohn, *Colonialism*, p. 160–1.
5. Quoted from Plunkett, *Queen Victoria*, p. 57.
6. *Staatsbürger-Zeitung*, August 1906. Quoted from Pohl, 'Der Kaiser', p. 11.
7. Plunkett, *Queen Victoria*, pp. 36–67.
8. Barman, *Citizen Emperor*.
9. Sieg, 'Wilhelm II.'.
10. Geisthövel, 'Wilhelm I.'.
11. Baedeker, *Northern Germany*, p. 14.
12. Geisthövel, 'Wilhelm I', p. 171.
13. Klaußmann, *Kaiser Wilhelm der Große*.
14. Klaußmann, *Kaiser Wilhelm der Große*, p. 15.
15. Giloi, *Monarchy, Myth, and Material Culture*, chapter 7.
16. Kohlrausch, 'Monarchische Repräsentation', p. 106.
17. Bredekamp, *Image Acts*, p. 160.
18. Bredekamp, *Image Acts*, pp. 137–92.
19. Benner, *Strahlen*, p. 359.
20. Taylor, *Empress*. p. 232.
21. Taylor, *Empress*, p. 243.
22. Taylor, *Empress*, pp. 90–1, p. 233.
23. Mansel, *The Eagle*, p. 23.
24. Porterfield and Siegfried, *Staging Empire*, p. 57.
25. Telesko, *Geschichtsraum Osterreich*, pp. 161–2.
26. Ormond and Blackett-Ord, *Franz Xaver Winterhalter*, p. 47.
27. *Spectaculaire Second Empire*, p. 89. The originals of this portrait and the companion portrait of Empress Eugénie are lost, probably destroyed in the fire in the Tuileries in 1871, so that all we have are copies.
28. Ormond and Blackett-Ord, *Franz Xaver Winterhalter*, p. 48.
29. Ormond and Blackett-Ord, *Franz Xaver Winterhalter*, p. 47.
30. Barta, *Maximilian*, pp. 39–40.
31. Acevedo-Valdés, 'La Historia', p. 5.
32. Moritz Schwarcz, *The Emperor's Beard*, p. 60.
33. Moritz Schwarcz, *The Emperor's Beard*, p. 60.

34. The offence Pedro II's underdressed appearance gave at formal court events in Potsdam and Windsor is discussed in chapter III.
35. Unowsky, *Pomp and Politics*, p. 97.
36. Telesko, *Geschichtsraum Österreich*, p. 212.
37. See László, *Catalogue Raisonné*.
38. Clark, *Iron Kingdom*, p. 600.
39. Müller, *Our Fritz*.
40. Röhl, *Wilhelm II, A Concise Life*, p. 25.
41. Hasselhorn, 'Nach dem Königstod', p. 39.
42. Pohl, 'Der Kaiser', p. 9.
43. Moritz Schwarcz, *The Emperor's Beard*, pp. 260–63.
44. Pohl, 'Der Kaiser', p. 10.
45. Müller, *Unser Fritz*, pp. 113–14.
46. Pohl, 'Der Kaiser', p. 10.
47. Müller, *Unser Fritz*, p. 114.
48. Laforgue, *Berlin*, pp. 12–13.
49. Clark, *Iron Kingdom*, p. 589.
50. Kirschstein, *Aus Allerhöchster Schatulle*.
51. Kohlrausch, 'Monarchische Repräsentation', p. 100.
52. Asser and Ruitenberg, *Der Kaiser im Bild*.
53. *Der Kaiser im Bild*, p. 28.
54. *Der Kaiser im Bild*, p. 48.
55. Kirschstein, *Aus Allerhöchster Schatulle*, p. 84.
56. Kirschstein, *Aus Allerhöchster Schatulle*, p. 86.
57. *Der Kaiser im Bild*, p. 13.
58. Giloi, 'Copyrighting the Kaiser', p. 448.
59. Giloi, Copyrighting the Kaiser', p. 449.
60. Zweig, *Die Welt von Gestern*, pp. 283–5. The first edition was published jointly in 1942 by Hamish Hamilton in London and Bermann-Fischer Verlag in Stockholm.

VI

Harnessing Religion to the Imperial Cause

Religion plays a central role in any monarchical system, for it is God Himself who is considered the fount of monarchical power. Imperial regimes, therefore, like monarchical ones, used religion to legitimate as well as to project their power. Individual emperors may have been personally pious, but whether they were or not, they had to demonstrate that they were mandated by God, to be seen to share in the religious practices of their subjects in an official and visible way, and to call the blessings of God down on all their most important endeavours.

Religion played a central role in the staging of the short-lived reign of Agustín I of Mexico. On 16 November 1821, the date of his departure from the capital to begin his military campaign for independence, the anniversary was celebrated in the church of St Francis in Mexico City with a service in honour of Mary's Immaculate Conception, followed by a procession through the streets. There was a service of thanksgiving on 30 December in the shrine of Our Lady of Piety to the south of the city. On 24 February 1822, the anniversary of the date on which Iturbide had proposed the Plan of Iguala and on which the Congress was initiated, the date was also celebrated with a Mass and there was yet another on 2 March to commemorate the date on which the Plan of Iguala was promulgated and on which the army swore loyalty to Iturbide.

Napoleon I and Religion

Emanuel Las Cases reports the following utterance from Napoleon I on St Helena:

> Always, said the emperor, from the moment that I had power, I hastened to re-establish religion. I used it as foundation and root. It became the support of good morals, of true principles, of good manners.[1]

Michael Broers paints a very different picture of Napoleon's dealings with the pope and the church and explains why these ultimately failed. This failure stemmed from his inability to understand 'the religious culture of his times, and . . . popular piety above all', which led to 'his utterly deaf ear to the spiritual sensibilities of the Vatican and the higher clergy'.[2] Napoleon's first dealings with the papacy occurred when, as a young general, he invaded Italy in 1796. He had Pope Pius VI (Giovanni Angelo Braschi, 1717–99, pope from 1775) arrested and transported to France in

Projecting Imperial Power: New Nineteenth-Century Emperors and the Public Sphere. Helen Watanabe-O'Kelly, Oxford University Press (2021). © Helen Watanabe-O'Kelly. DOI: 10.1093/oso/9780198802471.003.0007

1798, where he died in 1799 in Valence. 'In the eyes of the world Pius VI died a martyr', writes Eamon Duffy.[3] The new pope, elected in 1800, was Barnaba Niccolò Chiaramonte (1742–1823), who took the name of Pius VII. Napoleon needed an agreement with the church to enable him to pacify France, but, writes Broers, 'Napoleon's whole view of the world baulked at the prospect of the Church exercising real, independent influence over society.'[4] During his time as First Consul, after a series of difficult negotiations, he reinstated the Catholic religion in France, suppressed during the French Revolution and still anathema to Republicans, by signing a Concordat with Pius VII on 15 June 1801. This allowed Sunday worship again and clergy who had gone into exile were allowed to return, but the church was to be subordinate to the state, confiscated church property was not returned, feast days and processions were cut to a minimum, only a handful of teaching and nursing orders were allowed to exist, and, though Catholicism was recognized as the religion of the majority of French people, it was to have equal status with Judaism, Lutheranism, and Calvinism. Napoleon kept the right to appoint bishops and oversee church finances.[5] On the first Easter Sunday after the signing of the Concordat, 18 April 1802, Napoleon went to Notre-Dame to Mass in a glittering procession with trumpets blaring, accompanied by the papal nuncio Cardinal Caprara.[6]

Napoleon, for all his contempt and mistrust of religion and of the church, needed it to project his power. Although he had already been elected emperor by the French people in a plebiscite, he organized the coronation ceremony in Notre-Dame, discussed in chapter I, to demonstrate that he was also God's chosen ruler, going so far as to bring the pope to Paris to preside over it and to anoint him and his consort. Just how important the Catholic Church was to a majority of the population was demonstrated by the pope's triumphal journey to Paris for the coronation, with crowds of people kneeling at the roadside for his blessing.[7] In 1806, Napoleon issued the Imperial Catechism as the basis for religious instruction in French schools. Lesson VII of this document states:

> God [...] has established him [=Napoleon, HWOK] as our Sovereign, and has made him the minister of His power and image on earth. To honour and serve our emperor is then to honour and to serve God Himself.[8]

Napoleon's claim to a divine mandate could not be more clearly stated.

Napoleon went further in his instrumentalization of religion by creating the feast of St-Napoleon as a public holiday in 1806.[9] The decree, promulgated on 19 February 1806, called the new holiday 'the feast of St Napoleon and of the re-establishment of the Catholic religion in France' and proclaimed that it was to be celebrated on 15 August throughout the empire with a church service and a Te Deum. This date was Napoleon's birthday, but it was also the Feast of the Assumption of the Blessed Virgin, already a popular feast day. By choosing

15 August, Napoleon was not only celebrating himself but piggybacking on an existing religious festival. In the very same decree, he also called for a church service on the first Sunday of December to commemorate both his coronation and the Battle of Austerlitz as an occasion for 'each citizen to dedicate his life to his prince and to his fatherland'.[10] In both cases, Napoleon was linking homage to God with celebration of his person and his military victories and with dedication to his political aims. Whether St Napoleon ever existed is doubtful.[11] His name was said to be a variant of that of Neopolis, a third-century Roman martyr who resisted Emperor Maximianus (*c*.250–310 CE) and whom the Papal Legate Cardinal Giovanni Battista Caprara (1733–1810) produced when Napoleon I wanted a patron saint to enable him to celebrate his name day. St Napoleon was very suitable for the emperor's purposes, for he could be presented as the patron saint of warriors and as someone who was prepared to die for his people.

This instrumentalization of religion for his own ends in France did not stop Napoleon's ambitions to annexe the Papal States. If a concordat could be signed with Pius VII as ecclesiastical ruler, as a temporal ruler he stood in the way of Napoleon's intention to conquer Italy. In January 1808, French forces occupied Rome and took the pope prisoner, bringing him to Savona on the French Riviera, and later to Fontainebleau. He remained Napoleon's prisoner for five years. Though he excommunicated Napoleon in September 1809 and annulled the Concordat, Napoleon carried on using the church to provide ceremonial on important occasions and to give them legitimacy. The singing of a Te Deum in every church throughout the land was de rigueur on the occasion of a military victory, for instance.

Napoleon divorced Joséphine de Beauharnais, who could not give him a son, and married Marie-Louise of Austria on 2 April 1810 in a church ceremony in a specially decorated room in the Louvre.[12] He could not be married in Notre-Dame because the See of Paris was vacant, and Pius VII had not appointed an archbishop. Napoleon and his bride processed from St-Cloud in a grand cortege of carriages through the only partially completed Arc de Triomphe and down the Champs-Elysées. Napoleon had decided to move the Holy See and the College of Cardinals from Rome to Paris and had already transported the Vatican archives. He now ordered all twenty-seven cardinals to attend his wedding in the Louvre, but thirteen of them staged a revolt and did not attend. Napoleon was still married to Joséphine in their eyes, and the cardinals were not prepared to endorse a ceremony which was against the laws of the church nor to lend credence to the man who had imprisoned the pope. Napoleon punished them by removing them from their bishoprics, forbidding them to appear as cardinals, and depriving them of their pensions. A year later, Marie-Louise gave birth to the son Napoleon needed to establish his dynasty. He was christened Napoleon François Charles Joseph (1811–32) and Napoleon gave him the title of 'Roi de Rome', King of the Romans, the title used by the son and designated heir of the Holy Roman

Emperor. He needed the church again for a suitably grand christening ceremony, which took place in Notre-Dame on 9 June 1811.

Ultimately, Napoleon failed in his attempt to bend the church to his will. When he returned to Fontainebleau in January 1813 after his defeat in Russia, he met his prisoner, the pope, who was isolated without any advisers or any news of the outside world, and so Napoleon was able to talk him into another concordat, the Concordat of Fontainebleau. In this document, the pope renounced his temporal power and gave up the Papal States. He soon revoked it, however, and in 1814 returned to Rome, his journey again resembling a triumphal procession. In April 1814, Napoleon abdicated, while Pius VII continued to hold office until his death in 1823.

Napoleon III, Religion, and the Feast of Saint-Napoleon

After Napoleon's departure for St Helena in 1815 until 1848, during both the Bourbon restoration and the July monarchy, only scattered Bonapartist groups continued to mark the feast of Saint-Napoleon.[13] Louis-Napoléon (1808–73), Napoleon I's nephew revived it, playing on his uncle's reputation, as he did on every other occasion. After the 1848 revolution and the end of the reign of King Louis-Philippe, Louis-Napoléon, whom scarcely anyone in the country knew personally, was elected the first President of France—or Prince-President, as he preferred to be called. He filled this position from December 1848 until late 1851. When he could not be re-elected president according to the constitution, he seized power in a *coup d'état* on 2 December 1851. Less than three weeks after the coup, on 21 and 22 December, Louis-Napoléon asked all adult males in a plebiscite to allow him to draw up a new constitution, one which would allow him to remain in power for much longer. Seven and a half million men voted in favour and the new constitution gave him sweeping powers, as well as allowing him to rule for consecutive terms of ten years. The resounding victory of the plebiscite was celebrated with a Te Deum in Notre-Dame on 1 January 1852 and bishops and prefects throughout France were requested to organize similar services in all the cathedrals and churches nationwide.[14]

Certain aspects of the Te Deum in Notre-Dame are reminiscent of Napoleon I's coronation. The decorations were designed by the medievalizing architects Eugène Viollet-Le-Duc (1814–79) and Jean-Baptiste-Antoine Lassus (1807–57). The interior of the cathedral was hung with red velvet embroidered with gold Ns and stands were erected on both sides of the nave to provide seating for dignitaries and the national delegates. Ninety flags representing the ninety departments hung from the upper part of the nave. Louis-Napoléon sat on a large dais in the centre of the transept beneath a velvet canopy. Outside above the entrance, an awning bore the letters 'L-N', paintings of Charlemagne, Saint Louis, Louis XIV, and

Napoleon I decorated the two towers of the cathedral, and in large gilded figures across the front of the cathedral was inscribed the number 7,500,000, indicating the number of yes votes in the plebiscite.[15] The cannon at the Invalides boomed out seventy-five times, again a reference to the plebiscite. Louis-Napoléon was escorted to his throne-like seat in the transept, and three hundred singers and two hundred musicians played music from Napoleon's coronation. After the church service, Louis-Napoléon returned not to the Elysée Palace where he was actually living, but to the Tuileries, the palace of the kings of France.

Louis-Napoléon was proclaimed Napoleon III, Emperor of the French, on 2 December 1852—the anniversary of the coronation of Napoleon I, of the Battle of Austerlitz, and of the coup of 1851. He had been elected emperor in another plebiscite, this time by 7,800,000 million men. Following so soon after the proclamation, Napoleon III's marriage to Eugénie de Montijo on 30 January 1853 in Notre-Dame, again lavishly decorated by Viollet-Le-Duc and Lassus, can be seen as a substitute for the coronation the new emperor never had, as Truesdell points out (Figure 28).[16] Equestrian statues of Napoleon I and Charlemagne flanked the portico to the cathedral erected for the occasion and the marriage procession was designed to resemble that of Napoleon I and Marie Louise of Austria as closely as possible. Paintings of Charlemagne, Saint Louis, Louis XIV, and Napoleon I decorated the towers of the cathedral. On 14 June 1856, the baptism of Napoleon III's son, called the Prince Imperial, took place again in Notre-Dame performed by the papal nuncio Cardinal Patrizzi, representing the pope who was the baby's godfather. The same team designed the decoration of the cathedral, which was again the theatre in which a religious sacrament was made the pretext for a show of imperial grandeur, linking the second emperor with his uncle.

In a move reminding the populace and the army of the glory days of Napoleon I, it was decided to replace the gallic rooster which had crowned regimental standards under King Louis-Philippe with Napoleonic eagles. The new standards were distributed on 11 May 1852 in a ceremony on the Champ de Mars, where the original ceremony had taken place in 1806 under Napoleon I. Sixty thousand soldiers from forty-eight infantry battalions and fifty-six cavalry battalions, as well as some other units, gathered for the distribution. The essentially military ceremony was again given ecclesiastical legitimacy by the presence of a thousand clerics from all over Paris led by the archbishop. They processed to 'an elaborate canopied altar platform'[17] where they had to wait while Louis-Napoléon in a general's uniform reviewed the troops and presented the eagles. Then Mass was said, after which the archbishop blessed the new standards and the kneeling generals. As Hazareesingh points out, under Napoleon III, Te Deums were also held to celebrate the military successes of the Crimean War in 1855 and the Italian campaigns in 1859, the emperor's survival after the assassination attempt by Orsini in 1858, and the annexation of Nice and Savoy in 1860.[18]

THE MARRIAGE CEREMONY IN NOTRE DAME.

Figure 28 Napoleon III, Marriage to Eugénie de Montijo, Countess of Teba, in 1853 in Notre-Dame Cathedral, Paris. Engraving. Private Collection Look and Learn/ Illustrated Papers Collection/Bridgeman Images

Louis-Napoléon went further in his use of religion to endorse political actions. In a decree of 16 February 1852, he reinstituted the feast of St Napoleon and made 15 August not only a national holiday but *the* sole national holiday, ordering that it was to be celebrated in every commune throughout France.[19] The decree stated that this feast day was chosen because celebrations of political anniversaries often led to civic discord, whereas the Saint-Napoleon would 'reunite everyone in the common sentiment of national glory'. As Truesdell comments: '15 August was to be an annual reminder that what unified France as a nation in the nineteenth century was the glorious memory of the First Empire.'[20] The past was being used to underpin the present. The first celebration of the Saint-Napoleon in Paris began with Mass at the church of the Madeleine and a military review on the Champs-Elysées, followed by an extraordinarily lavish festival in which all could take part. Temporary theatres on the Champs-Elysées gave free performances, as did a number of the permanent theatres, the city centre was illuminated with coloured lampions, there was a naval battle on the Seine, there were greasy poles to be climbed in order to carry off valuable gifts, and there was an impressive firework display showing Napoleon I crossing the St Bernard Pass and besieging the Bard Fortress. The centre of Paris was decorated with all kinds of ephemeral architecture: an enormous eagle on the Arc the Triomphe and four more eagles surmounting the Vendôme Column. The lamp posts along the Champs-Elysées were decorated with N's and eagles, there were sixty-two seven-metre-high fountains decorated with statues along the avenue, and a large equestrian statue at the rondpoint. At the Marché des Innocents, a ballroom big enough to accommodate 20,000 people was erected with an almost baroque façade in which a huge N and an eagle figured prominently. Figure 29 depicts a scene from the Saint-Napoleon of 1853.

The Saint-Napoleon was celebrated every year, apart from 1870. Describing the festival of 1859 in the *Moniteur Universel* on 16 August, Théophile Gautier praises the fireworks and the illuminations but focuses also on the fact that the opening of all the regular theatres for free gave ordinary people ('the unlettered mob', as he calls them) the opportunity to experience great art: Corneille, Racine, Molière, Mozart, Rossini, and Meyerbeer, and he describes with fulsome praise the religious silence in which people listened to Corneille's verse drama *Polyeucte*.[21]

All the Saint-Napoleon celebrations throughout France began with a church service, and the involvement of the church was a key element. Church and secular authorities often worked hand in hand in a seamlessly harmonious way, the local priest blessing the bonfire at Tourtour (Var) in 1859 and the archbishop blessing the standard of the 14th Artillery Regiment in Rennes in 1860.[22] As well as the church service, the celebration of the Saint-Napoleon embodied an important element of charity to the poor and always also consisted of a military parade or

Figure 29 Fête of the Saint-Napoleon on 15 August in the Champs-Élysées in Paris. *Illustrated London News*, 20 August 1853. Engraving. Private Collection Look and Learn/Illustrated Papers Collection/Bridgeman Images

review, free entertainments of all kinds, and a firework display. Hazareesingh shows, however, how the celebrations varied in different parts of the country both from each other and from those in Paris, how inventive different communes could be in what they provided by way of entertainment, and how the celebrations could foster forgiveness and compassion, patriotism and communal pride, but could also provide opportunities for dissent. The Catholic Church (and its legitimist faithful) were not always happy that the Feast of the Assumption of the Blessed Virgin should be taken over by the Saint-Napoleon. When both ecclesiastical and civic authorities worked together, however, 'the celebrations took on an added dimension, becoming instruments for the promotion of a distinct civic order.'[23] The festival meant 'an incorporation of the religious sphere by the state.'[24]

When the Second Empire came to an end after the Franco-Prussian War of 1870–71, this festival, which honoured an invented saint in a national celebration called into being by governmental decree and which used the name of Napoleon I to bolster the power of Napoleon III, came to an end. The Saint-Napoleon continued to be celebrated by certain groups in Paris, in Marseille, in the southwest and in Corsica during the 1880s and 1890s, even though by now the official celebration of the Third Republic had been declared to be 14 July, Bastille Day.[25]

Franz Joseph and Austrian Piety

For the House of Habsburg, that overt and visible religious devotion known as the *pietas austriaca* was part of the dynasty's self-definition. This piety had three main elements: devotion to the Cross, to the Virgin Mary, and to the Eucharist.[26] From the sixteenth to the eighteenth century, the Habsburgs believed that the Virgin Mary as the *Magna Mater Austriae* helped them to win battles against the Protestants, for instance, at the Battle of Mühlberg in 1547 and against the Turks at Lepanto in 1571 and at the Siege of Vienna in 1683. As they saw it, it was their devotion to the Cross and to the Eucharist that enabled them to re-catholicize those parts of their dominions that had gone over to Protestantism. The practice of their religion played a large part in their daily ceremonial. All the members of the dynasty engaged in frequent rituals of penance and devotion to the Virgin Mary and the saints, they went on pilgrimages, and for them Catholicism was the state religion. Though the Enlightenment rationalism of Joseph II (who reigned from 1765 to 1780 together with his mother Maria Theresia and from 1780 to 1790 alone) brought a halt to many manifestations of Counter-Reformation piety, the imperial family renewed its association with Catholicism during the almost seventy-year reign of Emperor Franz Joseph from 1848 to 1916. He had been brought up a strict Catholic by his mother, Sophie of Bavaria (1805–72), and was also personally devout. It is recorded, for instance, that he attended Mass daily in private as an act of personal piety, not just for reasons of convention.[27]

He had come to the throne as the consequence of the suppression of a popular uprising, and regarded conservative Catholicism as a bulwark against dangerous revolutionary ideas which might burst forth again at any moment.[28] He was not a bigot and in the course of his imperial duties came into contact with Orthodox Christians, Jews, and Muslims. However, Catholicism was for him the only true religion and he was confirmed in this attitude by his first conservative prime minister and foreign minister Felix Prinz von Schwarzenberg (1800–52), whose brother was a cardinal, and also by his own tutor Joseph Otmar von Rauscher (1797–1875). Rauscher became Archbishop of Vienna in 1853, a post he held until his death, and was made a cardinal in 1855. In that year, on his twenty-fifth birthday, Franz Joseph signed a Concordat with Pope Pius IX, giving the church complete control over the theological faculties in the universities, as well as over education in primary and secondary schools, where Catholic pupils had to be taught by Catholic teachers. The church was also given control over marriage law, and Catholicism became the official state religion, superior to other confessions and religions. Franz Joseph revoked the laws passed by Joseph II in the eighteenth century which had curtailed the power of the pope over subjects of the emperor. The church was given considerable power, but Franz Joseph nonetheless saw it as the servant of the state.[29] Ruling as a neo-absolutist monarch without a parliament, he saw the church and the army as the pillars of his power.

That he himself was genuinely pious was visible to all who were present at his entry into Jerusalem on 9 November 1869—one of his titles after all was 'King of Jerusalem'. This occurred during his sojourn of about a week in the Holy Land, in the course of which he also visited Bethlehem, Jericho, the River Jordan, the Dead Sea, and Jaffa. This was part of a trip to the Middle East from 25 October to 6 December 1869, the immediate impetus for which was the opening of the Suez Canal on 17 November 1869. When Franz Joseph reached the point from which he could see Jerusalem, he knelt down, prayed, and kissed the ground. Wearing dress uniform, he processed into the city, visited the Holy Sepulchre, Mary's tomb, the Garden of Gethsemane, the Mount of Olives, and the Tomb of Lazarus, and, in the chapel of the Holy Sepulchre, he took communion. The whole visit clearly made a deep impression on him, as his letters to his wife attest.[30]

Habsburg piety was also visible in the public participation by the imperial family and the court in the major religious ceremonies of the Catholic Church. In her memoirs, published in 1932, Princess Nora Fugger (Eleonora Fugger von Babenhausen, 1864–1945), who had been at the centre of Viennese society since she came to court in the late 1880s, relates how the ceremonial year began at the Viennese court with the religious devotion known as the Quarant'ore, forty hours of prayer spread over four days and lasting from eight in the morning to six in the evening.[31] On Maundy Thursday in Holy Week, the imperial couple washed the feet of thirteen poor men and thirteen poor women, a ceremony watched by members of the court. The imperial couple and the court venerated the cross on Good Friday and on Holy Saturday celebrated the Resurrection in the 'Auferstehungsfeier'.[32] The celebration of the Resurrection consisted of a service in the Hofburg chapel and a procession through the Hofburg complex. Princess Nora describes the procession led by three clerics followed by about a hundred court officials, twenty priests, a large number of gentlemen of the bedchamber, important public figures, privy counsellors, government ministers, the prime minister, and all the archdukes (uncles, brothers, or sons of the emperor). They were followed by the imperial chaplain holding the monstrance with the host under a baldachin. Behind that came the Lord Chief Marshal and then the emperor in his field marshal's dress uniform wearing the collar of the Golden Fleece. He was accompanied by his chief courtiers and followed by the Chief Marshal of the empress, by the empress herself with her ladies of the bedchamber, followed by the archduchesses. Everyone wore their most splendid uniforms, jewels, and decorations.

Where imperial piety was on public display in the streets of Vienna was in the Corpus Christi procession which took place in either May or June, depending on the date of Easter. Seeing the imperial family taking part in it reminded people of how faith in the Eucharist was part of Habsburg myth and, as mentioned above,

Franz Joseph's younger brother Maximilian, Emperor of Mexico, transported the ceremonial of the Corpus Christi procession to Mexico City, setting it out in detail in his printed handbook of court ceremonial and etiquette in 1867.[33] Two important legends which were part of the myth of Habsburg veneration of the Eucharist are depicted in the Franzensburg, Franz I's early nineteenth-century dynastic monument discussed in chapter I. One tells how, in 1268, Count Rudolf of Habsburg (1218–91) gave his horse to a priest to enable him to cross a flooded river and bring the Eucharist to a dying man. In another legend, Emperor Maximilian I, while out hunting in 1484, was trapped on a rock face known as the Martinswand near Innsbruck. Various versions of the episode relate either that he was blessed with the sacrament from below or was given the Eucharist on a long pole or that he simply prayed to the Eucharist, whereupon an angel came and showed him the way down.[34]

At the Corpus Christi procession, archdukes and their retinues, court officers, the heads of all the first families of the realm, and the emperor drove up to St Stephen's Cathedral in the centre of Vienna in magnificent carriages.[35] From here the immense procession set off on foot, winding its way through the streets, accompanying the sacrament held aloft in a monstrance under a baldachin. Members of all the religious orders, secular priests, representatives of parishes, the members of the cathedral chapter, members of knightly orders, and many others made up the procession. Behind the sacrament came the emperor on foot, followed by the archdukes. There was singing, incense, and the ringing of church bells. Like the foot-washing at the Maundy Thursday ceremony, the emperor processing on foot, as he did at Easter, was meant to express not just piety and devotion but also humility before God. Catholic belief created a real problem for the dynasty when Crown Prince Rudolf (1858–89) killed his lover Mary Vetsera (1871–89) at his hunting lodge at Mayerling and then shot himself. If the true events were admitted, Rudolf, as a murderer and a suicide, could not be buried in consecrated ground. One might say that Austrian imperial piety was rewarded when the last Habsburg emperor, Karl I (1887–1922), was beatified in 2004.

The Hohenzollern Emperors as Defenders of Protestantism

If the two Bonaparte emperors instrumentalized Catholic ritual and a supposed Catholic saint's day to project their imperial power, the Hohenzollerns constituted themselves the guardians of Protestantism. This took on a new dimension when they became German emperors in 1871, but it goes back to 1815 when the Treaty of Vienna assigned the northern two fifths of Saxony to Prussia. This meant that all the sites associated with Martin Luther—Eisleben, Mansfeld, Magdeburg, Erfurt, and especially Wittenberg—were now under the jurisdiction of the Hohenzollern kings of Prussia. Saxony had always been proud of its status as the cradle of the Reformation, but since, under Lutheran administrative structures, the territorial ruler always functioned as the 'summus episcopus', the head of the church in his lands, from 1815 on, the Prussian king had jurisdiction over the most important sites of the Lutheran Reformation.

There is an irony in this for, from 1613 to 1817, the Hohenzollerns were Calvinists and not Lutherans. In 1817, Friedrich Wilhelm III, King of Prussia (1770–1840), merged the Lutheran and Calvinist confessions in his kingdom into one single so-called 'evangelisch-christliche Kirche', later known as the Preussische Unionskirche. This was not uncontroversial, especially for orthodox Lutherans, but after the merger had gone through, two Hohenzollern kings, Friedrich Wilhelm III and Friedrich Wilhelm IV (1795–1861), and three German Emperors—Wilhelm I (1797–1888), Friedrich III (1831–88), and Wilhelm II (1859–1941)—were in turn 'summus episcopus' of the United Protestant Church of Prussia.[36] They used this position to present themselves and their dynasty increasingly as the champions not just of German Protestantism, but of European, and in the case of Wilhelm II, even world Protestantism. Prussia could claim to have a track record here, for it had not only accepted considerable numbers of Huguenots expelled from France in the late seventeenth and in the eighteenth century but had even provided a refuge for Lutherans who were expelled from the Archbishopric of Salzburg in 1732.[37]

The absorption of all the key Lutheran sites into Prussia coincided with a change in the way Luther was regarded by Germans.[38] The Napoleonic Wars, with the widespread suffering occasioned by the French occupation of Prussia in particular, led to an upsurge in German national feeling, so that Luther became a symbol of German nationalism, a representative of the ordinary German people who had had the courage to stand up to foreign domination. The development of this cult of Luther as courageous national German hero coincided with Prussia's pride in its defeat of the French enemy at the Battle of Waterloo. With the reassignment of territory at the Treaty of Vienna, the heroic Prussian nation could now claim the heroic German Luther as one of its own.

Inaugurating the Schlosskirche in Wittenberg in 1892

If Wittenberg was the key Lutheran town, the Schlosskirche or Castle Church was the key Lutheran site in that town, for it was here that Luther was said to have nailed the ninety-five theses to the church door and it is here that he and Melanchthon are buried. The Schlosskirche had, however, suffered considerably during the Napoleonic Wars: on 27 September 1813 the church tower had caught fire, though the church itself remained largely undamaged, but Wittenberg was besieged three times and French troops used the Castle and the Castle Church as a fortress, for instance boarding up the church windows. Very soon after

Wittenberg became Prussian in 1815, the architect Karl Friedrich Schinkel (1781–1841) was sent to make a report on the state of the building. The interior of the church as he found it had been altered in the mid-eighteenth century after the church had burned down in the Seven Years War (1756–64). Schinkel proposed to renovate the church so as to make it a 'a monument to its significance as the premier church of the Reformation'.[39] By this he meant that it should be restored in a Gothic style, Gothic being regarded as the national style that symbolized the German spirit but also because it corresponded to that in use in Luther's own day. Friedrich Wilhelm III died in 1840 and his son Friedrich Wilhelm IV succeeded him, a monarch who saw himself as God's anointed with a special mission to promote the Protestant religion in Prussia. Though a full restoration in the Gothic style was again under discussion, Friedrich Wilhelm IV's main contribution to the Schlosskirche was to commission massive bronze doors—nowadays known as 'die Thesentür'—on which the Latin text of the ninety-five theses was inscribed, surmounted by a tympanum painted by August von Kloeber, depicting Christ on the cross, flanked on one side by Luther holding his Bible translation and on the other by Melanchthon holding the Augsburg Confession. Above the painting the original figures of Friedrich the Wise and Johann the Steadfast, the two Saxon dukes who had supported Luther, were placed on pedestals. The lintel over the doors, however, bears an inscription commemorating Friedrich Wilhelm IV as the king who commissioned them, with the Prussian eagle in the middle of the inscription. In his speech at the inauguration of the doors in 1858, 375 years after Luther's birth, Superintendent Sander spoke of Friedrich Wilhelm IV as 'walking in the footsteps of Friedrich the Wise'.[40] The Saxon dynasty of the Wettins was thus superseded by the Prussian dynasty of the Hohenzollerns. The church itself had still not been renovated, however, and it took a groundswell of popular opinion and the fact that the kings of Prussia had become German emperors in 1871 for the renovation to be properly taken in hand.

The man responsible for overseeing the planning of the renovation was not Kaiser Wilhelm I, by now in his eighties, but his heir, Crown Prince Friedrich Wilhelm. The plans for the renovation by the Berlin architect Friedrich Adler (1827–1904) were completed in 1883, the 400th anniversary of Luther's birth. The Crown Prince was a fervent Protestant who was devoted to the idea of the United Protestant Church of Prussia but who, influenced by his English wife Victoria, dreamed of turning the Schlosskirche into 'a second Westminster Abbey' containing monuments of all the famous German Protestants, or, in the words of Friedrich Adler, into 'a Pantheon of German heroes of faith and of intellect'.[41] The Schlosskirche was to become a memorial to Protestantism, but also a monument to the Hohenzollern dynasty. The church tower was rebuilt to the gigantic height of 88 metres, with the words of Luther's hymn 'Ein feste Burg ist unser Gott' (a mighty fortress is our God) inscribed below the dome. A rib-vaulted ceiling, a large Gothic altarpiece framing the figures of Christ, Peter, and Paul, and a pulpit in the Gothic style were installed inside the church. The upper part of the walls of the nave was decorated with twenty-two medallions honouring notable European Protestants down the ages—the monarchs Gustav Vasa, king of Sweden, and Christian, king of Denmark, Joachim II, duke of Brandenburg, a Hohenzollern ancestor who had reluctantly become Lutheran in 1539, the Swiss reformers Zwingli and Calvin, the painters Albrecht Dürer and Lucas Cranach, the poet Hans Sachs, the churchmen Martin Bucer, Savonarola, and John Wyclif. Below them in front of each pillar are nine larger than life-size statues of important Reformers: Luther, Melanchthon, Johannes Bugenhagen, Georg Spalatin, Julius Jonas, Johannes Brenz, Urbanus Rhegius, Nikolaus von Amsdorf, and Caspar Cruciger. Fifty-two coats of arms of Protestant princes and knights were carved in stone along the galleries on either side of the nave, and 198 coats of arms of Protestant towns were depicted in the stained-glass windows. On either side of the altar were placed the original free-standing figures of the Saxon Electors who were Luther's protectors: Friedrich the Wise (1463–1525) and Johann the Steadfast (1468–1532). The new interior decoration of the Schlosskirche is therefore a monument to the Reformation.

Wilhelm I died in 1888 aged ninety-one, the Crown Prince reigned for only ninety-nine days as Friedrich III and never lived to see the Schlosskirche renovated as he had planned it. In the same year, the 'Year of the Three Emperors', Wilhelm II (who reigned from 1888 to 1918) succeeded as King of Prussia and German Emperor. He was concerned to increase the status of the Protestant Church in Prussia as a bastion against Catholicism, but he wanted it even more to be a bulwark against the rising Social Democratic movement.[42] However, as Thomas Harmut Benner shows conclusively, he was personally extremely devout, and saw himself not just as 'summus episcopus' of Prussia but as 'imperator christianus' and as God's instrument.[43] He gave sermons on board ship on his annual 'Nordlandreisen', for instance, which he published.[44] He used the ceremonies for the consecration of the newly renovated church in 1892 to present himself to his subjects and to the invited guests not just as the leader of German but of European Protestantism.[45] He commissioned twenty-two choir stalls, the so-called 'Fürstengestühl', for the twenty-two Protestant German princes and Free Imperial Cities whose representatives he had invited, and had them installed in the choir of the church. He also commissioned a separate imperial throne for himself, on the left as we look at the altar, and had it decorated on the front with Prussian eagles and with the imperial crown and with the Hohenzollern coat of arms on the back, as well as heraldic decoration on the top (Figure 30). Actual Renaissance choir stalls to seat the representatives of the queens of England and the Netherlands as well as the kings of Sweden and Denmark, who were guests at the opening ceremony, were lent by the Berlin Museum of Applied Art.

Figure 30 Wilhelm II's imperial throne
in the Schlosskirche in Wittenberg
1892. Photo © Ekkehard Henschke

Wilhelm chose 31 October 1892, the 375th anniversary of the nailing of the
ninety-five theses to the door of the Schlosskirche, as the date for the inauguration
of the renovated church, and he commanded all the churches in his lands to ring
their bells at the same hour as the inauguration in Wittenberg. On the day of the
ceremony, he arrived by train and, in a modern version of the solemn entry or
adventus, processed up a street lined with militia and decorated with flags and
garlands, arriving at a triumphal arch crowned with a huge Prussian eagle and the
letter W. The arch was decorated with figures representing Catechism with the
tablets of Moses and Luther's Bible translation. It was also decorated with trophies. In keeping with this military aspect, the emperor wore the uniform of the
Prussian Lifeguards with its characteristic helmet crowned with a silver eagle, and,
as his first action, reviewed his guard of honour, the First Company of the Third
Brandenburg Infantry Regiment, who then marched past. He then entered a
pavilion erected in front of the 'Thesentür' where, before the busts of his grandfather and father, he accepted the golden key to the church before presenting it to
Dr Barkhausen, the head of the Protestant Church Council in Prussia, the
'Evangelischer Oberkirchenrat'. The religious service of dedication was therefore
prefaced with dynastic and military elements.

After the service with its hymns, sermon, and prayers, Wilhelm went to Luther's house in Wittenberg where, drinking a toast from the cup which the University of Wittenberg had given Luther and Katharina von Bora as a wedding gift, he launched into his own profession of faith, stressing again the unity of all German and European Protestants. He and all the princes present signed a copy of the so-called 'Wittenberg Profession of Faith'. Then the Kaiser and his party watched a procession of costumed figures and floats, commemorating the Reformation, in which almost a thousand people took part, and a performance of Hans Herrig's popular play *Martin Luther*, before returning to Berlin.

Church-Building in the Prussian Lands

In the meantime, the imperial couple had become associated with a massive programme of church-building in Berlin to cater for the spiritual needs of the expanding capital city, and throughout Prussian territory, which included the Catholic Rhineland. Their involvement began with the founding of the 'Evangelisch-Kirchlicher Hilfsverein' at what is known as the Waldersee Meeting on 28 November 1887. This took place before Wilhelm II succeeded as emperor, but when it was already clear that he would shortly do so. It is named after Alfred Graf von Waldersee (1832–1904), a reactionary and anti-Semitic general in whose quarters it took place. It was intended to raise funds for the poor of the city under the aegis of the City Mission. The City Mission was led by Adolf Stoecker (1835–1909), who, though court chaplain, was at the same time a rabble-rousing anti-Semitic right-wing politician who saw the building of churches as a weapon against socialist, liberal, and democratic tendencies and as a way to bring the workers back to the church. Also involved in this meeting was Ernst Freiherr von Mirbach (1844–1925), a Prussian officer who had served in the three wars of Unification and who in 1882 had become Gentleman of the Bedchamber to the then Princess Auguste Viktoria (1858–1921). Out of the 'Evangelisch-Kirchlicher Hilfsverein' emerged a 'Kirchenbau-Verein', in which Baron Mirbach found his true calling.[46] In 1888 he became head of the Empress's household, a post he held for over twenty-five years. He ran her private office, corresponded on her behalf with various institutions and ministries, administered her financial affairs, and represented her on many important bodies of which she was patron. This included above all the building of churches, for which Baron Mirbach became the chief fundraiser.

Bismarck managed to detach Wilhelm and Auguste Viktoria from Stoecker and his reactionary agenda, but the empress became the patron of the 'Kirchenbau-Verein', founded on 2 May 1890, and made it one of her chief causes to promote the building of churches in the newly created parishes in Berlin and further afield. In 1903, Baron Mirbach could report with satisfaction that, in only fifteen years, fifty-three churches had been built, thirty-nine of which had the Empress as their patron.[47] During the reign of Wilhelm II, 112 churches were erected in Greater Berlin, the majority of them Protestant churches.[48] These buildings with their imposing towers, often built of red brick and situated in a prominent position in the midst of the parishes they were built to serve, are a characteristic feature of Berlin today.

Prestigious Imperial Church Projects

If the empress became more and more involved with the building of parish churches, often donating the land and attending the inauguration, Wilhelm II was concerned with three more prestigious Protestant church projects: the Church of the Redeemer ('Erlöserkirche') in Jerusalem, the Emperor Wilhelm Memorial Church ('Kaiser Wilhelm-Gedächtnis-Kirche') in the centre of Berlin in honour of his grandfather, and, most prestigious of all, the erection of a new and imposing cathedral for Berlin opposite the Imperial Palace at the end of the ceremonial avenue of Unter den Linden.

The Church of the Redeemer in Jerusalem

Benner provides by far the fullest account of the so-called 'Orientreise' (Journey to the Middle East), which took the imperial couple first to Constantinople and from there to Palestine, where they visited Haifa and Jaffa before going on to Jerusalem (Figure 31). They set off on 11 October 1898 accompanied by some eighty-three servants and courtiers.[49] Two hundred delegates of the German and Scandinavian Protestant churches took part on a kind of pilgrimage to the Holy Land, organized so that they would arrive in Jerusalem in time for the inauguration, in the presence of the emperor, of the newly constructed 'Erlöserkirche' or Church of the Redeemer on Reformation Day, 31 October. The church was built on land on which stood the ruins of the medieval church and hospital of St John. It had been given by the Sultan to Wilhelm II's father, Crown Prince Friedrich Wilhelm, in 1869, when he, like Franz Joseph of Austria, had visited Constantinople on his way to attend the opening of the Suez Canal.[50] Friedrich Wilhelm also rode into Jerusalem in early November through the Damascus Gate and had this event painted later by Wilhelm Gentz (1822–90), who travelled to Jerusalem in 1873 to make some preparatory sketches. The completed painting showing the prince on his white charger above the Holy City, which won a gold medal at the Academy Exhibition in 1876, played an important role in building the image of the crown prince, as well as underlining the newly imperial Prussia's role in the Middle East.[51]

Figure 31 Henri Meyer, The German Emperor on his travels, *Le Petit Journal*, 6 November 1898. Colour lithograph. Private Collection © Look and Learn/Bridgeman Images

Wilhelm II, keen to outdo his late father in all things, wished his solemn entry, his *adventus*, into Jerusalem on 29 October to be a splendid one. So that he could do it in style on horseback, the authorities made a gap in the city wall next to the Jaffa Gate. Benner writes: 'Wilhelm II's entry is a key scene for the comprehension of the modern imperial cult, for the monarch's self-understanding, and for the expectations of those surrounding him.'[52] His route led through two triumphal arches erected in his honour, one by the Ottomans and the other by the Jews. Jewish schoolchildren sang a song with the refrain 'Blessed is He who comes in the name of the Lord', which could also be read on the Jewish arch. Wilhelm is being greeted as though he were the Messiah. The imperial couple went on foot to the Church of the Sepulchre and visited the Church of the Redeemer for the first time. On 30 October they went to Bethlehem where they attended a service in the Protestant Christmas Church, the construction of which had been promoted by the empress.

Then, on Reformation Day, 31 October, the Church of the Redeemer was inaugurated, the high point of the whole trip. As well as the church delegates, other groups of Germans had also arrived in Jerusalem for the inauguration, so that roughly one thousand Germans were present on the day. The Kaiser's presence at the inauguration of this German Protestant church was meant to emphasize his role not only as the protector of the German colony in Palestine but of Protestantism worldwide.

He had worn tropical clothing and a pith helmet on 29 October, but on this occasion he wore the uniform of the Lifeguards with a silver-gilt breastplate and the eagle-topped helmet. Over this he wore a gold woven burnouse and a silk veil floated down from his helmet.[53] He was greeted by a delegation from the Order of St John, the German Protestant branch of the Knights Hospitallers, and at the door of the church by the trustees of the Protestant Jerusalem Foundation, founded by Wilhelm in 1889, by the architect Friedrich Adler (the same architect as in Wittenberg), the builder Paul Ferdinand Groth, and church representatives. Here the Kaiser was presented with the key to the church, which, as in Wittenberg, he passed to Dr Barkhausen, the head of the Protestant Church Council in Prussia. In his sermon, Ernst von Dryander (1843–1922), the Berlin court preacher, spoke of how divine providence and the events of history had made the Hohenzollerns the guardians of the Reformation faith. After the end of the service, Wilhelm surprised the congregation by ascending the altar steps, kneeling down to pray, and then from the lectern reading a speech expressing with great fervour his personal piety and beliefs but also his role as the leader of German Protestantism. Among other things he said:

> From Jerusalem came the light, the blessed light, in whose radiance our German people has become great and glorious. What the Germanic people have become, they have become under the banner of the cross on Golgotha, the sign of self-sacrificing love of one's neighbour.[54]

If Protestantism was at the heart of the trip, Wilhelm did not neglect the German Catholics in Palestine. During his visit, he donated a piece of land to them so that they could build what is today the Benedictine Abbey of the Dormition. The Kaiserin Auguste Viktoria Foundation—a church and hospital on the Mount of Olives—was also inaugurated.

The journey to Palestine was regarded positively by many German Protestants, but not by all. As John Röhl points out, politically it was a minefield. The emperor received Theodor Herzl in Jerusalem, he telegraphed to the Pope, expressing his willingness to become the protector of the Catholics in the Holy Land, and he praised the Sultan in Damascus, proclaiming that the German Kaiser would be the friend for all time of 'the 300 million Mahomedans who live scattered throughout the world', thus arousing great nervousness among the European great powers.[55] Baroness Hildegard von Spitzemberg (1843–1914), that candid observer of Berlin court life over fifty years, commented exasperatedly: 'One can really shudder at all kinds of tactlessness! And in addition, the emperor himself, puffed up with memories of the Crusades, of the German emperors of the Middle Ages.'[56]

The Emperor Wilhelm Memorial Church

The second major church building project was the Emperor Wilhelm Memorial Church, designed by Franz Schwechten (1821-1924), to honour Wilhelm I or, as his grandson Wilhelm II liked to call him, 'Wilhelm the Great'. The church was consecrated on 1 September 1895, on the eve of the national festivity known as Sedan Day ('Sedantag'), which commemorated the Prussian victory over Napoleon III and his troops on 2 September 1870 at Sedan, a victory which led to the founding of the German Empire four months later in January 1871. The most striking thing about the Emperor Wilhelm Memorial Church in our context, apart from its name, is the antechamber, not finished until 1906, which glorifies Wilhelm I as warrior and emperor and celebrates the Hohenzollern dynasty. The church was badly bombed in World War II, but the antechamber survived.[57] Four marble reliefs on the walls illustrate four scenes from the life of Wilhelm I: his commissioning as an officer, his participation in the battle of Bar-sur-Aube on 27 February 1814 during the Napoleonic Wars, his consultation with Field Marshals Albrecht Graf von Roon (1803-79) and Helmut Graf von Moltke (1800-91) and with the Chancellor Otto Prince von Bismarck (1815-98) during the Franco-Prussian War in 1870-71, and finally, as emperor, dressed in Roman garb and accompanied by his son and grandson.

Over what would have been the entrance to the church, depicted in glorious colourful mosaics on the ceiling, are two groups of life-size Hohenzollerns, processing from two different directions towards two angels holding a paten and a chalice who lead them towards the cross. On the left-hand side are Burgrave Friedrich VI of Nürnberg (1371-1440), who from 1415 was the first Margrave and Elector of Brandenburg, and his wife Else. In front of them are Elisabeth of Denmark (1485-1555), widow of Elector Joachim I (1484-1535), holding a Bible to signify that she was the first convert to Lutheranism. She is accompanied by her two sons Joachim II Hector (1505-55), Elector of Brandenburg, and Johann, Margrave of Brandenburg-Küstrin (1513-71). Ahead of her is Albrecht of Prussia (1490-1568), the last Grand Master of the Teutonic Order dressed in its robes. He introduced the Reformation to Prussia. Then come Johann Sigismund, Elector of Brandenburg (1572-1619), through whose conversion the Hohenzollerns became Calvinist for two centuries, and Friedrich Wilhelm, the Great Elector (1620-88). Processing towards them from the right (see the cover illustration of this book) are Wilhelm I's parents Friedrich Wilhelm III, King of Prussia (1770-1840), wearing his coronation robes, and his wife Queen Louise (1776-1810). Then come King Friedrich Wilhelm IV (1795-1861) and his younger brother, Wilhelm I, King of Prussia and the first German emperor. Behind him stands his son Friedrich III (1831–88), and after him come Wilhelm II and his consort Auguste Viktoria, followed by Crown Prince Wilhelm (1882–1951) and, barely visible, his consort Cecilie of Mecklenburg-Schwerin (1886–1954).[58] Auguste Viktoria is dressed in a shimmering silver court dress with a long train, to celebrate the fact that this antechamber was inaugurated on 2 February 1906, the silver wedding of the imperial couple. A notable omission is the widowed Victoria, Empress Friedrich (1840–1901), Wilhelm II's mother. The Hohenzollerns are presented as warriors and guardians of Protestantism, who lead those coming for worship into the church.

Berlin Cathedral

Wilhelm's third major ecclesiastical building project was the new Berlin Cathedral, whose foundation stone was laid in 1894 but which was not inaugurated until 1905. Designed by Julius Raschdorf (1823–1914), its massive size, neo-baroque style and overwhelming interior decoration led to criticism from the beginning.[59] The dome is designed to echo the dome of St Peter's in Rome, indicating that this is not just a cathedral for Berlin, but is the motherhouse of worldwide Protestantism. The building has a centralized plan with the emperor's gallery with its throne situated over the main door and directly opposite the altar. Life-size figures of such important reformers as Luther, Melanchthon, Calvin, and Zwingli are placed high up on the walls to indicate that this is a church for all Protestants. The whole interior is a rich mixture of carving, mosaics, stained glass, marble, and gold leaf.

In contrast to the cathedral's role as a motherhouse for all Protestants, it also houses the official burial vault of the Hohenzollerns. Their tombs were originally placed in the so-called 'Denkmalkirche' or memorial chapel, a chapel on the same level as the main church which is known as the 'Predigtkirche' or sermon church. A third chapel, known as the 'Festkirche' or celebratory chapel, is for weddings and christenings. The memorial chapel no longer exists, so the ninety-four tombs of Hohenzollerns from the sixteenth to the early twentieth century are all in the crypt beneath the church.

The cathedral was inaugurated with great fanfare on 27 February 1905, on a far larger scale than was possible in Wittenberg or Jerusalem, because the ceremony was taking place in the middle of a capital city where tens of thousands of Berliners could line the streets to see the imperial party drive past.[60] As usual with Wilhelm II, the ceremony began with a strong military accent. The Household Guards marched up with banners and military music to take up position in front of the cathedral, and the first action of the Kaiser, who was wearing uniform as usual, was to review the troops. He was presented with the key to the cathedral, which he passed to Court Preacher Dryander, who then opened the doors of the cathedral. Led by the members of the cathedral consistory, the imperial couple entered the church to the sound of the organ playing the Halleluja Chorus from Handel's Messiah. To underline the cathedral's hoped-for status as Protestant motherhouse, Wilhelm had invited not just representatives from the Protestant churches of England, Denmark, Switzerland, Sweden, Norway, Austria, and the Netherlands but even from the United States.

This constant alignment of the Hohenzollerns with Protestantism must be seen against the background of the 'Kulturkampf' of the 1870s, that is, the struggle between the Prussian and imperial governments and their many Catholic citizens. This struggle led to a large number of laws being passed which discriminated against Catholics and were only rescinded in the late 1880s. It was precisely this exclusive focus on Prussian Protestantism and the claim to universal validity that went against the grain with such insiders in Berlin court and political circles as Hildegard von Spitzemberg. She writes in her diary:

> Why for such purely Prussian, at most German Protestant events is there this exaggerated pomp, this cosmopolitan exaggerated posturing in the truth of which no one believes, and which therefore arouses inward contradiction?[61]

Why indeed? The Habsburgs, in particular Franz Joseph, saw Catholicism as part of Austrian identity, practised it out of personal belief, but also regarded it as a bulwark against revolution. For Napoleon I and Napoleon III, religion was a useful tool to be used for purposes of legitimation, national cohesion, self-promotion, and social control. For Wilhelm II, religion went far beyond that. For him, the Hohenzollerns were the guardians of the Reformation, and he saw himself as a kind of Messiah who had been chosen by God to unite German, European, indeed world Protantism. Those of his subjects who had read his profession of faith in the Church of the Redeemer in Jerusalem and seen the large number of churches being built throughout the Empire will have seen him—at least until it all began to go wrong during World War I—in the same light.

Notes

1. Las Cases, *Le Mémorial de Sainte-Hélène*, p. 501.
2. Broers, *Napoleon*, vol. I, p. 341.
3. Duffy, *Saints*, p. 260.
4. Broers, *Napoleon*, vol. I, p. 329.
5. Aston, *Religion and revolution*; Roberts, 'Napoleon, the Concordat'; Vilmer, 'Commentaire du Concordat'.
6. Broers, *Napoleon*, vol. I, p. 285.

Plate 1 François Gérard, *Napoleon I in his coronation robes.*

Plate 2 Louis Le Coeur, Napoleon I swearing the constitutional oath on 2 December 1804.

Plate 3 Jacques-Louis David, *The Distribution of the Eagle Standards, 5 December 1804,* detail.

Plate 4 Franzensburg, Vienna, exterior.

Plate 5 The Habsburg Hall in the Franzensburg, Vienna.

Plate 6 Jean-Baptiste Debret, *The Coronation of Emperor Pedro I of Brazil.*

Plate 7 Pedro Américo de Figueiredo e Melo, *Pedro II, emperor of Brazil.*

Plate 8 *Entry of the Army of the Three Guarantees into Mexico City on 27 September 1821.*

Plate 9 *Agustín de Iturbide, emperor of Mexico, in his coronation robes.*

Plate 10 John Watson Nicol, Wilhelm II, German emperor.

Plate 11 Friedrich von Amerling, *Franz I, emperor of Austria, in his imperial robes.*

Plate 12 William 'Crimea' Simpson, The Begum of Bhopal at the first investiture of the Star of India in 1861.

Plate 13 Hans Bitterlich, Statue of Elisabeth, empress of Austria, in the Volksgarten in Vienna.

Plate 14 Bust of Empress Augusta by Theodor Litke after a model by Bernhard Roemer.

Plate 15 Jean-Auguste-Dominique Ingres, *Napoleon I in his coronation robes.*

Plate 16 Franz Xaver Winterhalter, *Portrait of Napoleon III, emperor of the French.*

Plate 17 Albert Gräfle, *Maximilian I, emperor of Mexico.*

Plate 18 Jacques-Louis David, *Napoleon I in his Study at the Tuileries.*

Plate 19 Franz Xaver Winterhalter, *Franz Joseph I, emperor of Austria.*

Plate 20 Auguste Roubille, *Wilhelm II* from his series of 13 caricatures of political figures around 1900.

Plate 21 Wilhelm II's imperial throne in the Schlosskirche in Wittenberg.

Plate 22 Henri Meyer, The German Emperor on his travels, *Le Petit Journal*, 6 November 1898.

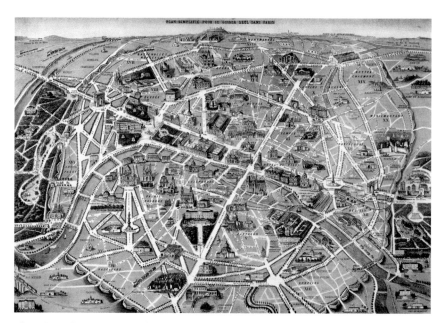

Plate 23 Hilaire Guesnu, Map of Paris during Baron Haussmann's 'Grands Travaux'.

Plate 24 The Museum of Art History in Vienna with the Maria Theresia monument.

Plate 25 A postcard showing Wilhelm II and Auguste Viktoria on the Siegesallee in Berlin.

Plate 26 The Krupp pavilion at the World Exposition in Vienna in 1873.

Plate 27 Victoria Memorial Hall, Kolkata.

Plate 28 Christopher Clark, *King George V at Delhi.*

Plate 29 Edwin Lutyens, Rashtrapati Bhavan, formerly the Viceroy's House, New Delhi.

Plate 30 Bust of Wilhelm II in front of Huis Doorn, Netherlands.

Plate 31 Jean Magrou, Pedro II as scholar-king in Petrópolis.

Plate 32 Raymond Kittl, Wilhelm I, German emperor (1993), Deutsches Eck, Koblenz.

 7. Duffy, *Saints*, p. 266.
 8. Dwyer and McPhee, *The French Revolution*, p. 160.
 9. *Décret Impérial*, 19 février 1806.
10. *Décret Impérial*, 19 février 1806, Titre II.
11. George, 'Saint-Napoléon'.
12. Broers, *Napoleon*, vol. II, pp. 447–54.
13. Hazareesingh, *Saint-Napoleon*.
14. Truesdell, *Spectacular Politics*, pp. 35–8.
15. *Le Moniteur Universel*, 2 Janvier 1852.
16. Truesdell, *Spectacular Politics*, p. 67.
17. Truesdell, *Spectacular Politics*, p. 39.
18. Hazareesingh, *Saint-Napoleon*, p. 140.
19. Décret portant qu'à l'avenir', 16 Février 1852.
20. Truesdell, *Spectacular Politics*, p. 41.
21. *Le Moniteur Universel*, 16 August 1859.
22. Hazareesingh, *Saint-Napoleon*, p. 151.
23. Hazareesingh, *Saint-Napoleon*, p. 10.
24. Hazareesingh, *Saint-Napoleon*, p. 223.
25. Hazareesingh, *Saint-Napoleon*, p. 221.
26. See Coreth, *Pietas Austriaca*; Vocelka and Heller, *Die Lebenswelt der Habsburger*, pp. 13–38.
27. Coreth, *Pietas*, p. 32.
28. See Vocelka and Vocelka, *Franz Joseph*, pp. 110–13.
29. Bled, *Franz Joseph*, p. 81.
30. Vocelka and Vocelka, *Franz Joseph*, p. 236.
31. Fugger, *Im Glanze*, p. 78.
32. Fugger, *Im Glanze*, p. 36. Winkelhofer, in *Der Alltag des Kaisers*, confuses this description of the Easter procession with Nora Fugger's description of the Corpus Christi procession.
33. *Reglamento*, p. 267.
34. Telesko, *Geschichtsraum Österreich*, pp. 181–2.
35. Fugger, *Im Glanze*, p. 92.
36. Pollmann, *Landesherrliches Kirchenregiment*; Nipperdey, *Religion im Umbruch*.
37. Clark, *Iron Kingdom*, pp. 142–4.
38. Steffens, *Luthergedenkstätten*, p. 51.
39. Steffens, *Luthergedenkstätten*, p. 263.
40. Steffens, *Luthergedenkstätten*, p. 272.
41. Steffens, *Luthergedenkstätten*, p. 280.
42. Lepp, 'Summus episcopus', pp. 77–114, pp. 77–8.
43. Benner, *Strahlen*, p. 120.
44. Giloi, 'Copyrighting the Kaiser', p. 449.
45. Witte, *Erneuerung der Wittenberger Schloßkirche*.
46. Gundermann, *Mirbach*.
47. Gundermann, *Mirbach*, p. 17.
48. Barth, *Kaiserliches Berlin*, p. 248.

49. Benner, *Strahlen*, p. 177.

50. See Lepp, 'Summus episcopus', pp. 107–10; Benner, *Strahlen*, pp. 266–7.

51. Müller, *Our Fritz*, p. 111. See https://smb.museum-digital.de/index.php?t=objekt&oges=144225

52. Benner, *Strahlen*, p. 282.

53. Benner, *Strahlen*, p. 293.

54. Translated from Benner, *Strahlen*, p. 297. The whole speech is reprinted on pp. 296–8.

55. Röhl, *Wilhelm II* (2014), pp. 76–7.

56. Spitzemberg, *Tagebuch*, p. 371.

57. Nowadays the ruined church is known simply as the 'Gedächtniskirche'. It has a modern chapel and belfry by Erich Eiermann (1904–70) erected between 1959 and 1963. It is now a memorial to war and a place to pray for peace.

58. Staudinger, *Gedächtnis-Kirche*.

59. Lemburg, 'Julius Raschdorf'.

60. Lepp, 'Summus episcopus', pp. 110–13.

61. Spitzemberg, *Tagebuch*, p. 445.

VII

Creating the Imperial City

Remodelling Paris

At the beginning of his diary for the years 1854 to 1869, the lawyer Henri Dabot (1831–1907), the 'bourgeois du quartier latin' as he calls himself, writes: 'For nearly a year cholera has been reigning in Paris and is almost endemic.'[1] Quite matter-of-factly, mixed with other snippets of news for 1854, he tallies the dead: 125 on 21 May, 53 on 30 June, 182 on 8 July, 77 on 12 August. Then on 7 September he writes: 'the cholera is decreasing but typhoid fever seems to have taken its place.'[2] Donald J. Olsen points out that 'the same cholera epidemic that in 1832 killed 5,500 of London's 1,778,000 in habitants, killed 20,000 of Paris's 861,000.'[3] Across the Seine from where Dabot was living was the oldest part of Paris, the Île de la Cité, which was particularly overcrowded and insanitary. Violent crime, prostitution, and disease were rife, and here as well as elsewhere traffic could not move through the city because of the narrow dark streets. Indeed, some of the streets were so narrow that two people could not even walk abreast, and contemporary photographs show houses in such bad repair that they appear virtually derelict and on the verge of collapse.

Forty years before, during his short reign, Napoleon I had begun to rebuild Paris, constructing the church of the Madeleine and the Stock Exchange, the Pont d'Iéna and the Pont des Arts, and creating the Rue de Rivoli, lined with a regular row of arcades, as a thoroughfare running eastwards from the Place de la Concorde along the north side of the Tuileries and the Louvre. He had also planned to create two broad intersecting streets running north–south and east–west respectively through the centre of the city but did not reign long enough to put the plan into action. When Louis-*Napoléon* Bonaparte was elected president of France in December 1848, it was clear that Paris needed cleaning up and drastic restructuring, as the population of the city had doubled since the beginning of the century due to inward movement of workers for the new industries, facilitated by the railways.[4] The prince-president's first projects were the extension of the Rue de Rivoli eastwards so that it would reach the Hôtel de Ville; and the creation of a new public park on the western outskirts of the city, the Bois de Boulogne. However, the then Prefect of the Seine, Jean-Jacques Berger, was making slow progress, so, after Louis-Napoléon had carried out his *coup d'état* to extend his presidency at the end of 1851 and had been elected Emperor of the French as

Napoleon III a year later, he appointed Georges-Eugène Haussmann (1809–91) to Berger's post. Haussmann filled it from 1853 to 1870. He was a qualified lawyer with twenty years as an administrator behind him and at the time of his appointment was Prefect of the Gironde, the largest Prefecture in Metropolitan France whose capital is Bordeaux.

The transformation of Paris was an imperial project. In volume II of his *Mémoires*, published at the end of his life, having been forced out of office in 1870, Haussmann describes how, having reluctantly taken on the post of Prefect of the Seine and having sworn his oath as a public servant, placing his right hand between those of the emperor, he was later that day taken away for a private conversation, during which the emperor showed him 'a map of Paris on which could be seen, drawn by the emperor himself, in blue, red, yellow and green, according to how urgent they were, the different new roads which he wanted to have made'.[5] Napoleon III, having personally chosen Haussmann, gave him his wholehearted and continuing support until he himself was forced to abdicate and go into exile. He chose well. Haussmann was a Parisian who had attended school and university in the city and had walked every street in the centre in his youth. Without this extraordinary man, his ruthless drive, and his ability to find a way around difficulties, his insight into people, his ability to pick the right specialists and get them to work for him, and his perception that committees only slow things down, the imperial vision would never have been accomplished. The transformation of the city was a practical necessity, but the ambition of the two men was to create 'a modern-day Rome'.[6]

Haussmann was a gifted administrator, who writes: 'I love administration, for its own sake. It is my vocation.'[7] He was more than that, however. He writes in the preface to his *Mémoires* that the Prefect of the Seine under the Empire had to double as an artist who had to be 'passionate about the Beautiful, the excellent artistic manifestation of the Good and considering much of the rest to be secondary'. Then, in a characteristic qualification he goes on: 'but knowing through experience that secondary matters cannot be neglected'.[8]

Haussmann's *Mémoires* could be used as a manual for how to arrive from outside to head a large bureaucracy, tasked with accomplishing a huge infrastructure project of great political and social importance, as well as national and international visibility. He describes how, before anything else could be accomplished, the whole city had to be surveyed and measured in great detail by Eugène Deschamps, Conservateur du Plan de Paris, using huge wooden triangulation towers erected at key points. A law had been passed on 3 May 1841 allowing the expropriation of buildings and land in the cause of 'public utility'. This was to facilitate the building of railways, but Haussmann was able to use it in the transformation of Paris. A further law was passed on 26 March 1852 permitting the expropriation of whole lots for the sake of 'healthfulness'.[9] Without these two laws, Paris could not have been transformed at all, never mind in the space of seventeen years.

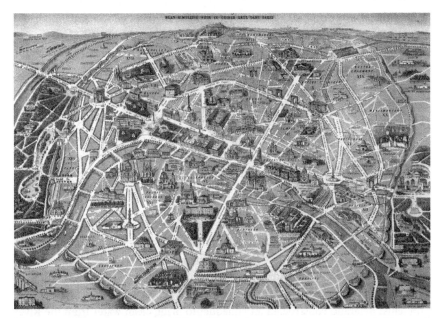

Figure 32 Hilaire Guesnu, Map of Paris during Baron Haussmann's 'Grands Travaux'. 1864. Coloured engraving. Bibliothèque Historique de la Ville de Paris, Paris/ Bridgeman Images

What Haussmann accomplished is staggering, even if several of his plans had to be completed by the Republic after his demission in 1870 (Figure 32). He cut two axes through the city which cross at the Place du Châtelet in the city centre. The north–south axis begins on the right bank at the Gare de l'Est and continues along the Boulevard de Strasbourg until it debouches at an angle into the new Boulevard de Sébastopol. This runs down to the Seine, across the place du Châtelet and over into the left bank. From here it continues south for 1.38 kilometres as the Boulevard Saint-Michel. The east–west axis on the right bank was created by extending the Rue de Rivoli from the Hôtel de Ville to the Rue Saint-Antoine and finally to the Place de la Bastille. On the left bank Haussmann constructed another east–west axis, the Boulevard Saint-Germain, which crosses the Boulevard Saint-Michel at right angles but curves down to the Seine at the Pont de la Concorde at the western end and to the Pont Sully at the eastern. By 1854, under Haussmann's direction Jacques-Ignace Hittorff, mentioned in chapter IV as the architect of Empress Eugénie's Maison Eugène Napoleon, had built houses on six of the twelve streets radiating out from the Arc de Triomphe at the Étoile (now the place Charles de Gaulle) at the top of the Champs-Élysées and had begun four more. A circular street running round across the twelve axes, called variously the Rue de Tilsit and the Rue de Presbourg, had been created, and Charles Rohault de Fleury had been commissioned to design grand private residences in uniform style at each of the points of the star created by the circular street. Two other important new thoroughfares were the Boulevard Malesherbes running from the church of the Madeleine up to and beyond the Parc Monceau to the north-west and the Boulevard du Prince Eugène (named after Eugène du Beauharnais, Napoleon III's uncle) in the east of the city, running south-eastwards from the present place de la République to what is nowadays called the place de la Nation but was then the place du Trône. In all, Haussmann constructed twelve bridges and built eighty kilometres of streets, widening existing ones by demolishing 20,000 buildings and erecting 43,000 new ones.[10] He imposed the uniform look that is so characteristic of Paris: buildings of the same height, faced with cream-coloured stone and of a similar design. He also insisted on property owners cleaning the façades of their houses.

At least as important as the new streets and thoroughfares were two essential services which were constructed underground. Before Haussmann, water for drinking and washing had been taken directly from the Seine, into which sewage also flowed. In 1855, Haussmann appointed the hydrological engineer Eugène Belgrand (1810–78) to the post of Director of Water and Sewers to tackle these problems. Belgrand constructed an aqueduct to bring clean water from the River Vanne in Champagne and stored it in a huge reservoir near the future Parc Montsouris. He increased the water supply of Paris from 87,000 to 400,000 cubic metres of water a day, distributing water around the city through two networks totalling 1,500 kilometres of pipes: one for drinking water and one for impure water that could be used to wash the streets and water the parks. Belgrand also built the huge underground network of sewers immortalized by Victor Hugo in his novel *Les Misérables* (1862). Under each of the new streets a sewer was built, and these large tunnels could also accommodate gas pipes for heating and light, so that the consumption of gas tripled between 1855 and 1859. By 1870 'the city was illuminated by nearly 40,000 gas lamps, which in most of the central area were not only efficient but ornamental.'[11] Haussmann also paved the streets with macadam.

Napoleon III insisted on there being oases of green in every *quartier*, called, using the English word, 'squares', so twenty such small gardens were created where to this day children go after school to play and adults to chat or picnic. He had lived in exile in London, so, having enjoyed the amenity of Hyde Park himself, he had a large park created at each of the four points of the compass: the Bois de Boulogne to the west (1852–58), the Bois de Vincennes to the east (1860–65), the Parc des Buttes-Chaumont (1865–67) to the north, and the Parc Montsouris (1865–78) to the south. In the layout of these parks, with their lakes and cascades, statues, paths, and flower beds, the garden designer Jean-Charles Adolphe Alphand (1817–91) was a key figure, and his designs can be seen in the delightful richly illustrated volume *Les Promenades de Paris*.[12] The Parc Monceau and the Jardin du Luxembourg were also refurbished and replanted and the new boulevards were lined with trees and furnished with 8,428 benches. The new wide boulevards were to be enjoyed as spaces in which to walk and sit. Haussmann's concept of a complete urban environment also meant that he built churches, seventy schools, six new district town halls ('mairies') and enlarged others and, as well as the spectacular glass and iron central market of Les Halles designed by Victor Baltard (1805–74), a further eleven smaller markets were scattered round the city. The second wing of the Louvre was completed, linking it with the Tuileries. Five new theatres were constructed as well as the spectacular Opéra Garnier, though that was not completed until 1875. From 1867, a major renovation of the old hospital known as the Hôtel Dieu on the Île de la Cité was begun. Once the emperor had decided that the indigent should not be buried one on top of another but that even they should each have a separate grave, Haussmann had to find enough land around Paris for new cemeteries.

Railway stations were prominent buildings that symbolized the new age, and the influx of passengers that they brought into Paris made it all the more essential to enable traffic to flow. The Gare de l'Est had been completed in 1849 and was formally opened by Louis-Napoléon in 1850. The Gare Saint-Lazare, inaugurated in 1837, was completed in 1853. The Gare de Lyon was built in 1855. The Gare d'Austerlitz was rebuilt between 1862 and 1867, and during the same period, between 1861 and 1866, the Gare du Nord, first opened in 1846, was rebuilt to three times its original size, under the direction of Hittorff.

Another important action taken by the emperor was the expansion of the city boundaries in order to accommodate its increasing population. In 1859, he decreed that eleven communes around Paris were to be taken into the city, making twenty arrondissements instead of twelve. The population of Paris had been almost a million in 1851 but, by the end of the Second Empire, and taking into account an additional 400,000 from the new arrondissements, it was two million. After so much construction and disruption caused by living for seventeen years in the midst of a building site, the Parisians had had enough and, because of political opposition to Napoleon III, the rising costs and out of control finances of the building work, and the displacement of some 350,000 Parisians from the central area, Haussmann, like his master, was forced to go in 1870. It is a testament to his achievements that his programme was carried on for at least another ten years very much as he had planned it and that collaborators of his such as Alphand and Belgrand continued to work for the city on major projects. Haussmann's legacy is also visible beyond Paris in the cityscapes of Lyons, Marseilles, Bordeaux, Nantes, Lille, Besançon, Blois, and Rouen, thanks to what Pierre Milza calls 'Haussmannian contagion'.[13]

Inaugurating the New Paris

To show the inhabitants what all the upheaval was achieving and to remind them that the rebuilding of Paris was an imperial project, Napoleon III staged theatrical inauguration ceremonies for three important thoroughfares: the Boulevard de Sébastopol on 5 April 1858, the Boulevard Malesherbes on 13 August 1861, and the Boulevard du Prince Eugène (now the Boulevard Voltaire) on 7 December 1862.[14] The ceremony, which in each case involved the emperor riding or driving up the grand new carriageway in solemn procession accompanied by members of his court to be greeted by municipal officers at the top, had strong overtones of the royal entry of the *ancien régime*, a ceremony which traditionally expressed a contract of mutual obligation between sovereign and people. The inaugurations of the Boulevard Malesherbes and the Boulevard du Prince Eugène gave Haussmann the opportunity for lengthy speeches setting out in detail his larger vision for the rebuilding of Paris and countering the criticisms and objections that had been uttered in the press. Though few people will have been able to hear these speeches, they were afterwards disseminated in the press for all to read.

The official organ of the Empire, the *Moniteur Universel*, describes the inauguration of the Boulevard de Sébastopol in the issue for 5 and 6 April 1858. It was also reported on in the foreign press, as we see in Figure 33. The siege of 1854–55 which gave the boulevard its name and its appalling loss of life must have been in the minds of the crowds of onlookers when the emperor, accompanied by his military household, the minister of war, the commandants of the army of Paris, of the imperial guard, and of the national guard, as well as a great number of other officers, rode out of the Tuileries and along the Seine to the place du Châtelet at the bottom of the boulevard, where they were met by Baron Haussmann and the Prefect of Police. The emperor and empress had come within a hair's breadth of being assassinated on 14 January 1858 by three bombs thrown at their carriage by Felice Orsini (1819–58) just as they were on their way to the opera. At the inauguration of the new boulevard the emperor riding out alone in front of his guard was seen as a public demonstration of courage.[15] We might add that Empress Eugénie driving in an open carriage with her ladies was showing equal courage. Under the direction of Victor Baltard, the architect of Les Halles, the boulevard had been lined on both sides with flagpoles from which hung alternate tricolours and green banners covered in Napoleonic bees. At the point where the Boulevard de Sébastopol meets the Boulevard de Strasbourg leading to the Gare de l'Est, a huge gold lamé curtain twenty metres high and covered with gold stars had been stretched across the street between two decorative towers. At a signal from Haussmann, the curtain was pulled back on each side, so that the full prospect of the street could already be seen from below as the imperial party moved up towards it to where they were received by the members of the municipality and

Figure 33 Inauguration of the Boulevard de Sébastopol, Paris. *Illustrated London News*, 17 April 1858. Engraving. Private Collection Look and Learn/Illustrated Papers Collection/Bridgeman Images

other dignitaries. Henri Dabot, who was present, was impressed: 'suddenly the curtains opened and folded back towards the towers; then, as in a magic spectacle, the Gare de l'Est became visible; a very successful decoration.'[16] Once he reached the top, the emperor reminded his listeners of the economic benefits which the railways would confer by bringing producers and consumers closer together. Then, with great tact, he thanked the municipal council and the legislature for what *they* had done not just to beautify Paris but to build housing, hospitals, churches, schools, and markets and to sanitize the city by building underground sewage tunnels, 'worthy of the works which exist in ancient Rome'. He wanted the assembled worthies to feel part of a great enterprise because he needed them to agree to finance the next stage of his and Haussmann's grand plan.

The next great ceremony inaugurated the Boulevard Malesherbes on 13 August 1861, just in time for the celebrations of the Saint-Napoleon two days later described in chapter VI. Construction of this street had begun under Napoleon I in 1808 and had continued under several rulers up to 1840. It began at the church of the Madeleine and, before Haussmann's intervention, had ended at the place Saint-Augustin. Haussmann doubled the street in length and changed the angle of the new portion so that it now led up diagonally towards the Parc Monceau and eventually to the Place de Wagram and beyond. The boulevard was again lined with flagpoles from which fluttered tricolour pennants and which were decorated with large shields containing the letter N. Baltard, whose church of Saint-Augustin at the bottom of the new portion of the street was still only a building site, covered it with a scaffolding, decorated with garlands, flags, and plaques, outlining the planned dimensions of the church. The emperor and his entourage rode up to where, near the Parc Monceau, a huge ephemeral triumphal arch of an unusual square shape had been erected and behind it a large circular tent, flanked by covered stands for a thousand guests. Photographs of this *mise en scène* survive, but it is not until we see the watercolours of Léon Leymonnerye (1803–79) in the Musée Carnavalet that we realize how colourful the scene was. The arch, composed of two high turrets at each side with a broad transverse lower down between them surmounted by a golden eagle, was white and gold, and the three tents were a rich crimson, while points of colour were added everywhere by garlands and pennants. 'Urbs renovata', it said on one side of the frieze across the arch, reminding those present of the Rome of Augustus, and 'Paris embelli et agrandi' (Paris embellished and enlarged) on the other. Haussmann opened his speech by reminding his listeners that this new street was merely bringing to a conclusion the plans of Napoleon I and praising 'the grandeur of the conception of 1808'.[17] In his long address he answered and refuted his critics on a whole range of contentious points to do with the building programme so far and at the end he compared what was happening in Paris to the Rome of Augustus, saying that in that era carrying out public works was the best way to gain public recognition. The supreme praise accorded to 'Caesar's nephew' was that he had beautified Rome, the capital of the Empire, and Haussmann finished by quoting, in Latin, Suetonius's statement that Augustus had found Rome a city of brick but had left it a city of marble. The listeners were reminded by this rhetoric that, not only was Napoleon III the nephew of the first Napoleon, he was the new Augustus and the renovation of Paris was an imperial project.

Yet another grand inauguration was that of the Boulevard du Prince Eugène (now the Boulevard Voltaire) on 7 December 1862. As the newspaper *La France* emphasized, in contrast to the boulevard Malesherbes which led through the richest *quartiers* of Paris, this boulevard crossed the industrial quartiers and is 'the Appian Way of the people of Paris'. The purpose of all the renovation is not vanity or love of luxury, 'it is not only the beautification, it is above all the clean-up of Paris.'[18] No more shall there be dark streets without light or air, epidemics, sickness and death, 'infected cesspools' where the families of workers suffer great misery and privation. The article goes on to remind its readers that these same people have the Bois de Vincennes on their side of town which equals, even surpasses, the Bois de Boulogne. The Boulevard du Prince Eugène was not just honouring a man who was Napoleon III's uncle but someone who had been viceroy of Italy under Napoleon I and a successful general, thus underlining both the imperial and the military themes of the inauguration.

What many of the newspapers, for instance, the *Moniteur*, *Le Constitutionnel*, and *La France*, do not do, is to describe the lavish ephemeral architecture of the place du Trône (now the place de la Nation) which we know from contemporary illustrations. The entire space was surrounded by a colonnade with a huge fountain in the centre and a triumphal arch, designed by Baltard and resembling the Arc de Triomphe. The monumental fountain had a globe in the centre supporting a statue of Glory which in turn held a figure of Victory and a laurel wreath. Two tall victory columns stood at the exit from the space behind the arch. The triumphal arch, some twenty metres high and again designed by Baltard, was a monument to Napoleon III as military commander and a celebration of his ten years as emperor. A victor on a quadriga surmounted the arch, there were figures of trumpeters at each corner and of French soldiers round the cornice. The text at the top announced that it was dedicated to 'Napoleon III, Emperor of the French, and the victorious armies of the Crimea, Italy, China, Cochinchina,[19] and Algeria' with the dates 1852 and 1862. The names of Napoleon III's military victories were written on either side of the arch. Had this complex ever been built, it would have been Napoleon III's answer to the Arc de Triomphe erected by his uncle Napoleon I, and the place du Trône would have corresponded to the Étoile. In his speech, however, even Haussmann sounded cautious about actually erecting these bombastic structures. They never were constructed, but this glorification of Napoleon III as a military commander is reminiscent of the equally bombastic *Apotheosis of Napoleon III* at Compiègne, painted by Guillaume-Alphonse Harang Cabasson (1814–84). Harang Cabasson's painting of 1854 depicts the emperor in a quadriga driven by France, one of whose hands supports his right hand, while her other hand holds a tricolour on a pole surmounted by a golden eagle. Fame with her trumpet flies before them, Victory holds a wreath over the emperor's head with one hand and an olive branch with the other, Justice and the arts follow. Up above in the clouds stands the shadowy figure of Napoleon I, raising his hat to salute his nephew. If Napoleon III believed his own propaganda, then it is no wonder that he engaged in the ill-fated 'Expédition du Mexique' in 1864 and the disastrous war with Prussia that brought the Second Empire to an end in 1870. This led immediately after to the Prussian bombardment of Paris, and then to the violence and destruction of the Paris Commune and its defeat, so vividly described by Philip Mansel.[20]

Rethinking Vienna

During the same decades that Napoleon III and Haussmann were transforming Paris, Vienna was also undergoing its own metamorphosis. The construction of the Ringstrasse, the wide tree-lined boulevard on which stand such grand build-ings as the opera house, the parliament, the town hall, the art history and natural history museums, and the university, will be forever associated with the reign of Franz Joseph, emperor of Austria from 1848 to 1916. When the readers of the *Wiener Zeitung* opened their newspapers on Christmas Day in 1857, the first thing they saw was a long memorandum from the emperor, addressed to Alexander von Bach, the Interior Minister (1813–93) and dated 20 December 1857. In it, Franz Joseph decreed that the city of Vienna should be extended in such a way as to connect the inner city within the walls with the districts beyond them. This inner city was a small tightly packed conglomeration of streets containing the imperial palace (the Hofburg), the cathedral of St Stephen and other old churches, and the baroque residences of the high aristocracy. Unlike other capital cities, at this late date it was still surrounded by a defensive wall dotted with bastions and pierced by eleven gates. Around this wall was the so-called glacis, a wide, open, park-like space with trees and benches, where citizens could walk or drive and which incorporated a large military parade ground on what was called the 'Josefstädter Glacis' on one side. Surrounding this green space were the suburbs which had been incorporated into the city of Vienna in 1850. Franz Joseph decreed that the defensive wall should be torn down, that the ditches around them should be levelled, and that the glacis should be available for building. The emperor wanted a wide street running around the inner city: 'a ring of at least 75,6 metres wide, consisting of a carriageway with bridle paths and paths for pedestrians at either side.' This ring, or rather horseshoe, should meet the Danube canal at each end, where a quay—the Franz-Josefs-Kai—was to be built for boats to dock, with a broad carriageway running along it and thus completing the ring. The decree listed the public buildings that should be built along the new street: a war office, a headquarters for the city commandant, an opera house, a federal archive, a library, a town hall, museums, and galleries. The neo-Gothic Votivkirche, already begun on the glacis in 1856 to commemorate Franz Joseph's escape from a Hungarian assassination attempt and intended to function as a garrison church, was also to form part of the Ringstrasse. (In fact, the church was not completed until 1879.) The emperor was careful to specify which spaces were to be kept clear—the parade ground just mentioned, for instance, and the space around the Hofburg—and to stipulate that the new public buildings should alternate with open gardens. Plots of land between these buildings were to be sold to private investors and the proceeds to be paid into a development fund controlled by the Ministry of the Interior, not the city. These investors would be exempt from property taxes for thirty years,[21] provided they began building within a year and completed the building within four years.

But this civilized vision of grandeur, space, and elegance is not where Franz Joseph began to make his mark on his capital city. He came to the throne after a bloodbath of his own future subjects in Vienna in October 1848. Since the death of his grandfather Franz I in 1835, the Empire had been run by a Council of State, led by Prince Clemens von Metternich (1773–1859), because the legitimate emperor, the epileptic Ferdinand I (1793–1875), was not capable of ruling alone. During his reign, swathes of the population became more and more dissatisfied under the restrictive Metternich System of social control. The economically successful middle class and the students wanted freedom of expression, freedom of association, and a constitution, the workers needed better living conditions, secure jobs, higher wages, and shorter working hours, and the peasants demanded freedom from the feudal ties, the 'Grunduntertänigkeit', that bound them to their estate owners. The revolution, which began in Paris in February 1848, spread in March to Berlin, and, in the lands under Austrian control, to Hungary and Vienna, Prague, and northern Italy. This first phase of the revolution in Vienna was quelled when the anti-liberal general, Archduke Albrecht, Duke of Teschen (1817–95), shot into the crowd on 14 March. Metternich fled to England and the emperor quickly agreed to freedom of the press and increased representation for the middle classes. Revolution broke out again in May, however, when students and workers marched in protest to the Hofburg, leading to the flight of the imperial family to Innsbruck. In September, the emperor agreed to emancipate the peasants. On 6 October 1848, troops were preparing to leave Vienna for Hungary to suppress the revolution there, when some of the soldiers mutinied and, with students and workers, tried to prevent the troops from leaving. Fighting broke out and the Minister of War, Theodor Graf Baillet von Latour (1780–1848), was lynched and his naked body strung up from a lamp post. The insurgents barricaded sixteen streets in the crowded inner city and tore up paving stones. The imperial family fled again, this time to the Archbishop's Palace in Olmütz (Olomouc) in Moravia, where they stayed for the next six months. On 26 October, Alfred Prince Windisch-Graetz (1787–1862) and the Croatian Field Marshal Count Josip Jelačić von Bužim (1801–59) began to bombard the city and were able to storm it on 31 October. The bombardment set the Imperial Library in the Hofburg on fire, some two thousand people were shot in the streets in the course of the battle, and prominent members of the uprising were subsequently executed by the military government, including Robert Blum, a member of the Frankfurt Parliament, who should have been protected by parliamentary immunity. Emperor Ferdinand was persuaded to abdicate and his legitimate successor, his brother Archduke Franz Karl, renounced his claim to the throne in favour of his own eldest son who took the regnal name of Franz Joseph. He was proclaimed Emperor of Austria on 2 December 1848 at the age of eighteen.

This conflict at the inception of his reign explains why the first building erected in the reign of the new emperor was the Arsenal (1849–56), a huge fortified complex of some thirty buildings, among them a barracks, a weapons factory, a military headquarters, a cadet school, and a church. Artillery fired from the Arsenal could reach right into the heart of the city to the Stephansplatz in front of the cathedral. The Arsenal was but one element in a defensive system to protect the emperor and his capital city against his own subjects. In 1854–57 he built the Franz Joseph Barracks, a fortified military barracks on the Danube canal at the north-eastern end of what was to become the Ringstrasse, and a second one at the other end of it, built between 1865 and 1869 and named the Crown Prince Rudolf Barracks. Both of these barracks complexes were strategically placed near railway stations.[22] Two further fortified barracks were planned but never built.

Prominent in the Arsenal complex is the museum of military history, called in a guidebook to Vienna from 1873 simply the 'Waffenmuseum' or weapons collection.[23] Also known as the 'Heeresmuseum' or army museum, it was conceived as a monument to the glory of the Austrian military tradition.[24] Visitors enter it through the Feldherrenhalle (the Hall of the Military Commanders), a veritable forest of fifty-six life-size statues of noted Austrian rulers and military leaders going back to the Middle Ages grouped around pillars, four at a time. As Werner Telesko says, they were conceived as a textbook of Austrian history and great emphasis was placed on lifelike and accurate representation of these historic personages.[25] Visitors then mount the grand stairway and are greeted on the way up by life-size statues of the commanders who crushed the 1848 uprising in Vienna (Windisch-Graetz and Jellačič), Budapest (Haynau), and Italy (Radeztky). A huge statue of Austria with sword and shield spreads her cloak over figures representing spiritual and material culture.[26] Visitors then enter the Ruhmeshalle (the Hall of Glory), a richly painted pillared hall in which the colourful ceiling frescoes present a historical programme of the glorious victories achieved by the Austrian army mostly in the seventeenth to the nineteenth centuries.

There were other monuments to Austria's military glory. In front of the imperial palace, the Hofburg, was an open space, the 'Äußerer Burgplatz' or Outer Palace Square, which had been created when Napoleonic forces breached Vienna's defensive wall in 1809. This space had been used as a parade ground in the past, so it was not unfitting that two bronze equestrian statues should be erected there to commemorate two of Austria's most successful military commanders. In 1860 the monument to Archduke Karl, Duke of Teschen (1771–1847), the victor of the Battle of Aspern against Napoleon I in 1809 (and father of the Archduke Albrecht just mentioned), was unveiled, and in 1865 it was the turn of the companion piece representing Prince Eugen of Savoy-Carignan (1663–1736), one of the outstanding European commanders of his day, who had won victories against the Turks in Hungary and the Balkans, in the Wars of the Spanish Succession and the Polish Succession. Because of these two monuments, the area became known from 1879 as the 'Heldenplatz'—Heroes Square.[27]

All this adulation of military success as the foundation of Franz Joseph's power made all the more painful the disastrous defeats that Austria had to undergo at the hands of the French in Italy in June 1859 at the battles of Magenta and Solferino and of the Prussians in July 1866 at the battle of Königgrätz. The inexperienced

Franz Joseph had even led the Austrian troops himself at Solferino. The statue of Archduke Karl, which should have been unveiled on 22 May 1859 on the fiftieth anniversary of the Battle of Aspern, could only be unveiled on that date a year later after the defeats in Italy.[28] These failures by the army were in spite of the fact that almost two thirds of state income had been spent on the military between 1848 and 1859.[29] The defeat at Königgrätz, where the Austrians were numerically superior, led to the inescapable conclusion that the Prussians were both better trained and better equipped and that the modern needle gun, which the military establishment in Austrian had refused to introduce, was a significant factor in their victory. These defeats with their loss of life and financial and reputational consequences forced the emperor, unwillingly, to give his people more say in how they were governed, beginning with the Laxenburg Manifesto of 1859. This was followed by what is called the October Diploma, a document published on 20 October 1860 which instituted a system of aristocratic federalism. Though it did guarantee certain rights such as equality before the law, freedom of religion, and some participation in the legislative process, ultimately it satisfied neither the German-speaking Austrians nor the Czechs and Hungarians. Franz Joseph was forced to amend it in the February Patent, which established a bicameral imperial parliament, the Reichsrat, with an upper chamber appointed by the emperor and an indirectly elected lower chamber. The lower chamber consisted of delegates from the diets of the various provinces of the empire, but the emperor could always block its decisions by appointing more members to the upper chamber which consisted of important aristocrats and bishops whose tenure was for life. The new Reichsrat was divided into a 'greater' and a 'lesser' parliament—the latter without the Hungarian delegates who could regulate their own affairs in the Hungarian Diet. Under the February Patent, the parliament had more decision-making power than it had before, but it was still subject to the emperor, who could dissolve it and who had to sanction its laws. He, on the other hand, could make political and military decisions without the consent of the Reichsrat and had complete power of decision-making in an emergency whenever the parliament was not sitting. In 1867, after losing another war, the emperor was forced to go further and agree to a constitution for Hungary as well as for the rest of his territory, giving full rights to Jews for the first time.[30] What is called the 'Hungarian Compromise' is discussed more fully under Empress Elisabeth's political involvement in chapter IV.

The October Diploma provided, for the first time since 1851, for the election of a city council in Vienna, the 'Gemeinderat', with 120 members.[31] The franchise, based on taxable income or a university qualification, was so restricted that only 3.3 per cent of the inhabitants of Vienna were eligible to vote. Furthermore, the voters were divided into three tax groups and each group could elect forty councillors, which gave the richest and smallest portion of the voters proportionately far more influence than their numbers warranted. From 1861 until 1879 the

Gemeinderat was dominated by Liberals who favoured a free market economy. This led to an economic boom, but also to the stock market crash of 1873. Dr Cajetan Felder (1814–94), a lawyer who was elected mayor four times and was in post from 1868 to 1878, played an important role in pushing through such projects as the first pipeline bringing drinking water into the city from the mountains south of Vienna, the 'regulation' of the Danube ('Donauregulierung') to prevent the city from flooding, and the building of the new neo-Gothic town hall.

Two years before Franz Joseph was forced to give his subjects a constitution, the Ringstrasse was officially inaugurated on 1 May 1865, though with far less pomp than Napoleon III would have thought necessary. Two covered stands for dignitaries such as government ministers and the mayor of Vienna had been erected in front of the 'Äußeres Burgtor' or Outer Palace Gate, the five-arched stone gate which commemorated Napoleon I's defeat at the Battle of Leipzig. This area was decorated with four tall pyramids covered with pine branches and inscriptions giving the dates of the inauguration and of the 1857 decree to build on the glacis. Between them, on a tall pedestal and holding a wreath, stood a huge winged figure of Vindobona, representing the city of Vienna. The emperor and empress drove up in their carriage and were greeted by the mayor who lauded the new street and its initiator, the emperor. The emperor replied, announcing that he was making the people a present of the Kaiserbrunnen, a source of spring water in southern Austria that was needed to give the city clean drinking water. For various administrative reasons, construction on this project did not begin officially until 1870, but it was completed in 1873 in time for the international exhibition.

The mayor, the emperor and empress, members of the imperial family and of the court then drove round the Ring, past the new opera house which was almost completed, and crossed the Danube canal at the Aspern Bridge. They then drove to the Prater, the spacious park on the other bank, to dine. Many of the grand residences for aristocrats and wealthy manufacturers were already built or almost completed on the half of the Ring that they traversed. Building on the Ring in the other direction from the Hofburg could only be undertaken after 1868 once the large parade ground stretching from the palace to the Votivkirche was designated building land. It was Mayor Felder who, by working behind the scenes 'with the calm of a practised chess player', as he says himself, persuaded the emperor to allow the city to buy the parade ground from the military, though they then had to be persuaded to relinquish it.[32] Felder already had a vision of how a new town hall, a parliament building, the university, and a new court theatre could all be built on this space. In his memoirs, he relates with great enjoyment how he persuaded all the important players in turn. He tackled figures close to the emperor first and then convinced Friedrich Schmidt (1825–91), the architect who had won the competition to design the new town hall on a different site entirely, of the virtues of the parade ground. Then he got Schmidt to show the plan for the whole area, including the other major buildings, to the Buildings Committee of the city council and the City Expansion Commission, telling the members that of course this grand plan would never be approved. The full city council then voted overwhelmingly in favour of the plan, believing and hoping that it would be turned down, and was horrified when the emperor approved it. Construction on the new town hall began in 1872 and was inaugurated in 1883, the same year as the new parliament building. The university was opened in 1884 and the new Imperial and Royal Palace Theatre, the 'K.K. Hofburgtheater', was opened opposite the town hall in 1888.[33]

A major event that functioned as a second inauguration of the Ringstrasse was the costumed procession in honour of the silver wedding anniversary of Franz Joseph and Elisabeth held on 27 April 1879.[34] It was organized by the city, not the court, and was as much a celebration of the citizens, their organizations, and their activities as it was of the emperor and empress. The procession began with students, members of shooting and gymnastics clubs, and representatives of various civic organizations, and ended with firemen from 168 different fire stations with their hoses, fire wagons, and bands as well as veterans from seventy-nine towns in Austria and Hungary. The main part of the procession was the spectacular costumed pageant designed by the artist Hans Makart (1840–84). Some forty-three groups dressed in colourful and intricate sixteenth-century costumes, most of them accompanying a festival car resembling those used in early modern processions, represented a wide range of trades and crafts. There were hunters and miners, bakers and vintners, carpenters and butchers, millers and weavers, saddlers and coopers, shipbuilders and goldsmiths, printers and artists, some 8,000 of them in all, all gorgeously dressed. There was even a group representing the railways and another the mechanics and machine-makers. The festival cars were extremely elaborate, with that of the tailors surmounted by a huge pair of scissors, for instance, and that of the shipbuilders with a ship, while the patissiers had a Guglhupf, the traditional Austrian sponge cake, on top. Stands for the onlookers were built all the way along the Ringstrasse, while the Secessionist architect Otto Wagner designed a special one for the imperial family in front of the Äußeres Burgtor. A lengthy account in the *Neue Freie Presse* on Monday, 28 April 1879, relates that the sun shone, that the procession was marshalled in perfect harmony in the Prater on the other side of the Danube canal, and that it proceeded in good order round the Ringstrasse, greeted with great enthusiasm by the spectators.[35] The reporter complains, however, that a photographic studio, which had set itself up on the Schwarzenberg Platz, kept holding the procession up before it reached the imperial stand, in order to photograph each individual group—a sign of things to come.

It bears repeating that this lavish and sophisticated event, requiring great logistical skill, was not only organized by the citizens but paid for by them too. The city financed the costumes of the heralds and standard-bearers, those who wanted to take part paid for their own costumes, many firms painted and decorated the festivals cars for free, and 120 of the stands were privately financed.[36]

Imperial Planning

Two striking buildings on the Ringstrasse today are the natural history museum and the art history museum, placed symmetrically across from each other on the far side of the boulevard opposite the Hofburg. Once the planning of the Ringstrasse began in 1858, it was decided to bring the imperial collections together and display them in a worthy manner and, for this, new museums were needed. It was not until 1867, however, that a competition was launched to find a suitable design. Many of the noted Viennese architects of the day took part, but it proved impossible to agree on a winner, so in 1868 the well-known German architect Gottfried Semper (1803–79) was called in to settle the dispute. In Dresden, he had designed a gallery to house the Old Masters collection of the Saxon court, as well as the opera house that still bears his name. The emperor asked Semper to complete Carl Freiherr von Hasenauer's designs for the museums, but Semper went further and placed them in a grandiose imperial forum ('Kaiserforum'), bounded on one side by the Hofburg, extending over the Ringstrasse to include the museums, and then continuing up to the impressive imperial stables designed by Johann Bernhard Fischer von Erlach (1656–1723) in 1713.[37] At the Hofburg end, this would have meant constructing a huge ceremonial tract with an impos-ing central throne room surmounted by a cupola parallel to, and in front of, the seventeenth-century Leopoldine Wing ('Leopoldinischer Trakt'). This would then have been flanked on each side by a new curving wing, each of which would be joined to a 'corps de logis'—an apartment building—to provide accommodation for members of the imperial family and for important guests. Grand symmetrical triumphal arches would lead on over the Ringstrasse to the museums. Comparisons have often been made between this plan and the grand complex consisting of the Louvre and the Tuileries, completed in the 1850s under Napoleon III.[38] Semper's plan for the Kaiserforum was never realized and, had it been, it would have made necessary 'a rethinking of ceremonial procedures or a new imperial mise-en-scène'.[39]

Work began on the museums in 1871, though it was not until 1889 and 1891 respectively that the natural history museum and the art history museum were formally opened to the public (Figure 34). Another part of the Hofburg that needed to be tackled was the façade of the 'Michaelertrakt' at the back of the Hofburg towards the old city. Plans for this by Joseph Emanuel Fischer von Erlach (1693–1742) (the son of Johann Bernhard Fischer von Erlach) existed. However, it still took until 1895 for this successful project to be completed. Semper had died in

Figure 34 View of the entrance and north façade of the Museum of Art History designed by Gottfried Semper and Karl von Hasenauer, 1871–91, with the Maria Theresia monument in the foreground. Photograph. Kunsthistorisches Museum, Vienna/Bridgeman Images

1879 and Hasenauer was left to carry the entire scheme for the Kaiserforum forward. Construction had begun in 1881 on the new wing now known as the 'Neue Hofburg' or New Palace. This is joined at right angles to the 'Leopoldinischer Trakt' and consists of a connecting building on that side and a curving façade that leads to the 'corps de logis' and ends at the Ringstrasse. Construction was well advanced when Hasenauer died suddenly in 1894. The façade was completed and decorated with twenty life-size figures representing different territories in the Austrian lands (a Roman soldier, a Slav, a Hungarian, a Bavarian, a Pole, and a Tyrolean, for instance) and different avocations from Austria's past such as a crusader, a knight, a missionary, a peasant, a merchant, a miner, and a sailor. The interior was fitted out, but after many changes of architect and project managers, as construction dragged on and costs rose, it was decided in 1913 not to complete the rest of Semper's grand scheme. Today, the Neue Hofburg houses the Austrian National Library, various important collections, and several museums. Over on the other side of the Ringstrasse, between the two museums and surrounded by lawns and fountains, is an imposing monument which was not part of Semper's plan at all. This is the monument by Caspar Zumbusch (1830–1915) to Maria Theresia, archduchess, empress and king of Hungary and Bohemia (1717–80), depicting her as a unifying figure, the mother of all the nations in the Empire, and the embodiment of the Enlightenment. This is discussed more fully in chapter XI. She ruled for forty years from 1740 to 1780, and it is not an accident that the monument was unveiled on 13 May 1888, in the fortieth year of Franz Joseph's reign.

Modern visitors to Vienna experience imperial Austria in the historicist nineteenth-century public buildings on the Ringstrasse, in the Neue Hofburg, the monuments on Heroes' Square, the two museums, and the façade of the Michaelertrakt. Imposing as they are, they are only a fragment of what would have been built if the plan for an imperial forum had been completed. Visitors who enter the Hofburg soon come to the Schweizerhof dating to the thirteenth century. This is where they will find the Schatzkammer or Treasury in which the insignia of the emperors of Austria are displayed alongside the insignia of the Holy Roman Emperors, demonstrating a seamless imperial tradition from the fifteenth to the twentieth century.

Expanding Berlin

In the early 1850s, when Napoleon III and Haussmann were planning the restructuring of Paris and Franz Joseph was constructing military buildings to defend himself against revolution in Vienna, the city of Berlin was changing from a royal residence into a metropolis. When Friedrich Wilhelm IV of Prussia (1795–1861), the older brother of the first German emperor Wilhelm I, came to the throne in 1840, his capital city had some 330,000 inhabitants. At its heart was the Royal Palace, dating largely to the first half of the eighteenth century. The Palace Bridge led from it to one end of a broad avenue shaded by lime trees and known therefore as 'Unter den Linden'. Unter den Linden is bounded at the far end by the late eighteenth-century Brandenburg Gate (1791) surmounted with a quadriga dating to 1793. The avenue continues on beyond the Brandenburg Gate for nearly four kilometres to the eighteenth-century Charlottenburg Palace. At the Palace end of Unter den Linden was the 'Forum Fridericianum', an ensemble planned by Frederick the Great from 1740 and comprising an elegant group of palaces, the opera house, opened in 1742, the Catholic Hedwigskirche consecrated in 1773, and the Baroque Zeughaus or armoury, for which the foundation stone was laid in 1695. One of the palaces, the Prinz-Heinrich-Palais constructed between 1748 and 1753, became the new university of Berlin founded in 1810. Berlin's first museum, the Altes Museum for Greek and Roman art, built by Karl Friedrich Schinkel (1781–1841) opposite the Royal Palace, was opened in 1830. Next to it, Schinkel redesigned the cathedral in his classicist style in 1820–21 and what later became known as the Kaiser Wilhelm Palais in 1837. Nearby was the Gendarmenmarkt with its twin churches from the early eighteenth century, modified in 1785: the French church for the Huguenots and the German church for the Lutherans. Between them, from 1821, was Schinkel's 'Königliches Schauspielhaus' or royal theatre. Restrained classical elegance characterized this urban ensemble.

Berlin was changing, however. The Borsig factory to build steam locomotives opened in 1837, the Siemens factory was founded in 1847, the Berlin Rubberware Factory (Berliner Gummiwaarenfabrik) opened in 1849 and Schering, the pharmaceutical company, in 1851. The first railway line in Prussia from Berlin to Potsdam was opened in 1838 and from then on stations and lines were opened at breakneck speed, many of them connecting Berlin to Poland and East Prussia. These railway lines brought workers for the new factories and, whereas the population of Paris and Vienna grew by 50 per cent between 1825 and 1850, in Berlin it doubled in the same period and continued to double every twenty-five years from then up to 1900. The population of Berlin was 222,000 in 1825 and by 1900 it was 2,424,000.[40] Jens Bisky points out that in 1860, every second inhabitant of the city had been born elsewhere.[41] As in the other cities discussed above, infrastructure projects were carried out with increasing speed during the second half of the nineteenth century, beginning with gas lighting, running water, and railway stations. A 'Ringbahn' or circle line to link the termini had been built in 1850–51 but had to be redesigned and greatly enlarged when the war against Denmark in 1864 showed that it was inadequate for military purposes.

The speed of the city's expansion led the Prussian Ministry of the Interior to set up a committee in 1858 to plan the growth of Berlin out into the surrounding countryside. The committee was chaired by a young engineer named James Hobrecht (1825–1902), who first travelled to Hamburg, Paris, and London to assess those cities' urban planning. The ensuing plan, which still determines how parts of Berlin are structured today, has been known ever since as the Hobrecht plan.[42] The achievement for which Hobrecht has been universally praised, however, is Berlin's sewage system. He had inspected those in Paris and London and, after gaining experience designing a sewage system for Stettin, in 1871 he presented the city authorities in Berlin with a comprehensive plan for twelve so-called 'Radialsysteme', each of which would collect wastewater and pump it out of the city with steam-driven pumps. His main aim, like Belgrand's in Paris, was to combat disease, for, as in Paris, sewage and wastewater ran down the streets along open gutters. In getting the agreement of the city fathers for his plan, he was supported by the famous doctor Rudolf Virchow (1821–1902), the father of modern pathology, and greatly aided by the fact that his older brother, Arthur Hobrecht (1824–1912), became Lord Mayor of Berlin in 1873. It took twenty years for Hobrecht's sewage system to be completed, from 1873 to 1893, and it cost Berlin a third of all tax revenue during that time, but it is substantially the system still in use today.[43] It was so successful that he was brought in to design the sewage systems in thirty other German cities, as well as in Moscow, Tokyo, and Cairo. The doctor and journalist Isidor Kastan (1840–1931), looking back on the Berlin of the mid-century, describes a poorly lit, stinking town with evil-smelling canals and rivers, badly paved roads, bridges about to collapse, and substandard railway stations.[44] It was not until the city took over the administration of its own affairs from the Prussian state that these evils could be remedied.

Prussian or Imperial Capital?

In 1871, Berlin metamorphosed from a royal into an imperial capital. This was achieved by Prussian victories in three wars: the Danish War in 1864, in which Austria was Prussia's ally against Denmark, the Austrian War in 1866, in which Prussia fought against Austria, and the Franco-Prussian War in 1870–71, which brought the French Second Empire to an end and led to Wilhelm I (1797–1888), king of Prussia since 1861, being proclaimed German emperor in the Hall of Mirrors in Versailles on 18 January 1871. This was only possible because of financial dealings that were kept secret from Wilhelm and which Fritz Stern explains in full.[45] Bavaria, the largest kingdom in southern Germany, had to be convinced to agree to German unification. Ludwig II of Bavaria, desperately in need of money for his building projects and his theatre, was induced to sign what is known as the 'Kaiserbrief', urging Wilhelm to accept the title of German Emperor. Ludwig already signed this letter, drafted by Bismarck, in November 1870 and received in return an annual secret gift of 100,000 taler.

As Christopher Clark points out, the German constitution of 1871 was really a treaty between twenty-five states of hugely varying size.[46] Prussia was by far the largest in terms of both area and population and could always outvote the others. In addition, its administration underpinned the imperial administration, just as the offices of Imperial Chancellor and Prussian prime minister were united in one person, that of Otto von Bismarck (1815–98), the creator of the German Empire. On the face of it, the role of the emperor was simply that of president of the Federal Council or Bundesrat. However, he had supreme command over the army and the power to name all commanding officers and could dissolve or prorogue the Reichstag or imperial parliament. This was elected by universal male suffrage in a direct secret ballot, whereas the Prussian bicameral parliament, which continued to exist in the same way that the parliaments in each of the constituent territories of the Empire did, had a three-class indirect franchise with public ballots, which ensured the dominance of the agrarian sector. Clark remarks that Wilhelm I, born in 1797, was in his seventies when he became German emperor and ninety when he died and always felt and acted more as a Prussian king than as German emperor.[47]

That Berlin was now the imperial capital was brought home to its inhabitants on 16 June 1871 when the Prussian army, 42,000 strong, entered Berlin in triumph. The procession was led by generals and ministers of war who were followed by Bismarck and the two most outstanding Prussian generals, Albrecht von Roon (1803–79) and Helmuth von Moltke (1800–91). Then came Wilhelm I on horseback accompanied by his sons and the rulers of other territories in the Empire such as Saxony and Bavaria. They marched up through the city from the Tempelhofer Feld, the big parade ground to the south, through the Hallesches Tor to the Brandenburg Gate and from there along Unter den Linden, which was decorated like the route as a whole with flags, greenery, and garlands, to the Palace. At the Hallesches Tor they were greeted by a twenty-metre-high figure of Berolina, the personification of Berlin; at Potsdamer Platz there was a structure made of captured cannon on which stood a huge statue of Victoria, flanked by female personifications of the cities of Strasburg and Metz, the cities gained by Prussia as part of the peace treaty. Opposite the Royal Palace was a figure of Germania, welcoming her two new children, Alsace and Lorraine.[48] Half a million visitors came to Berlin to see the parade, and emotions ran high. Even Baroness Hildegard von Spitzemberg (1843–1914), who as a South German was often critical of Prussian attitudes, was carried away:

> The proudest sight for a German heart was the non-commissioned officers from all regiments who carried 81 French flags and eagles in front of the troops! The guards looked magnificent, so manly, sun-burned, bearded, their overly stiff Prussian nature somewhat relaxed by the campaign. Truly they were the most beautiful sight for a patriotic heart. Every individual regiment, every individual ragged banner was cheered...[49]

These captured trophies and banners were placed at the foot of an equestrian statue of King Friedrich Wilhelm III, Wilhelm I's father, unveiled on that day in front of the Altes Museum opposite the Palace. This was a highly symbolic gesture, for Friedrich Wilhelm III was the Prussian monarch whom Napoleon I had humiliated in 1806 when he occupied Berlin, forcing the king to flee to Königsberg in East Prussia and quartering French troops in the city until 1813. That night the principal buildings and monuments were illuminated.

One of the decorative features during the procession along Unter den Linden was painted canvases hung up between columns surmounted by Victory figures. One of them, by Anton von Werner (1843–1915), the Prussian history painter, depicted the myth of Emperor Barbarossa (1122–90), who was said to have been asleep for seven hundred years inside the Kyffhäuser mountain with his red beard growing down through the table he was sitting at, waiting for the time when he could awake. Ravens circling overhead indicated the site of his long slumber. He could now arise, since his empire had been founded anew by Prussia. Baroness von Spitzemberg tells us that, on the evening after the victory parade, the emperor, his generals, all the notables of Berlin, many officers and their families, and she herself attended a performance in the opera house of Barbarossa, a short opera by

Ludwig Bernhard Hopffer (1840–77) with a libretto by Julius Hein. Barbarossa was sung by Albert Niemann (1831–1917), a leading Wagner tenor of his day. The opera depicts Barbarossa deep inside the mountain, witnessing in a dream five key moments from Prussian history, until in 1870 he sees Germania carried on a shield supported by Prussian, Bavarian, and Württemberg soldiers. He sings:

> Das Deutsche Reich erschuf auf's Neue
> Ein großes Reich der Einigkeit,
> Der Hohenzollern deutsche Treue
> Und deutscher Heere Taferkeit![50]

The final scene, which was loudly cheered, showed an equestrian monument of Wilhelm I in front of a backdrop of the city of Paris.

When the Reichstag, the Federal Parliament, was opened for the first time on 1 March 1871 in the White Hall in the Berlin Palace, Wilhelm I sat on a throne which had been brought specially from the town of Goslar, where there was a complex of buildings connected to the Salic dynasty whose members had ruled as Holy Roman Emperors from 1024 to 1125. The throne, called the 'Kaiserstuhl' or imperial seat, consists of a sandstone base dating to the thirteenth century with a back and sides of cast bronze dating to 1070. Crown Prince Friedrich Wilhelm persuaded his father that the Salic Emperor Heinrich III had sat on this throne— something he later discovered was not the case—and had it brought to Berlin for the inauguration of the German Empire.[51] The point was to connect the new Hohenzollern emperors to an ancient imperial dynasty that predated that of the Habsburgs.

The first monument erected in Berlin to celebrate the newly created Empire was the Siegesäule or Victory Column, and it too picks up on the Barbarossa legend. It began life as a monument to glorify Prussia's victory in the Danish War in 1864 and was to have had an inscription praising 'our noble ally, the emperor of Austria'.[52] After Prussia had defeated that ally two years later, the monument was redesigned in 1869 and again redesigned after the victory over the French in 1871. It was originally a column 60.5 metres high, crowned by a golden winged Victory holding a laurel wreath in one hand, a staff with the insignia of the iron cross in the other, and with an eagle on her head. Originally too, the column was decorated with three rows of gilded captured cannon standing upright along the flutes of the column, Danish ones at the bottom, Austrian ones in the middle, and French ones at the top.[53] The column stands on a granite base with a bronze relief on each side made from melted down captured cannon depicting scenes from the three wars. Above this base and surrounding the bottom of the column is a colonnade decorated with a mosaic designed by Anton von Werner and based on four canvases which had adorned Unter den Linden in June 1871.[54] The mosaic depicts Germania taking up arms to protect Germany against the French menace

(Napoleon I appears in the clouds); the German princes supporting their ally Prussia against Napoleon III; Germania, who is simultaneously Borussia, the embodiment of Prussia, accepting the imperial crown; and, of course, the Emperor Barbarossa, ravens circling above, waking from his 700-hundred-year sleep to welcome the new Empire.

This same mythology linking the Empire and its new emperors to a medieval past was to the fore again in the 'Ruhmeshalle der brandenburgisch-preußischen Armee' (Hall of Fame for the Army of Brandenburg-Prussia).[55] This was con-structed in the Zeughaus in Berlin, the Baroque armoury on Unter den Linden not far from the palace. The inspiration for this came from Vienna, for, when Wilhelm I went there in 1873 to see the international exhibition, he visited the Arsenal with its weapons collection and Hall of Fame glorifying the Austrian army, as described above. In 1875 he signed an order to remodel the Berlin armoury and turn it into something similar. Work began on the costly project on 1 August 1877. The inner courtyard was covered over, and a 4.5-metre-high marble figure of Borussia was placed there, in the midst of artillery and flags captured from the French in 1870–71. From this courtyard, a curving double staircase led the visitor up to the first floor into a domed hall known as the 'Herrscherhalle' or Hall of the Rulers. Opening out of this on each side was a 'Feldherrenhalle'—a Hall of the Army Commanders. The Hall of the Rulers contained a 3.9 metre-high marble statue of Victoria and eight life-size bronze statues depicting all the rulers of Brandenburg-Prussia from the Great Elector, whose reign began in 1640, through the first king in Prussia, Friedrich I, and Frederick the Great down to and including Wilhelm I. Thirty-two bronze busts of generals peopled the Halls of the Commanders, those from the seventeenth and eighteenth century in the western Hall and those from the nineteenth century, among whom was Crown Prince Friedrich Wilhelm, in the eastern Hall. These rooms were decorated with sixteen murals by the leading painters of the day. Anton von Werner painted *The Coronation of Friedrich I in Königsberg* and *The Proclamation of the Empire in Versailles* and Friedrich Geselschap *The Reception of the Fallen Heroes into Walhalla* (1879/83)—the heroes being a mixture of medieval and modern Prussian figures. Geselschap was also responsible for the *Triumphal Procession*, which was divided into three parts—*The Outbreak of War*, *The Subjugation of the Enemy*, and *The Crowning of the Victor with a Wreath*.[56] King Friedrich Wilhelm III's *Call to his People* to fight against Napoleon I in 1813 was the subject of a painting by Georg Bleibtreu, and Emil Hünten depicted the Battle of Königgrätz in another. Apart from the coronation of Friedrich I in 1701, all the other subjects are to do with conquest in war and in the rest of the building weapons and trophies from these very conquests were displayed.

The pendant to all this emphasis on war, conquest, and death was, as Eva Giloi has shown, the Hohenzollern Museum in the Monbijou Palace in Berlin, opened by Wilhelm I on 22 March 1877, his eightieth birthday.[57] This collection, which no longer exists, was devoted to sentimental displays of mementos, what one might call relics, many of them donated by members of the public, showing the private and intimate side of the Hohenzollerns. The museum was extremely popular with the public and constantly augmented. According to the Baedeker for 1877, the museum had fourteen rooms.[58] By the 1904 edition of Grieben's guidebook to Berlin, it had forty-two rooms, thirty-nine of them devoted to members of the dynasty, beginning with the Great Elector in the seventeenth century and finishing with the current emperor Wilhelm II and his empress Auguste Viktoria. In contrast to the Zeughaus, the female members of the dynasty had an important place in the Hohenzollern Museum, with nine of them being commemorated. Given her status in Prussian mythology, it is not surprising that no fewer than four rooms were devoted to Queen Luise.

In 1888, Wilhelm I died and shortly afterwards so did his heir Friedrich Wilhelm, who reigned for only ninety-nine days as Friedrich III. Müller relates that Friedrich Wilhelm was so enamoured of the notion that he was the latter-day embodiment of the Holy Roman Emperors (whose empire came to an end, as we know, in 1806) that he wished to take the regnal name of Friedrich IV, in succession to the last Habsburg emperor of that name, Friedrich III, who reigned from 1452 to 1493.[59] Bismarck had to put his foot down and insist that the only possible designation for a Hohenzollern who would become king of Prussia as well as German emperor was Friedrich III, following on from Prussia's most famous king Friedrich II, better known as Frederick the Great.

In 1888, the year of the three emperors, Wilhelm I's grandson Wilhelm II came to the throne. Wilhelm II was extremely interested in art and architecture and had very firm old-fashioned views on them both. John Röhl points out the extraordinary extent to which the new emperor influenced buildings all over the Empire, not just in his capital city.[60] One of the areas in which he and his consort Auguste Viktoria were particularly active was in church-building, a subject that is discussed in detail in chapter VI. By 1903 , fifty-three churches had been built in the Berlin area, among them the emperor's own prestige projects such as the Emperor Wilhelm Memorial Church, in honour of his grandfather, inaugurated on 1 September 1895, and the Berlin cathedral, consecrated on 27 February 1905. During Wilhelm II's reign, 112 churches were erected in Greater Berlin, the majority of them Protestant churches,[61] and he frequently visited the building sites while the churches were under construction to discuss the design.[62]

But this was not the only kind of building in which Wilhelm had a hand. According to article 50 of the 1871 constitution, the emperor was head of the Imperial Postal Service and all its civil servants had to obey his orders. He therefore thought nothing of correcting the architectural plans for some sixty post offices scattered across the Empire, and he did the same with railway stations. As Röhl explains, he had the designs submitted to him and wrote very full comments in the margins, correcting even relatively minor details such as window shapes, mouldings, balconies, columns, and cartouches.[63] The one building he did not manage to influence was the Reichstag, the new imperial parliament, designed by Paul Wallot (1841–1912) (Figure 35). It had already been built up to the eaves by the time Wilhelm II ascended the throne. The emperor assumed that here too he would be able to alter the design at will and, at an audience with Wallot in Potsdam in 1889, was about to start amending the plans for the building in his usual manner. He was completely taken aback when Wallot stopped him in his tracks, saying: 'Majestät, das geht nicht' (which in colloquial English would translate as 'Your Majesty, that's not on').[64] The Reichstag itself was the client, not the emperor or the government, so the emperor had no power over the plans for the building. Naturally, he wrote to the Reichstag building committee to express his views, but Wallot persuaded the committee to stand firm. The emperor never ceased to criticize the building publicly after it was opened in 1894 and took his revenge on Wallot by denying him honours that were his due.

Much could be said about Wilhelm II's love of monumental sculpture, which, combined with his glorification of his grandfather Wilhelm I as 'Wilhelm the Great', led to the erection of between three and four hundred state-funded monuments to Wilhelm I throughout the Empire.[65] The most prominent example

Figure 35 The Reichstag Building in Berlin in 1904, with the monument to Bismarck prominently in front of it. This monument is now in the Tiergarten in Berlin.
Photograph. Private Collection Look and Learn/Elgar Collection/Bridgeman Images.

in Berlin was the 'Kaiser-Wilhelm-Nationaldenkmal', erected on the Spree Canal to one side of the Royal Palace. The nine-metre-high equestrian statue of Wilhelm I, in uniform and wearing a spiked helmet, accompanied by a female figure representing peace holding his bridle, was by Wilhelm II's favourite sculptor Reinhold Begas (1831–1911) and was unveiled in 1897 on his hundredth birthday. The statue was placed on a high pedestal flanked by four great lions, so that in total its height was twenty-one metres. This was placed on a terrace built out into the canal and surrounded by a semi-circular neo-baroque colonnade designed by the architect Gustav Halmhuber (1862–1936). The colonnade ended in a pavilion at each end, surmounted by the quadrigas of Bavaria and Borussia respectively. As Thomas Nipperdey pointed out, this monument, financed by the state to the tune of 4 million marks, is not a monument to the nation, as the term 'Nationaldenkmal' would suggest, but rather a monument to the monarchy and its power.[66]

Wilhelm II had even bigger plans to present the history of his dynasty in monumental form and they were revealed on his thirty-sixth birthday, 27 January 1895, in the official newspaper, the *Deutscher Reichs=Anzeiger und Königlich Preußischer Staats=Anzeiger*. He announced that he wanted to make his capital city a gift, to be paid for from his privy purse, as a thank you to the German people for rising up against foreign aggression and making great sacrifices to bring about the unity of the fatherland and to refound the Empire. He wanted to present the 'the development of national history from the foundation of the Mark Brandenburg to the re-founding of the empire' by means of a series of marble statues of the princes of Brandenburg and Prussia, to be erected on the Siegesallee or Avenue of Victory. They would begin with Margrave Albrecht the Bear (*c*.1100–70) and finish with Emperor and King Wilhelm I (significantly not with the most recent emperor, his own father, Emperor Friedrich III). Next to each of the statues he envisaged a representation of an important man (and he did mean a man) from the same era. His didactic conception of a history lesson in stone reduced the history of the German Empire to the history of Brandenburg-Prussia, identified from the beginning of the fifteenth century onwards with the history of the Hohenzollerns. Wilhelm II regarded himself as a sculptor *manqué* and involved himself with every detail of the project, just as he did with buildings.[67] Reinhold Koser (1852–1914), director of the Prussian state archives and official historian of Prussia, had the oversight of the historical details, Begas was entrusted with the artistic supervision of the project and was asked to complete some of the statues himself, and Halmhuber, the architect of the colonnade round the Kaiser Wilhelm monument, was in charge of the architectural conception. Twenty-five other sculptors were chosen by the emperor, who approved their models before they could be carved and who visited their studios to see the work in progress.

For 750 metres along the Siegesallee, the avenue leading through the wooded Tiergarten from the Victory Column, which was then in front of the Reichstag, up to Kemperplatz, were placed thirty-two life-size marble statues of rulers and princes in Brandenburg-Prussia from the twelfth to the late nineteenth century, sixteen on each side along a wide path separated by a hedge from the carriageway. Each figure was placed on a pedestal, so that it was 2.75 metres high, and placed in a marble bay. Steps led up to each pedestal, behind which was a semi-circular bench, also of marble, divided into three by two busts of figures placed on the back of the bench. These figures were chosen either for their relationship to the ruler or for their significance in the era of his reign. The marble bays with their benches, busts, and statue were spaced out with flowerbeds between them, and the whole ensemble was intended as a place for a pleasant stroll, while at the same time providing a lesson in Prussian history (Figure 36). The first ten figures were margraves of Brandenburg, before the first elector of Brandenburg, Ludwig II (r.1356–1365), made his appearance in group eleven. The first Hohenzollern, Friedrich I, elector of Brandenburg (r. 1415–1440), arrived in group fifteen. The

Figure 36 A postcard saying 'Greeting from Berlin' with Wilhelm II and Empress Auguste Viktoria walking on the Siegesallee in Berlin. Chromolithograph. Private Collection Look and Learn/Valerie Jackson Harris Collection/Bridgeman Images

first three monuments to be completed were unveiled on 22 March 1898, Wilhelm I's birthday. John Röhl, quoting Uta Lehnert's classic study,[68] describes how the emperor carefully chose the guests for each of the unveiling ceremonies, seeking out descendants of the figures portrayed, and how he himself wore the costume of the period in question. He is reported to have stood to attention for a full minute before the statue of Frederick II the Great.

The whole ensemble ended at the Roland Fountain on Kemperplatz. This was another monumental creation financed by the emperor, unveiled in 1902. The Berliners' ancient rights and political autonomy were symbolized by the figure of Roland, which Elector Friedrich II, known as Irontooth (r.1440–70) (group sixteen on the Siegesallee), had thrown into the river Spree as a sign that his authority was paramount. The story of the citizens' defeat was a favourite of Wilhelm II's. In 1894, he commissioned Ruggero Leoncavallo (1857–1919) to compose an opera entitled *Der Roland von Berlin*. Its long gestation period meant that it could not be performed in the Royal Opera House in Berlin until 13 December 1904, where it met with a very negative critical reception. In 1899, as part II of a projected tetralogy based on great figures from Hohenzollern history, Josef von Lauff's play *Der Eisenzahn* (Irontooth) was premiered in 1899 in Wiesbaden at the annual Imperial Festival there. The clear message of the clash between Irontooth and the self-governing craftsmen who made up the citizenry, transposed to the late nineteenth century, was that monarchical authority trumped the self-determination of the people. The monarch was the guarantor of peace, justice, and the welfare of his subjects.[69] The colourful fountain, in neo-Gothic style, consisted of an octagonal basin, surrounded by four smaller ones. It was surmounted by a figure of Roland, 3.75 metres high and carved from granite, wearing full armour and holding the sword of justice in his right hand and a horn in his left. Reliefs depicted representatives of crafts and guilds, as well as a knight and a scholar. The Roland figure may be imposing, but this was surely not 'a goodwill gesture' to the people of Berlin,[70] rather a reminder of their subordinate position, particularly as the statue of Irontooth stood immediately next to the fountain at the end of the Siegesallee.

Wilhelm's didactic purpose for this celebratory sculpture park was partly fulfilled in that school classes were taken to visit it and made to write essays about it afterwards. A group of these essays, written by students in the top class, were found in the archives, annotated with comments from the emperor himself. It seems that their teacher must have had a sense of humour, for the topic he set was 'The Hohenzollerns' Legs'. He asked the students to examine the legs of the various figures and judge their characters from what they found.[71]

The Siegesallee was a target for criticism of all kinds, either taking issue with individual groups or with the project as a whole. The question was asked why the figures were all of men. Where were such notable women in Prussian history as Electress Sophie Charlotte and Queen Luise? And the satirists had a field day. In the *Lustige Blätter* in 1899 Franz Jüttner depicted Otto V the Lazy (r. 1365–73) having a nice lie-down, having descended from his pedestal. A verse in the satirical magazine *Simplicissimus* on 27 May 1901 said that the white marble groups looked like figures on a wedding cake,[72] while on 14 October 1901 the cover illustration of *Simplicissimus*, headed 'Childish Game' and subtitled 'Little Willy plays Berlin', depicted two rows of toy soldiers standing on cotton reels with stiff white curving shirt collars behind them to indicate the marble bays. Toy trees separated them and down the middle marched another group of toy soldiers following their officer on horseback, while a little closed wagon drives in front. A small hand comes down from the top left-hand side of the picture to adjust one of the little soldiers.[73] Berlin wits called the ensemble the 'Puppenallee'—Dolls' Avenue or Puppets' Parade—and shook their heads at the vanity of their emperor.

London as Latecomer

By the time of Queen Victoria's Diamond Jubilee in 1898, those who knew about architecture and urban planning such as Henry Heathcote Statham, architect and editor of *The Builder*, were appalled by London's haphazard urban layout, especially by contrast with Paris, Vienna, and Rome. In an article in 1897, Statham lamented the absence of the 'palatial dignity' of Paris and the fact that 'the shortcoming of London, as a capital city, is that it is almost entirely devoid of the qualities of spaciousness and stateliness. It is not so much like a capital city as like a very large and overgrown provincial town'.[74] Statham noted exasperatedly that a new north–south thoroughfare had been mooted but not yet carried out and proposed that 'the Mall should be carried through and opened into Charing Cross',[75] lamenting at the same time that no monument to the queen's reign was being planned. These deficiencies had finally been remedied by the time of George V's coronation in 1911. The north–south thoroughfare, named Kingsway, was opened in 1905 by King Edward VII, and it formed part of a planned development which included the Aldwych crescent, a street that meets the east–west thoroughfare of the Strand on both sides.[76] A monument to the late queen, the Victoria Memorial, began to be planned very soon after her death in 1901 and was unveiled by George V and Kaiser Wilhelm II, two of Victoria's grandsons, on 16 May 1911. This was placed in a setting that finally gave London a ceremonial focus.

The Victoria Memorial by Thomas Brock (1847–1922) was erected in front of Buckingham Palace, which was given a new façade, and the Mall, leading from the Palace down towards a new monumental opening into Trafalgar Square called Admiralty Arch, was redesigned as a processional street. The memorial consists of a golden winged Victory standing on a globe, accompanied by figures of

Constancy and Courage, Justice and Truth, while two eagles with outspread wings represent Empire. The enormous enthroned figure of Queen Victoria faces down the Mall, while the much more intimate figure of Motherhood faces the Palace. On the plinth beneath the queen can be read the words 'Victoria Regina Imperatrix'. At the four corners of the monument are fountains with the figures of Peace, Progress, Agriculture, and Manufacture, accompanied by huge bronze lions. The monument was placed in an architectural setting by Aston Webb (1849–1930), not completed until 1924, which included formal gardens. As Tori Smith points out, the Memorial was financed by public subscription, with about a third of the cost coming from the colonies. She also points out that those same colonies did not feature prominently either on the monument or in the Mall. Canada, Australia, South and West Africa are represented on what are called the Dominion Gates,[77] but, because Lord Curzon had gone ahead with his scheme to erect a Victoria Memorial in Calcutta, India did not contribute to the London monument, so was not represented on it at all!

Mexico City and Petrópolis

When Ferdinand Maximilian of Habsburg, Archduke of Austria, arrived in Mexico in 1864 as its new emperor, the capital was a Spanish colonial city with a cathedral, an imposing viceregal palace, and a town hall grouped around the main square and with many handsome colonial buildings in the grid of streets roundabout. At this time, the city contained some 300,000 inhabitants and had been built by the Spanish conquistadores on top of the Aztec settlement of Tenotichlan, which they had razed to the ground in 1521. Maximilian and his consort Charlotte of Belgium sometimes resided in the Viceregal Palace but decided to make Chapultepec Castle, situated on an eminence outside the city centre and with a wonderful view, their second residence. Bernardo de Gálvez (born 1746, viceroy from 1785) had begun to construct the Castle in 1785 but died in 1786. Plans were then made to turn it into an archive—presumably on the model of the Royal Spanish Archives housed in the hilltop fortress of Simancas near Valladolid in Spain—but in the end it was decided to sell the building. When no buyer could be found, the authorities started to tear out the windows and doors and sell them, something that Alexander von Humboldt described in his account of New Spain, castigating it as vandalism because it left the building open to the elements on a windy promontory.[78] It then had a period as a military college and became the site of the heroic stand made by a group of twelve cadets against the US army in 1847, the so-called 'Niños Héroes'. When Maximilian and his consort took over the building, they commissioned the Viennese architect Carl Gangolf Kayser (1837–95) to plan the renovation and Julius Hofmann (1840–96) to design the interiors. Wilhelm Knechtel (1837–1924), who had designed the gardens at

Maximilian's neo-Gothic castle on the sea at Trieste, was brought to Mexico to plan the gardens.[79] Easy access was now needed from the old city to the castle and a straight road of some three and a half kilometres was constructed, running diagonally towards the beginning of the existing streets. Called by Maximilian the 'Paseo de la Imperatriz' or Promenade of the Empress, it is now the 'Paseo de la Reforma' and has been extended into a major thoroughfare nearly fifteen kilometres in length. Nowadays, it is adorned with statues of notable Mexicans, punctuated with impressive monuments, lined with fine buildings from later periods, and planted with trees and flowers. Photographs taken during Maximilian's reign, however, simply show a very straight country road running through fields. As to who designed the road, Pruonto writes that two Austrian engineers were involved, Alois (or Luis) Bolland Kuhmackl and Colonel Ferdinand von Rosenzweig, while Nizza Santiago Burgoa also names the Mexicans Luis Robles Pezuela, Miguel Iglesias, and Benito León Acosta.[80] After Maximilian's execution, the road was broadened by adding paths for pedestrians on both sides.

Santiago Burgoa discusses a rough draft she found in the Haus- Hof- und Staatsarchiv in Vienna setting out Maxmilian's plans to embellish Mexico City and give it the grandeur of a European capital: an independence monument, a monumental fountain honouring Christopher Columbus, other fountains like those in front of St Peter's in Rome on the Plaza Major near the cathedral, improvements to the Palacio Nacional, the Teatro Nacional, museums, and a national library are all mentioned.[81] An important figure here was Ramón Rodríguez Arangoiti (1830–82), who won the competition to design both the independence monument and the Columbus monument. In the Alameda, the park in the centre of Mexico City, zinc copies of antique statues made in Berlin were to be installed. There were to be rows of trees and iron benches on the Paseo de la Emperatriz. Maximilian also envisaged improving the infrastructure by installing a water supply and gas lighting throughout the city, and hospitals and orphanages, public water pumps, and cemeteries were also to be constructed.

Maximilian was, of course, influenced by the European capitals he knew. He had visited Paris from 17 to 28 May 1856, when he saw the Champs-Élysées and Haussmann's *grand boulevards*. He had also seen Brussels at the time of his marriage to Princess Charlotte in 1857, at a period when plans to regulate the river Senne and construct wide boulevards were being discussed there, and of course he knew the Ringstrasse in Vienna. Had he reigned for twenty or thirty years and had he had sufficient funds, Mexico City would doubtless have become an imperial city with many of the features of its European models. As it is, the Paseo de la Reforma is 'probably the most visible remnant of the Empire'.[82]

If Maximilian was dreaming of a Mexican Paris, Pedro II was building Petrópolis, a Brazilian Bad Ischl, a comparison Barman makes.[83] Two separate elements combined to create this new imperial town in the lush green hills above Rio de Janeiro. The first was the desire of the imperial family and the court to escape the heat of the capital during the summer months from December to the beginning of May and move up into the lush vegetation of the hills. The second was Brazil's need to import hard-working white settlers to come to the country and work the land. Pedro I had bought an estate called the Fazienda de Córrego Seco in 1830, but, after he left Brazil, it had to be assigned to his creditors and was then bought back in 1840. In order to colonize the area, it was decided to bring settlers from Germany, giving them free passage and a grant of land. They 'were expected to be white, industrious, literate and reliable'.[84] Towards the end of June 1845, the first 160 settlers arrived, and by March 1847 there were almost 3,000 of them living in Petrópolis. They were settled in twelve districts scattered around the area and each district was named for the area of Germany in which the settlers originated. The Museu Casa do Colono in the town today illustrates the history of these settlers and displays many touching examples of typical everyday objects that the settlers brought with them from home. These immigrants quickly settled down and began to farm the land.

The imperial palace, on a site chosen by Pedro II himself, is a modestly sized neoclassical building, which is now the Imperial Museum. Because the imperial family spent almost half of every year at Petrópolis, members of the court, the diplomatic corps, and wealthy coffee barons also began to spend time in the town, building pastel-coloured villas with gardens along the streets, among the canals and bridges that criss-cross the town. Inhabitants of Rio also moved to Petrópolis during the summer to escape outbreaks of yellow fever. Brazil's first railway, built in 1854, took visitors part of the way, and from 1883 the whole way, to the town, which made commuting down to Rio easier and quicker. In 1874 Princess Isabel, the heir to the throne, moved up there permanently and had her own residence. She was extremely pious and was instrumental in founding the imposing neo-Gothic cathedral, dedicated to St Peter of Alcántara. Building commenced in 1884, though it was not completed until 1925.

It was at the Imperial Palace in Petrópolis on 15 November 1889 that Pedro II received the telegram informing him of a military uprising in Rio. To quote Barman: 'He ordered a special train and went down to the capital, to dethronement and to exile in Europe.'[85] He died in 1891. Almost immediately, Brazil seemed to regret his departure. Pedro's afterlife in Petrópolis is described in the last chapter of this book.

Another museum in Petrópolis commemorates the Jewish writer Stefan Zweig (1881–1942), a Viennese through and through, who had to flee in 1934 and, after years of homeless wandering, was given asylum in Brazil, arriving in Petrópolis on 22 August 1940. On 21 February 1942, he finished his memoir, *Die Welt von Gestern* (The World of Yesterday) in a little house almost buried in lush green vegetation halfway up a hill half an hour on foot outside the centre of the town. Here, on 22 February 1942, he and his wife took their own lives. If Petrópolis marks the end of the Brazilian Empire, it also stands for the end of the European 'world of yesterday', in which the imperial cities discussed above achieved their self-confident apogee.

Notes

1. Dabot, *Souvenirs*, p. 1.
2. Dabot, *Souvenirs*, p. 2.
3. Olsen, *The City*, p. 37.
4. Loyer, 'La ville en représentation'.
5. Haussmann, *Mémoires*, pt. II, p. 53.
6. *Haussmann* (1867), p. 8.
7. Haussmann, *Mémoires*, pt. II, p. 8.
8. Haussmann, *Mémoires*, pt. II, xii.
9. Zanten, *Building Paris*, p. 19.
10. For a critical view of Haussmann's activities see Jones, *Paris*, pp. 344–68.
11. Smith, *Napoleon III*, p. 67.
12. Alphand, *Les promenades de Paris*.
13. Milza, *Napoleon III*, p. 518.
14. Zanten, *Building Paris*, pp. 204–11 and Truesdell, *Spectacular Politics*, pp. 88–99. Van Zanten's dates are not always correct.
15. Hübner, *Neun Jahre*, vol. II, p. 81.
16. Dabot, *Souvenirs*, p. 38.
17. *Le Moniteur universel*, 13 August 1861, p. 1222.
18. *La France*, 8 December 1862, p. 1.
19. Cochinchina was a French colony in the southern part of Vietnam. It included Saigon and was invaded by the French in 1859.
20. Mansel, *Paris between Empires*, pp. 423–32.
21. Schorske, *Fin-de-Siècle Vienna*, p. 54.
22. Schorske, *Fin-de-Siècle Vienna*, p. 30. The Crown Prince Rudolf Barracks still exists, though under another name.
23. *Wegweiser durch Wien*, p. 11.
24. Czeike, *Historisches Lexikon*, pp. 370–1.
25. Telesko, *Geschichtsraum Österreich*, p. 416.
26. Telesko, *Geschichtsraum Österreich*, p. 415.
27. Telesko, Kurdiovsky, and Sachsenhofer, 'The Vienna Hofburg'.
28. Gottfried, *Das Wiener Kaiserforum*, p. 62.
29. Vocelka and Vocelka, *Franz Joseph*, p. 106.
30. Stickler, 'Die Herrschaftsauffassung Kaiser Franz Josephs.
31. Öhlinger, 'Kommunale Oligarchie'.
32. Felder, *Erinnerungen*, p. 400.

33. Though it is now known simply as the Burgtheater, it still has the old name K. K. Hofburgtheater in gold letters over the entrance.
34. Rehbock, *Festzug der Stadt*.
35. *Neue Freie Presse*, 28 April 1979.
36. Fischer, *Hans Makart's Festzug*, p. 1.
37. Kurdiovsky et al., 'Legitimacy through History'.
38. Kurdiovsky, 'Die Wiener Hofburg'.
39. Kurdiovsky, 'Zeremonielle Räume', p. 208.
40. Figures taken from *Experiment Metropole*, p. 13.
41. Bisky, *Berlin*; Bienert and Buchholz, *Modernes Berlin*.
42. Bernet, 'The 'Hobrecht Plan'.
43. Bisky, *Berlin*, p. 298.
44. Isidor Kastan, *Berlin wie es war* (Berlin: Mosse, 1919) quoted in Glatzer, *Berlin wird Kaiserstadt*, p. 37.
45. Stern, *Gold and Iron*, p. 133.
46. Clark, *Iron Kingdom*, p. 556–62.
47. Clark, *Iron Kingdom*, p. 588.
48. Glatzer, *Berlin wird Kaiserstadt*, p. 25.
49. Spitzemberg, *Tagebuch*, p. 126.
50. 'The German Empire was created anew by a great empire of unity, the German faithfulness of the Hohenzollerns and the bravery of German armies!'. Hein and Hopffer, *Barbarossa*, p. 20.
51. Müller, *Our Fritz*, p. 91.
52. *Siegessäule Berlin*.
53. In the Third Reich, the column was increased in height by 6.5 metres by adding a fourth row of cannon. It was moved from its original position in front of the Reichstag to where it stands now, in the middle of the 'Großer Stern' or Great Star, the intersection of four axial roads, one of which is the continuation of Unter den Linden mentioned above.
54. *Siegessäule Berlin*, n. pag.
55. *Die Ruhmeshalle*.
56. *Führer durch das Königliche Zeughaus*, pp. 24–7.
57. Giloi, *Monarchy, Myth*, p. 221.
58. Baedeker, *Northern Germany*, p. 42.
59. Müller, *Our Fritz*, p. 92.
60. Röhl, *The Kaiser's Personal Monarchy*, pp. 894–925.
61. Barth, *Kaiserliches Berlin*, p. 249.
62. Röhl, *The Kaiser's Personal Monarchy*, p. 899.
63. Röhl, *The Kaiser's Personal Monarchy*, p. 896.
64. Röhl, *The Kaiser's Personal Monarchy*, p. 904.
65. Hasselhorn, 'Der Kaiser und sein Großvater'.
66. Nipperdey, 'Nationalidee und Nationaldenkmal', p. 543.
67. Röhl, *The Kaiser's Personal Monarchy*, pp. 915–23; Richie, *Faust's Metropolis*, pp. 231–2.
68. Lehnert, *Der Kaiser und die Siegesallee*.

69. Förster, *Kulturpolitik*, pp. 62–4.
70. Richie, *Faust's Metropolis*, p. 231.
71. Caspar, *Die Beine der Hohenzollern*.
72. *Simplicissimus*, 6, no. 10 (1901), p. 77.
73. *Simplicissimus*, 6, no. 30, cover.
74. Statham, 'London as a Jubilee City', p. 595.
75. Statham, 'London as a Jubilee City', p. 599.
76. Finding, 'London 1911', p. 5.
77. Smith, '"A grand work"', p. 34.
78. Humboldt, *Versuch*, p. 81.
79. Pruonto, 'Did the Second Mexican Empire', p. 103.
80. Santiago Burgoa, 'Forjando la cara del imperio', p. 380. Tenenbaum also mentions Francisco Somera as the architect of the road in 'Streetwise history'.
81. Santiago Burgoa, 'Forjando la cara del imperio', pp. 381–2.
82. Pruonto, 'Did the Second Mexican Empire', p. 103.
83. Barman, 'Imperial Cities'. Bad Ischl was Franz Joseph's summer residence.
84. Barman, 'Imperial Cities', p. 8.
85. Barman, 'Imperial Cities', p. 14.

VIII

Showcasing the Empire

International Exhibitions

The second half of the nineteenth century and the first half of the twentieth were remarkable for large-scale international exhibitions of agricultural products, manufactured goods, technological inventions, and artworks that were staged in major cities in purpose-built buildings and visited by very large numbers of people. These events enabled demonstrations of national pride, functioned as engines of modernity, and promoted the global exchange of knowledge, global competition, and global trade. Raymond Isay, in a work which is still worth reading for its verve and comparative focus, sees one of these exhibitions, the 1855 Exposition Universelle in Paris, as both a symbol and a synthesis of its own period as well as of the entire nineteenth century. The exposition was based, he writes, on many notions that were fanciful:

> Belief in material progress and in indefinite moral progress; the conviction that the development of science and industry could and must bring happiness and wisdom to people; confidence in the regime, the certainty that France, after many storms, had finally come to rest; the conception of the rapprochement of the classes, hope in a European peace, faith in the harmony between the nations associated with the great task of civilisation.[1]

These hopes were reiterated again and again at exhibitions held in Paris, London, Vienna, and Philadelphia and were expressed not just by the countries staging the exhibitions but by the Empire of Brazil which was taking part in them. There is a huge literature on international exhibitions, often devoted to particular aspects or individual countries. Of the standard works that attempt to cover the whole subject those by Paul Greenhalgh and Pieter van Wesemael are two of the best known and discuss a wide range of relevant questions.[2] The first question being asked here is to what extent emperors in France, Austria, and Brazil used these exhibitions to project themselves to the world as modern monarchs, promoting progress in the territories they ruled over. How Britain exhibited India in national and international exhibitions is discussed in chapter IX.

Projecting Imperial Power: New Nineteenth-Century Emperors and the Public Sphere. Helen Watanabe-O'Kelly, Oxford University Press (2021). © Helen Watanabe-O'Kelly. DOI: 10.1093/oso/9780198802471.003.0009

Imperial Pomp in Paris—the Exposition Universelle of 1855

The grand inaugurations of streets, discussed in chapter VII, were directed in the first instance at the citizens of Paris. Two other events, the Expositions Universelles held in Paris in 1855 and 1867 respectively, were showcases in which France, her capital city, and her emperor presented themselves to the world. France had a tradition of industrial exhibitions going back to 1797, the two most recent before 1855 being held in 1844 and 1849. These were, however, exhibitions of national products, whereas the immediate model and competitor for the Paris exhibition of 1855 was the Great Exhibition of the Works of Industry of All Nations held in London in 1851, an international event at which the products of various nations could compete and be compared with one another. On 8 March 1853, Napoleon III decreed that a so-called Exposition Universelle, an international exhibition of agricultural and industrial products, would take place in Paris from 1 May until 31 October 1855. A second decree of 22 June 1853 established what became the distinguishing feature of French exhibitions, namely, the inclusion of a separate fine art exhibition. According to the decree, this would contribute to the progress of the arts by means of a competition between 'all the artists in the world' and would remedy a lack in previous exhibitions, including London. It was especially the task of France, said the decree, whose industry owed so much to the fine arts, to give them the place they deserved in the forthcoming exposition. Haussmann, having only taken up his post in 1853 as Prefect of the Seine, had to complete the rue de Rivoli in time and a grand hotel had to be built on the street big enough to house prestigious visitors to Paris.[3] Three thousand workers laboured day and night and the Grand Hôtel du Louvre with its seven hundred rooms and two steam-driven lifts, designed by Alfred Armand (1805–88), was able to open in time.

The purpose-built Palais de l'Industrie on the Champs de Mars where the main exhibits were shown was not finished by the opening on 15 May, a date two weeks later than originally planned.[4] Though it was 250 metres long and 180 wide, it turned out to be too small to house the machinery that exhibitors wanted to show, so a 'Galerie des Machines', 1.2 kilometres long, was constructed between the Palais de l'Industrie and the Seine, with a rotunda, designed by Jacques-Ignace Hittorff, enabling visitors to pass from one to the other. This rotunda, called the Panorama, was cleverly used to display the crown jewels, the emperor's Sèvres dinner service, Gobelin and Beauvais tapestries, and Aubusson carpets. On the gallery could be seen other items of French manufacture such as musical instruments, arms, cutlery, and fine furniture—and a Colt pistol.[5] Among the exhibits in 1855 there were innumerable inventions of note from Foucault's pendulum to Cockerill's steam engine, from the first examples of cement and reinforced concrete to Singer sewing machines and the saxophone. The Palais de l'Industrie was not a wholly satisfactory building, for it had insufficient ventilation and not enough light on the ground floor.[6] The fine art exhibition was housed in a separate building, also specially constructed, on the avenue Montaigne and an international jury was appointed to judge the exhibits. [7] Delacroix and Ingres, two artists of the First Empire who were still active, were given a room each, Winterhalter's *Empress Eugénie Surrounded by her Ladies* was shown for the first time, and, though eleven of Courbet's paintings were accepted, two of his most important, *The Studio* and *The Burial at Ornans*, were rejected.[8]

The entrance to the exposition was already meant to impress visitors with the glory of the Second Empire and its head of state. They entered the Palais de l'Industrie through an enormous portal surmounted by a 6.5-metre-high sculptural group by Élias Robert entitled *France Crowning Art and Industry*, a design that was also used on many of the medals presented to prizewinners at the final ceremony. This was flanked on each side by a pair of putti leaning on a cartouche bearing Napoleon III's arms. Beneath the feet of the figure of France was an eagle and, on the frieze below that, a bust of the emperor with another far larger eagle below that again.[9] That the Bonaparte emperor was the presiding genius over the exposition was underlined by this means before the visitor ever entered the exhibition. Prince Napoleon, the emperor's cousin and the head of the imperial commission which organized the exposition, began his speech at the opening ceremony, attended by the emperor and empress, the diplomatic corps and other notables, by reminding those present that the exhibition was taking place during the Crimean War in which several of the exhibiting nations were involved. Indeed, he himself had been absent from Paris for several months, commanding a division at the front. Addressing the emperor, he said:

> France, engaged for the last year in a serious war 800 leagues from her frontiers, is battling against her enemies with glory. It was not until the reign of Your Majesty that France showed herself worthy of her warlike past and greater than she has ever been in the arts of peace. The French people are showing the world that every time that their genius is understood, and they are well led, they will always be 'la grande nation'.[10]

In a fortunate turn of events, before the closing ceremony on 15 November, French troops under General MacMahon had won the battle of Malakoff on 8 September 1855 and the Russians had retreated from Sébastopol on 9 September, thereby enabling Prince Napoleon to laud France as a successful military power and as a peacemaker.

The exposition, like all similar exhibitions, had been conceived as a celebration of national superiority, which the comparison with the products of other nations was expected to confirm. As one of the guidebooks to the 1855 Paris exhibition states confidently: 'in the design arts, in luxury articles France has no rival anywhere; that good taste which reigns in the works of our artists and the general feeling for form have imprinted their influence for a long time on most French industries.'[11] This superiority of French manufacture and agricultural produce was intended to shed its lustre on the emperor who had called such an outstanding display into being. Though there were five million visitors and 24,000 exhibitors, the exposition made a heavy loss (8 million francs out of a total cost of 11 million), yet in terms of international prestige it was a great success. Queen Victoria and her consort Prince Albert visited between 18 and 26 August, for instance, and were able to admire not just the exhibits but also the transformation of Paris. The queen graciously allowed a street running between the rue de Rivoli and the quai de Gesvres to be named after her.

The real show of imperial pomp took place at the closing ceremony on 15 November, when the emperor distributed prizes and medals to some 12,000 prizewinners. It took place in the Palais de l'Industrie, which by then had been emptied of all the exhibits and turned into a huge theatre with raked seating for 40,000 guests and a dais for the imperial party, on which stood a throne covered in red velvet with an enormous N on the back. A baldachin surmounted by the imperial crown hung overhead and an eagle standard was positioned at each side. The highpoint of the ceremony was the concert given by 1200 musicians organized and conducted by Hector Berlioz (1803–69).[12] Berlioz had been recruited as a member of the jury to judge the musical instruments in the exposition, a task that meant spending all day from nine to five during most of the months of August and September listening to examples of a whole range of different instruments. He bemoaned this duty vigorously in letters to his friend, the bedridden poet Heinrich Heine, to his sister Adèle, and to the composer Stamaty. Having finished the judging, he thought his involvement with the exposition was at an end, until Prince Napoleon asked him at three weeks' notice to arrange the concert. Berlioz told his sister that a businessman was funding it and would only do so if he, Berlioz, was in charge. The programme he arrived at comprised three movements of his own *Te Deum*, the last movement of his *Symphonie Funèbre et triomphale*, and the cantata *L'Impériale*, dedicated to the emperor. This latter was supposed to receive its premiere on this occasion, but it was thought too long, at ten to twelve minutes, and Berlioz was forced to break off in the middle, so as to allow time for Prince Napoleon to make his speech. It was therefore not performed in its entirety until a second concert the next day. Yet another concert, at which the entire programme was performed, was held on 24 November. The text of *L'Impériale* by Pierre-Chéri Lafont (1797–1873) is a victory hymn, in which the triumphant souls of the French answer the cry of destiny uttered by the cannon and in which an eagle with burning wings bears the battle standard aloft and returns to the skies:

> Car du sépulcre est sortie,
> Comme autrefois le Messie,

L'impériale dynastie
Que Dieu même suscita
Et que la gloire enfanta.[13]

Here we surely have a reference to the many depictions of Napoleon I rising from the tomb, for instance, by Horace Vernet, which were circulating at the time in various versions and media. Napoleon III may not be the Messiah himself, but he is the latter-day incarnation of his uncle, and he and his dynasty have a messianic mission to lead France.

Social Purpose and Glamour—the 1867 Exposition Universelle in Paris

The Universal Exposition of 1867! What a memorial to the glory of France and her sovereign Napoleon III, who invited all the peoples of the earth to give each other their hands in a brotherly embrace within the immense perimeter of the Champ-de-Mars, that vast space of iron, cast iron and glass open to the products of the entire universe and [which is], in conformity with the grandeur of its role and the majesty of its civilizing mission, the first step towards that universal peace that will cease to be a dream on the day that all peoples will be in direct and perpetual communication.

Guide Général, pp. 199–200.

This is the claim made in an official guidebook, published by the administration of the Exposition Universelle in 1867 (Figure 37). Once again, Paris was in competition with London, which had organized its second international exhibition in 1862. As in 1855, Frédéric Le Play (1806–82), engineer and social thinker, was the 'Commissaire Générale' for the Paris event of 1867. This meant that he was the man responsible for the overall concept and its implementation, though he was assisted by another engineer, the economist Michel Chevalier (1806–79) who had helped to prepare the free trade agreement between France and Great Britain in 1860. They were both strongly influenced by the ideas of the political philosopher and social thinker Claude-Henri de Rouvroy de Saint-Simon (1760–1825) and the theme they chose for the exposition was that of 'work'.[14] This meant not just showing the glories of technological advance and the outstanding products of various industries but considering the place of the worker in the new society technology was bringing about. Their perception was that the worker was more and more cast adrift in society and was less and less attached to the concern he was working for, as could be seen in the flood of peripatetic craftsmen of all kinds who had come to Paris to assist in its rebuilding. This detachment also meant that

Figure 37 The Arrival of the Emperor and Empress at the Grand Entrance for the opening of the Paris Exhibition of 1867. *Illustrated London News*, 13 April 1867. Engraving. Private Collection Look and Learn/Illustrated Papers Collection/ Bridgeman Images

unrest broke out at intervals and that socialist thinking was on the rise. As a response to this, the exhibits in Group X consisted of 'Objects exhibited especially in order to improve the physical and moral state of the population', classes 89–95). These objects were supposed to counterbalance all the luxurious furnishings, clothes, domestic appurtenances, and jewellery exhibited elsewhere in the exposition.[15] Group X had seven subgroups: class 89 contained materials and methods for children's education; class 90 demonstrated teaching materials and libraries for adult education; class 91 contained furniture, clothing, and foodstuffs, both useful and affordable; in class 92 'costumes populaires' (folk costumes) of various countries were exhibited; class 94 consisted of products made by master craftsmen; and 95 tools and procedures to help such craftsmen.

Class 93 was dedicated to what is nowadays called 'affordable housing'—dwellings for workers, either single or family men, which would be cheap to build but hygienic and well equipped. Prince Albert, consort of Queen Victoria, had led the way here, promoting the erection of model houses by the Society for Improving the Condition of the Labouring Classes at the Great Exhibition in London in 1851.[16] Housing for workers was a subject dear also to the emperor's heart. He had had Henry Roberts's *The Dwellings of the Labouring Classes* (1850) translated into French shortly after it appeared and had also had two different types of workers' housing built in Paris, in the rue de Montessuy and in the boulevard Daumesnil, the second of which he designed himself. For these efforts he was awarded the Grand Prix in this class.[17] He also gave 20,000 francs to a committee of workers to build the so-called 'House of the Workers of Paris' on the exposition site, which contained twelve independent small dwellings for workers. Workers were also encouraged to visit the exposition, free travel was available to the peasantry from numerous provinces, and free lodging for 67,000 people was also provided on the site. In Paul Greenhalgh's words, 1867 was 'one of the most hopeful exhibitions ever staged, a strange mixture of imperial-economic ambition and of Saint-Simonian paternalism, it projected a notion of society as a beautifully tuned machine capable of resolving conflicts and harnessing the world to its own ends.'[18]

The main exposition was staged on the Champs de Mars and consisted of a new Palais de l'Industrie in the shape of a huge oval building open in the middle like a modern Coliseum (resembling, said the emperor, 'the largest gasometer in the world').[19] The objects were grouped in seven concentric circular galleries, each of which was devoted to a different category of exhibit, and these galleries were intersected longitudinally by rows of exhibits representing the various nations.[20] Visitors could thus, if they wished, compare all the exhibits in one category or examine all those submitted by one nation. Eleven million people visited the exhibition ground between 1 April and 3 November 1867, many of them waiting until the gardens and the various pavilions were finished. For this reason, the inauguration on 1 April was a low-key affair. The *Illustrated London News* reported that there was a grand imperial entrance to the park 'with lofty standards richly painted and gilt, the summits of which were crowned with gigantic golden eagles with outspread wings' and 'a gorgeous green canopy, spotted over with golden bees and intersected with golden cords', that the imperial cipher, the huge N, was everywhere to be seen, that there were bands and soldiers and what amounted to an honour guard of workmen, holding their picks and shovels aloft.[21] However, many exhibits were still missing and many of the galleries were full of unopened packing cases. The same paper reports, too, that the park was in chaos, with 'the scores of unfinished structures rising up in every direction, the trodden-down grass-plots, the trampled-over flower beds and the muddy pathways.' Surely for this reason the *Grand Album de l'Exposition Universelle 1867* only gives a brief description of the opening, devoting more space to a catalogue of the crowned heads who had visited the exhibition.[22] The catalogue begins with the Sultan Abdul-Aziz, the emperors of Russia and Austria, the king and queen of Prussia, the queen of the Netherlands, the king and queen of Belgium, and goes down a list of some seventy imperial, royal, princely, and ducal names (Figure 38). The *Grand Album* only begins to convey the sheer glamour and excitement of a visit to the exposition when it gets to the outermost gallery of the Palais de l'Industrie, lit up at night with hundreds of gas lamps. This gallery was devoted to food, which meant not just foodstuffs to look at or purchase and take home, but a huge range of cafes and restaurants devoted to the characteristic food of the various nations. Here one of the attractions was the young waitresses wearing their national costume, to which the author devotes almost half a page of leering admiration, seeming to regard the young women as fodder too. Proceeding on into the Palais, huge noisy machines transforming the world of work could be examined in Gallery VI, raw materials extracted from nature were

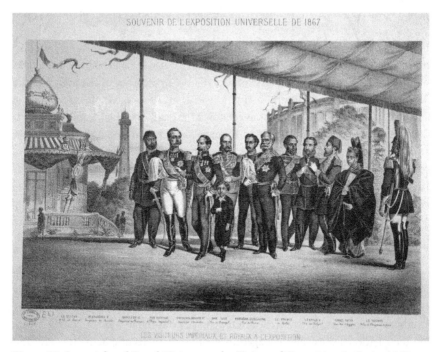

Figure 38 Imperial and Royal Visitors to the Universal Exposition in Paris, 1867. Lithograph. Archives du Ministère des Affaires Étrangères, Paris. Archives Charmet/ Bridgeman Images

shown in Gallery V, clothing, including jewellery, was exhibited in Gallery IV, with furniture in Gallery III. Gallery II presented what were called 'Matériel et l'application des arts libéraux': printing, papermaking, photography, musical, medical, and precision instruments, before the visitor arrived in Gallery I, where the fine arts were displayed. Here too he or she could visit an exhibit explaining the history of work before proceeding into the central garden, where visitors could rest among fountains and flowers and in the shade of the arcades.

The Palais was surrounded by a park, crowded with structures of various kinds. There were Turkish, Egyptian, and Tunisian palaces, a mosque, a yurt from Kyrgyzstan, a Pharanoic and an Aztec temple, Russian, Danish, and Norwegian houses, a Chinese theatre, a lighthouse, a Gothic and a Romanesque church, a Japanese teahouse and a Russian stables, to name but some of these separate buildings.[23] Surveying this and a number of other world fairs, Zeynep Çelik comments:

> The site planning also graphically signified power relations among the exhibiting countries. It portrayed a world where races and nations occupied fixed places determined by the exposition committees of the host countries. Thus the host nation occupied the center; the other industrial powers surrounded it; colonies and other non-Western nations were relegated to the peripheries.[24]

In Paris in 1867, the horticultural engineer Adolphe Alphand, who contributed so much to the beautification of Paris, had worked his usual magic with planting and water features round the various exotic pavilions. In a corner of the park was the 'Jardin Reservé', a horticultural exhibition with grottos, waterfalls, greenhouses, and an aquarium. Five kilometres away down the Seine was the Île de Billancourt, the site of an agricultural show with steam-driven farm machinery and farm animals of all kinds, as well as horses, dogs, and fowl. From the main site visitors could saunter over the pont d'Iéna and up the Trocadero hill, from the summit of which fireworks were let off on 15 August, the national holiday of the Saint-Napoleon discussed in chapter VI.

Following in the footsteps of the British exhibitions discussed below, the 1867 Exposition emphasized France's claim to be a colonial power, devoting much more space than in 1855 to her Empire in North Africa, with Algeria, Tunisia, and Morocco each having a section of their own. In each of these, spectators were provided with a wealth of factual information about, among other things, their respective history, geography, commerce, produce, and population. The exotic structures mentioned above were often peopled with living human beings, wearing their national dress and engaged in various characteristic activities. The 150 plates of the *Grand Album* convey a good impression of this. In the Bardo, for instance, the palace of the Bey of Tunis, plate 93 shows Nubians working as barbers, serving in a café, and grooming camels in a stable. The waitresses from different nations wearing their national costumes have already been mentioned, and plate 105 which depicts them shows eleven different nationalities. Plate 97 presents a Chinese giant, his average-sized wife, and a so-called 'Tartar dwarf'. Siberians are shown on the same plate. These 'exotic persons' were not in general exhibited as admirable examples of superior cultures to be emulated, but rather as curiosities to be gaped at by passers-by, who were likely to find them and their doings strange and probably smile at that strangeness.

As in 1855, there was a grand prize-giving ceremony, not at the end of the exposition this time but on 1 July. A huge dais was erected in the Palais de l'Industrie with an imposing baldachin erected over it, topped by the imperial crown. Many crowned heads were present at the presentation, among them the Sultan, the Prince of Wales, the Crown Prince of Prussia, the Prince of Orange, the Grand Duke and Grand Duchess of Baden, and the half-brother of the Japanese Shōgun. This time it was not Berlioz but Rossini who composed and conducted a *Hymne à Napoléon III et à son vaillant peuple* (A Hymn to Napoleon III and his Valiant People). It is a prayer to protect France and her emperor which mentions peace, but which has a very warlike middle section in which a battle is depicted:

> Au bruit du canon,
> Quand les blessés
> Tombent pressés,
> À leur secours
> On risque ses jours.
> Pour nos amis bat notre cœur,
> Aide au vaincu, gloire au vainqueur![25]

This exposition with its social purpose, its exciting presentation of technological and artistic progress, the rich variety of experiences it offered the visitor, the beauty of its gardens, the glamour of the royal visitors and of the social events and opera performances, was a high point of the reign of Napoleon III. The world came to his door and, in the person of his young son, the succession was assured. Paris had never been more brilliant, with four hundred balls being given during the period of the exposition by the various embassies and other members of high society.[26] In her memoirs Pauline Metternich, the wife of the Austrian ambassador, describes the ball she gave at the embassy, attended by the emperor and empress. She was able to enlist the assistance of no less a person than Alphand for the general organization and garden design.[27] Only the behaviour of Friedrich Wilhelm, Crown Prince of Prussia, clouded her pleasure in the evening. She reported him as saying that 'it was a great source of satisfaction to him to think that his first appearance in Paris was taking place at the Austrian Embassy. It was just a year ago that his father, King William, had declared war against the Emperor of Austria!'.[28] Since this had resulted in Prussia defeating Austria at the Battle of

Königgrätz, it would have been more tactful of Friedrich Wilhelm to have kept silent on the subject of the war.

The princess also gives an insight into the extent to which the visits of foreign heads of state could serve the cause of peace. Franz Joseph, emperor of Austria, came to Paris on 23 October 1867, accompanied by his brothers, the archdukes Karl Ludwig and Ludwig Victor. His visit had been planned for June, but on 19 June, Franz Joseph's other brother Maximilian, emperor of Mexico, was executed at Querétaro—a debacle for which Napoleon III was partly responsible—and Franz Joseph was in mourning. Princess Metternich contrasts Franz Joseph's visit to Paris with the first time he had met Napoleon III in what she euphemistically calls 'very trying circumstances'. This was on 11 July 1859 at Villafranca, after the French had defeated the Austrians at the battles of Magenta and Solferino. In 1867, when Franz Joseph arrived at the Gare de l'Est, he stretched out his two hands to Napoleon, who took Franz Joseph publicly into his arms. The Austrian emperor was acclaimed by the French wherever he went, a military review was held in his honour at Longchamps and a shooting party at Compiègne, and the two emperors were also able to talk in private.[29]

But Napoleon III was not a well man, and Prussia's power and ambition were on the rise. With the benefit of hindsight, we may well regard with misgiving Plate 47 of the *Grand Album* which depicts the enormous fifty-ton Krupp cannon that Prussia exhibited in Paris (Figure 39). Only three years later, Prussia defeated the French at the Battle of Sedan on 2 September 1870, Napoleon III was taken prisoner, and the French Second Empire was at an end. Beginning on 19 September, the victorious Prussians besieged Paris for five months during an extremely cold winter and drove many people to starvation. In January 1871, with the same cannon or with others like it, they bombarded the city for three weeks with some 12,000 shells. Paris surrendered on 28 January but already on 18 January the German Empire had been declared in Versailles. Krupp staged a similar display at the next exhibition to be discussed, that held in Vienna in 1873.

International Diplomacy in Vienna—the *Weltausstellung* of 1873

The 1848 uprising in Austria led to the emancipation of the peasants which, in turn, created rapid industrial growth.[30] The estates to which the peasants were tied were assessed and the peasants had to pay one third of the value of the land, which they then owned, the state paid another third, and the landlords had to renounce the rest. This had two separate effects: the estate owners now had liquid capital which they could invest in banks or in new industries such as breweries or weaving mills, while the peasants who could not afford to pay for land moved into the city to work in these new factories. This boosted the Austrian economy, as did the

Figure 39 The Krupp pavilion at the World Exposition in Vienna in 1873. Coloured engraving. Private Collection Tarker/Bridgeman Images

building of the Ringstrasse, and, as we saw already, the population of Vienna doubled in the twenty years after 1850 and was to double again by the end of Franz Joseph's reign. Austria had exhibited at the London and Paris exhibitions in 1862 and 1867 respectively, but Vienna now wanted to organize an exhibition of its own to demonstrate Austria's economic and technical progress and to put the city on the map as a tourist destination. The emperor signed the decree establishing the exhibition in May 1870 and it was held in 1873, the twenty-fifth anniversary of his accession to the throne. Wilhelm Freiherr von Schwarz-Schönborn (1816–1903), who had been responsible for Austria's exhibits in London and Paris, was commissioned to organize it. The patron was Archduke Karl Ludwig, the emperor's brother, and the organizing committee was presided over by Archduke Rainer. We see here the same involvement of figures close to the emperor that we saw in Paris. What was new was the enormous scale of the exhibition, bigger than any that had yet been held. It had 53,000 exhibitors, 194 pavilions, an 800-metre-long Machine Hall, and a Palace of Industry that was almost a kilometre long with a rotunda in the middle which had the largest dome in the world, 108 metres in diameter, topped by the imperial crown. The whole complex, situated in the Prater park, occupied an area five times bigger than that of the Paris exhibition of 1867.

It was not just its size that made this exhibition remarkable. As the authors of the exhibition catalogue *Experiment Metropole: 1873: Wien und die Weltausstellung* show, the exhibition gave added impetus to many infrastructure projects of lasting value to the city of Vienna.[31] Four new railway stations were constructed and five new bridges were built over the Danube for both ordinary and railway traffic, horse trams were installed in the city, the pneumatic post system was added to the telegraph, a new channel was dug for the Danube to make it flow faster and avoid flooding (the 'Donauregulierung'), a new water system, bringing clean spring water from the mountains south of Vienna, was inaugurated. The exhibition presented technical innovations as well as design and art objects of all kinds, and the new Meiji government brought an exhibit designed to present Japan for the first time as a modern nation. Vienna put itself on the map as a tourist destination with elegant hotels, luxury industries, a flourishing theatrical and musical culture.

To what extent did the exhibition enable Franz Joseph to project imperial power as Napoleon III had done in Paris? It was formally opened on 1 May 1873 in the presence of the emperor, empress, and the mayor of Vienna, Cajetan Felder. The court orchestra and 600 singers under the baton of Johann Strauss played the imperial hymn 'Gott erhalte, Gott beschütze unsern Kaiser, unser Land' (May God sustain, may God protect our emperor, our country). The Crown Prince and Princess of Prussia were present, as was the Prince of Wales, and the Crown Prince of Denmark. As in Paris in 1867, many buildings, not to mention displays, were not ready, commented on again and again sarcastically in his dispatches for the periodical *Pester Lloyd* by the twenty-four-year-old Max Nordau (1849–1923).[32] Even the elegant 'Kaiserpavillon', the imperial pavilion, to which the emperor and other members of the imperial family were supposed to be able to withdraw and receive guests, was not formally handed over to the emperor until the end of August.[33] In the course of the six months that the exhibition ran, thirty-three monarchs, thirteen royal heirs, and twenty other princes came to Vienna to visit the exhibition. This enabled Franz Joseph to extend his political contacts, for, as the host, he not only received each of them on arrival at the railway station, but showed them round the exhibition, took them to the opera, and entertained them with banquets, balls, and military parades.[34] Tsar Alexander (1818–81) visited Vienna in June 1873 and concluded a military agreement with Franz Joseph on 2 June, the so-called 'Schönbrunner Konvention'. Because of illness earlier in the summer, Wilhelm I, German emperor, was not able to visit the exhibition until October, when it was nearly over. Empress Augusta had represented Prussia instead. Wilhelm arrived in Vienna with Otto von Bismarck, the Federal Chancellor and Prussian prime minister, and on 22 October 1873 he, Franz Joseph, and the Tsar concluded what became known as the Three Emperors' Treaty ('Dreikaiserabkommen'), an agreement to keep the peace and to consult each other on important matters of policy, thus building on Franz Joseph's visit to Berlin in September 1872. What Franz Joseph had to be very careful about, in contrast to the French and to a far greater extent, the British, was claiming imperial hegemony over the many territories he ruled over. He was the king of Hungary and of Bohemia, for instance, not their emperor. In June 1867, he and Elisabeth had been crowned king and queen of Hungary, thus confirming the Dual Monarchy of Austria and Hungary, often referred to as Cisleithanien and Transleithanien (that is, the territories to the west and the east of the River Leitha respectively). That they thought of themselves as two separate nations was made visible by their separate exhibition areas in the Rotunda in Vienna in 1873. They did not exhibit as one nation until the Paris exhibition of 1878.[35]

The exhibition has gone down in historical memory for some of its failures: though twenty million visitors had been hoped for, the exhibition only attracted seven million; it made a huge loss; and, just after it opened on 1 May 1873, the stock market collapsed and that summer cholera broke out in the city, so that 1,230 people died. However, as the authors of *Experiment Metropole* remind us, for the first time since the Congress of Vienna in 1814–15, the city was able to bring itself to worldwide attention and Vienna now stood alongside London and Paris as a metropolis that could organize such an impressive event.[36] Exhibitors were able to bring their products to the notice of the public and were able to learn from other exhibitors, so that knowledge transfer was an important outcome.[37] And the emperor of Austria was able to use the exhibition to build bridges with the emperors of Germany and Russia.

Pedro II and the Brazilian Exhibits in 1862, 1867, and 1873

The Empire of Brazil used its participation in international exhibitions to promote itself to Europe and the United States as the source of valuable raw materials crying out to be exploited, and as a country offering great opportunities to immigrants. Emperor Pedro II was a key figure in the increasingly prominent presence of Brazil at international exhibitions during his reign. We see how things changed if we look at Brazil's minimal participation in the Great Exhibition in London in 1851. On that occasion only four exhibitors presented what the official catalogue calls 'productions of Brazilian industry' and visitors must have regarded as ethnographic curios: a bouquet of flowers made of the feathers of Brazilian birds, a model of a native craft, some reins and a cap made of leather from Pernambuco, and 'leaves and butterfly' (*sic*) made from beetles' wings.[38] At the Exposition Universelle in Paris in 1855, Brazil still had only a very small presence, mostly represented by raw materials such as skins, tobacco, and rubber which had been processed by other nations and were therefore exhibited by them. Brazil was not represented at all in the Galerie des Machines on this occasion. France also took a protectionist stance towards products that were in competition with imports from its own colonies. Tresca, in his guide to the exposition, explains for instance that France does not want its markets to be invaded ('envahi') by coffee from India, Brazil, and Java.[39] It was not until 1861, when Brazil accepted the invitation to take part in the London Exhibition of 1862, that the Empire began to be officially represented by a wide selection of exhibits organized from Rio and with the involvement of the emperor. From 1861 on, writes Livia Rezende,

> Brazilian imperial exhibitions were a matter of the state. Participations were financially supported by it and organised by politicians, museum directors, artists and scientists closely linked to the government and personally associated to the emperor.[40]

Preparation was also systematic, for regional and national exhibitions were organized in Rio de Janeiro the year before each of the big international events: in 1861 before the London Exhibition of 1862, in 1866 before the Paris Exposition Universelle of 1867, in 1872 before the Vienna Weltausstellung of 1873, and in 1875 before the Philadelphia Centennial International Exhibition of 1876. Schwarcz emphasizes the emperor's personal involvement, helping to select the products to be exhibited, for instance.[41] This preparation showed. In London in 1862 Brazilian products were entered in thirty-one out of thirty-six categories, concentrating on agricultural produce such as coffee, sugar, tobacco, rubber, cotton, wood, and fibres of various kinds, and minerals such as diamonds, rather than on manufacture, machinery, or technological innovation, as was the case with European nations.[42] Brazil demonstrated that it could manufacture some commodities, such as agricultural implements and ship's compasses, boots and hats, and school books and educational materials, but it mostly presented itself as a treasure trove of natural resources, only waiting to be exploited by those who had the technical knowhow to process them. A surprising item was displayed in class XXXIII by J.M. Dos Reis: 'Eye-glass, the property of His Imperial Majesty'.[43]

Was this intended to remind the host nation that Brazil too was ruled by an emperor?

Brazil moved into a higher league in Paris in 1867. In his *Relatório Sobre a Exposição Universal de 1867*, Julio Constancio de Villeneuve, who acted as secretary to the organizing commission of six titled members and five specialist advisers, gives a full account of every aspect of Brazil's participation. As an insider, he is able to recount the difficulties of accepting the invitation, caused by the fact that Brazil was engaged in the Paraguayan war, and the tardiness of the decision-making, but he also stresses the support that the emperor gave throughout.[44] Other difficulties awaited them in Paris. The organizers had expected to be able to group all the Latin American countries together, not taking into account the enormous size of Brazil, when compared with some of the other countries in the region, or the fact that some of them were at war with each other. In the end, Brazil succeeded in acquiring 785 square metres of exhibition space compared to only 603 square metres for all the other Latin American nations put together. If we are to believe Villeneuve, the other Latin American nations put on a folkloric display with figures of gauchos on horseback or dressed in national costume. Brazil had two very different aims at this exhibition, in both of which it succeeded: to promote its natural products, for they were 'mais indispensaveis ao comercio do mundo' (more indispensable to world trade) than those of other Latin American nations;[45] and to attract immigrants from Europe.

The success of Brazil's displays and the excellence of its raw materials were confirmed by Raoul Ferrère's report in Ducuing's official guide.[46] One of the displays was so spectacular that it is depicted in an engraving and, according to Villeneuve, was also reproduced everywhere in the press.[47] In front of a backdrop depicting a mysterious forest painted by no less a person than Auguste Rubé (1817–99), the foremost scene painter of the day for the Parisian stage, stood a huge decorative pyramid of 400 large blocks of exotic timber from the Brazilian forests. The wood was cut in such a way as to show off the grain and the fibre and apparently aroused great interest from the carpenters who were setting up the various stands in the Palais de l'Industrie.[48] The painted forest came to be called 'The Virgin Forest', and in the engraving it indeed looks like a Romantic *Urwald* of huge trees, tangled vines, and exotic plants with glimpses of a blue sky through gaps in the foliage. This was a virgin only waiting to be despoiled.[49] Interested parties were assured that access would not be difficult by reminding them, 'em letras gigantescas' (in huge letters) on a transparent blind in front of one of the huge windows looking onto the gallery, of the decree that opened the Amazon to international navigation: 'BRAZIL. Decreto de 7 de Dezembro de 1866. *Liberdade de navegação*'. In a series of rooms designed by Alfred Chapon (1834–93), the architect of many of the exotic pavilions on the exposition site such as the Tunisian Bardo, the Egyptian pavilion, and the Suez Canal Pavilion, Brazil showed its other raw materials—coffee, tobacco, rubber, sugar, diamonds, and coal—, its products such as leather, hats, and ironwork, and even its artworks. The Brazilian stand was entered through a carved archway in the Brazilian colours of green and gold and was decorated with the imperial crown and the arms of the Braganzas, as well as with leaves of the tobacco and coffee plants. The walls were covered with tiles alternating the imperial crown and the Braganza two-legged dragon known as the wyvern. Though Ferrère declares the Brazilian leather the finest in the whole exhibition, it was Brazilian cotton that was given a special prize.

Brazil took another special prize, this time in a special category for institutions or organizations that promoted social harmony.[50] This was for the colony of Blumenau in the province of Santa Caterina in Southern Brazil. It had been founded in 1850 by the German pharmacist and chemist Dr Hermann Blumenau (1819–99).[51] His interest in Brazil was awakened by meeting Alexander von Humboldt in the 1840s, and he first came to Brazil in 1846–48, where he laid claim to 200 square kilometres of forest. He returned in 1850 with seventeen Germans to found his colony, which was integrated into the state in 1860. By 1880 it had grown to at least 13,000 inhabitants, most of them Germans. This colony, together with the German colony in Petrópolis discussed in chapter VII, was part of a deliberate official policy to make Brazil whiter and more European.

Brazil also reminded visitors to the 1867 exhibition that it, like France, was an imperial nation, with an emperor born of a Braganza father and a Habsburg mother. We have already seen how the Brazilian stand copiously used the imperial crown and the Braganza symbol of the wyvern as a decorative element. The organizers also brought to Paris a 2.8 metre-high equestrian statue of Pedro II by Francisco Manoel Chaves Pinheiro (1822–84), Professor of Sculpture at the Imperial Academy of Fine Arts in Rio and one of the expert advisors to the organizing commission. The statue was a plaster cast, to be cast in bronze later, which depicted the emperor on campaign at the siege of Uruguaiana, wearing boots, spurs, a cloak, and a flat hat. It was supposed to be cast in bronze, but the emperor decided to use the money for educational purposes instead. Raoul Ferrère finds the sculpture lacking in inspiration, but it is in fact an impressive work, as can be judged by anyone who views it today in the entrance to the Museu Historico Nacional in Rio de Janeiro. Thanks to the British giving up some of the outdoor area allotted to them, the statue was able to be erected in the exposition park. The equestrian statue of Pedro I, the first emperor of Brazil, waving the constitution, by Louis Rochet (1813–78) was erected in another part of the exhibition park near the Rapp Gate.[52] This can only have been a copy, for the work, in bronze, had been inaugurated in Rio de Janeiro in 1862.[53] By presenting its two emperors in this way and making them the subject of a eulogy by Ferrère in the official guidebook, Brazil was putting itself on a par with a major European nation such as Prussia which had also brought an equestrian statue of its monarch to Paris, that of Wilhelm I by Friedrich Drake (1805–82).

Brazil took part again in the World Exhibition held in Vienna in 1873 and exhibited its products in seventeen classes over a wider range than before: mining, agriculture and forestry, the chemical industry, foodstuffs, textiles, leather, metals, wood, glass and stoneware, haberdashery, graphic art, scientific instruments, military matters, naval matters, the influence of museums on industry, fine art, and educational materials. The first of the two main articles on Brazil's participation in the exhibition by an anonymous reporter writing in the daily *Wiener Weltausstellungs-Zeitung* on 21 October 1873 consists of a depiction of Brazil as an earthly paradise, where everything grows in great abundance and from whose soil diamonds spring, followed by a fulsome eulogy of Pedro II. According to the newspaper, Brazil has become so powerful and important and has arrived so triumphantly at the height of culture because it has cultivated the academic disciplines.

> And who has Brazil to thank for this respect for learning? No less a person than the gloriously reigning emperor Dom Pedro II himself, whose government places the greatest weight on the cultivation of the sciences and makes their care one of the most important tasks of the individual ministries.[54]

The newspaper goes on to list the various scholarly institutions and colleges founded by D. Pedro, saying that he himself is learned in many disciplines and has placed scholars in many high positions of state. This is then illustrated with reference to the current Brazilian ambassador to Austria, Francisco Adolfo de Varnhagen, Baron de Porto Seguro (1816–78), who was indeed an eminent historian of Brazil. Brazil is praised for making a model contribution to the exhibition, attributable to the emperor and his fatherly ('landesväterliche') care. On 28 October, the same newspaper explains how the timber industry is flourishing under the 'aegis of the gloriously reigning emperor Dom Pedro II'.[55] Is the reason for this eulogizing an implied comparison of D. Pedro with his first cousin, Emperor Franz Joseph, both of them in power since the 1840s?

Pedro II and the Philadelphia Centennial Exhibition of 1876

The high point of Pedro II's engagement with international exhibitions was the Philadelphia Centennial Exhibition of 1876. This event celebrated the centenary of the American declaration of independence, which had, as Roderick Barman writes, 'overthrown a monarch to create the first republic in the New World', and D. Pedro attended in person.[56] No head of state, still less a monarch, had previously paid a visit to the United States, and D. Pedro's visit caused great excitement. On 10 May 1876, he and President Grant formally inaugurated the exhibition by going to the Machinery Hall where, in the presence of its American inventor, George Henry Corliss, together they started the huge steam engine known as the Corliss engine, which powered eight miles of shafting and many other machines in the hall.[57] The empress then went to the Women's Pavilion, where she set a six-horse-power Baxter engine in motion which powered the looms in that building.[58] As was the case at every exhibition, many of the stands were not yet ready, so D. Pedro returned to Philadelphia on 21 June where he visited the exhibition every day for two weeks, starting at seven in the morning. It was here on 25 June that he was able to draw the judges' attention to Alexander Graham Bell and his invention of the telephone, which led to Bell being given a gold medal.[59] Back in Brazil, Dom Pedro had one of the first telephones in a private residence installed in his palace in Petrópolis, where it can still be seen on his desk.

Ingram describes the 'beautiful and brilliant' Brazilian stand which won a prize for its architecture, the work of the Philadelphia architect Frank Furness (1839–1912). Illustrations show that it was a striking and decorative building of painted wood in what Ingram called the 'Moresque' style, where 'festoons formed of the hides of boas and of wild and domestic animals' can be seen next to exhibits of wood, cotton, coffee, sugar, tobacco, silk, and rubber. Long showcases containing school textbooks and work by pupils from various schools were placed down the centre of the stand. In spite of this, Brune comments that 'striving to portray Brazil as civilized, the exhibition organizers did not recognize the negative consequences of defining the nation solely in terms of natural resources.'[60] Bruno Giberti is even more severe, saying that the display 'was a motley display of things—a cabinet of curiosities illustrating the resources of a nation'.[61]

Brazil took part in yet another international exhibition in Paris, the 1889 Exposition Universelle, commemorating the centenary of the French Revolution, which many monarchies refused to attend for this reason. D. Pedro was again involved in the preparation of the exhibition but was forced to abdicate four months after it opened on 6 May 1889. He died in exile in Paris in 1891.

Notes

1. Isay, *Panorama*, p. 71.
2. Greenhalgh, *Ephemeral Vistas*, pp. 14–15; Wesemael, *Architecture*, pp. 221–330.
3. Hancock, '*Capitale du plaisir*'.
4. Poisson, '1855. France's First International Exhibition'.
5. Tresca, *Visite à l'exposition*, p. 64; Calonne, *Exposition universelle*; Darjou, *À l'exposition nouvelle*.
6. Matthieu, 'Le Palais de l'Industrie', p. 66.
7. *Le Moniteur Universel*, 22 June 1855.
8. Murphy, 'Becoming Cosmopolitan'; Cabanès and Laisney, *L'Année 1855*.

9. Truesdell, *Spectacular Politics*, fig. 5.1, p. 107.

10. *Le Moniteur Universel*, 16 May 1855.

11. Tresca, *Visite à l'exposition universelle*, p. 66.

12. See http://www.hberlioz.com/Paris/BPIndustrieF.html,where there is a lot of contextual material, including extracts from Berlioz's letters.

13. 'Because the imperial dynasty, which God Himself sustained and to which Glory gave birth, has emerged, as once the Messiah did, from the tomb.' See http://www.hberlioz.com/Libretti/vocal4.htm/

14. Isay, *Panorama*, pp. 86–134; Wesemael, *Architecture*, pp. 221–330; various contributors in Babelon, Bacha, and de Andia, *Les expositions universelles*, pp. 68–86.

15. See *The Illustrated Catalogue*.

16. Shears, *The Great Exhibition*, p. 155.

17. Sellali, 'Les habitations', in Babelon, Bacha, and de Andia, *Les expositions universelles à Paris*, p. 76.

18. Greenhalgh, *Ephemeral Vistas*, p. 35; Le Play, *Rapport sur l'exposition universelle*.

19. *Illustrated London News*, 13 April 1867, p. 350.

20. *Guide officiel de 1867*; *Exposition universelle de 1867*.

21. *Illustrated London News*, 6 April 1867, p. 327.

22. *Grand Album*.

23. *Grand Album*, p. xii.

24. Çelik, *Displaying the Orient*, p. 51.

25. 'At the sound of the cannon, when the wounded fall pressed together, we risk our lives to help them, our heart beats for our friends, help to the vanquished, glory to the victor!'

26. Radetz, 'L'Exposition de 1867', p. 249.

27. Metternich, *My Years*, pp. 142–5.

28. Metternich, *My Years*, p. 145.

29. Metternich, *My Years*, chapter XIV, 'The Emperor of Austria in France', pp. 155–71.

30. Vocelka and Vocelka, *Franz Joseph*, p. 107, pp. 244–8.

31. Kos, Gleis, and Aigner, *Experiment Metropole*.

32. Ujvári, 'Feuilletons über die Wiener Weltausstellung'.

33. See www.wiener-weltausstellung.at, launched by the Austrian Academy of Sciences in 2014.

34. Vocelka and Vocelka, *Franz Joseph*, pp. 249–52.

35. Kos, Gleis, and Aigner, *Experiment Metropole*, p. 128.

36. Kos, Gleis, and Aigner, *Experiment Metropole*, p. 570.

37. Kos, Gleis, and Aigner, *Experiment Metropole*, p. 573.

38. Ellis, *The Official Descriptive and Illustrated Catalogue*, vol. 3, p. 1429.

39. Tresca, *Visite à l'exposition*, p. 484.

40. Rezende, 'Manufacturing the Raw', p. 124.

41. Schwarcz, *The Emperor's Beard*, p. 289.

42. *The International Exhibition of 1862*.

43. *The International Exhibition of 1862*, vol. 3, p. 41.

44. Villeneuve, *Relatorio*.

45. Villeneuve, *Relatorio*, xxxiii.

46. Ducuing, *L'Exposition Universelle*, p. 278.

47. Villeneuve, *Relatorio*, p. xliii.

48. Villeneuve, *Relatorio*, p. xxxix.

49. Rezende, 'Of Coffee, Nature and Exclusion'; Inés Dussel, 'Between exoticism and universalism'.

50. Villeneuve, 'Il Premio Blumenau', *Relatorio*, pp. lxviii–xciii.

51. Oliveira, 'Festejos do Progresso'; Cizeron, *Les representations du Brésil*. Cizeron mostly discusses French exhibitions.

52. Villeneuve, *Relatorio*, p. xlviii.

53. Kraay, *Days of National Festivity*.

54. *Wiener Weltausstellungs-Zeitung*, no. 283, 21 October 1873, p. 2.

55. *Wiener Weltausstellungs-Zeitung*, no. 289, 28 October 1873.

56. Barman, *Citizen Emperor*, p. 275.

57. Ingram, *The Centennial Exposition*.

58. Ingram, *The Centennial Exposition*, p. 116.

59. Barman, *Citizen Emperor*, p. 280.

60. Brune, 'Retranslating the Brazilian Imperial Project', p. 18.

61. Giberti, *Designing the Centennial*, p. 111.

IX

Inventing Empire in Twentieth-Century India and Britain

Victoria, queen of India since the 1857–58 rebellion, was awarded the title of empress of India by the British parliament in 1876. However, 'the title was not only not used in Britain but disowned altogether. The slightest intrusion of "empress" into domestic usage prompted hostility in the House of Commons', writes Miles Taylor.[1] This explains why, at the Colonial and Indian Exhibition which was staged in and around the Royal Albert Hall in 1886, the title of empress did not occur, in spite of the central role of India in the exhibition. If Victoria's imperial title was not used in London in 1886, one might expect it to have been prominent at the Calcutta International Exhibition held in the capital of the Raj from December 1883 to March 1884 three years before. Surprisingly, it only makes a brief appearance in the Official Report, so brief that it could easily be missed. At the opening ceremony on 4 December 1883, performed by the viceroy Lord Ripon and attended by Queen Victoria's son Prince Arthur, Duke of Connaught, who was in India as a military commander, the line of a cantata sung in Italian by members of the Italian opera, 'Dio salve la Regina', was translated as 'God Save our Empress-Queen'.[2]

At Victoria's two jubilees, her golden jubilee in 1887 and her diamond jubilee in 1897, celebrating fifty and sixty years on the throne respectively, she herself made her role as ruler of India visible by being accompanied by a guard of honour of Indian cavalry officers at all the various public events that took place during the celebrations, by ensuring that the Indian princes who had come to London for her jubilee celebrations in 1887, gorgeously dressed in their native costumes, rode in front of her carriage on the way to Westminster Abbey; and that they sat in the choir stalls during the service.[3] Queen Victoria's interest in India became more pronounced during her last years, when she took Indian servants into her household, learned Hindustani, and had the so-called 'Durbar Room' constructed at Osborne House, her residence on the Isle of Wight. In these years too, her status as Mother of India was celebrated all over India. But it was during the reign of her three successors in the twentieth century that the notion of India, Britain's most important colony, as an empire was invented and promoted by means of imperial architecture, ceremonial, and a new capital city.

Projecting Imperial Power: New Nineteenth-Century Emperors and the Public Sphere. Helen Watanabe-O'Kelly, Oxford University Press (2021). © Helen Watanabe-O'Kelly. DOI: 10.1093/oso/9780198802471.003.0010

Impressing the Indians—the Victoria Memorial Hall and the 1903 Durbar

Victoria died in 1901 and her son Edward VII (1841–1910), by then a man of sixty, succeeded her. Miles Taylor describes the outpouring of grief from Indians at the news of Victoria's death, mourning her according to their own customs as an Indianized empress whom they linked to the goddess Lakshmi and incorporated into Indian mythology.[4] Lord Curzon (George Nathaniel Curzon, 1859–1925), viceroy since 1889, had quite different ideas of how mourning for Victoria should be expressed and immediately leapt into action. What he proposed was a building to be called the Victoria Memorial Hall, whose ostensible purpose was to commemorate the late empress but whose equally important purpose was to serve as a museum of, and therefore monument to, the history of the Raj (Figure 40). Brushing aside suggestions that a hospital or a technical college might be a more suitable monument to Victoria, he conceived of his pet project as follows:

> Nothing had struck me more painfully than the almost complete lack in that country [India] of relics or memorials of the great events through which it had passed, the thrilling scenes that it had witnessed, the famous men, English and Indian, by whom it had been served. Whereas every European Capital that I had ever visited possessed and treasured in its galleries or museums trophies of such incidents and such men—exercising a potent influence on the imagination and stimulating the patriotism of succeeding generations—in Calcutta and indeed in India... there was little to show that the Indian scroll of history had been one on which immortal characters had been inscribed, or that the Victorian Era in particular had witnessed the growth of India from a scattered complex of heterogeneous states and territories into a powerful and consolidated Empire

Figure 40 Victoria Memorial Hall, Kolkata. Photo © Ekkehard Henschke

...I felt that the lack of this historical sense—the surest spring of national self-respect—was injurious in its effect both upon English and Indian interests.[5]

This meant, therefore, not just a memorial but a museum. Lord Curzon, ever the pedagogue, describes it thus:

It was proposed to erect upon the Calcutta Maidan a magnificent building, to be known as the Victoria Memorial Hall, the central feature of which should be a marble statue of the Queen standing under the central dome. In immediate proximity to this would be a hall or halls consecrated to personal memorials of Her Majesty, her family, and her reign. In the remainder of the building would be a number of galleries, corridors, and apartments, which would be filled with statuary, paintings, personal relics, prints and engraving, documents, models and every variety of historical trophy, illustrating the period since the Moghul rule, during which British connection with India had begun, grown, and reached its zenith.[6]

Curzon immediately received large financial contributions from the maharajas of Jaipur, Kashmir, and Mysore, and all over India other contributions began to pour in, both of money and of objects for the display. Sir William Emerson (1843–1924) was chosen as the architect, to be assisted by Vincent Jerome Esch (1876–1950). Lord Curzon left India in 1905 and Lord Minto, his successor as viceroy, was not enthusiastic about the scheme, but Curzon kept up the pressure after his return to England and construction began in 1906. The result was the building we see today, an impressively large white marble domed palace fifty-six metres high at its highest point, situated in landscaped gardens at one end of the large open space known as the Maidan. The first thing the visitor sees on approaching the Hall is a seated bronze statue of Empress Victoria in old age, two and a half-times life size, by George Frampton (1860–1928). Marble panels in the entrance porches depict her signing the Declaration of 1858 on becoming queen of India, the durbar of 1877 at which she was proclaimed empress, the Golden Jubilee procession of 1887 in London, and the laying of the foundation stone of the Memorial Hall by the future George V in 1906. Above the main entrance porch are figures of Motherhood, Prudence, and Learning. A revolving bronze figure of Victory almost five metres high adorns the dome, though it only revolves nowadays on special occasions. Inside the building a marble statue of the young queen by Thomas Brock (1947–1922) stands, just as Lord Curzon envisaged it, in the middle of the circular hall under a domed ceiling.[7] Around the cornice of this ceiling are depicted twelve scenes from the life of the queen by Frank Salisbury (1874–1962)—her acceptance of the British crown and her marriage to Prince Alfred, for instance. Outside at the back of the Memorial Hall in the gardens, a statue of Lord Curzon himself by Frederick William Pomeroy (1857–1924) looks towards a stone arch on which stands a bronze equestrian statue of Edward VII by Bertram Mackennel (1863–1931). A Latin inscription chiselled on the arch under the figure of the king proclaims 'EDWARDUS VII REX IMPERATOR' and beneath that again are four figures representing the pillars of British power in India: Naval Power, Agriculture, Civil Government and Law, and Military Power on Land. The grand scale of the building, the figure of Victory on the roof, the glorification of the queen-empress and of notable administrators of the Raj, and the Latin inscription on Edward VII's monument all proclaim that this is a European imperial building transposed to India. It might have sprung from the imagination of a Napoleon III or a Wilhelm II. That the history of India displayed in the museum within begins with the Moghul Empire, a link made again and again up to and including the building of New Delhi, is another of the legitimation strategies with which we are now so familiar from the other empires discussed.

The Memorial Hall was not finished until 1920. Lord Curzon, still the viceroy, wanted to celebrate Edward VII's accession as emperor by bringing him to India for the Imperial Durbar he organized in Delhi in 1903. Edward refused to travel himself and sent his brother, Prince Arthur, Duke of Connaught (1850–1942), to represent him. Curzon, with his customary perfectionism, organized the durbar almost single-handedly.[8] The Duke was accompanied by his wife Princess Louise of Prussia (1860–1917) and his nephew Ernst Ludwig, Grand Duke of Hesse (1868–1937). The prince and his wife knew India well, for he had held several military commands there in the 1880s, including as commander-in-chief of the Bombay army from 1886 to 1890. Though based on the first durbar organized by Lord Lytton in 1877 and discussed in an earlier chapter, this one differed in six respects from its predecessor: it eschewed the medieval ceremonial and iconography employed by Lytton; it was much larger, with one hundred Indian princes in attendance instead of sixty-three, as well as representatives of other Asian territories, many spectators and official guests; the Indian princes were treated like great lords who were the colleagues of the viceroy rather than his underlings; there was some sensitivity towards native culture and religion; Indian arts and crafts were showcased and Indian monuments restored; and, finally, in spite of the sensitivity just mentioned and the presence of Indian princes, 'Mutiny' veterans were publicly celebrated.

On 29 December 1902, the Curzons travelled by train from Calcutta and the Duke of Connaught's party from Bombay and both arrived in Delhi within fifteen minutes of each other, a feat of railway timetabling that the twenty-first century would struggle to emulate. On arrival, they were met by the Indian princes who had come for the durbar. The official account of the events was composed by Stephen Wheeler, the son of the man responsible for the official account of the 1877 durbar, and he begins by explaining the current status of the native princes in British India:

The Imperial Assemblage held at Delhi on January 1st, 1877 [...] brought home to the Indian public in a way which no mere written pronouncement could have done, the nature and reality of the process by which India had become incorporated in the British dominions, and which in the course of the reign of a single Sovereign had converted the Native States from isolated and quasi-independent Powers into powerful and contented feudatories of a common sovereign.[9]

Both the British grandees and the Indian chiefs mounted richly caparisoned elephants and processed together through the city to the tented camp on the Ridge. This collegial treatment was underlined at the Imperial Proclamation, the main ceremony, on 1 January. Instead of the Indian chiefs, as in 1877, sitting in two horseshoes opposite the viceroy who was raised above them on a dais, this time a much bigger horseshoe was constructed with the viceroy's dais in the middle between the princes facing, as they did, the pavilion in which the Duke and Duchess sat. This was meant to show that the Indian chiefs were

> colleagues and partners as it were of the Sovereign's representative. They had come to Delhi not to pay a reluctant homage to alien rulers; but to take their part, with the Viceroy, as the chief actors in the performance of an Imperial function. In the presence of the King-Emperor's brother, and in the eyes of India and the world, they were to appear as the trusted supporters of the Indian Government and as the foremost of the feudatories of the Crown ... there were no prouder or more contented actors in this memorable scene than the more than a hundred ruling Chiefs who had responded to the invitation of the Viceroy, and had come to Delhi to join him in rendering honour to the Sovereign.[10]

All are now 'performing an Imperial function' and, seen through British eyes, are happy to do so. Each of the Indian chiefs was presented to the Duke of Connaught after the Proclamation and many of them were given honours in the Order of the Indian Empire and the Order of the Star of India.

Sensitivity to Indian religion and language was shown by delaying the proclamation of the new emperor until 1 January 1903, the date of Eid-ul-Fitr bringing the month of Ramadan to an end and so enabling Muslims to end their fast. Also, the start of the ceremony was put off from 12.00 to 12.30 so that Muslims could attend prayers beforehand, and everyone was given an Urdu translation of the viceroy's speech. Lord Curzon, whose record in preserving and restoring outstanding examples of Indian architecture is well known, restored the Diwan-i Am and the Diwan-i Khas in the Red Fort, and he organized an exhibition of traditional Indian arts and crafts to showcase their skill and beauty and save them from being destroyed by cheap imports. He also got the Victoria and Albert Museum in London and some Indian princes to loan outstanding examples of various crafts to act as an inspiration to Indian craftsmen. As he said in one of his speeches:

> For powerful Empires existed and flourished here, while Englishmen were still wandering painted in the woods, and when the British Colonies were wilderness and jungle. India has left a deeper mark upon the history, the philosophy, and the religion of mankind than any other territorial unit in the universe.[11]

There is no doubt that Curzon appreciated Indian art and architecture, but Indians did not feel that they needed an Englishman to show them how to appreciate their own artefacts. Curzon's exhibition was the target of much criticism in a broad section of the Indian press as 'a glorified bazaar'.[12] The National Congress Party, founded in 1885 to work for greater Indian autonomy, staged its own exhibition in Ahmedabad in December 1902, two weeks before Curzon's. The Gaekwad of Baroda, Sayajirao III (1863–1939), an enlightened and progressive ruler, said in his speech at the opening that the Congress's exhibition was designed 'to bring back prosperity to the masses by revival of industries and manufactures, almost wholly killed by the selfish policy of the early rulers of British India themselves'.[13]

Whatever we think of Curzon's reverence for Indian culture, the 'Mutiny' was not forgotten. The spectators were forcibly reminded of this key event in the history of the British conquest of India by 'the entry of the Mutiny veterans—27 Europeans and Eurasians and 387 Indians', officers and non-commissioned officers, who marched into the amphitheatre before the arrival of the viceroy, the vicereine, and the Connaughts.[14] These men, 'this little band of war-scarred heroes', had been brought to the durbar by the government and were entertained there as official guests. They entered to the strains of 'See the Conquering Hero comes', and when Auld Lang Syne was played in memory of fallen and deceased comrades, 'few eyes were dry, and there was a choking in many throats.' The painter Mortimer Menpes (1855–1938) was sent to India, along with other artists, to paint what he saw, and he published a richly illustrated account of the durbar with a text by his daughter Dorothy. His account of the entry of the veterans is equally emotional:

> All eyes were fixed on a shuffling, shambling band of white-haired old men . . . some of them on the verge of the grave . . . A thrill ran round the audience as they approached; for these were the Mutiny veterans of Delhi and Lucknow, the men who held India for the Empire on the Ridge at Delhi through heat and battle and pestilence and hardships . . . this rickety collection of old gentlemen, some in weatherbeaten tunics stained and faded with the sun, others in frock-coats of ancient pattern buttoned up the wrong way, but on every coat a medal! And the people! They stood up and cheered and shouted until they were hoarse; women

wept hysterically, and strong men sobbed. The whole assemblage rose to do them honour. One felt that but for these men there would have been no brilliant pageant to-day, no Delhi Durbar.[15]

And there is more in the same vein. One wonders whether the Indian chiefs were also expected to stand up and cheer and sob at this performance of victory over them and their compatriots as a defeated and colonized people.[16] Again, as in 1877, those present at the durbar were reminded of British military might in India. Instead of the roughly 14,000 British soldiers in 1877, this time 39,500 members of the British army marched past.[17] This was not the only element of this second durbar that was bigger than the first. Wheeler peppers his account with awe-inspiring facts and figures. Immense tented apartments for both living and entertaining had been constructed for the viceroy and the Connaughts. The viceroy's camp consisted in total of 1400 tents and 'covered an area of upwards of 93 acres'. A census of the main or central camps showed a population of 12,983 persons, including 1,222 Europeans, 159 native and other Asiatic guests, and 11,202 followers. Seven and a half miles of twelve-foot road, and three and a quarter miles of sixteen-foot road, were made in the central camp, which was also connected with the city and the Durbar Amphitheatre by means of a two and a half feet gauge light railway, seven miles in length, which carried over 100,000 passengers in the course of the two weeks of the durbar. The whole of the central camp was lit with electricity, more than one hundred arc lamps being placed along the principal thoroughfares, and 9,300 incandescent lights elsewhere and in the tents. Fifty-four tons of bare copper wire and over twelve miles of insulated wire were used.[18] Wheeler writes that the Colosseum at Rome embraced 40,495 square feet, while the Delhi Amphitheatre covered 101,828 square feet and that there were 4,000 guests at the State Ball on 6 January. A huge firework display was organized by Messrs. C.T. Brock and Co of the Crystal Palace London, as well as many sporting contests. On 9 January, before everyone left, the viceroy gave an evening party for the Indian chiefs, whose territories were in some cases thousands of miles apart, so that they could meet each other. The Durbar 'showed to the world that unity has at last been achieved among the millions of India, and that the mysterious influence that has accomplished this result is no other than the British Crown'.[19]

George V's Coronation Durbar in 1911

In 1910 Edward VII died and his son George V (1865–1936) succeeded him.[20] His coronation as king of Great Britain and Ireland took place in Westminster Abbey on 22 June 1911. In December 1911 he and his consort Mary of Teck (1867–1953) travelled to India to be acclaimed as emperor and empress at the third of the great durbars, the so-called Coronation Durbar, the only time that an empress or emperor came to India. They landed in Bombay on 2 December, where they were welcomed by a large ephemeral triumphal arch, which contemporary photographs show to have been a gleaming white battlemented structure in the Mughal style with a dome and a central pointed arch. In commemoration of the visit, it was decided to build a permanent triumphal arch of stone to be designed by the same architect, George Wittet (1878–1926). The massive fortress-like arch of honey-coloured basalt in the Indo-Saracenic style, twenty-six metres high, is known today as the Gateway of India. It is positioned right on the sea and, had Wittet's plans been carried out in full, a grand processional way would have led from it into the city.[21] It has a large central archway and rooms at each side for civic receptions. It is not an entrance into a building or into a complex of buildings, as is the case with Mughal arches, but is simply there to do honour to the arrival of the sovereign. It is imperial architecture transposed to India and, though the foundation stone was laid in 1913, the arch was not completed until 1924.

As the only reigning British emperor to visit his Empire, George V's visit had great symbolic importance and a special crown was made the occasion, the Imperial Crown of India. It is made of gold and silver and covered in diamonds, rubies, emeralds, and sapphires. According to John Fortescue, the Royal Librarian and Archivist and son of a peer who accompanied the royal party on the visit and published a detailed account of it, the princes and people of India sent a message to the British prime minister after the visit conveying 'an assurance of their warm attachment to the worldwide Empire of which they form a part, and with which their destinies are now indissolubly linked', saying also that they are 'conscious of the many blessings which India has derived from the connection with England'.[22] His own conclusion was that 'India is proud of her place in the British Empire; and to prove herself worthy of it she will try to quench old internal animosities, and to co-operate heartily with England in working out her future.'[23] Fortescue is clearly aware of 'internal animosities', even while he insists on harmony. By this date, the Indian National Congress was twenty-six years old, and four years later Gandhi was to return to India from South Africa.

The viceroy in 1911 was Charles, First Baron Hardinge (1858–1944), who had only just arrived in India when the durbar was announced. All those who had been part of the organization in 1903 had left by then, so he formed a committee which this time actually included four Indian princes: the Maharajas of Gwalior, Bikaner, Idar, and Rampur. The ceremonial resembled that of 1903 and was held in another huge tented camp in the same place on the Ridge above Delhi, though the celebrations were shorter. The imperial couple arrived in Delhi on 7 December, the durbar was held on 12 December and they left for Agra on 16 December (Figure 41). The official account contains much condescending rhetoric on the lines of the following: 'To the Indian…a great public ceremony

Figure 41 Christopher Clark, *King George V at Delhi*, 1915. Watercolour on paper. Brown University Library, Providence, Rhode Island, USA/Bridgeman Images

naturally means more than it ever can to the matter-of-fact European.'[24] Queen Victoria, according to the author, 'sought to soothe the wounds of India by drawing it more closely to herself', which gave India to 'the guardianship of a single person'.[25] This meant that 'Indian troops went gladly to the wars beyond the seas; Indian Princes journeyed to England to take a prominent part in the Jubilee rejoicings.'[26]

On this occasion the state entry began at the Red Fort where the king-emperor met all the 148 Indian princes who had accepted the invitation to attend. They all then wound their way to the camp on the Ridge in a procession five miles long which no longer consisted of ceremonial elephants. The emperor decided to ride on horseback, which meant that many people did not recognize him, while many of the Indian princes drove in barouches and landaus. The numbers of visitors had grown again and those visiting Delhi were estimated at over a million. At the 1903 durbar there had been a press camp, described in glowing tones by Mortimer Menpes,[27] but this time PR and communications had also increased in size:

Between the two [camps] came the camp of the central telegraph bureau, fully equipped with accommodation for the pressmen and the public, and with all the latest appliances for rapid transmission of state and press messages between India and England. The camp of the press representatives lay just beyond. The King-Emperor, knowing how much interest would be excited, in other parts of the Empire, by the events at Delhi, attached great importance to the arrangements for reporting them, and showed a constant solicitude for the welfare of the pressmen, who numbered ninety in all, forty-one being Indians of all castes and creeds, and seven foreigners.[28]

The pressmen, like the veterans, were guests of the government of India, showing how essential their role had become.

The emperor gave an individual audience to each of the Indian princes at his camp and the empress received the ladies. This time the durbar was held on 12 December to avoid 'the Mohurram', another important Muslim month in which adherents would have had to fast. Two semi-circular amphitheatres were built to allow as many people as possible to see the emperor and the proceedings. The massed band of 1,600 performers drawn from seventeen British and twenty-six Indian regiments played, the veterans of the 'Mutiny' entered the amphitheatre again to the strains of 'See the Conquering Hero Comes', and 'Auld Lang Syne' was played again. The emperor and empress, placed on an elevated stage under a canopy, had brought their coronation robes with them from London and George V wore the new Imperial Crown of India which he had had made specially for the occasion. India was being presented not just with a representative of their monarch far away but with their emperor, costumed appropriately. Each of the chiefs came forward individually wearing their most gorgeous attire and all their jewels, except for the Gaekwad of Baroda, one of the most senior princes who was now attending his third durbar. He wore a simple white costume, carried a stick, and, having bowed briefly to the emperor and his consort, walked off to the side, then turned his back and trotted down the steps—actions that created a scandal in both India and London when they became known and which, as discussed more fully in chapter III, were clearly an act of protest.

At this durbar, the emperor announced that the capital of India would be moved from Calcutta to Delhi, a decision that had been kept secret from the public. After the emperor and the other dignitaries had left, spectators swarmed up to the dais with the thrones 'and men of all races and religions prostrated themselves before the empty Thrones.' They then formed queues and it is 'estimated that over 200,000 persons thus passed before the Thrones'.[29] As in 1903, there was a military parade and an investiture in the Indian Orders.

Did the durbars mean anything to ordinary Indians? Miles Taylor points out that Queen Victoria's new title of empress was proclaimed all over India and was often associated with acts of charity, famine relief, and public works. At the other durbars too, festivities were held in many centres, at which the poor were fed in their thousands. In 1911 in Madras, 14,000 portraits of the king-emperor were distributed. However, Mortimer Menpes sheds an interesting light on the reaction of the crowd in Delhi in 1903. He was able to move around the various important sites with his paint box and easel so as to see and record as much as possible. Down in the old city among the crowd, waiting for the procession to pass by, he describes the reaction of ordinary Indians to the imperial event that meant so much to the British crown and to the Indian princes:

> The crowd of natives remained passive. Nothing seemed to affect them. They showed no emotion, made no demonstration, throughout all the long hours of waiting. You couldn't tell what they were thinking about. They were just a dignified crowd. You felt that it was not their show—that it roused no enthusiasm in them. Some of their own smaller processions would have interested them infinitely more.[30]

John MacKenzie cites two passages in Fortescue's account of the 1911 Durbar where the Indian crowds were completely silent, once at the King-Emperor's entry into Delhi and again during the durbar at a point where the Europeans cheered themselves hoarse. MacKenzie asks:

> To what extent was this grand display, intended to impress Indians and demonstrate the might of the British and the futility of opposing them, actually an imported sight that moved them very little, particularly when the educated leadership was developing the nationalist movement as never before?[31]

The durbars were not directed at the ordinary Indians lining the streets, however, but at the Indian princes who, in David Cannadine's words, 'were probably at the peak of their power and prestige' not long after this, so that they 'gave generously to the imperial war effort in terms of money and men'.[32] The official account in 1911 points out that one third of the Empire of India 'or an area more than three times the size of France, with a population of 71 millions, is governed by the Indian Chiefs and Princes'.[33] The British installed a so-called 'Resident' or 'Political Agent' in each territory who was a representative of the viceroy, but nonetheless, says the account, 'The [princely] States have been raised from a position of subordination to the position of partners...' Given how powerful the British Residents were, with the power even to depose an Indian ruler, this is a piece of contradictory logic that is hard to comprehend today.[34]

Impressing the British—the Festival of Empire in London in 1911

Before George V was presented to his Indians subjects in all his imperial glory in Delhi in 1911, the king-emperor's subjects back home were invited to a show designed to educate them about that empire.[35] This was the Festival of Empire and Imperial Exhibition, which exhibited India but placed it into the context of all the colonies that made up the British Empire. The Festival was held in and around Paxton's Crystal Palace, which had been moved from Hyde Park and erected in an enlarged form in Sydenham in Kent in 1854.[36] The Festival was opened by the king and queen on 12 May 1911—their first official engagement since coming to the throne and before their coronation—and ran until 28 October 1911.

In the exhibition itself, India was presented in a space opening out of the central nave of the Crystal Palace with a dome which was described by the guide book as 'only 11 inches less in diameter than the great mosque of Mohamad Shah at Bijapur which is larger than that of the Pantheon in Rome', thus linking the British, the Mughal, and the Roman empires.[37] This strategy of alignment with past glory is by now familiar to us from all the other empires discussed in this book. In 231 glass cases the visitor could admire 1752 objects, many of them outstanding craft objects, lent not just by the king and the duke of Connaught but also by twenty Indian princes and by public bodies from Oxford to Bangalore. They included manuscripts, swords, carpets, wooden and ivory carvings, bronzes, textiles and embroideries, as well as twelve miniature historical tableaux depicting scenes from the enthronement of Rama and Sita to Victoria's proclamation as empress of India in 1876, the four-month-long visit of the prince of Wales, George V's father, in 1875–76, and the signing of the Treaty of Lhasa in 1904. One section illustrated India's progress under British rule, which meant the coming of the railway and the steamship. Nor was the 1857 uprising forgotten, for case 96 displayed what are referred to as 'relics' relating to the Willoughby Memorial at Delhi, when nine Englishmen defended a powder magazine for four hours and then fired it when they could defend it no longer.[38] In the section called the Art Gallery hung 641 paintings. The catalogue went out of its way to explain many of the objects and their context to the British visitor and to show the high standard of Indian arts and crafts, but the basis for doing this was, of course, what Bernard Cohn calls 'European interpretative strategies for "knowing" India'.[39]

In the grounds of the Crystal Palace, a landscape representing the British Empire was constructed, through which visitors could be transported for a mile and a half on an electric train called the All Red Tour, the name picking up on the 'All Red Line', the common designation for the telegraph cable that linked all the territories of the British Empire. The reporter in *The Gentlewoman* describes on 20 May 1911 how, beginning in 'Newfoundland' and ending in 'South Africa', the train took her through mountains, forests, and water representing Canada, Jamaica, Malaya, India, Australia, and New Zealand. She was taken past three-quarter-size models of the parliament buildings in the so-called 'dominions' of Canada, Australia, New Zealand, and South Africa, remarked that real sheep were grazing and real men toiling in 'Australia', while noting 'real Maoris at work and play round their quaint *whares*' (meeting houses). There were also a Malay village on stilts, a Jamaican sugar plantation, and an Indian tea plantation. The vast expanse of the British Empire was reduced here to an accessible playground, with just enough strangeness to make it an entertaining object of wonder. This was the empire as theatre with its colonial subjects as performers, while its British subjects formed the audience, measuring with their eyes the colonies of which they were the masters.

The Pageant of London and the Masque Imperial—1911

In the spacious grounds at Sydenham where the 1911 Festival of Empire was held there was room for an open-air amphitheatre in which fifteen thousand amateur actors performed a huge historical pageant, the Pageant of London, directed by Frank Lascelles (1875–1934).[40] The pageant was divided into four sections, so that an audience member had to attend on more than one day to see it all. It began with 'the dawn of British history' and went from there in forty scenes to the depiction of Britain as a colonial power. Many notable historians and writers of the day were involved in composing the individual scenes and ensuring that they were historically accurate, and each scene was performed by a group from a different London borough. The first section presented Roman London and the arrival of the Vikings; the second covered the fourteenth to the sixteenth centuries, from what was called the 'Age of Chaucer' to Elizabeth I's reign; the third section showed how trade with the Indies commenced and how the Pilgrim Fathers departed for north America; then came 'the meeting of the Old World and the New', when Pocahontas visited the court of King James I, followed by the execution of Charles I, and the Restoration of 1660. This section finished with the period of the Napoleonic Wars. There were two magnificent set-pieces: the funeral of Admiral Nelson in 1806 and the meeting of the allied sovereigns in London in 1814 after the defeat of Napoleon. These three parts were originally planned to take place in 1910, but the pageant was postponed to 1911, where it became part of the Festival of Empire. At this point, a fourth section was added, directly addressing the theme of empire.

In this fourth section, six scenes depicted the British arriving successively in Newfoundland, Australia (where Captain Cook gives the natives beads, mirrors, cloth, and knives), New Zealand, South Africa, Canada, and India. The colonization of India is represented not as a conquest but as the respectful meeting in 1616 of Sir Thomas Roe, King James's ambassador, with the Mughal emperor Jahangir, thus enabling Roe to acquire trading concessions. The souvenir booklet explains that after this, the Honourable East India company became a mighty power, that Britain took over the direct rule of India in 1858, and that Queen Victoria was proclaimed empress in 1877.[41] There is no mention of the uprising of 1857, making it seem as if India gladly gave herself to Britain. Representatives of all the so-called Overseas Dominions then gathered round a majestic figure wearing a helmet and holding a huge trident. She is the Mother Country, Britannia.

The show was not yet over, however, for it culminated in the *Masque Imperial*, subtitled 'an Allegory of the Advantages of Empire', by Francis Hartman Markoe. This was where history was left behind, and allegory took over. The opening scene was a meadow with a Grecian temple on one side. The Genius of the World, knowing that 'old Empires forgot the virtue that established them', has come to see if Britannia, the new nation that wishes to rule an empire, is up to the task. He summons seven 'Queens of Need' to test her. She has to learn that acquiring an empire demands sacrifice. He tells her:

> First you shall see the pageant of the Pain
> That Empire brings, the immolating toil,
> The holocaust of body and of brain
> That patriots suffer, in the wild turmoil
> Of nation-founding; when each foot of soil
> Is bought with blood and dreams as ransome price.[42]

Legions of weary people are shown, appearing from all directions, 'soldiers, sailors, scholars, workers, thinkers', who have sacrificed themselves to acquire an empire. Then, with the help of Hope, Britannia overcomes the ten Damozels of Death, whereupon the Genius of the World says to her:

> Nobly, Britannia, have you proved your worth
> To rank among the glorious ones of earth
> And having metamorphosized its pain,
> Behold, triumphant, the Imperial Gain.[43]

Trumpets ring out, the Damozels of Death and the Queens of Need are transformed. Then, in 'the Pageant of the Gain of Empire', there appear seventy-five groups of citizens from each of the territories of the British Empire and their provinces. All the groups ascend the steps to the temple and vanish inside. The masque ends with the singing of Psalm 24—'The earth is the Lord's and the fulness thereof'—and with the recitation of a prayer from the Book of Common Prayer: 'O Lord save the King and mercifully hear us when we call upon thee'. This is the only mention of the king in the entire pageant, something that would have been impossible in either Austria or Germany. The show was not about the king-emperor but about the Empire. It demonstrated to the British audience that the history of Britain led up to its role as an imperial power, that that role was sanctioned by Divine Providence, and that the entire population of the home country and the Empire was involved in this great endeavour. It was so successful that, instead of running from 6 June to 21 July as originally planned, its run was extended to 16 September, so that over a million people saw it.

At the back of the illustrated souvenir booklet of the pageant a revealing advertisement shows a photograph of about a dozen dark-skinned men, mostly naked from the waist up, busily hoeing among bushes. It is headed 'PURE INDIAN TEA' and the text proclaims:

> It must be remembered that Indian Tea is British Tea. British capital is invested in the Indian Tea Industry: the gardens are owned or managed by British planters; the tea is manufactured by ingenious machinery of British make; and it is dispatched to the United Kingdom in British ships. Indian Tea, then is of especial interest to the patriotic Briton.

Eric Hobsbawm points out that 'Britons, who had consumed 1.5 lb of tea per head in the 1840s and 3.26 lb in the 1860s, were consuming 5.7 lb in the 1890s.'[44] By exporting certain foodstuffs to Britain, India remained an agrarian society, and a backward and stagnant one at that, and it did not industrialize. Its role, like the other colonies, was to complement the British economy, not compete with it, as Hobsbawm says.

Setting the Empire in Stone—Building New Delhi

The royal visit of 1911 initiated another far larger architectural endeavour than the Gateway of India. Because the capital was scheduled to move from Calcutta on the east coast to Delhi in northern India, this meant designing a completely new viceroy's palace, a complex of administrative buildings for the officials and the various ministries, and living accommodation for many of these officials, virtually a new city. Edwin Lutyens (1869–1944) was chosen as the chief architect with Herbert Baker (1862–1946) as his collaborator. Herbert Baker explained how he saw his task in an article in *The Times* in 1912:

> First and foremost it is the spirit of British sovereignty which must be imprisoned in its [i.e. the capital's] stone and bronze. The new capital must be the sculptural monument of the good government and unity which India, for the first time in its history, has enjoyed under British rule. British rule in India is not a mere veneer of government and culture. It is a new civilization in growth, a blend of the best

elements of East and West. The effect of this will remain even should British sovereignty ever depart from the shores of India.[45]

New Delhi was to be the embodiment in stone of the invention that was the Empire of India. Baker goes on to quote an article in the *Round Table* which compares Britain's hegemony over India to empires of old: 'Thothmés and Sennacherib, Alexander and Napoleon never did the like. Only Rome in her greatest days did what England has been doing, as a matter of course, for one hundred years.'[46] On the one hand, this speaks volumes about the arrogance and overweening confidence with which the architects tackled their task; on the other hand, there is an uneasy recognition that Britain may not be in India for ever. According to C. Northcote Parkinson, when an organization builds itself a splendid, perfectly planned headquarters, that is an unfailing sign that that organization's best days are over. He cites New Delhi as one such example, in which 'the stages of its progress toward completion correspond with so many steps in political collapse. [. . .] What was finally achieved was no more and no less than a mausoleum.'[47] Planning began early in 1912 and the first idea was to build the new city on the northern ridge where the uprising of 1857 had been defeated. George V and Queen Mary even laid the foundation stone of New Delhi there during their stay in 1911. It was not until 1913 that the present site south of the old city of Delhi was finally decided upon.

In 1914, World War I broke out and 1.3 million Indians fought on the British side in various theatres of war with a huge loss of life. Work on the new city had to wait until after the war, so that New Delhi was not inaugurated until February 1931. What strikes the visitor today is the spacious grandeur of the whole layout. At one end of the broad formal avenue flanked by trees, lawns, and canals originally called Kingsway and now renamed Rajpath stands the huge stone arch, designed by Lutyens, and originally called the All India Memorial. Forty-two metres high, it commemorates the 70,000 Indians who died in World War I, fighting for Britain. Rajpath leads to the imposing secretariat buildings and the Viceroy's House on the hill, three kilometres away. Only from up close can one appreciate the impressive scale of the buildings. Placed on stone platforms, the two symmetrical secretariat buildings, designed by Herbert Baker, loom above the visitor, who has to mount a flight of stone steps to the terrace where the entrances are located. Set further back behind the secretariats is the Viceroy's House of pink and red stone, surmounted by an enormous black dome for which the inspiration was the Buddhist stupa at Sanchi in Madya Pradesh Figure 42). With its colon-naded entrance, this monumental building, Lutyens's masterpiece, combines a European style with many Indian features, far different from the fussy Indo-Saracenic style of many nineteenth-century buildings in India. The Indian elem-ents include the 2.5 metre jutting ledge or *chujja* below the level of the roof giving shade to the interior, the pierced screens or *jaalis* that allow air to circulate, and

Figure 42 Edwin Lutyens, Rashtrapati Bhavan, New Delhi. It is now the official residence of the President of India but was built as the Viceroy's House and completed in 1929. In front is the Jaipur Column completed in 1930, also by Lutyens, with bas-reliefs at the base by Charles Sargeant Jagger. Pictures from History/David Henley/Bridgeman Images

the umbrella-like towers or *chattris* and the fountains adorning the roof. Among the 355 rooms are a Durbar Hall, a throne room, and a ballroom. The building, now the residence of the President of India and officially called the Rashtrapati Bhavan, backs onto the Mughal Gardens with their pools and canals. At the other end of Rajpath, 150 metres beyond India Gate, is a stone canopy, again designed by Lutyens, which was erected in 1936 to house a statue of George V who died in 1936. The fate of this statue is described in chapter XI. After the Government of India Act was passed in 1919, New Delhi needed a Council Chamber, so Baker designed a circular structure off to one side of the central axis. It is now the Lok Sabha, the lower house of the Indian parliament. All these official buildings are set in a garden city with avenues radiating out from Rajpath lined with bunga-lows set in spacious grounds, the size of the bungalow reflecting the status of the inhabitant. It was said to be 'the first city specifically designed to the scale of the motorcar'.[48] Lord Hardinge insisted that one principal avenue should lead to the sixteenth-century Purana Qila fort and another to the seventeenth-century mosque, the Jama Masjid, thus emphasizing, yet again, the Mughal Empire as the forerunner of the British Raj.[49]

The monumental secretariat buildings, the Viceroy's House, and the India Gate are imperial in scale and ambition. They confidently assert that the British will be in India for the foreseeable future, if not forever. This was how New Delhi was perceived at the time. Robert Byron, in a lengthy assessment in *The Architectural Review* in January 1931, illustrated with many photographs and plans, was deeply impressed by what he saw and says that the complex, exuding 'such an expression of irrefragable permanence, of the monumental function transcending all considerations of adornment or utility, recalls the architectural intentions of Antiquity, of Egypt, Babylon and Persia'.[50] The days of Britain's rule over India were numbered, however, something that was clear at the time, not just with the benefit of hindsight. Thomas Metcalf writes:

> Like so much Edwardian building elsewhere, the product of an anxious Britain determined to assert itself against newly powerful rivals, the monumental classicism of the Viceroy's House, with its huge dome and seeming endless ranks of columns, can be seen as a device to mask a growing insecurity by shouting forth an assertive magnificence. Sheer size, so this mammoth palace seemed to say, could help obscure, if not deny altogether, the waning of Britain's authority over its premier dependency. Lutyens's use of Indic features too, while innovative, reflected the loss of imperial self-confidence.[51]

At the same time as the Gateway of India, the Victoria Memorial Hall, and New Delhi were striving to convince the Indians that the Raj would last forever, the British Empire Exhibition and the Pageant of Empire of 1924, held at Wembley, were doing their best to impress on the British back home that their hegemony over India was built on rock-solid foundations. India was allowed to play a prominent role in the exhibition, but its history and its contribution to World War I were strikingly downplayed in the pageant.

The British Empire Exhibition of 1924

The British Empire Exhibition of 1924 held at Wembley and the Pageant of Empire that was performed to accompany it were designed to convince the British people of their mission to rule vast swathes of the globe.[52] Though the exhibition had been mooted as early as 1902, the actual organization, which began in 1912 under the leadership of Lord Strathcona, had to be paused during the war and then restarted in 1919. It was due to open in 1921, was postponed until 1923, and was finally opened by George V, the king-emperor, on St George's Day, 23 April 1924. It ran until 1 November and, in order to reduce its deficit, was reopened in May 1925 and ran until the end of October of that year, though without the participation of India during this second year for financial reasons. Twenty-seven million people visited the exhibition over the two years that it was open.

The exhibition displayed the manufactures, produce, engineering, arts, and crafts of Britain and her colonies. On a site of 88 hectares, there were two large Palaces of Industry and Engineering respectively, a much smaller Palace of Arts, conference halls, a government building with apartments for the King and Queen, and separate pavilions for each of Australia, Bermuda, Burma, Canada, Ceylon, East Africa, Fiji, Hong Kong, India, Malaya, Malta, New Zealand, Palestine and Cyprus, Sarawak, South Africa, West Africa, West Indies, and the Atlantic Group. David Simonelli shows how the 'concept of a "Greater Britain" consisting of Britain and its white-governed colonies of emigration had been enshrined in the idea of "commonwealth" throughout the latter part of the nineteenth century' and how, after World War I, the concept of a commonwealth began to be promoted as a way of redefining the notion of empire.[53] The only territories in this 'commonwealth' not to be represented were Gibraltar and the Irish Free State, which had come into existence in 1922. Though the term commonwealth suggests an association of autonomous territories, it was taken for granted that Britain would lead this association, since the British were members of the superior Anglo-Saxon race and therefore considered by themselves to be more evolved than many members of the colonies. Simonelli shows how transparent racism, as well as overt British nationalism, informed many aspects of the exhibition. We remember that *A Passage to India*, E.M. Forster's devastating critique of the British in India and their racist attitudes, was published in 1924.

The Indian Pavilion at the exhibition was the most impressive ever to be built in Britain, a visually stunning white structure made of concrete whose style was based on that of the Taj Mahal in Agra, the Jama Masjid in Delhi, the Golden Mosque at Lahore, and the Victory Gate at Fatehpur Sikri.[54] It was not a foregone conclusion that India would take part at all and it was only at a debate in the Indian Legislative Assembly on 25 March 1922 that it agreed to do so, on condition that a preliminary exhibition would be held beforehand in Calcutta and that the Indian exhibit would be organized not by the India Office in London but by the Government of India in cooperation with the various newly established provincial councils, which were one of the outcomes of the Government of India Act of 1919. The Commissioner for India tasked with organizing the Indian exhibit was Sir Thiruvalayangudi Vijayaraghavacharya (1875–1953), an experienced administrator who had been dewan or prime minister of the kingdom of Cochin and represented Udaipur in the Constituent Assembly.[55] He describes in vivid detail the diplomatic efforts he had to engage in and the huge distances he had to travel within India in order to persuade the various kingdoms and the provinces to agree to take part at all. Then they had to be persuaded to decide in a timely fashion on which objects they were sending to London and how those would be transported. The Indian Pavilion was divided into seventeen sections or courts to show off such structural achievements as the railways and the telegraph service, which could be chalked up as British achievements, and to exhibit commodities such as tea and cotton. Models of the Gateway of India and of the Victoria Memorial Hall were also displayed.

However, there were also twenty separate courts for individual kingdoms and provinces, each of which had a free hand in designing, decorating, and furnishing their own section, which necessitated further decision-making and logistical organization. The pavilion also contained a restaurant where visitors could consume Indian dishes, served by Indian waitresses. A 344-page illustrated guide to the Indian pavilion was published, which in effect constitutes a handbook to India, since it contains details of every aspect of India's trade with graphs making international comparisons, information about Indian railways and about important raw materials such as cotton, as well as fifty pages on geology detailing all the ores and minerals the country offers. In addition, a section is devoted to each province or kingdom, giving its population and size, its chief architectural and landscape features, its raw materials, and its industries. Anyone reading this handbook would be seized by the sense of a vast, exotic, and multifarious continent and by the huge opportunities for trade that it presented. As Greenhalgh comments, 'obsession with India obviously had its basis in economic dependence, the extraordinary attention given to the Indian continent at exhibitions exposing both a pride in possession and a terror at the thought of loss.'[56]

The official guide proclaims that the purpose of the exhibition was to be 'a Family Party of the British Empire', continuing: 'The Exhibition has a mission to foster that friendship and good feeling which make the sure bond holding together the broad Dominions of the King-Emperor.'[57] Here at last was a reference to the monarch's imperial title in an official publication in a British context. The *Times*, in a special supplement on 23 April 1924, got quite carried away in the introductory article headed 'Wembley—Gateway to Empire':

Entering the Exhibition at Wembley, millions of British subjects will ascend the Heights of Empire. Spread before them is the wondrous reality of Britain's might and magnitude—her grandeur and her glory. Riches and romance, ancient civilisation flowering in modern enterprise, the limitless range of activity and achievement—the scene is without parallel in the history of mankind. Within the master-gateway of Wembley are a hundred inner gates of Empire. They give access to the five continents and all the seas: to the mystic East, the stirring West, the sterner north, the romantic South. They lead to tropical gardens, to groves of palm, banana and orange; to plantations of coffee, tea, sugar, rubber and cotton; to goldfields and diamond mines; to ostrich farms and sheep stations; to busy Oriental bazaars and the lonely haunts of trappers. No less challenging in their compelling interest are the gates of Science: of Stephenson, Watt, Faraday and Arkwright; or the great Gates of Industry: of Wool, Cotton, Steel and Leather. Wembley throbs with variegated life—a vivid, unforgettable realisation of Empire.[58]

The capital letters and superlatives are typical of the whole article: the UK is 'the greatest manufacturing country in the world', the Palace of Industry is 'the largest building ever erected for exhibition purposes', the power station providing light and power is 'the world's finest' and so on. A weekly newsletter sent to teachers from January to July 1924, *The Weekly Bulletin of Empire Study*, was designed to teach schoolchildren about the Empire, 1.2 million of whom would visit the exhibition in 1924 alone.

One of the aims of the exhibition was to encourage emigration, partly to alleviate unemployment at home and partly to make sure that there was a sufficiently large proportion of white people in every part of the British Empire or commonwealth.[59] Simonelli mentions the Oversea Settlement Committee founded in 1920 which established an Oversea Settlement Gallery in the Government Building when the exhibition reopened in 1925. While the Empire Settlement Act of 1922 devoted funds to help those, especially veterans, who wished to emigrate to Canada, Australia, New Zealand, or South Africa, the handbook accompanying the Indian Pavilion sells India so well that a reader might well be moved to investigate opportunities for service in or trade with India, even without a subsidy.

In order to encourage people to visit the exhibition, an amusement park was built next to the exhibition ground. It contained restaurants and cafes, a theatre, a switchback railway, a dance hall, an aquarium, a working colliery, and more. Instruction was combined with entertainment and the presence of the latter may explain the high number of visitors.

The Pageant of Empire in 1924

Just as he had organized the Pageant of London in 1911 to accompany the Festival of Empire, in 1924 Frank Lascelles organized the Pageant of Empire, another historical pageant with fifteen thousand lay participants to accompany the British Empire Exhibition. It was performed in the newly constructed Empire Stadium at Wembley, beginning on 25 July in such heavy rain that four episodes had to be abandoned.[60] The pageant was divided into three parts, each of which consisted of several scenes and the whole show was so vast in its conception that the following can only be a sketch.[61] The first part, labelled Westward Ho!, began in 1497 with Cabot setting off for Newfoundland, and then presented what were called 'the pioneers'—early colonizers accompanied by native inhabitants from the countries they arrived in. This was followed by the 'Pageant of Newfoundland' (the first colony), the 'Pageant of Learning', which presented the Universities of Oxford and Cambridge, the coming of printing to Britain, and Shakespeare, and 'the Pageant of Canada'. Eastward Ho! began with Elizabeth I celebrating the defeat of the Spanish armada and the clearing of pirates from the seas, went on to the 'Pageant of South Africa' with the Portuguese, the Dutch, and the French arriving before the British but the latter concluding a treaty with the Dutch in 1903, Wilson's last stand in 1893 against the Matabele, and Cecil Rhodes making peace with them in 1896. The 'Pageant of India', the last in this section, began with a teeming bazaar, presented Sir Thomas Roe at the court of the emperor Jahangir in 1616, and culminated in an elephant procession, called in Spencer Pryse's illustration in the souvenir volume 'The Rajah's Progress'.[62] Southward Ho! showed Captain Cook arriving in New Zealand and battling the Maoris. This was followed by the 'Pageant of Australia' showing the British arriving in Australia and its 'Era of Development, 1813–1860' culminating in Australia becoming a nation, where-upon the audience were shown the sinking of an artesian well and the land being planted with vineyards, orchards, cotton, and sugar.

The story that was told is that of the English, for the other nations of the United Kingdom are virtually ignored, fanning out over the globe, but the Great War was not forgotten. It was depicted as showing the unity of the different nations of the Empire and their sacrifices on Britain's behalf. The 'Pageant of Newfoundland', for instance, ends by saluting 'the magnificent services of the Newfoundland Regiment at Gallipoli and on other bloody fields in that Great War of 1914–18, which witnessed the final welding together of the British Empire beyond the seas'.[63] The 'Pageant of New Zealand' culminates in the inhabitants of New Zealand, including the Maoris, hearing the declaration of war on Germany in 1914 and stripping off their outer garments to reveal khaki and nurses' uniforms, whereupon they all march off to 'answer the Call of Empire'. The whole pageant ends with the 'Pageant of Heroes', beginning with Richard Coeur de Lion and his crusaders, Cromwell and his Ironsides, Drake, Grenville, and many others, who line up to salute Nelson's coffin. When the coffin is halfway across the stadium, the whole group of naval and military heroes fall in behind it, the chorus sings 'Toll for the Brave'; and the Pageant becomes a thanksgiving for what are called 'the Glorious Dead'. The account of what happens next deserves to be quoted in full:

> Small groups from the Dominions, India and the Crown Colonies come to show to the Motherland what they have done, of their sacrifice, their loyalty and love, and their hope for the future. Amongst them are some wounded and blinded soldiers, and a woman shrouded in black, with her orphan children to represent sacrifice; they group around her with arms outstretched. There is a complete silence for a few seconds, everyone is motionless, and then in the distance is heard the Reveille. Then from every entrance, as the music crashes, bells ring and the choirs sing, there streams into the Stadium a procession displaying all the countless units of the Great British Empire, who in a Thanksgiving Service, showing the glories, the wealth, the opportunities and resources of Greater Britain, that mighty commonwealth of Free Nations. They depart as the choir

intones the reverent words of Kipling's 'Recessional', the warning against pride, which bids us remember that 'unless the Lord build the house, the builders labour but in vain'.[64]

Frank Lascelles was an accomplished showman, using every resource of the theatre to entertain and to educate, but he was also a master at manipulating the emotions of his audience, many of whom must still have been grieving for the menfolk who never came back from the Great War. The music from an orchestra of 110 musicians and 400 singers, with compositions by among others Granville Bantock, Eric Coates, Percy Grainger, Arthur Sullivan, and, above all, Edward Elgar, contributed greatly to the drama and the emotion. Nalini Ghuman shows how important Elgar's contribution was in tying the whole pageant together. She comments, however, that the music he composed for it returns

> to a *fin-de-siècle* musical language and performing forces, [and so] participates triumphantly in the attempt of the whole British Empire Exhibition to return to a prewar sense of the spectacle of empire—the *Empire March* could have been written in 1897; nothing in it suggests a musical vintage of 1924.[65]

It is noticeable how the depiction of India concentrated on presenting its exoticism. As *The Times* put it on 26 July 1924, the day after the opening, referring to the scene showing the court of the Mughal emperor Jahangir in the late sixteenth and early seventeenth centuries, the pageant reminded the audience that 'then as now, the Orient was a mysterious and sun-soaked place.' While the sections depicting the dominions brought their history up at least to the nineteenth century and often almost to the present, there was no mention of any event in Indian history after Jahangir! Contested events in the history of British India such as the 1857 uprising, whose veterans were lauded as recently as 1911 at the Coronation Durbar for having fought for the British against their own compatriots, were not mentioned in 1924. The absence of an acknowledgement of the extraordinary contribution that Indians had made to the war effort in World War I must have been deeply hurtful, and the reference to the 'Free Nations' that made up the commonwealth surely rang hollowly in Indian ears. The pageant ended with Kipling's poem 'Recessional' with its admonition to give up vainglorious boasting, to trust in God, and to realize that sacrifice remains after military might has faded away. This resembled, in other words, the ending of the 1911 pageant with its religious message and reflective and prayerful tone.

George V died in 1936, and in 1937 his second son was crowned George VI, after the abdication of his older brother, Edward VIII. For this occasion the *Illustrated London News* produced the lavish folio-size Coronation Record Number, costing five shillings and containing both colour and black and white photographs.[66] In a double-page colour spread on plates XX and XXI, showing the fourteen 'Capitals of Empire' (including strangely both Dublin and Belfast, but excluding London), by far the biggest illustration is reserved for the Viceroy's House in Delhi. Though the corresponding special number for George V's Silver Jubilee in 1935 included the meeting in 1931 between Gandhi and the viceroy Lord Irwin accompanied by a photograph of Gandhi in his usual costume,[67] there is no indication as yet in 1937 that George VI was to be the last emperor of India, thus bringing the series of emperors and one empress with which this book is concerned to an end.

Notes

1. Taylor, *Empress*, p. 171.
2. *Official Report*, p. 8.
3. Taylor, *Empress*, p. 235.
4. Taylor, *Empress*, pp. 259–61.
5. Curzon, *British Government in India*, vol. I, pp. 178–9.
6. Curzon, *British Government in India*, vol. I, pp. 179–80.
7. Thomas Brock also created the statue of Queen Victoria in front of Buckingham Palace.
8. Gilmour, *Curzon*, pp. 239–46.
9. Wheeler, *History of the Delhi Coronation*, p. 4.
10. Wheeler, *History of the Delhi Coronation*, p. 107.
11. Wheeler, *History of the Delhi Coronation* pp. 139–40.
12. Codell, *Power and Resistance*, pp. 38–9.
13. Quoted from Codell, *Power and Resistance*, p. 38.
14. Wheeler, *History of the Delhi Coronation*, pp. 111–12.
15. Menpes, *The Durbar*, pp. 58–9.
16. Goyle, 'Tracing a Cultural Memory of 1857'.
17. Wheeler, *History of the Delhi Coronation*, pp. 177–94.
18. Wheeler, *History of the Delhi Coronation*, p. 57.
19. Wheeler, *History of the Delhi Coronation*, p. 238.
20. Cannadine, 'The Context, Performance and Meaning of Ritual'; Cannadine, *Ornamentalism*.
21. Davies, *Splendours*, p. 180; see in general Metcalf, *An Imperial Vision* and Banerjee, 'British India and Victorian-Era Architecture'.
22. Fortesque, *Narrative of the Visit*, pp. 263–4.
23. Fortescue, *Narrative of the Visit*, p. 265.
24. *The Historical Record*, p. 3.
25. *The Historical Record*, pp. 5–6.
26. *The Historical Record*, p. 7.
27. Menpes, *The Durbar*, pp. 113–19.
28. *The Historical Record*, p. 111.
29. *The Historical Record*, p. 174.
30. Menpes, *The Durbar*, p. 42.

31. MacKenzie, 'Exhibiting Empire', p. 205.
32. Cannadine, p. 54.
33. *The Historical Record*, p. 127.
34. *The Historical Record*, p. 128.
35. Auerbach, 'Empire under Glass'.
36. Hassam, 'Portable iron structures'.
37. *Indian Court*, p. x.
38. *Indian Court*, p. 50.
39. Cohn, *Colonialism*, p. 78.
40. Ryan, 'Staging the imperial city'; Lomas, *Festival of Empire*.
41. Lomas, *Festival of Empire*, p. 143.
42. Lomas, *Festival of Empire*, p. 154.
43. Lomas, *Festival of Empire*, p. 157.
44. Hobsbawm, *The Age of Empire*, p. 64.
45. Baker, 'The New Delhi', p. 7.
46. Baker, 'The New Delhi', p. 8.
47. Parkinson, *Parkinson's Law*, pp. 96–7. Evenson, *The Indian Metropolis*, p. 108, picks this up too.
48. Evenson, *The Indian Metropolis*, p. 153.
49. Davies, *Splendours*, p. 224.
50. Byron, 'New Delhi', p. 11.
51. Metcalf, *An Imperial Vision*, pp. 237–8.
52. *His Imperial Majesty*.
53. Simonelli, '"[L]aughing nations"', p. 3.
54. *India. Catalogue*, p. 2.
55. Vijayaraghavacharya, *The British Empire Exhibition*.
56. Greenhalgh, *Ephemeral Vistas*, p. 62.
57. Cook, *The British Empire Exhibition*, p. 10.
58. *The Times*, Exhibition Supplement, 23 April 1924, p. 1.
59. Simonelli, 'Laughing nations', p. 11.
60. *The Times*, 26 July 1924.
61. It is based on the account given by Angela Bartie et al, 'The Pageant of Empire'.
62. Lucas, *Pageant of British Empire*, p. 45.
63. Quoted from Bartie et al., The Pageant of Empire.
64. Quoted from Bartie et al., The Pageant of Empire.
65. Ghuman, 'Elgar's *Pageant of Empire*'.
66. Equivalent to at least £253 in today's currency, according to the National Archives Currency Converter.
67. *Illustrated London News, Silver Jubilee Record Number 1910–1935*, p. 33.

X

Staging Empire as History and Allegory in Austria and Germany

The ritual and ceremonial, costumes and palaces, courts and images, religious observances and public appearances discussed above were 'the *theatrical* elements; those which appeal to the senses, which claim to be embodiments of the greatest human ideas—which boast in some cases of far more than human origin' of which Walter Bagehot wrote in 1867.[1] Many of these elements were only directly accessible to the aristocracy or to those involved in government, so what about the mass of the emperor's subjects? From the middle of the nineteenth century on, more and more of them were living in cities, were demanding a better standard of living and more control over their own destiny, were joining political parties, and becoming ever more fractious. They no longer simply accepted the will of a ruler said to be appointed by God. Some of them had the vote and hoped by doing so to choose their own rulers. The ubiquity of affordable newspapers meant that they were better informed than they had ever been and could read critical as well as adulatory assessments of their monarchs' behaviour. The expansion of the railways, not to mention the development of the bicycle and the motorcar, meant that they could move around in a way that would have been impossible in the first half of the nineteenth century and could experience other societies and other modes of living. In addition, in an age of growing nationalism, each of the empires contained large numbers of subjects who belonged to other ethnic groups and confessions and did not necessarily feel an emotional connection to the capital city or the court. 'The widespread progress of electoral democracy and the consequent emergence of mass politics therefore dominated the invention of official traditions in the period 1870–1914', writes Hobsbawm.[2]

Those in power needed to persuade all their subjects that the nation's destiny and therefore their own, regardless of their own origins or traditions, was tied in an indissoluble bond to the monarch who ruled over them, a monarch who looked down on his people benevolently from an imperial height. A version of national history had to be promulgated that focused on a number of key episodes which had been declared to be foundational. Throughout the territories of the two European empires that continued to exist at the end of the nineteenth and the beginning of the twentieth century, school books and cheap popular publications promoted this official version of national history, as did the statues and monuments that were erected in increasing numbers. Theatrical presentations of these

Projecting Imperial Power: New Nineteenth-Century Emperors and the Public Sphere. Helen Watanabe-O'Kelly,
Oxford University Press (2021). © Helen Watanabe-O'Kelly. DOI: 10.1093/oso/9780198802471.003.0011

foundational myths, either as costumed processions and pageants or as specially commissioned plays for the theatre, were staged on anniversaries and important jubilees. In these events the imperial present was presented as the inevitable, divinely ordained fulfilment of a destiny that had been working itself out for centuries. Britain, too, presented its hegemony over India as the working out of destiny and also used pageants for the purpose. Two that were performed in 1911 and 1924 respectively are discussed in chapter IX.

In 1908, on the sixtieth anniversary of Emperor Franz Joseph's accession to the throne, a huge costumed procession involving 12,000 amateurs was staged in Vienna. The first part depicted the glorious historical development of the Habsburgs as rulers of Austria and as Holy Roman Emperors, while the second part presented huge groups representing most of the nationalities that made up what was called 'Cisleithanien', that part of the Austrian Empire west of the river Leitha. 'Both parts came together to demonstrate the Austrian idea of the state, to present the kingdom of Austria as a sacred empire ("sacrum imperium") in a centuries-old tradition', writes Elisabeth Grossegger.[3] Just as important as presenting a national historical myth was the elevation of the emperor onto a higher plane, making him timeless, untouchable, the guarantor of the national destiny and therefore beyond criticism. In both Austria and Germany this was accomplished by means of historical and allegorical dramas, performed on the occasion of important jubilees. In Franz Joseph's case, this meant his Golden Jubilee in 1898 and his Diamond Jubilee in 1908. In the case of the German Empire, Emperor Wilhelm II chose Wilhelm I's hundredth birthday in 1897 to glorify his late grandfather as a way of glorifying himself. Wilhelm II strongly believed in the power of the theatre to inculcate certain values and to promote a vision of Prussian history. To this end, he had initiated an annual theatre festival in Wiesbaden, a so-called 'Kaiserfestspiel', held each year in May between 1896 and 1914. It was only to be expected, therefore, that Wilhelm I's centenary should be marked by the performance in the court theatre in Berlin of an allegorical play.

Franz Joseph's Diamond Jubilee in 1908

Franz Joseph had ascended the throne in 1848 at the age of eighteen and he reigned for almost seventy years, dying in 1916 in the middle of World War I. As the successor to sixteen Holy Roman Emperors and two emperors of Austria, he had been taught from his earliest years that he was an emperor not because he had been chosen by the people, as, for instance, Napoleon I and III had been, but because he was 'emperor by the grace of God'. Though he was forced to become a constitutional monarch in 1867, the year in which the so-called December Constitution gave his subjects in Cisleithania new rights and the parliament and government new powers, he was still supreme commander of the armed forces, had the right to make foreign policy, to dissolve the government, and to name the prime minister. He was also the head of the senior dynasty in Europe and he exercised complete control over all the members of all its branches according to the powers given to him by the confidential Habsburg Family Statute, agreed on 3 February 1839 during the reign of his predecessor and uncle, Ferdinand I. This allowed him to determine where they lived and whom they married and, as many of them were financially dependent on him, he could enforce these decisions. Various family members such as his nephew Archduke Leopold Ferdinand, who formally left the family in 1902, took the name Leopold Wölfling and wrote several volumes of memoirs, report that, even in the bosom of his family, Franz Joseph was always 'the emperor' and was addressed as Your Majesty and in the third person.[4]

This unassailable position, which formed part of his aura and contributed over the years to his unapproachability, meant that, unlike the insecure and narcissistic Wilhelm II, he did not feel the need for major celebrations on his birthday or other dynastic occasions and he only rarely authorized them. He did not wish to be personally feted, preferring the money to be devoted to charitable causes. One of the few major events that he did allow was the costumed procession in celebration of his Silver Wedding in 1879, discussed above in chapter VII in connection with the building of the Ringstrasse. The only formal public event that could be considered a celebration of his fortieth jubilee as ruler was the inauguration of the statue of Maria Theresia in Vienna in 1888, discussed in the same chapter. 1898 was another matter, for this was the year in which he celebrated fifty years on the throne and such a notable anniversary could not be ignored.[5] Daniel Unowsky has set out in illuminating detail how this Golden Jubilee was instrumentalized by a number of institutions and groups within the empire. The church presented him as a 'Christ-like martyr and sublime moral model' in a pastoral letter to be read out in all churches in Cisleithania on 27 November 1898, the first Sunday of Advent.[6] He was presented as the suffering father because his son and heir Crown Prince Rudolf had killed himself and his young lover Mary Vetsera in the hunting lodge at Mayerling on 30 January 1889. From the point of view of the army he was the First Soldier of the realm, their patron saint, devoted to the welfare of the soldiers, each of whom received a special Jubilee Commemorative Medal.[7] Though the Hungarian government did not recognize the jubilee at all, since he had only been their king officially since his coronation in 1867, the Cisleithanian government portrayed him as a symbol and guarantor of state unity. The conservative Catholic Christian Social party—rabidly anti-Semitic and led by the charismatic demagogue Karl Lueger (1844–1910)—achieved a majority in the Viennese City Council in 1895 which meant that Lueger was chosen as Lord Mayor. Franz Joseph, who disapproved of his views, refused to confirm him as mayor no fewer than four times, until he finally had to agree to his election in 1897. Lueger remained Lord Mayor until his death in 1910 and was therefore at the head of the City Council at the time of the Golden Jubilee. He and his party used this opportunity to position themselves as the party of Christian charity by contributing to a 'Franz Joseph Jubilee Children's Hospital', as the party of piety by supporting the building of a Jubilee Church, and as the patriotic party by becoming involved in the organization of the Kaiser Jubilee Exhibition held in the Prater on the site of the 1873 world exhibition. Lueger achieved his greatest propaganda coup, however, by organizing a procession of 70,000 schoolchildren around the Ringstrasse in homage to the emperor. On 24 June, the children marched twenty-four abreast along the broad avenue, the first row of boys lowering their flags as they passed the emperor and all the children turning towards him and doffing their hats and caps. As Unowsky puts it: 'In Lueger's choreography the emperor became a prop affirming his and his party's patriotic credentials.'[8]

On 6 May, Alfred Freiherr von Berger's so-called 'fairy tale play', *Habsburg*, was performed in the Deutsches Volkstheater in Vienna. This competent blank verse drama is set in 1278, just after Rudolf I of Habsburg has defeated and killed the Bohemian king Ottokar on the Marchfeld. Rudolf, the first Habsburg to be elected Holy Roman Emperor, was the foundational figure of the dynasty and the play shows Austria and the crown lands longing for a unifying figure. The old soldier Liechtenstein calls for 'a real German man like you and the princes of your house' to rule these lands.[9] Figures from the world of fairy tale, representatives of the ordinary people, the ghost of Ottokar, the saints, of whom St Hubertus, the patron saint of hunting, is the most important, and Lucifer show Rudolf different visions. Lucifer tries to convince him that his dynasty ended with Empress Maria Theresia, of whom he is also shown a vision. Unsure whether he should really take over the crown lands, St Hubertus brings him to the present where he meets Old Sepp, Franz Joseph's huntsman, who tells him how beloved the emperor is, who is much wiser than the politicians, and how he is 'the heart of the empire'.[10]

Archduke Franz Ferdinand of Austria-Este (1863–1914), now the designated successor to Franz Joseph, was given the task of organizing the court's own homage to the emperor, which was to begin with a Mass and Te Deum in St Stephen's Cathedral in Vienna on 29 November 1898, a theatre production on 1 December, a homage by the imperial family on 2 December, the actual date of the accession to the throne, and another act of homage by the provinces. However, Empress Elisabeth was assassinated on Lake Geneva on 10 September in 1898, so most of these events had to be cancelled. Her coffin was brought back to Austria by train and she was buried next to her son in the Habsburg burial vault in the Capuchin church in Vienna. Because of this new blow of fate, Franz Joseph appeared even more as the suffering martyr, carrying on stoically for the sake of his people.

Ten years later, Franz Joseph was still on the throne, since Queen Victoria's death in 1901 the senior monarch not just in Europe but in the world. His subjects and above all the city of Vienna wished to celebrate such an important anniversary with a procession around the Ringstrasse. The emperor refused to countenance it or any other large-scale celebration, however, requesting that any money that might have been spent should go to alleviate the widespread poverty in Vienna. As late as 9 March 1908 he was still refusing to give permission for the procession, planned for June, to go ahead.[11] The city council finally persuaded him to allow it by arguing that the procession would give tourism and the local economy a boost and provide much-needed employment. Medals, charitable giving, local celebrations, formal addresses, commemorative publications of all kinds formed part of a huge national celebration, but the first formal event of the Diamond Jubilee took place at Schönbrunn on 7 May 1908. Wilhelm II, German emperor and king of Prussia, led a delegation of eleven of the federal princes of the German Empire and the mayor of the Free City of Hamburg to Vienna bringing the Austrian emperor official greetings on his birthday. A painting by Franz Matsch (1861–1942) depicts the group, which included the kings of Saxony and Württemberg, the prince regent of Bavaria, and the grand duke of Baden in their gala uniforms, flanked by the Lord Mayor and President of the Senate of the Free City of Hamburg in his long black robe and starched ruff, standing in front of the aged Franz Joseph. As Harm Hinrich Brandt explains, this gesture particularly moved Franz Joseph because he clung, throughout his long reign, to the notions of a German 'Fürstenbund' or union of princes and of Austria and Prussia standing together as brothers.[12] This had not prevented the 'German war' of 1866, in which Prussia fought against Austria and comprehensively defeated it at the battle of Königgrätz. The relationship was repaired in the Dual Alliance of 1879 and cemented in 1897 when Wilhelm II, nearly thirty years younger than Franz Joseph, paid a state visit to Budapest as the latter's guest. When the two emperors toasted each other at the formal banquet there on 20 September, Franz Joseph referred to Wilhelm as his 'faithful friend and ally' who shared his views and attitudes ('Gesinnungen'), while Wilhelm in reply said that he looked up to his fatherly friend in the manner of a son (Figure 43).[13] In his reply to the homage of the German princes in 1908, Franz Joseph said that he saw in it 'a formal proclamation of the monarchical principle'.[14] Monarchy was the only political system that he recognized. On 21 May, Karl Lueger, still in post as Lord Mayor, used the occasion of the jubilee to show off his loyalty and patriotism again by leading a homage of 82,000 school children at Schönbrunn. On 25 June, four thousand huntsmen saluted the devoted hunter Franz Joseph at Schönbrunn.

The most impressive event of the summer celebrations was, however, the enormous costumed procession, seven kilometres long, officially called 'Der Kaiser-Huldigungs-Festzug' (Procession of Homage to the Emperor), which took place in excellent weather on 12 June 1908 on the Ringstrasse in Vienna.[15] The Viennese satirist Karl Kraus, in one of his savage phrases, called it 'The Triumphal Procession of Sycophancy', claiming—rightly, as we know—that the

In Treue fest!

Figure 43 Steadfast in Loyalty! Wilhelm II of Prussia with Franz Joseph I of Austria. Photograph. Private Collection © Arkivi UG All Rights Reserved/Bridgeman Images

emperor did not want such a procession but was forced to allow it.[16] As in 1879, the podium for the imperial family, designed this time by the architect Josef Urban, was positioned in front of the Äußeres Burgtor, with stands for important guests opposite it on the other side of the Ring. Hans Graf Wilczek (1837–1922), a friend and close collaborator of the late Crown Prince Rudolf, was the Honorary President of the organizing committee. According to Grossenegger, it was his vision of a Greater Austria animated by the Enlightenment ideas of Joseph II, a vision shared by Crown Prince Rudolf, that underpinned the conception of the procession.[17] It was divided into two parts. In the first part, nineteen enormous costumed groups performed the history of Austria entwined with that of the Habsburg dynasty, beginning with Rudolf I (1218–91) and culminating in the year 1848, when Franz Joseph came to the throne. This half of the procession with its 4,000 participants, many of them on horseback, demonstrated the continuity and *ancienneté* of the Austrian aristocracy, for many of the historical figures were played by their descendants. This began with the very first group depicting King Rudolf I accompanied by his German nobles, dressed as medieval knights. Only those who could trace their genealogy back to the thirteenth century were allowed to take part in this group. The forty-one descendants of such famous families as Auersperg, Fürstenberg, Hardegg, Harrach, Herberstein, Stillfried, and Trauttmansdorff represented 'the famous, proud, loyal, ancient original nobility of Austria'.[18] The same principle obtained in all the other groups. In group IX depicting the siege of Vienna, for instance, Ernst Rüdiger Fürst zu Starhemberg

(1638–1701), who had led the defence of the city in 1683, was played in 1908 by his descendant of the same name. Field Marshal Joseph Radetzky (1766–1858), leader of the group at the end of the historical half of the pageant, was played by his descendant Josef Graf Radetzky.

While one group presented the founding of St Stephen's Cathedral in Vienna in the Middle Ages, the double marriage of the grandchildren of Emperor Maximilian in 1515 which brought the kingdoms of Bohemia and Hungary to Austria, and peaceful scenes from the reigns of Empress Maria Theresia and Joseph II, eleven of the nineteen groups in the historical panorama either depicted such military triumphs as the two Turkish sieges of Vienna in 1529 and 1683 respectively and the defeat of the Protestant Swedes at the Battle of Nördlingen in 1634 or else Austrian military heroes such as Prince Eugen, Archduke Karl, and Field Marshall Radetzky. Austrian history was still military history and largely aristocratic history, and of course there was no reference to the Austrian defeats of the nineteenth century.

The second part of the pageant with its 8,000 participants depicted the present. Huge groups represented the city of Vienna and fifteen of the so-called crown lands of Austria, each group wearing its own colourful national dress, often accompanied by decorated wagons and bearing flags and banners. They processed in the order in which they were listed in Franz Joseph's official title: the kingdoms of Bohemia, Dalmatia, and Galicia came first, followed by the duchies of Austria, Styria, Carinthia, Carniola, Silesia, and Bukovina, and the margravates of Moravia, Istria and Trieste, the county of Tyrol, and the Vorarlberg. Hungary did not take part at all, because, as far as the Hungarians were concerned, Franz Joseph had only been king of Hungary since 1867. The kingdom of Bohemia was only represented by a tiny deputation, as contemporary photographs show. The Czech National Theatre was supposed to put on five theatrical performances beginning on 30 April, but from various remarks by Lueger and his deputy, the Czechs felt the atmosphere in Vienna was hostile towards them and they refused to take part in the procession. The Poles also threatened to boycott the procession when it seemed as if their king Jan III Sobieski (1629–96), whose support had been vital in defeating the Turks at the gates of Vienna in 1683, would be expected to ride behind Emperor Leopold I. This problem was solved by agreeing that the two leaders would ride side by side! Ruthenians complained about what they saw as the over-representation of Poles.[19] If the procession was meant to express the unity in diversity of the Austrian Empire, it also exemplified its tensions.

On the actual anniversary of Franz Joseph's accession, 2 December, a Te Deum was sung in St Stephen's Cathedral and that evening the allegorical history play, *Des Kaisers Traum*, by Christiane Countess Thun-Salm (1859–1935), was performed. This was an amended and shortened version of the work that had had to be cancelled in 1898 because of the empress's assassination.[20] In some of its aspects and in its main message it resembles Berger's *Habsburg*, but it is a far worse play. Where Berger introduces humour and shows Rudolf to be a straight-talking soldier, with refreshingly few purple passages, Thun-Salm's work is cloyingly adulatory. Unowsky vividly describes the manner in which a committee of the most important courtiers and politicians in Austria decided on its content. They 'sought to exalt Franz Joseph and the imperial house without making references that could exacerbate national tensions or be used by political factions for partisan advantage'.[21] As performed in 1908, the play begins, like the procession, in 1281 with Rudolf von Habsburg investing his sons Rudolf and Albrecht with his Austrian lands. After they have been greeted by the citizens of Vienna, Rudolf, worried about the future of his dynasty, wishes to know the future. The figure of Future appears and shows him tableaux of five key moments of Austrian history: the double marriage in 1515 that enabled the Habsburgs to inherit the kingdoms of Bohemia and Hungary; the meeting between Emperor Leopold I and Jan Sobieski, king of Poland, in 1683; the proclamation of the Pragmatic Sanction in 1725; Empress Maria Theresia and her children listening to the five-year-old Mozart at Schönbrunn; the Congress of Vienna in 1814. These five incidents, some of them identical with episodes depicted in the procession, were selected by the committee from a list of fifteen drawn up by Joseph Alexander von Helfert (1820–1910), the most important patriotic Austrian historian of the day, who greatly influenced the design of the history curriculum in Austrian secondary schools (*Gymnasien*).[22]

In *Des Kaisers Traum*, though he has seen the tableaux, Rudolf is not yet satisfied. He wants to see a future successor who loves all his peoples as he does and who is loved by them. Future vanishes and the figures of Love and Loyalty appear. They describe for Rudolf a blooming and happy land rejoicing in gratitude and loyalty towards its beloved emperor on his jubilee. Rudolf, raising his arms in blessing towards the imperial box, salutes this day. Love and Loyalty then address the audience, reminding them that the young emperor whom they greeted in the springtime of his youth is the same man whom they now see before them in the golden light of his autumn. They call on the audience to celebrate him and to sing the national anthem, a hymn that calls on God to sustain and celebrate the emperor and the nation. In 1898, a magnificent apotheosis was planned in which figures such as 'Bohemia', 'Hungaria', and 'Galicia' representing the different crown lands would have appeared 'wearing provincial colours and bearing the shields of the Habsburg provinces'.[23] This stirring scene was omitted in 1908; instead, the second half of the programme consisted of a series of folk dances from each of the crown lands, and the evening culminated in the entire audience singing 'O thou my Austria'. The Viennese newspaper, *Die Neue Freie Presse*, reviewing the evening, proclaimed that on this evening 'one felt the whole dynastic and national ("staatliche") significance and greatness of the jubilee.'[24] Karl Kraus, never tired of satirizing this very newspaper, had already pronounced earlier in the jubilee year that 'we have never lived in a more servile era.'[25] Victor Hahn's verse drama *Felix Austria*, put on in Graz on 1 December 1908, does nothing to dispel this view. It provides another panorama of Austrian history, beginning with the legend of the pious Emperor Maximilian trapped on a rockface near Innsbruck in 1484 and ending in the year 1908. In the last scene, Austria and Germania celebrate together as sisters and Maximilian does homage to the bust of Franz Joseph, taking the laurel wreath from his own head and laying it at Franz Joseph's feet.

Wilhelm II and Imperial Theatre

Wilhelm II did not need a committee to design theatrical performances for him, for this was one of the areas of artistic endeavour which he considered particularly important and in which he was often directly involved.[26] On 16 June 1898, ten years after his accession, in a speech to the actors and creative personnel of the three Royal Theatres in Berlin, he explained that the theatre should be

> a tool of the monarch ... like the school and the university, which have the task of forming the next generation and preparing them to work for the support of the highest spiritual values of our magnificent German fatherland. In the same way, the theatre must contribute to form the spirit and the character and to ennoble moral attitudes. The theatre is also one of my weapons.[27]

The theatre should 'cultivate idealism in our people', he said on the same occasion. In other words, he saw the theatre as a pedagogical instrument which would inculcate elevated values—values to be determined by himself, of course. One of the most important of these was the divinely ordained imperial mission of the Hohenzollerns.

Wilhelm II inherited no fewer than six theatres: three in Berlin and one each in Kassel, Hanover, and Wiesbaden—the three last-named in territories acquired by Prussia after 1871. All of them needed substantial subventions from the Privy Purse. Impressed with Bayreuth and its Wagner festival, Wilhelm established a competing festival, the so-called 'Kaiserfestspiele' or Imperial Festival, in Wiesbaden, which took place each year in May from 1896 to 1914.[28] Crucial for this endeavour was Georg von Hülsen (1858–1922), who was named director of the Wiesbaden theatre in 1893, becoming director general of all the theatres in Prussia in 1903 as Count von Hülsen-Haeseler. By 1890 Wiesbaden was becoming a fashionable spa, prosperous enough to be able to build a new theatre in 1892–94, a new town hall in 1897, and a new railway station in 1906. The presence each year of the emperor and his court, the standard of the productions, and the attendance of a large number of critics from all over Germany who came to see and report on them increased the town's fashionable reputation. For the duration of the festival, the whole town became the stage on which the emperor was the principal actor, feted wherever he went. In the theatre itself, he was patron and director, often attending rehearsals and making suggestions, but he was also audience and actor, matching the uniform he wore to the work he was going to see that night.[29]

If Wiesbaden were to become a second Bayreuth, it needed a grand tetralogy to rival Wagner's *Der Ring des Nibelungen*, so the emperor commissioned a 'Hohenzollern-Tetralogie' from Josef Lauff (1855–1933) (from 1913 Josef von Lauff), a popular novelist. Lauff only ever completed two of the projected four plays: *Der Burggraf* (The Burgrave), about the twelfth-century Hohenzollern Friedrich I, burgrave of Nürnberg, and *Eisenzahn* (Irontooth), about the fifteenth-century elector of Brandenburg Friedrich II and his victory over the independent-minded and rebellious citizens of Berlin discussed in chapter VII. The plays were premiered at the festival in 1897 and 1899 respectively, with 1897 being a particularly significant year, as it was the hundredth birthday of Emperor Wilhelm I. Stephanie Kleiner comments that 'the figure of the burgrave can be read as a scarcely concealed double portrait of Wilhelm I and his grandson.'[30] She also reports how involved in the production Wilhelm II was, designing costumes and sets, including that of the grand finale on the battlefield. While conservative critics praised the two plays, many others found the promotion of state-sponsored violence as the basis for government hard to stomach. Neither play had any lasting success with the public, which explains why the third and fourth dramas in the tetralogy, which had been planned to depict two other important Hohenzollerns, the Great Elector and Frederick the Great, were never written.

In 1897, Wilhelm II went to great lengths to establish the soubriquet 'Wilhelm the Great' for his beloved grandfather, hoping to counter the widespread cult of Bismarck, the imperial Chancellor and prime minister of Prussia whom he had dismissed in 1890 and whose reputation he tried to diminish at every turn. In a famous speech given on 26 February 1897 at the banquet of the Brandenburg Provincial Parliament, Wilhelm II suggested that, had he lived in the Middle Ages, his grandfather would have been canonized and people would have gone on pilgrimages to pray in front of his remains. Indeed, he went on, people were even now visiting his tomb! If this idea was a strange one to utter in a gathering of Protestants, his suggestion in the same speech that Wilhelm I had conceived of the German Empire all by himself was even stranger. Thanks to divine providence, said his grandson, Wilhelm I had had by his side 'many a good, competent adviser, who had the honour to carry out his ideas, but who were all the tools of his noble will, filled with the spirit of this noble emperor'.[31] This slighting reference to Bismarck and Generals Moltke and Roon, revered figures whom Wilhelm I himself would have said were crucial to the creation of the Empire, was considered disrespectful in the extreme, made worse by the fact that in another version of the speech, Wilhelm II was said to have called them henchmen ('Handlanger') and even pygmies. Wilhelm I would have turned in his grave, comments Hildegard von Spitzemberg, who believed that Wilhelm II had indeed used the term 'pygmies'.[32]

We have already seen in chapter VII how Wilhelm II erected an impressive monument to this grandfather in the centre of Berlin. In John Röhl's analysis, Wilhelm II's cult of his grandfather was 'a projection of the vision he cherished of his own role as ruler, and of his supposed historical mission, on to the revered, transcendental figures of his Hohenzollern ancestors'.[33] The theatre was particularly suited for this projection, which can be seen from the four categories into which Michael A. Förster divides the works that Wilhelm II promoted in his theatres: those depicting the monarch as the guarantor of peace, justice, and the good of the people; those representing Prussia's destiny; those celebrating the army and the military; and those presenting the destiny of the monarch.[34] All four of these themes are present in *Willehalm*, the verse drama commissioned from the historical dramatist Ernst von Wildenbruch (1845–1909) and performed in the Royal Theatre in Berlin on 22 March 1897, Wilhelm I's hundredth birthday.

The play, which is couched throughout in a heightened poetic and archaic language, opens on the banks of the Rhine at the court of a bloodthirsty despot called simply the 'Imperator', who wears a vaguely Roman costume. He has conquered the German lands and has enslaved a beautiful maiden who is the German Soul. He appears on a black stallion to the cheers of his warriors, boasting of how he has destroyed German culture and deprived the Germans of their history. He has taken the sons of all the German princes hostage and intends his own people to interbreed with them. He lures them by giving them wine, served by beautiful maidens, and gets them to kiss the foot of the seductive Amazon Parisina—not Byron's or Donizetti's Parisina but in this context the hussy from Paris. Only the young Willehalm is immune to this seduction. He proclaims that he will be revenged on the man who took his father's crown and broke his mother's heart. When Parisina's sandal breaks, Imperator calls for the maiden he has captured and enslaved (the German Soul) to come and mend it and makes her kneel before Parisina. Willehalm, alone of the German princes' sons, stops her, recognizing that she is not a servant but a queen. A clap of thunder rings out and the stage goes dark. Then a white light reveals the Imperator in a trance on his throne and all the other characters lying on the floor as though asleep. Standing in the light is the Maiden, stately and tall, dressed in splendid robes covered in jewels with a crown of reeds on her hair. Willehalm kneels before her and gazes up at her. She tells him that she is 'the soul of the destroyed German lands'. She has been taken captive 'because weakness and disgrace broke Germany's manly arm.'[35] She asks Willehalm to go to Germany and awaken the dreamers who must fight to free her. The white light vanishes, the Imperator and his court awake, and the Maiden is dragged off to prison as a witch. The Imperator boasts that he has broken the courage of Germania's men, so that not one of them will save Germania's soul. From offstage comes the voice of the Maiden calling on Willehalm to remember his promise to save her. The princes' sons, ordered to take him prisoner, find that they cannot. Offstage, a stallion is described leaping out of the water of the Rhine and galloping towards the Imperator's camp. As Willehalm rushes off to mount this fiery steed, he is followed by all the other princes' sons. The last word of the first act is 'revenge'.

The second act reveals a divided landscape with a ravine running through the middle and sheer cliffs on each side. The bridge across the ravine is broken and a whole group of so-called Wise Men cannot see how to repair it, even though they consult their learned books. On each side of the ravine is a cave, in one of which sits the Powerful One ('der Gewaltige'), and in the other the Wise One. A voice is heard calling on Willehalm to remember his promise, and the Wise One recognizes it as the voice of the German Soul and says that a steed will bring their saviour out of the forest. Willehalm appears riding on a white horse, dressed as a Germanic warrior and wearing a helmet with two huge golden wings. He reports on the sad state of Germany and awakens the warriors to take part in the sacred work. He gets the Powerful One to open his arms, whereupon under his feet a mountain raises him up to the level of the top of the cliffs on either side of the ravine and the two sides are no longer divided. Willehalm then tells the warriors to position themselves all down the sides of the new mountain. With the sword of the Wise Man, Willehalm opens a vein in his arm, fills his helmet with his blood, and gives it to all the warriors to drink blood-brotherhood.

The third act is set in a walled town. To one side of the town square is a tower so high that we cannot see the top. Gold and silver, artworks and precious objects, are piled up on the steps, and in the midst of the space is a bench covered with animal skins. The Imperator, now older and greyer, is haunted by all the corpses buried under his feet and worries that they will arise and take revenge. Tortured by his memories, he can no longer enjoy his booty, his wine, or his women. He alone hears a prophesy that the Germans will break the yoke that he has forged round the earth and that a strong man will emerge from among them. The custodian of the tower hears countless footsteps coming from the Rhine, but the Imperator believes that the Germans are powerless and that the German Soul is now an old woman. He has her brought out of the tower where she has been imprisoned but is horrified to find that she has remained a young and beautiful woman. When the Imperator's henchman tries to behead the Maiden, his sword shatters in two. As the Imperator and his troops begin to arm themselves, Willehalm appears on the battlements, lit up by the sun. He has come to avenge his mother and with one blow dispatches the Imperator. The Powerful One and the Wise One greet him as the bringer of light and justice and as the restorer of the German race. Willehalm is the saviour of the German Soul, he is the German king who places the Maiden before him on his saddle and rides off into the German lands.

In the fourth and final act Willehalm is now an old man with white hair and a white beard, communing with the German landscape but wondering if his people are happy. The German Soul appears to answer this question, telling him that the house he has built stands firm, that the Empire he unified stands strong. She launches into a hymn of praise, calling him 'King Willehalm, Father Willehalm, he who awakened the people, the counsellor of the land'.[36] Looking into her eyes, he bequeaths her to his beloved country as an inheritance and breathes his last in the Maiden's arms. The Maiden and the chorus sing of how he rests in the hearts of his people, crowned with laurels. Originally the play was supposed to have ended with the aged king being borne off to Valhalla to join the heroes, but fortunately, for this really would have been a step too far, the Kaiser's adjutant and friend Kuno von Moltke (1847–1923) and Georg von Hülsen were able to prevent this.

The parallels between the plot and the life and career of Wilhelm I are obvious. Napoleon—the Imperator—entered Berlin in October 1806 and the Prussian king Friedrich Wilhelm III fled to Königsberg in East Prussia. In 1807, his second son Wilhelm, then aged ten, became an officer in the Prussian army. The French continued to occupy Berlin until 1813 and forced Prussia to cede large portions of its territory. At the age of seventeen, Wilhelm took part in the Napoleonic wars, won the Iron Cross at the battle of Bar-sur-Aube in February 1814, and, with the victorious troops, marched into Paris. As a younger son, the army was an obvious career and he rose through the ranks, until he succeeded his childless brother as king of Prussia in 1861. Even then, he continued to command the army in the three wars of unification. The child Willehalm, defying the imperial conqueror who has trampled the Germans into the dust, is therefore a reflection of the young Wilhelm going to battle against the emperor of the French.

It is, however, still hard to understand how Wilhelm II could have considered this overblown tribute to his beloved grandfather in any way appropriate. Wagner's influence is unmistakeable in the high-flown language and the mythic dimension of the plot, but where Wagner shows us the limitations and failures of Siegfried and Wotan, Wildenbruch elevates Willehalm to the level of a visionary and heroic warrior saint. He alone has the courage to break the hold of the foreign usurper over the Germanic race, he alone recalls the other German warriors and princes to their duty and gives them back their courage. This was a monumental piece of tactlessness, for honoured guests at the performance were, among others, the kings of Saxony and Württemberg, the prince regent of Bavaria, and the grand duke of Baden. Their forebears had joined Napoleon's Confederation of the Rhine, so they were being castigated in the play for their pusillanimity. Only Prussia retained a vision of the German Soul, according to this version of history. Prince Chlodwig von Hohenlohe-Schillingsfürst (1819–1901), the Federal Chancellor and Wilhelm II's uncle, had spent the afternoon before the performance on a series of diplomatic visits to many of these princes, trying to iron out various clashes between what his own monarch was demanding and what they were prepared to accept. He described the play in his memoirs with the one word 'regrettable', recording that many people thought that Wilhelm II had collaborated on the composition.[37] Hildegard von Spitzemberg was not present at the performance but writes 'the drama "Willehalm" must be dreadful, an allegory laid on thick, banal, wearisome, in parts actually producing a comic effect.' She too reports that the emperor collaborated on it.[38]

The reviewer in the *Königlich Privilegierte Berlinische Zeitung* (usually called the *Vossische Zeitung*), writing the day after the performance, found the German pathos, artificial symbolism, and continuously thunderous declamation too hard to take and remarked that, after two hours in the theatre, they were still only halfway through.[39] In his journal *Die Zukunft* Maximilian Harden, the theatre critic and opponent of Wilhelm II, tore the play to shreds.[40] This was not difficult, for he only had to relate the plot to show how ridiculous it was. He wondered in his article why the Royal Theatre in Berlin had not put on one of the Prussian author Heinrich von Kleist's masterpieces for the gala performance—*Prinz Friedrich von Homburg* or *Die Hermannsschlacht*, both historical plays—, or why the novelist Theodor Fontane, the great observer of Berlin and Prussian life, had not been asked to write something specially. It is obvious why not. Kleist's and Fontane's subtlety in dissecting moral questions and their ironic and multi-layered depiction of society were not at all what was wanted. History and allegory were not to be exposed to the harsh light of irony and subtlety. In Wiesbaden and Berlin in 1897, in Vienna in 1908 or, as discussed in the previous chapter, in Sydenham in 1911 and Wembley in 1924, the members of the audience were to be lifted out of their everyday reality where they might ask too many awkward questions and utter too many awkward demands. They were invited simply to accept that the imperial regimes under which they were living were God's will.

Notes

1. Bagehot, *Constitution*, p. 9.
2. Hobsbawm, 'Mass-producing Tradition', pp. 267–8.
3. Grossegger, *Der Kaiser Huldigungs-Festzug'*, p. 251.
4. Wölfling, *Habsburger*.
5. Shedel, 'Emperor, Church and People; Unowsky, 'Staging Habsburg Patriotism'.
6. Unowsky, *Pomp and Politics*, pp. 94–5.
7. Unowsky, *Pomp and Politics*, p. 100.
8. Unowsky, *Pomp and Politics*, p. 158.
9. Berger, *Habsburg*, p. 65.
10. Berger, *Habsburg*, p. 107.
11. Grossenegger, *Der Kaiser Huldigungs-Festzug'*, p. 29.
12. Brandt, 'Franz Joseph I'.
13. Herzig, *Viribus Unitis*, pp. 112–14.
14. Stickler, '"Erneuerung der deutschen Kaiserwürde"', p. 342.

15. Junk and Schiller, *Kaiser Jubiläums-Festlichkeiten*; Grossegger, *Der Kaiser-Huldigungs-Festzug*; Emmer, *Sechzig Jahre*; Hahn, *Felix Austria*.

16. Kraus, *Die Fackel*, 5 June 1908, p. 1.

17. Grossenegger, *Der Kaiser-Huldigungs-Festzug*, p. 37.

18. Grossenegger, *Der Kaiser-Huldigungs-Festzug*, n.pag.

19. Unowsky, *Pomp and Politics*, p. 180.

20. Thun-Salm, *Des Kaisers Traum*.

21. Unowsky, *Pomp and Politics*, p. 84.

22. Bruckmüller, 'National Consciousness'.

23. Unowsky, *Pomp and Politics*, p. 87.

24. *Neue Freie Presse*, 3 December 1908, p. 11.

25. Kraus, *Die Fackel*, 22 May 1908.

26. Bösch, 'Das Zeremoniell der Kaisergeburtstage'; Martin Kohlrausch, 'Monarchische Repräsentation'; Kohlrausch, *Der Monarch im Skandal*; Kohlrausch, 'Zwischen Tradition und Innovation'.

27. Wilhelm II, *Die Reden*, vol. II, p. 98.

28. Kleiner, *Staatsaktion im Wunderland*.

29. Kleiner, 'Der Kaiser als Ereignis', p. 356.

30. Kleiner, *Staatsaktion im Wunderland*, p. 170.

31. Wilhelm II, *Reden*, vol. II, p. 40.

32. Spitzemberg, *Das Tagebuch*, p. 352.

33. Röhl, *Wilhelm II. The Kaiser's Personal Monarchy*, p. 864.

34. Förster, *Kulturpolitik im Dienst der Legitimation*, pp. 62–4.

35. Wildenbruch, *Willehalm*, p. 33.

36. Wildenbruch, *Willehalm*, p. 108.

37. Hohenlohe-Schillingsfürst, *Denkwürdigkeiten*, pp. 321–2.

38. Spitzemberg, *Tagebuch*, p. 355.

39. *Vossische Zeitung*, 23 March 1897.

40. Harden, *Die Zukunft*, vol. 18, pp. 571–6.

XI

Ending and Remembering

From the beginning of the nineteenth century and into the twentieth, as we have seen, the emperors (and one empress) of Austria, Brazil, France, Germany, India, and Mexico used coronations, ceremonial, costumes, court organization, rules of precedence, medals and honours, portraiture, statuary, photography, film, and even religion to project their power and craft their imperial image. They redesigned the urban landscape in order to create imperial cities, they built triumphal arches, museums, and dynastic monuments, and they used such theatrical forms as the costumed procession, the historical pageant, and the stage to create a past which justified their present. They increased their prestige by staging large-scale exhibitions of goods and inventions, in which they also paraded their colonial conquests and, in some cases, their colonial subjects.

Ending—The Debit Side

War was what brought most of these imperial regimes to an end, even though in three of them—Austria, Britain, and Germany—dynastic succession seemed to promise indefinite continuity. The first French Empire came to an end in 1815 at Waterloo and the second French Empire in 1870 at Sedan, though Napoleon III did not abdicate until 1871. Both Mexican emperors were shot by the armies of their opponents, Agustín in 1824 and Maximilian in 1867. World War I brought the Austrian and the Prussian empires to an end. On 11 November 1918, the Armistice was signed in Compiègne in France. On 9 November 1918 the Imperial German Chancellor, Prince Max von Baden (1867–1929), had announced the abdication of Wilhelm II as German emperor and king of Prussia. Some weeks later, on 28 November 1918, from his refuge at Amerongen in the Netherlands, Wilhelm signed the Document of Abdication, abdicating his throne 'for all time to come'. Karl I, emperor of Austria, Károly IV, king of Hungary (1887–1922), refused to abdicate and signed a Declaration of Renunciation on 11 November. Two days later, in the Habsburg hunting lodge of Eckartsau to the east of Vienna, where he and his family had taken refuge, he signed a similar declaration with respect to his Hungarian crown but again did not abdicate.[1]

Franz Joseph, emperor of Austria, had died on 21 November 1916 after a reign of almost seventy years. His son and heir Archduke Rudolf had killed himself in 1889 and his nephew Archduke Franz Ferdinand, the next in line to succeed him,

Projecting Imperial Power: New Nineteenth-Century Emperors and the Public Sphere. Helen Watanabe-O'Kelly, Oxford University Press (2021). © Helen Watanabe-O'Kelly. DOI: 10.1093/oso/9780198802471.003.0012

was assassinated in 1914. This meant that his great-nephew Archduke Karl succeeded him at the age of twenty-nine. He and his consort Zita, Princess of Bourbon-Parma (1892–1989), were crowned king and queen of Hungary according to the ancient Hungarian ceremonial in Budapest on 30 December 1916.[2] Two years later Karl, Zita, and their five children (they went on to have three more) were forced into exile, first in Switzerland and then in Madeira, where Karl died on 1 April 1922. Wilhelm II, meanwhile, after his stay in Amerongen took up residence in 1920 in a small manor house in the Netherlands called Huis Doorn where he lived until his death in 1941 (Figure 44). The reluctance of the Austrian and German emperors to accept constitutional government and parliamentary democracy and their excessive esteem for the military contributed to the outbreak of World War I and the growth of national socialism that followed later.

Walther Rathenau (1867–1922), physicist, industrialist, writer, and German foreign minister at the time of his assassination in 1922, in 1919 in *Der Kaiser* (The Emperor), gave his summing up of the personality and the era of Wilhelm II:

> The era has come to an end in which a handful of elevated beings in warlike uniforms and solicitous morning coats hand out life and death, in the name of their peoples and of humanity, as they think, but in reality in the name of their classes and the interests of those classes, in the name of an old politics of balance of power...

Figure 44 Bust of Wilhelm II in front of Huis Doorn where he spent the last twenty-one years of his life. Marble. Photo © Ekkehard Henschke

He goes on to say that 'at this moment we Germans are defenceless, powerless, humiliated and violated, wiped out politically.'[3]

The wars that the emperors engaged in throughout the period led to a horrific loss of life. The Napoleonic Wars alone, at the start of the nineteenth century, caused at least three million casualties on the battlefield. The Crimean War from 1853 to 1856 led to the pointless loss of at least 715,000 men, more through disease than combat. 95,000 of these casualties were citizens of the French Empire. Agustín de Iturbide rose to become emperor of Mexico through the army and Maximilian of Austria was sustained, during his brief period as emperor of Mexico in the 1860s, by French troops. Pedro II of Brazil fought wars against Uruguay and Paraguay between 1864 and 1870, in which more than 50,000 Brazilians are thought to have died. Bismarck achieved the hegemony of the kings of Prussia over the other German territories by fighting three so-called wars of unification against Denmark in 1864, Austria in 1866, and France in 1870–71 respectively. Two million German soldiers are estimated as having died in World War I, led into war by their emperor Wilhelm II. Franz Joseph led his people into war against Prussia in 1866 and into World War I in 1914. In the latter, one and a half million of his subjects died.[4]

Not all our six empires ended as the immediate consequence of war. The Brazilian Empire came to a peaceful end when Pedro II abdicated and went into exile in 1889. But what of India, which on the face of it also ended peacefully when, on 28 February 1948, the British army departed through the Gateway of India in Bombay and sailed back to Britain? George V, king-emperor throughout World War I, had celebrated his Silver Jubilee in 1935 and died in January 1936. His eldest son succeeded him as Edward VIII in 1936, but he was never crowned and abdicated at the end of that year. In 1937 Edward's younger brother ascended the throne as George VI and it seemed as if the Empire of India might last for another seventy years at least. However, as Alex von Tunzelmann puts it, 'the mechanisms of Empire had primed India for revolution', whatever comforting fictions Britain now tells itself, and this ultimately ensured that the British had to allow the Indians to govern themselves.[5]

One of the many factors in the demise of British hegemony over India was the huge loss of life through man-made famines. Numbers vary according to the source, but at least six million and perhaps as many as eight million died in the 1876–79 famine, at the very moment that Queen Victoria was being pro-claimed empress of India at the 1877 durbar, and about the same number died in the Bengal famine of 1896–1900 shortly before her death in 1901. Maurice Talmeyr, writing about what he calls 'the English Indian pavilion' at the Paris Exposition Universelle of 1900, compared it to a department store, an opulent bazaar, that displayed beautiful objects but ignored the other side of the colonial coin, the famine victims: 'India is not just a warehouse, it is a graveyard ... a field of death spreads out behind the shop'.[6] In World War I at least 70,000 Indians died fighting for Britain, to be followed by 87,000 who lost their lives in World War II. In 1919, three things happened that strengthened the push for independence. The first was the passing into law on 21 March 1919 of the Anarchical and Revolutionary Crimes Act of 1919, one of two proposed so-called Rowlatt Acts. This continued the provisions of wartime martial law into peacetime, allowing those accused of political crimes to be tried without a jury and without the right of appeal. It allowed trials to take place behind closed doors and to admit evidence that did not meet the standards of the Indian Evidence Act. Suspects could also be interned without trial for renewable periods of up to a year. The second was the infamous Amritsar Massacre on 13 April 1919, in which Brigadier-General Reginald Dyer (1864–1927) commanded troops of the Indian army, Indians themselves, to fire into a group of some 15,000 unarmed peaceful citizens, many of them celebrating a local festival. They had gathered in an enclosed garden called the Jallianwallah Bagh in Amritsar and were not ordered to disperse before shooting began. Estimates differ as to how many were killed, with numbers ranging from 379 to 1,500. At least another thousand were injured. There had been riots in the city a few days before, and Derek Sayer shows that Dyer had decided to shoot before ever arriving in the garden.[7] He had also arranged a ritual humiliation in order to avenge an attack on Miss Sherwood, the manager of the City Mission School, during these riots. Dyer

> closed the street where she had been assaulted, erected a whipping triangle at one end, posted pickets and ordered that any person wishing to pass through the street (including its residents) had to do so on all fours. In practice people had to squirm through the filth of the lane on their bellies, prodded along by the boots and bayonets of the soldiers. Prisoners were deliberately routed through the 'Crawling Lane'.[8]

Even Sir Michael O'Dwyer, the tough governor of the Punjab, found the 'Crawling Lane' unacceptable. Insult was added to injury when Dyer was defended by many Anglo-Indians at the time and subsequently by members of the British Parliament in the House of Commons debate on 8 July 1920. The poet, painter, and Nobel prizewinner Rabindranath Tagore returned his knighthood in protest.

The third major event of 1919 that impacted negatively on Indians was the Government of India Act which was given royal assent on 23 December.[9] Indians had hoped for greater autonomy as a reward for having supported Britain not just with men but with money and supplies during the war, but the act only allowed for limited self-government. It instituted a diarchy, that is, a dual form of government in which provincial councils had local control over what were called 'transferred' matters such as agriculture, health, and education, while the viceroy remained in control of everything else: defence, military matters, foreign affairs, and communications. The Imperial Legislative Council was enlarged and reformed and had two chambers, the Legislative Assembly and the Council of State, but in the lower chamber only two thirds of the members were elected, while in the Council of State slightly over half were elected and the franchise was in any case limited to those paying a certain sum in tax. The viceroy retained the power to veto any bill passed by the Legislative Council and had the right to enact bills of his own. The Council could only vote on one third of the expenditure of the government and the viceroy could restore any grant that the Council had thrown out or refused. This was in sharp contrast to the greater autonomy of Australia, Canada, New Zealand, Newfoundland, and South Africa, which were classed as dominions and not colonies. British officials' rule in India was

> predicated on their construction of Indians as unfitted to govern themselves. The Mutiny, which loomed large in their imagination, was a recurrent symbol of what could happen when order broke down; a symbol too of Indian untrustworthiness and British vulnerability.[10]

A third of India was still ruled by the native princes, of whom two are represented in Figure 45. Their problem, as Sunil Khilnani puts it, is that they 'were required to be at once conservative and liberal, to blend eastern splendor and western constitutional propriety, to sport turbans and read Bagehot' and that they were expected to inhabit a 'twilight world of spectacular impotence'.[11] They were finally given a forum in which to articulate their views collectively when the Chamber of Princes was established in 1920 after the Government of India Act. It first met on 8 February 1921 and initially consisted of 120 members. Before 1920, 'as princes on sufferance they could not afford to defy their colonial masters on any issue the latter defined as being of some consequence.'[12] Of the 120 members, 108 represented the more significant states and were members in their own right, while the remaining twelve seats represented a further 127 states. That left 327 minor states unrepresented and it is worth noting that the important rulers of Baroda, Gwalior, and Holkar declined to join.

The provisions of the Government of India Act led to widespread protests and riots and, in 1920, Mohandas Karamchand Gandhi (1869–1948) became the leader of the Indian National Congress and formulated his policy of non-violent non-cooperation. In 1929 India was refused dominion status by the British. In December 1929, Jawaharlal Nehru (1889–1964) was elected president of the Congress party and at midnight on 31 December 1929 he declared Indian independence and hoisted the flag of India on the banks of the river Ravi in Lahore. On 26 January 1930 Congress issued a public declaration of sovereignty and self-rule, called Purna Swaraj. Two months later, on 12 March 1930, Gandhi set out on his famous Salt March, walking 390 kilometres to the coast, to challenge British salt taxes in India. He and his followers, increasing in number all the time, reached the coast at Dandi in Gujarat on 6 April 1930. Here Gandhi proceeded to

Figure 45 Sir Bhupinder Singh, Maharaja of Patiala, and Sir Jagatjit Singh, Maharaja of Kapurthala, 20 July 1918. Photograph. Private Collection Peter Newark Pictures/ Bridgeman Images

make salt in defiance of British law in India. A year later, New Delhi was inaugurated in all its massive grandeur, but it was only a matter of time before the British would have to leave. The myth of the benefits that Britain has brought to India, another comforting British fiction, is not accepted by such Indian historians and commentators as Sunil Khilnani and Shashi Tharoor.

Remembering—Cities and Statues

It is seventy years since the British Raj came to an end, a hundred years since the demise of the Austrian and German empires, and even longer since those of Brazil, France, and Mexico. These regimes should by rights be forgotten, but their often monumental physical presence is used today in ways that keep the memory of their imperial past alive.

The first of these is that many imperial buildings have been repurposed and now provide an imposing backdrop for the democracies that have succeeded them. The Hofburg, the palace in the centre of Vienna, is the residence and workplace of the president of the Federal Republic of Austria. The Reichstag building is now the parliament of the Federal Republic of Germany. Its glass dome, designed by Norman Foster for the newly renovated building and inaugurated in 1999, is a symbol of Federal Germany's present-day democracy and transparency. The president of the French Republic lives and works in the Élysée Palace in Paris, where Napoleon I abdicated for the second time in 1815. The president of the Republic of India resides in what Lutyens designed as the Viceroy's House and which he also uses for state functions. Indian government ministries inhabit the grand secretariat buildings in front of it, while the Lok Sabha, the lower house of the Indian parliament, meets in Herbert Baker's Council House.

The second thing that keeps the memory of empire alive is tourism, because some cities are imperial creations to such an extent that even travellers who are not interested in history cannot avoid learning about the imperial past. Visitors to Paris encounter Napoleon I in the Arc de Triomphe du Carrousel near the Louvre, in the much larger Arc de Triomphe at the Étoile commissioned by him in 1806, in his mausoleum in the Invalides, and in urban features called after his victories such as the Pont d'Iéna and the Gare d'Austerlitz. If they visit the Louvre, they will see David's monumental painting of Napoleon crowning Josephine in 1804 and, if they go to the Louvre shop, they will be able to purchase an umbrella with David's depiction of Napoleon on horseback leaping over the Alps and a USB stick in the shape of the emperor. They will, of course, walk around the broad boulevards, squares, and parks of Paris, the creation during the 1850s and 1860s of Napoleon III and his Prefect of the Seine, Baron Haussmann. Vienna actively markets itself on the basis of its imperial past. In the arrival hall at the airport, travellers are greeted with huge transparencies of artworks from the great museums created in the 1880s and artefacts displayed in the Imperial Treasury in the Hofburg. Here, alongside the medieval vestments and coronation insignia of the Holy Roman Emperors, the costumes that were specially created for the emperor of Austria in 1830 are displayed. To visit the Hofburg in Vienna is to be urged to buy a ticket to visit the imperial apartments and the Sissi Museum, devoted to Empress Elisabeth. Everything from fridge magnets to biscuit cutters can be purchased in the shape of the empress, and Franz Joseph's portrait adorns everything from matchboxes to spoons. Pedro II's Imperial Palace in Petrópolis is usually packed with visitors and school groups, come to see not just his study but the imperial crown and toucan collar of the Brazilian Empire. Visitors to Mexico City go to Chapultepec Castle, in its present form largely a creation of Maximilian and his consort Carlota, whose life-size portraits are prominently on display. Anyone visiting Mumbai, whether a foreigner or an Indian, takes a selfie in front of its best-known monument, the Gateway of India, built to honour King-Emperor George V, in the same way that they visit the Victoria Memorial Hall in Calcutta and are photographed in front of the statue of Queen-Empress Victoria. Visitors to Berlin, having reached the end of Unter den Linden, usually visit the Cathedral with its Hohenzollern Burial Vault, or the Kaiser Wilhelm Memorial Church, now in its ruined state a war memorial, where the mosaics and bas-reliefs that Wilhelm II installed to glorify his grandfather and his dynasty can still be seen. The Victory Column or Siegessäule, with its golden victory figure on top and its mosaics around the base depicting the Hohenzollerns as the heirs to the medieval emperor Friedrich Barbarossa, dominates the skyline of central Berlin.

While tourists and other travellers can have an emotionally distanced response to imperial vestiges in countries not their own, how do Indians react to the remains of the British Raj in their own country? According to Maria Misra, the Raj has become 'commoditised' for Indian middle-class consumers, who like to stay in the hill station towns of Ootacamund and Simla with their archetypically British architecture and to eat in restaurants with names like 'The Solar Topee'.[13] The Raj and its customs have become exotic and therefore harmless. This can be observed in the Imperial Hotel, an art deco jewel from 1932 built as part of Lutyens's New Delhi and heavily used by well-to-do Indians. Here, life-size portraits of viceroys and Indian princes wearing rows of British medals adorn the principal rooms, and virtually every wall is covered in portraits, photographs, and documents relating to the Raj. Indian businessmen can enjoy a working lunch in front of these memorabilia because the regime that is on show has vanished and the guests need not think too deeply about the princes' collaboration in keeping that regime in power. Misra also points out how popular the British bungalow has become as a dwelling and how the colonial club, 'the archetypal symbol of British racial arrogance', has now been appropriated by Indians.[14]

The third and strongest reminder of the empires that have gone is their statues. Statues embody power and give it a face. A statue erected to a ruler or other public person is a political act which places the stamp of approval on the character and deeds of that person, imposing a certain vision on the viewer by elevating the subject of the statue above normal human beings. It literally places him on a pedestal, turns him (most often him) into a hero and promotes him as someone to be admired and emulated. Erecting a statue says as much about the regime or the person who commissions it as about the person being portrayed. When Maximilian, emperor of Mexico, unveiled a statue by Antonio Piatti (active in Mexico from 1855) of the freedom fighter and priest José María Morelos y Pavón (1765–1815) in 1865 in Mexico City, he, a newcomer to the country, was giving himself legitimacy by presenting himself as the guardian of Mexico's history and its struggle for independence. After Maximilian fell from power, the statue was moved not once but twice to less prominent positions.[15] Maximilian also planned to have a statue of another freedom fighter Vicente Guerrero (1782–1831) cast in bronze by Miguel Noreña (1839–1894), but he ran out of time to realize this project.[16] When Wilhelm II's enormous monument to Wilhelm I, whom he was trying to establish in his subjects' minds as 'Wilhelm the Great', was inaugurated in the centre of Berlin in 1897 on Wilhelm I's hundredth birthday, it was as much a statement about Wilhelm II's vision of his own role and importance as German emperor as it was a celebration of his grandfather.

Statues are often erected posthumously, which means that they are an interpretation of the past that is projected into the future, often underlined by the iconography, the inscriptions, and by carefully chosen allegorical or historical figures which set the interpretation in stone. Each of the first three emperors of Austria imposed an interpretation on one of their predecessors by erecting a statue to them in a prominent position in the centre of Vienna. Franz II/I, the last Holy Roman Emperor and first emperor of Austria, commissioned an equestrian statue by Franz Anton Zauner (1746–1822) of his uncle Joseph II (1741–90), his 'second father', as the inscription says. It was unveiled on 24 November 1807 on what is now called the Josefsplatz, a square behind the Hofburg.[17] The statue is inspired by that of Marcus Aurelius on the Capitoline Hill in Rome—an apt choice, since Marcus Aurelius died in Vienna in 180 CE. Joseph wears Roman dress and a laurel wreath and holds his hand out horizontally in a gesture that is both protective and commanding. Reliefs on the pedestal depict Joseph as the promoter of trade and of agriculture, and sixteen medallions on the four pillars which hold the chains around the monument bear witness to his tolerance, his charity and, as an Enlightenment monarch, his interest in science and learning. Joseph's reforms, which were not always popular with his subjects, are here being given the gloss of the actions of a benevolent ruler. Franz I had expressed a wish to be immortalized himself in a statue during his lifetime, but it was not until after his death in 1835 that Chancellor Metternich allowed his son Ferdinand I to erect one.[18] Ferdinand chose the Milanese sculptor Pompeo Marchesi (1790–1858) over possible Austrian candidates. The foundation stone was laid in the Innerer Burgplatz in the Hofburg on 18 October 1843, the anniversary of the Battle of Leipzig in 1813 in which Franz had taken part. The finished monument was finally unveiled on 16 June 1846. Franz stands on a tall pedestal wearing a toga, stretching out his hand to his people as lawgiver, connecting this statue to that of his uncle. Four seated life-size female figures represent Faith, Strength, Peace, and Justice, while reliefs on the plinth depict science, trade, mining, smelting, agriculture, cattle-rearing, art, and heroism. The inscription on the front of the pedestal is a quotation from Emperor Franz's will: 'to my peoples I bequeath my love.' Franz is depicted as the father of his people and as the 'Friedenskaiser', the emperor of peace, who brought the Napoleonic Wars to an end in 1814.

Forty-two years later, in 1888, Ferdinand's nephew Emperor Franz Joseph erected a monument to his great-grandmother Empress Maria Theresia (1717–80) on the fortieth anniversary of his accession to the imperial throne. Placed in the space between the two new museums, the Art History Museum and the National History Museum, the seated figure of the empress by Caspar

Zumbusch (1830–1915), six metres high, is elevated high above the viewer on a plinth, making the entire monument twenty metres high (see Figure 34). It was unveiled on 13 May 1888, the empress's birthday, in the presence of the whole court. She holds a sceptre and a copy of the Pragmatic Sanction, the legal document dating to 1713 that allowed her to reign as King of Hungary and of Bohemia and to rule in the Habsburg territories, even if, as a woman, she could not be elected Holy Roman Emperor. Four life-size equestrian figures of the most important generals of her reign are placed at each of the four corners of the plinth beneath her, while nineteen other standing figures of scientists, officials, military officers, and composers are located at the base of the pedestal. She is depicted as a unifying figure, the mother of all the nations in the Empire, and she and her era are also presented as the embodiment of the Enlightenment, which brings us full circle to the statue of Joseph II, her son. Summing up these monuments, Telesko stresses the extent to which the emperors of Austria looked at everything through what he calls 'dynastic spectacles', not making a distinction between the Holy Roman Empire and the Empire of Austria.[19] It was almost as if they were giving Maria Theresia the anachronistic title of 'empress of Austria', in a second *translatio imperii* transferring the imperial title from the Holy Roman emperors to the emperors of Austria, just as the title had been transferred from the Roman emperors in the first place.

Whoever commissions a statue cannot control its meaning forever. This changes if the political climate changes, as we have seen in the United States and the United Kingdom in 2020 with statues commemorating those who promoted and profited from slavery. When Emperor Ferdinand removed press censorship at the beginning of the 1848 revolution, this early success for the revolutionaries was celebrated in Vienna in front of the statue of Emperor Joseph, and it was decorated with flowers, with the black, red, and gold German flag, and with a sign saying 'press freedom'.[20] In contrast, when the revolutionaries were ordered to surrender by Prince Windisch-Grätz on 23 October 1848, Franz I's statue was attacked because it was regarded as symbolizing state authority.[21]

A telling example of how historical figures and their effigies can represent different things to different people in different generations and how they can be used for different political purposes is illustrated by the figure of Napoleon I on the Place Vendôme in Paris. The original idea came from Napoleon himself while First Consul. In 1803, he proposed erecting a column to celebrate the deeds of the French army modelled on Trajan's column in Rome. It was to be surmounted by a statue of Charlemagne. This proposal was not implemented, but, after the victory at Austerlitz in 1805, Vivant Denon (1747–1825), the Director of Museums, revived the proposal. A stone column was erected covered with bronze plaques depicting the campaign spiralling all the way to the top of the forty-two-metre-high monument. They are made from the 1,200 Austrian and Russian cannon captured on the battlefield. The column was crowned by the statue by

Antoine-Denis Chaudet (1763–1810) of Napoleon in the costume of a Roman emperor, wearing a laurel wreath and holding a small winged Victory on a globe in one hand and a lowered sword in the other. The monument was unveiled on 15 August 1810, Napoleon's birthday. Four years later, on 31 March 1814, the allied troops who had defeated Napoleon entered Paris. The statue was removed and melted down and replaced with a flag depicting the *fleur de lys*, the symbol of the Bourbons, who were now restored to power in the person of Louis XVIII. In 1831, during the so-called July monarchy, the new king Louis-Philippe (1773–1850), recognizing the strength of support for Napoleon among the French people, decided to replace the figure of Napoleon on the top of the column—not as a Roman *imperator* but as the *petit-caporal* that he had been in life. Charles-Émile Seurre (1798–1858) depicted him therefore wearing his characteristic bicorne, long overcoat, and Legion of Honour and striking his characteristic pose with his left hand stuck inside his waistcoat. During the same period, Louis-Philippe had Napoleon's remains repatriated from St Helena, and when they arrived in Paris in 1840, they passed under the Arc de Triomphe that Napoleon had commissioned in 1806 but that Louis-Philippe had caused to be completed. Napoleon's remains were brought to Les Invalides, where a splendid mausoleum was designed for them by Louis Visconti, though it was not yet ready. At the same time, the king was creating a history museum in the Palace of Versailles, in which Napoleon I's life and deeds are depicted in room after room on enormous canvases.[22]

The representation of his uncle in modern dress was not sufficiently heroic for Napoleon III when he became emperor in 1852. He commissioned Auguste Dumont (1801–84) to make a copy of Chaudet's sculpture of Napoleon I in Roman dress and had Seurre's figure in modern dress placed on a pedestal in the middle of the crossing in Paris called the 'Rondpoint de Courbevoie'. When the Second Empire came to an end in 1871, however, the Commune pulled the column down and smashed it. After the Commune was suppressed, the new government decided to repair and rebuild the column and restore Dumont's statue of Napoleon I in Roman dress, unveiling it on 28 December 1875. Naturally, this was controversial. Prince Pierre-Napoléon Bonaparte, Napoleon I's nephew, who had been elected deputy for Corsica after 1848 and claimed to be a republican, demanded in the National Assembly that the statue on the column should be of his uncle in modern dress,[23] while in January 1874, when it had already been decided what form the statue would take, another deputy asked why the imperial legend was being revived and proposed placing a statue of France on the column. Meanwhile, the figure of Napoleon in modern dress had been removed from the Rondpoint de Courbevoie to keep it safe during the Commune, and, after several vicissitudes, in 1911 was placed where it now stands, looking down into the courtyard of the Invalides.

Louis-Philippe's restoration of Napoleon I's statue, ten years after his death and sixteen years after his defeat at Waterloo, was a gesture of reconciliation towards the Bonapartists, which had only become possible because Napoleon himself no longer posed a threat and could now become a dehumanized myth. Something similar happened in Brazil in the case of Emperor Pedro II, who had been deposed in 1889 and who had died in exile in 1891. Lilia Moritz Schwarcz relates how, almost from the moment of his death the last Brazilian emperor began to be 'recovered not as a ruler but as a mystical, sacred being'.[24] In 1892, the Historical and Geographical Institute which he had founded started a campaign to have his mortal remains returned to Brazil and in 1916 the then President Venceslau Brás agreed to permit this on the centenary of Brazilian independence in 1922. In the meantime, on 5 February 1911, a life-size statue of the emperor by Jean Magrou (1869–1945) was unveiled in Petrópolis (Figure 46). It depicts him towards the end of his life, wearing ordinary attire and seated in an armchair with his legs crossed, his finger in a large book with another pile of books by his chair. This is not a representation of a timeless heroic figure nor of a powerful emperor, but of the wise, scholarly father of his people. It presents the man rather than the emperor, and in its charm is reminiscent of the bronze statue by Georg Leisek

Figure 46 Jean Magrou, Pedro II as scholar-king in Petrópolis. 1911. Bronze on granite base. Photo © Ekkehard Henschke

(1869–1936) of Franz Joseph of Austria towards the end of his life dressed as a huntsman, bare knees and all. He is depicted as though coming out of the forest and is standing on top of a craggy rock, with his staff in his hand and his gun slung on his back. At the bottom of the rock lies the magnificent deer he has supposedly tracked and shot. The monument, paid for by his fellow hunters, was unveiled on 24 August 1910 in Bad Ischl, his favourite summer residence, just as Petrópolis was Pedro's.

As 1922 approached, other statues of D. Pedro began to be erected on various public buildings in Rio de Janeiro and, in September 1922, his remains and those of his consort made a triumphal return to Brazil, with cannon sounding as the coffins were taken off the ship. At first the remains were housed in the cathedral in Rio, while the cathedral in Petrópolis was still under construction. The president declared 2 December 1925, D. Pedro's hundredth birthday, a national holiday and the emperor's grandchildren and great-grandchildren came to Brazil for it. 'Even traditional republicans were rehabilitating the emperor', writes Moritz Schwarz, for they were able to separate in their minds the emperor from the Empire.[25] His remains and those of the empress were finally transferred to the Imperial Mausoleum in Petrópolis Cathedral in 1939, where life-size marble effigies adorn the tombs of the imperial couple. In 1971, the remains of Princess Isabel and her husband, Gaston, Count d'Eu, joined them and their tombs lie on either side of those of the imperial couple. In 1972, the remains of Pedro I, of his second wife, Amélie of Leuchtenberg, and of his first wife Leopoldine of Austria were transferred from Lisbon and from Rio de Janeiro respectively to a specially built crypt and Catholic chapel underneath the Ipiranga Monument in São Paolo, the towering monument to Brazilian independence erected in 1922 on the centenary of independence.

This reconciliation with a departed, but in many ways admirable, monarch and imperial dynasty can heal old wounds. What is one to make of a popular movement that resulted in replacing a monument to the first German emperor, Wilhelm I, as recently as 1993 and which thereby opened such wounds? This monument was and is again sited at the confluence of the Rhine and the Mosel in Koblenz in a spot known as the 'Deutsches Eck' or German corner. Shortly after Wilhelm I's death in 1888, a general feeling arose among the German population that he should be commemorated in a major public monument for his role in founding the German Empire and bringing about German unity. This would, incidentally, be one of more than three hundred monuments to Wilhelm I, of which fifty-nine were equestrian statues. Koblenz, situated in the Rhine Province that had been ceded to Prussia in 1815, was associated with Wilhelm I, for he had resided there as the military governor of the Rhineland from 1850 to 1858.[26] His grandson Wilhelm II decided therefore that Koblenz would be a suitable site for the monument. A tongue of land was built between the two rivers, a million marks was collected by public subscription, and a square fortress-like hall twenty-three metres high in front of a semi-circular colonnade was constructed as the base, on which an equestrian statue by Emil Hundrieser (1846–1911), fourteen metres high and made of copper, was placed. The architectural elements were designed by Bruno Schmitz (1858–1916), who was responsible for a number of other huge monuments in Germany including the 'Völkerschlachtsdenkmal', commemorating the Battle of Leipzig of 1813 and inaugurated on its centenary in 1913. The monument on the Deutsches Eck was unveiled by Wilhelm II on 31 August 1897, his grandfather's hundredth birthday, the same year that another imposing monument to Wilhelm I was inaugurated in Berlin, discussed in chapter VII. Hundrieser depicted Wilhelm I on horseback, wearing a general's uniform and accompanied by a winged female figure holding out the imperial crown. An inscription on the base refers to 'Wilhelm the Great', the title that his grandson tried to promote. A quotation from the Koblenz writer Max von Schendorf (1783–1817) proclaimed: 'the empire will never be destroyed if you are united and true', dedicating the monument, therefore, not just to Wilhelm I but to the German Empire. After that ceased to exist in 1918, it bore witness to the glory that was gone and symbolized the sense of German humiliation expressed by Rathenau quoted above. It is no surprise, therefore, that the National Socialists used the site in 1934 and 1936 as a suitable backdrop for a public meeting and a military parade respectively.

The monument survived most of World War II intact until, on 16 March 1945, an American grenade hit the statue and destroyed it. After the war, the mangled copper was removed and ultimately stolen, and there were many suggestions as to what to do with the huge architectural structure that remained. In 1953, it was officially declared a national monument to German unity, at a time when Germany was divided into west and east. After reunification in 1989, however, the monument had lost its purpose. Already in 1987, Dr Werner Theisen (1927–1993), a lawyer and the wealthy publisher of the local newspaper, the *Rhein-Zeitung*, announced that he and his wife had decided, at a cost of three million marks, to have the statue reconstructed as a gift to the city of Koblenz to mark their thirtieth wedding anniversary and Dr Theisen's own sixtieth birthday. This plan to restore a monument commemorating a regime that had been achieved by three wars—all of them against nations that were now Germany's European partners—and that had contributed to the catastrophe of World War I aroused great controversy at both national and local level.[27] Since he was spending his own money and had enshrined the gift in law, Theisen went ahead anyway and commissioned the sculptor Raymond Kittl to make the statue in bronze, even before permission had been given either by the Land or the city for it to be erected at the Deutsches Eck. The Social Democrat government of the Land of Rhineland-Palatinate particularly objected to honouring a prince who had given the order to shoot the demonstrators of 1848 in the streets of Berlin and who had promulgated the Anti-Socialist Law that had been in force in the Empire between 1878 and 1888. The Protestant Church also opposed the recreation of the statue. The people of Koblenz, however, were broadly in favour of it, saying that it would boost tourism in the area! After much consultation with lawyers and monuments experts, the Land realized that it could not prevent the restoration of the statue and so presented the city with the site, washing its hands of the affair, and donating 1.1 million marks to prepare the site for the statue which, now made of bronze, was much heavier than the original. Wilhelm I, his huge steed, and the angel of victory holding the imperial crown were lifted into position on 2 September 1993, the anniversary of the Battle of Sedan in which Prussia had defeated the French army under Napoleon III in 1870 (Figure 47). This was the battle that led to the foundation of the German Empire and the destruction of the French Empire and which had been celebrated in Germany each year until 1918 as 'Sedantag'. The official inauguration of the restored monument took place on 25 September 1993, and the whole episode gave rise to a number of appalled reactions. Stefan Bouillon, reviewing the monument for the art history journal *Kunstchronik*, wrote: 'In its iconography and in the history of its inception and influence the equestrian statue of Wilhelm I is tied to values and to thinking which

Figure 47 The copy by Raymond Kittl, erected in 1993 at the Deutsches Eck, Koblenz, of Emil Hundrieser's 1897 equestrian statue of Wilhelm I, German Emperor. Bronze. Photo © Ekkehard Henschke

are in conflict with the moral order of the German constitution.'[28] It was the selective treatment of history that upset Udo Mainzer, as the title of his article indicates.[29] Why, he asks, are long-gone militaristic rulers on their steeds being solemnly restored in what was West Germany—Koblenz was not the only site in the Rhineland where an imperial statue was replaced—, while, at a cost of millions, monuments to such significant figures as Lenin, Marx, and Engels are being torn down in what was East Germany? The answer has to be that monuments, like history, are the creation of the victors.

The commonest European solution to the problem of monuments expressive of a regime that is anathema to its successors is to destroy them. The authorities in the GDR blew up the monument to Wilhelm I next to the City Palace in Berlin in the winter of 1949–50, so that only the base of the terrace remains, and in 1966, the fiftieth anniversary of the Easter Rising, Nelson's Pillar in Dublin was blown up by nationalists, just as they had previously blown up other statues of British monarchs in Ireland. Another solution is to export unwanted statues. In 1948, the three-metre-high bronze statue of Queen Victoria by the Irish sculptor John Hughes (1865–1941), unveiled in 1908, was removed from in front of the Irish parliament and put into storage. It was sent to Sydney, Australia, in 1986, where it stands in front of the beautifully restored Queen Victoria Building.

India has followed a different path in dealing with its monuments.[30] Travel up the Hooghly River from Calcutta to Barrackpore, the location of the summer residence of the governors-general and viceroys, and you will come to Old Flagstaff House, a small villa in the grounds of Barrackpore House. In 1815, in its leafy garden, the First Lord Minto (Viceroy from 1807 to1813) built a Greek temple, the Temple of Fame, as a memorial to twenty-four officers who died during the conquest of Java and what is now Mauritius. Here, in front of the temple stands the bronze statue of George V by William McMillan (1887–1977) dating to 1938 and at the side, tucked under the eaves, is the marble statue of Sir William Peel (1824–58) from 1860 by William Theed the Younger (1804–91). Peel, a naval officer who died of smallpox at the age of thirty-three, fought with great bravery at Sebastopol and during the uprising at Lucknow. Equestrian statues of Lord Mayo (viceroy 1869–72), Lord Lansdowne (viceroy 1888–94), the Fourth Lord Minto (viceroy 1905–10), Field Marshal Lord Napier (1810–90), Field Marshal Lord Roberts (1832–1914), and Sir John Woodburn (Governor of Bengal 1898–1902) are placed on two-metre-high plinths nearby (Figure 48). A little distance away across the garden, also raised up on plinths, are the standing life-size statues of Lords Lawrence (viceroy 1864–69), Northbrook (viceroy 1872–76), Curzon (viceroy 1899–1905), and Ronaldshay (governor of Bengal 1917–22) and of the only man without a title, Edwin Samuel Montagu (Secretary of State for India, 1917–22), one of the authors of the Montagu-Chelmsford Reforms. This statue by Kathleen Scott (1878–1947)—a rare statue by a woman sculptor—depicts Montague with bowed head, his arms crossed

Figure 48 Harry Bates, Equestrian statue of Henry Petty-Fitzmaurice, Fifth Marquess of Lansdowne, viceroy of India from 1888 to 1894, in front of the Temple of Fame in the gardens of Flagstaff House, Barrackpore. Bronze 1901. Photo © Ekkehard Henschke

across his chest, right over left, as though in penitence, and his legs crossed as well, though this time left over right. A short distance from Old Flagstaff House, the bronze equestrian statue of Lord Canning (viceroy 1856–62) by John Henry Foley (1818–74) is so positioned on his plinth that he can gaze down at the marble tomb of his beloved wife Charlotte Lady Canning who died of malaria in Calcutta in 1861. Lord Curzon, writing some twenty years after he left India, speaks with great nostalgia of Barrackpore as the place where the governor general 'could throw off some of the restraints, if few of the cares, of State, and where his wife or himself could find in the delights of the garden . . . some relief from the ceaseless persecution of official routine'.[31] He also describes very wistfully the evening journey upriver from Calcutta and the view from the deck of his steamship, a view that has remained remarkably unchanged a hundred years later. That the effigies of the viceroys and generals, all of them functionaries of a system that had been rejected, should be taken in 1969 to the one place which for these men meant refreshment and repose is remarkable. The careful positioning of Lord Canning's monument is the most striking of all.

The Victoria Memorial Hall in Calcutta is another site to which many statues have been moved. Either inside the Hall, within its purview, or in the gardens can be found statues of Lord Bentinck (governor-general 1828–35), Robert

Clive (1725–74), Lord Cornwallis (governor general 1786–93), Lord Dalhousie (governor general 1848–56), Sir Andrew Fraser (lieutenant governor of Bengal 1903–8), Warren Hastings (1732–1818), Lieutenant General Sir James Outram (1803–63), Lord Ripon (viceroy 1880–84), and Lord Wellesley (governor general 1798–1805). In addition to these and to the statue of Lord Curzon and the two of Queen Victoria, one Indian is represented: Sir Rajendra Nath Mookerjee (1854–1936), a pioneering engineer and industrialist in Bengal whose company Martin & Co helped to build the Memorial Hall. In other cities too, monuments have been moved into the grounds of museums, for instance, Lucknow Museum and the newly restored Dr Bhau Lad Daji Museum in Mumbai.

In Delhi, the solution was to create Coronation Park on the ridge above Old Delhi where the three durbars took place. The centrepiece of the park, on a stepped platform, is an obelisk commemorating the durbars. Scattered round the dry and dusty space are nineteen plinths, each about two metres high, of which only seven are occupied and none of which are labelled. Charles Sargent Jagger's George V from Rajpath is there, of which more below (Figure 49). Around him are the life-size standing figures of Lords Chelmsford (viceroy 1916–21), Hardinge (viceroy 1910–16), Irwin (viceroy 1926–31), and Willingdon (viceroy 1931–36) and two busts represent the civil servants Sir Guy Fleetwood Wilson (1850–1940) and Sir John Jenkins (1857–1912) respectively. The planning for the park clearly got so far and then ground to a halt. A small building was probably meant as an interpretation centre, but no display had been installed by 2019. The statues and their plinths provide a small amount of privacy for the young courting couples who have nowhere else to go. The park, which was at one time intended to be a tourist attraction, is not easy to find. Anyone driving up to it out of the city passes the red sandstone Mutiny Memorial in the Gothic style, thirty-three metres high, erected in 1863 to commemorate the British and Indian soldiers who suppressed the first Indian uprising. Astonishingly, this was not destroyed after Independence and it took until 1972 for a plaque to be added at the base pointing out that the 'enemy of the inscriptions on this monument were those who rose against colonial rule and fought bravely for national liberation in 1857'. They were 'immortal martyrs for Indian freedom'.

Thanks to the work of Mary Ann Steggles, we have a full, though not complete, catalogue of the statues of the Raj, with information on the subjects portrayed, the artists, the site for which they were commissioned, and their current location.[32] She has identified 170 marble and bronze statues in the territory covered by the Raj, which means the territories nowadays called India, Pakistan, Bangladesh, Burma, and Singapore. They were virtually all designed in Britain by the leading sculptors of the day, mostly carved or cast there[33] and shipped out to India at great cost. The statues are usually at least life size but can be a lot bigger, the figures can be seated, standing, or on horseback, and the majority are of monarchs, viceroys, governors of the three presidencies of Bengal, Madras, and Bombay, or else

Figure 49 Charles Sargeant Jagger, The statue of George V that once stood under Lutyens's canopy as the culmination of Kingsway (Rajpath) in New Delhi. It is now in Coronation Park, Delhi. The king's face has been smashed and he is no longing holding a sceptre and an orb. Photo © Ekkehard Henschke

generals. There were no fewer than thirty-five statues of Queen Victoria, the vast majority produced at the time of her Golden and Diamond Jubilees or after her death, often portraying her enthroned. There were at least eight statues of Edward VII and at least seven of George V. The statues were usually funded by public subscription, often with large contributions from the Indian princes. Sometimes, says Steggles, 'the Indian community was willing to fund a statue to a British individual when the British were not prepared to do so themselves', the example she cites being the two statues of the Liberal reforming viceroy George Robinson, Marquess of Ripon (1827–1909), in Kolkata and Chennai respectively.[34] Miles Taylor calls him the only radical viceroy during the British Raj.[35] He was unpopular with his compatriots because, during his time as viceroy from 1880 to 1884, he devolved some powers to local government and introduced an elective element for its members and, above all, because he introduced the so-called Ilbert Bill which would have allowed Indian judges to try Europeans.

In all the cities with a major British presence, statues were erected—Bangalore, Bombay, Calcutta, Delhi, Lahore, Lucknow, and Madras. Sometimes they were vandalized during the Raj, as happened no fewer than three times to Matthew Noble's marble of the young Queen Victoria on her throne erected in Bombay in 1869 and funded by Maharaja Khanderao Gaekwad of Baroda (1828–1870) to mark the British crown taking over the government of India.[36] Steggles reports that the statue was first vandalized in 1876 by two brothers who were disgruntled at failing to get into the army and who then poured tar over the statue. More often, statues were attacked after Independence. The same statue was apparently attacked again in the 1950s and in 1965. In 1965, another prominent statue was despoiled, this time in New Delhi, namely the white marble figure of King-Emperor George V by Charles Sargent Jagger, paid for by the Maharaja of Kapurthala and some other princes (Figure 49). It stood in a very prominent position under a *chattri* or stone canopy designed by Lutyens just beyond India Gate at the bottom of Kingsway or Rajpath, completing the vista from the top of the ceremonial way at the Viceroy's House. It depicted the king-emperor wearing his coronation robes and the imperial crown, with his cloak hanging down at the back almost to the base of the pedestal. Even though the statue is five and a half metres high and stood on a pedestal thirteen metres high, when in position it was beautifully framed by the arch of India Gate. In the early hours of 13 August 1965, members of the Samyukta Socialist Party 'carrying hammers, chisels, ladders, and buckets of tar' attacked the statue, smearing it with tar and hacking off its ear, nose, and crown.[37] The surprising thing is not that the statue was despoiled but that something so expressive of British domination over India should still be standing in such a prominent position almost twenty years after Independence.

Pressure was now building to remove the statues of the Raj, something that Nehru had resisted ever since Independence on the grounds that the statuary was part of India's history. As Maria Misra puts it in her illuminating article, the way India has dealt with its Raj monuments is a sign of the politicization and deeply contested nature of memory. She writes:

> Because there is no agreement on the meaning of empire in India, it has proved difficult to create cults of victimhood, villainy or heroism that might command common assent and thus facilitate memorialisation. Paradoxically, therefore, empire as memory seems to be absent because empire as politics is too present.[38]

She points out that Nehru's attitude towards the British was ambivalent, for he was sympathetic to the modernizing elements of the British legacy and indeed led India to join the Commonwealth in 1950. He refused the demand from the Hindu nationalist party, the Jan Sangh, to tear down the Mutiny Memorial and to erect one to the rebels instead.[39] He made a famous distinction between three groups of statues: those of historical importance, those with artistic merit, and those deemed offensive to Indian national sentiment, into which category fell the statues of the British generals Sir John Nicholson (1821–57) and Sir Alexander Taylor (1826–1912), each of whom had played a prominent role in putting down the uprising in Delhi in 1857 and whose effigies still stood opposite Delhi's Kashmiri Gate. In 1957 they were taken down and returned to the UK. Nicholson, an Ulsterman, is now in the grounds of the Royal School in Dungannon, Northern Ireland, and Taylor stands in the grounds of Brunel University. When pressure to remove statues generally began to build at the centenary of the uprising in 1957, those states with the greatest number of statues were asked to make a survey and to state their wishes, but no unified strategy emerged.[40]

McGarr chronicles the extent to which the British government, either directly or through the High Commissioner in Delhi, was involved in discussions about the statues, how eager the British were to preserve them, and how they saw the statues' fate as emblematic of Britain's international influence and global relevance. They were keen to strike a mutually acceptable compromise, but on 10 May 1957, the Praja Socialist Party attacked a number of British statues across Uttar Pradesh, and the Congress government in the state ordered that all statuary 'reminiscent of foreign domination' should be removed. Many statues in Agra, Allahabad, Kanpur, and Lucknow were then taken down.[41] Other states followed suit. In July 1959, the statue of George V near the Gateway of India in Bombay was removed and replaced with a statue of the Maratha warrior Chhatrapati Shivaji Maharaj. The statue of George V, uniquely, was by an Indian sculptor, G.K. Mhatre (1879–1947), and, at the time of writing, it seems that the figure is still languishing in a shed behind Elphinstone College in Mumbai. In Calcutta, statues of Queen Victoria and Lord Lawrence were replaced by statues of Bal Gangadhar Tilak (1856–1920) and Subhas Chandra Bose (1897–1945), both important activists for independence, and this went hand in hand with revisionist history writing.[42] Nehru died in 1964, and in that year a statue of Lord Irwin, viceroy from 1926 to 1931, was attacked at a Socialist rally and covered in tar. Congress finally agreed to remove all the Raj statues within two years. In Delhi, Viceroys Irwin, Chelmsford, and Willingdon were the first to be moved in August 1964 to the Exhibition Ground on the outskirts of Delhi. There they stayed until the construction of Coronation Park, where, as we saw above, they are now located.

Both Misra and McGarr show how regional differences played a part in the retention of existing statues and even led to the erection of new ones. Some regional groups looked to the Raj to bolster their identity in protest against cultural colonization by the Hindu north. From the point of view of the Tamils in Tamil Nadu, for instance, it was 'British philologists who had established that Dravidian languages were entirely separate from, but as sophisticated as, northern Sanskritic languages.'[43] After the election of 1967, the new DMK (Dravida Munnetra Kazhagam) government erected statues on the Marina in Madras to two pioneering Tamil scholars, both missionaries, Robert Caldwell, former Bishop of Tinnevelly

(1814–91), who produced the first *Comparative Grammar of Dravidian*, and George Uglow Pope (1820–1908), who wrote several Tamil textbooks and dictionaries before becoming lecturer in Tamil and Telugu at Oxford in the 1880s, where he translated various Tamil texts. Conflict between Tamils and the indigenous Kannada-speaking population in Bangalore developed into a quarrel about retaining or destroying a British cenotaph there. In 1964, the Kannada-speaking group had it destroyed and replaced by a statue of Kempe Gowda, who they claim founded Bangalore. Statues of Queen Victoria and Edward VII, as well as the equestrian statue by Carlo Marochetti (1805–67) of Lieutenant General Sir Mark Cubbon (1775–1861), still stand today in Cubbon Park in Bangalore, in spite of moves to replace them. Even though the park was renamed Sri Chamerajendra Park in 1927, it is still commonly called Cubbon Park, and Cubbon's statue is garlanded each year on his birthday on 23 August in recognition of his enlightened governance of Mysore. He took a deep interest in, and financially supported publications relating to, the Kannada language, for instance. Gordon Park in Mysore has also kept its name, and the bronze statue of Sir James Davidson Gordon (1835–89), Chief Commissioner and then Resident at Mysore between 1878 and 1883, by Edward Onslow Ford (1852–1901), still stands on the spot for which it was commissioned. India's relationship to its Raj statues is, therefore, not uniform, but depends on political and regional allegiance and, where locals have retained a knowledge of history, upon the worthy character and deeds of the person who is portrayed, even where they were members of the colonial government.

The point of all those figures of British monarchs and colonial administrators was not just to show the Indians who their masters were but to present them with exemplars of Britishness. As Herbert Baker, Lutyens's collaborator in building New Delhi, put it in an article in *The Times* in 1912: 'British rule in India is not a mere veneer of government and culture. It is a new civilization.'[44] British civilization is what the statues were designed to convey and, like the statues, after Independence it was either violently rejected, firmly but respectfully put aside, or absorbed into a new narrative.

As stated at the beginning of this chapter, all the empires discussed in this book came to an end. Kipling's famous poem 'Recessional', written in 1897, reads like a prophesy:

> The tumult and the shouting dies;
>   The Captains and the Kings depart:
>   . . . .
> Lo, all our pomp of yesterday
>   Is one with Nineveh and Tyre!
>   . . .
> For frantic boast and foolish word—
> Thy mercy on Thy People, Lord![45]

Notes

1. Watanabe-O'Kelly, 'The Last Habsburg Coronation'.
2. Meynert, *Das königliche Krönungszeremoniel.*
3. Rathenau, *Der Kaiser*, p. 52.
4. Keegan, *The First World War*, p. 423.
5. Tunzelmann, *Indian Summer*, p. 20.
6. Talmeyr, 'L'école du Trocadéro', p. 201.
7. Sayer, 'British Reaction'.
8. Sayer, 'British Reaction', p. 142.
9. Tharoor, *Inglorious Empire.*
10. Sayer, 'British Reaction', p. 131.
11. Khilnani, *The Idea of India*, p. 25.
12. Metcalf, *Imperial Vision*, p. 105; Jeffrey, *People, Princes*, pp. 389–90.
13. Misra, 'From Nehruvian neglect', p. 202.
14. Misra, 'From Nehruvian neglect', p. 203.
15. Zarate Toscano, 'El papel de la escultura', p. 422.
16. Zarate Toscano, 'El papel de la escultura', p. 432.
17. Telesko, *Geschichtsraum Österreich*, pp. 112–15. Franz II had already erected an equestrian statue of Joseph II in the Waffensaal of the Franzensburg in 1798.
18. Telesko, 'Kaiser und Reich', p. 383.
19. Telesko, 'Kaiser und Reich', p. 398.
20. Telesko, *Geschichtsraum Oesterreich*, p. 117.
21. Telesko, 'Kaiser und Reich', p. 388.
22. Bajou, *Louis-Philippe et Versailles*, pp. 242–87.
23. *Journal officiel de la République française*, 11 February 1872, p. 1003.
24. Moritz Schwarcz, *The Emperor's Beard*, p. 354.
25. Moritz Schwarcz, *The Emperor's Beard*, p. 364.
26. See the full account by the Koblenz City Archivist, Michael Koelges: 'Heroisches Kaiserdenkmal oder "Faustschlag aus Stein"?'
27. See *Der Spiegel*, 6 March 1989 and 25 May 1992.
28. Bouillon, 'Das Kaiser-Wilhelm-Denkmal'.
29. Mainzer, 'Denkmäler', p. 220.
30. When speaking about cities during the period of British rule, the British names are used, e.g., Bombay. When the names introduced during the last twenty-five years are used, they refer to the contemporary city.
31. Curzon, *The Government of India*, vol. II, p. 1.
32. Steggles, *Statues of the Raj*. Only four represented Indians, all important businessmen in Bombay, three of them Parsees and the fourth a Jew. All four were loyal to the Raj and notable philanthropists.
33. Two exceptions are the statue of George V in New Delhi, designed by Charles Sargent Jagger in England, but carved by Indian masons, and the statue of George V, formerly in front of the Gateway of India in Mumbai, designed by the Indian sculptor G. K. Mathre.
34. Steggles, *Statues of the Raj*, p. 9.

35. Taylor, *Empress*, p. 216.
36. Steggles, *Statues of the Raj*, p. 178; http://www.victorianweb.org/history/empire/india/sculpture.html
37. McGarr, '"The Viceroys are Disappearing"', pp. 787–8.
38. Maria Misra, 'From Nehruvian neglect', p. 188.
39. Misra, 'From Nehruvian neglect', p. 192.
40. McGarr, The Viceroys are Disappearing', p. 803.
41. McGarr, 'The Viceroys are Disappearing', p. 812.
42. McGarr, 'The Viceroys are Disappearing', p. 817; 'Surfeit of Statues', *The Times*, 12 May 1964.
43. Misra, 'From Nehruvian neglect', p. 194.
44. Baker, 'The New Delhi', p. 7.
45. https://www.poetryfoundation.org/poems/46780/recessional

Bibliography

General Works

Aldrich, Robert, and Cindy McCreery (eds.), *Crown and Colonies. European Monarchies and Overseas Empires* (Manchester: Manchester University Press, 2016).

Anderson, Benedict, *Imagined Communities: Reflections on the Origin and Spread of Nationalism*, rev. ed. (London, New York: Verso, 2006).

Bagehot, Walter, *The English Constitution (1867)*, edited by Miles Taylor (Oxford: Oxford University Press, 2001).

Berenson, Edward, and Eva Giloi, *Constructing Charisma: Celebrity, Fame, and Power in Nineteenth-Century Europe* (New York: Berghahn, 2010).

Berenson, Edward, 'Charisma and the Making of Imperial Heroes in Britain and France, 1880–1914', in *Constructing Charisma: Celebrity, Fame, and Power in Nineteenth-Century Europe*, edited by Edward Berenson and Eva Giloi (New York: Berghahn, 2010), pp. 21–40 and 185–88.

Berns, J.J., and Thomas Rahn, *Zeremoniell als höfische Ästhetik* (Tübingen: Niemeyer, 1995).

Blanning, T.C.W., *The Culture of Power and the Power of Culture: Old Regime Europe, 1660–1789* (Oxford: Oxford University Press, 2002).

Bourdieu, Pierre, 'Sur le pouvoir symbolique', *Annales. Economies, sociétés, civilisations* 31 (1977): 405–11.

Bredekamp, Horst, *Image Acts: A Systematic Approach to Visual Agency* (Berlin: De Gruyter, 2017).

Burbank, Jane, and Frederick Cooper, *Empires in World History: Power and the Politics of Difference* (Princeton: Princeton University Press, 2010).

Çelik, Zeynep, *Displaying the Orient. Architecture of Islam at Nineteenth-Century World Fairs* (Berkeley and Los Angeles: University of California Press, 1992).

Darwin, John, *After Tamerlane. The Global History of Empire since 1405* (London: Allen Lane, 2007).

Darwin, John, *The Empire Project. The Rise and Fall of the British World System, 1830–1970* (Cambridge: Cambridge University Press, 2009).

Duffy, Eamon, *Saints and Sinners. A History of the Popes*, 2nd ed. (New Haven: Yale, 2006).

Fischer-Lichte, Erika, 'Performance, Inszenierung, Ritual. Zur Klärung kulturwissenschaftlicher Schlüsselbegriffe', in *Geschichtswissenschaft und 'performative turn'*, edited by Jürgen Martschukat and Steffen Patzold (Cologne: Böhlau, 2003), pp. 33–54.

Geertz, Clifford, 'Centers, Kings, and Charisma: Reflections on the Symbolics of Power', in *Local Knowledge: Further Essays in Interpretive* Anthropology (New York: Basic Books, 1982), pp. 124–46.

Geppert, Dominik, and Franz Lorenz Müller, 'Beyond national memory. Nora's *Lieux de Mémoire* across an imperial world', in *Sites of Imperial Memory. Commemorating colonial rule in the nineteenth and twentieth centuries*, edited by Dominik Geppert and Franz Lorenz Müller (Manchester: Manchester University Press, 2015), pp. 1–18.

Goffman, Erving, *The Presentation of Self in Everyday Life* (Edinburgh: Ed. Social Sciences Research Centre, 1956).

Greenhalgh, Paul, *Ephemeral Vistas. The Expositions Universelles, Great Exhibitions and World's Fairs, 1851–1939* (Manchester: Manchester University Press, 1988).

Hobsbawm, Eric, 'Mass-producing Traditions: Europe 1870–1914', in *The Invention of Tradition*, edited by Eric Hobsbawm and Terence Ranger (Cambridge: Cambridge University Press, 1983), pp. 263–307.

Hobsbawm, Eric, *The Age of Capital, 1848–75* (London: Weidenfeld & Nicolson, 1975).

Hobsbawm, Eric, *The Age of Empire, 1875–1914* (London: Weidenfeld & Nicolson, 1987).

Hobsbawm, Eric, *The Age of Extremes, 1914–1991* (London: Michael Joseph, 1994).

Keegan, John, *The First World War* (New York: Alfred Knopf, 1999).

Natale, Simone, 'Photography and Communication Media in the Nineteenth Century', *History of Photography* 36, no. 4 (November 2012): 451–6.

Olsen, Donald J., *The City as a Work of Art. London, Paris, Vienna* (New Haven: Yale, 1986).

Ormond, Richard, and Carol Blackett-Ord, *Franz Xaver Winterhalter and the Courts of Europe 1830–70*, exh. cat. (London: National Portrait Gallery, 1987).

Osterhammel, Jürgen, *Die Verwandlung der Welt. Eine Geschichte des 19. Jahrhunderts* (Munich: C.H. Beck, 2009).

Parkinson, C. Northcote, *Parkinson's Law Or the Pursuit of Progress* (London: John Murray, 1961).

Pontificale Romanum Clementis VIII. Ac Urbani VIII. Jussu editum et a Benedicto XIV recognitum et castigatum (Rome: typis S. Congregationis de Propaganda Fide, 1849).

Rausch, Helke, *Kultfigur und Nation. Öffentliche Denkmäler in Paris, Berlin und London 1848–1914* (Munich: Oldenbourg Verlag, 2006).

Rehberg, Hans-Siegbert 'Weltrepräsentation und Verkörperung. Institutionelle Analyse und Symboltheorien—eine Einführung in systematischer Absicht', in *Institutionalität und Symbolisierung. Verstetigungen kultuerller Ordnungsmuster in Vergangenheit und Gegenwart*, edited by Gert Melville (Cologne: Böhlau, 2001), pp. 3–49.

Schwengelbeck, Matthias, *Die Politik des Zeremoniells. Huldigungsfeiern im langen 19. Jahrhundert* (Frankfurt: Campus Verlag, 2007).

Stollberg-Rilinger, Barbara, *Des Kaisers alte Kleider. Verfassungsgeschichte und Symbolsprache des alten Reiches* (Munich: C.H. Beck, 2008).

Stollberg-Rilinger, Barbara, Matthias Puhle, Jutta Götzmann, and Gerd Althoff (eds.), *Spektakel der Macht. Rituale im Alten Europa 800–1800* (Darmstadt: Primus Verlag, 2008).

Telesko, Werner, *Das 19. Jahrhundert. Eine Epoche und ihre Medien* (Vienna, Cologne, Weimar: Böhlau, 2010).

Textile Research Centre, Leiden. https://trc-leiden.nl/trc-needles/individual-textiles-and-textile-types/secular-ceremonies-and-rituals/robe-of-estate-uk

Watanabe-O'Kelly, Helen, 'The Consort in the theatre of power: Maria Amalia of Saxony, Queen of the Two Sicilies, Queen of Spain', in *Queens Consort, Cultural Transfer and European Politics, c. 1500–1800*, edited by Adam Morton and Helen Watanabe-O'Kelly (Abingdon: Routledge 2016), pp. 37–63.

Weber, Max, *Wirtschaft und Gesellschaft. Grundriss der verstehenden Soziologie*, edited by Johannes Winckelmann (Tübingen: Mohr, 1976).

Wesemael, Pieter van, *Architecture of Instruction and Delight: A Socio-historical Analysis of World Exhibitions as a Didactic Phenomenon (1798–1851–1970)* (Rotterdam: 010 Publishers, 2001).

Wilentz, Sean (ed.), *Rites of Power: Symbolism, Ritual and Politics since the Middle Ages* (Philadelphia: University of Pennsylvania Press, 1999).

Woolley, Reginald Maxwell, *Coronation Rites* (Cambridge Handbooks of Liturgical Study, Cambridge: Cambridge University Press 1915).

Austria

Ascher, Matthias, Thomas Nicklas, and Matthias Stickler (eds.), *Was vom alten Reiche blieb. . . Deutungen, Institutionen und Bilder des Frühneuzeitlichen Heiligen Römischen Reiches deutscher Nation im 19. und 20. Jahrhundert* (Munich: Bayerische Landeszentrale für Politische Bildungsarbeit, 2011).

Barta, Ilsebill, Marlene Ott-Wodni, and Alena Skrabanek, *Repräsentation und (Ohn)Macht: Die Wohnkultur der habsburgischen Prinzen im 19. Jahrhundert—Kaiser Maximilian von Mexiko, Kronprinz Rudolf, Erzherzog Franz Ferdinand und ihre Schlösser* (Göttingen: Vandenhoeck und Ruprecht, 2019).

Beke-Martos, Judit, 'After 1848: The Heightened Constitutional Importance of the Habsburg Coronation in Hungary', in *More Than Mere Spectacle. Coronations and Inaugurations in the Habsburg Monarchy during the Eighteenth and Nineteenth Centuries*, edited by Klaas Van Gelder (New York: Berghahn, 2021), pp. 283–302.

Beller, Steven, *Franz Joseph. Eine Biographie* (Vienna: Döcker, 1997).

Benedik, Christian, 'Der Zeremoniensaal', in *Die Wiener Hofburg 1705–1835. Die Kaiserliche Residenz vom Barock zum Klassizismus*, edited by Hellmut Lorenz and Anna Mader-Kratky (Vienna: Österreichische Akademie der Wissenschaften, 2016), pp. 205–9.

Berger, Alfred Freiherr von Berger, *Habsburg. Märchenspiel in drei Acten* (Vienna: Carl Konegen, 1898).

Bled, Jean-Paul, *Franz Joseph* (Oxford: Blackwell, 1992).

Brandt, Harm Hinrich, 'Franz Joseph I. von Österreich 1848–1916', in *Die Kaiser der Neuzeit 1519–1918: Heiliges Römisches Reich, Österreich, Deutschland*, edited by Anton Schindling and Walter Ziegler (Munich: C.H. Beck, 1990), pp. 341–81.

Briot, Marie-Odile, Georg Kugler, and Monica Kurzel-Runtscheiner, *Costumes à la cour de Vienne: 1815–1918*, exh. cat. (Paris: Palais Galliera, 1995).

Bruckmüller, Ernst, 'National Consciousness and Elementary School Education in Imperial Austria', in *The Limits of Loyalty: Imperial Symbolism, Popular Allegiances, and State Patriotism in the Late Habsburg Monarchy*, edited by Daniel Unowsky and Laurence Cole (New York: Berghahn, 2007), pp. 11–35.

Bürgler, Anna, et al., *Die Franzensburg. Ein Führer durch Geschichte und Gegenwart* (Laxenburg: Schloss Laxenburg, 1998).

Chapman, Tim, *The Congress of Vienna. Origins, Processes and Results* (London: Routledge, 1998).

Chatelain, Caesar von, *Patriotisches Gedenkblatt zur Enthüllungsfeier des Kaiserin Maria Theresia-Monumentes in Wien am 13. Mai 1888*, edited by Eduard Allmayer (Vienna: Gresser, 1888).

Coreth, Anna, *Pietas Austriaca. Ursprung und Entwicklung barocker Frömmigkeit in Österreich* (Munich: Oldenbourg, 1959).

Czeike, Felix, *Historisches Lexikon der Stadt Wien* (Vienna: Kremayr und Scheriau, 1992–2004).

Elze, Reinhard, *Die Ordines für die Weihe und Krönung des Kaisers und der Kaiserin* (Hannover: Hahn, 1960).

Emmer, Johannes, *Sechzig Jahre auf Habsburgs Throne. Festgabe zum 60-jährigen Regierungs-Jubiläum Sr. Majestät Kaiser Franz Joseph I.*, vol. 2 (Vienna: Pallas, 1908).

Etzlstorfer, Hannes, *Der Wiener Kongress: Redouten, Karoussel und Köllnerwasser* (Vienna: Kremayr & Scheriau, 2014).

Evans, R.J.W., 'Communicating Empire: The Habsburgs and their critics, 1700–1919', *Transactions of the Royal Historical Society* 19 (2009): 117–38.

Eynard, Jean Gabriel, *Der tanzende Kongress* (Berlin: Hafen-Verlag, 1923).

Felder, Cajetan, *Erinnerungen eines Wiener Bürgermeisters* (Vienna: Karolinger Verlag, 1984).

Feyerlichkeiten bei der Rückkehr Seiner Majestät des Kaisers von Österreich nach Wien im Jahre 1814: dann bey dem Empfange und während der Anwesenheit der fremden Souveraine in Wien, in den Jahren 1814 und 1815 (Vienna: J.B. Wallishauger, 1814).

Fischer, J.C., *Hans Makart's Festzug der Stadt Wien, 27. April 1879, als Huldigung zur silbernen Hochzeit des Kaiserpaares*, naturgetreu chromolitogr. dargestellt von E. Stadlin (Vienna: Moritz Perles, 1879).

Freifeld, Alice, 'Empress Elisabeth as Hungarian Queen: The Uses of Celebrity Monarchism', in *The Limits of Loyalty: Imperial Symbolism, Popular Allegiances, and State Patriotism in the Late Habsburg Monarchy*, edited by Daniel Unowsky and Laurence Cole (New York: Berghahn, 2007), pp. 138–61.

Fuchs, Martina, and Alfred Kohler (eds.), *Kaiser Ferdinand I. Aspekte eines Herrscherlebens* (Münster: Aschendorff, 2003).

Fugger, Nora, *Im Glanz der Kaiserzeit* (1st ed. 1932) (Vienna: Amalthea, 1989).

Gaul, Gustav, *Lebende Bilder aus der Geschichte des Oesterreichischen Kaiserhauses zur fünfundzwanzigsten Vermählungsfeier Ihrer Majestäten des Kaisers Franz Joseph I. und der Kaiserin Elisabeth Dargestellt von Mitgliedern des Durchlauchtigsten Erzhauses Bei seiner K.K. Hoheit Erzherzog Carl Ludwig am 22. April 1879* (Vienna: A. Angerer, 1881).

Godsey, William, 'Das Habsburgereich während der Napoleonischen Kriege und des Wiener Kongresses', in *Europa in Wien, Wien in Europa, der Wiener Kongress 1814/ 1815*, exh. cat., edited by Agnes Husslein-Arco, Sabine Grabner, and Werner Telesko (Munich: Hirmer, 2015), pp. 29–35.

Godsey, William, 'A Noblewoman's Changing Perspective on the World: The Habsburg Patriotism of Rosa Neipperg-Lobkowicz (1832–1905)', *Austrian History Yearbook* 47 (2016): 37–60.

Godsey, William, 'Pageantry in the Revolutionary Age: Inaugural Rites in the Habsburg Monarchy, 1790–1848', in *More than Mere Spectacle. Coronations and Inaugurations in the Habsburg Monarchy during the Eighteenth and Nineteenth Centuries*, edited by Klaas Van Gelder (New York: Berghahn, 2021), pp. 247–82.

Gottfried, Margaret, *Das Wiener Kaiserforum: Utopien zwischen Hofburg und Museumsquartier: imperiale Träume und republikanische Wirklichkeiten von der Antike bis heute* (Vienna: Böhlau, 2001).

Grossegger, Elisabeth, *Der Kaiser-Huldigungs-Festzug Wien 1908* (Vienna: Österreichische Akademie der Wissenschaften, 1992).

Grossegger, Elisabeth, '"Du kannst Dir keinen Begriff machen, wie toll es hier ungeachtet der ausserordentlichen Theuerung zugeht". Theater, Fest, Publikum im Wiener Kongress', *Römische Historische Mitteilungen* 58 (2016): 223–65.

Haag, Sabine (ed.), *Meisterwerke der Weltlichen Schatzkammer* (Kurzführer durch das Kunsthistorische Museum Wien 2) (Wien: KHM-Museumsverband, 2017).

Hahn, Victor, *Felix Austria. Ein Festspiel zu Kaiser Franz Josephs 60-jährigem Regierungs-Jubiläum* (aufgeführt in Graaz am 1. Dezember 1908) (Berlin: Paetel, 1908).

Hamann, Brigitte, 'Der Wiener Hof und die Hofgesellschaft in der zweiten Hälfte des 19. Jahrhunderts', in *Hof und Hofgesellschaft in den deutschen Staaten im 19. und beginnenden 20. Jahrhundert*, edited by Karl Möckl (Berlin: De Gruyter, 1990), pp. 61-78.

Hattenhauer, Christian, *Das Heilige Reich krönt seinen letzten Kaiser. Das Tagebuch des Reichsquartiermeisters Hieronymus Gottfried von Müller und Anlagen* (Frankfurt: Peter Lang, 1995).

Herzig, Max (ed.), *Viribus Unitis. Das Buch vom Kaiser* (Vienna: Verlag Max Herzig, 1898).

Hilscher, Elisabeth, '"Unserem guten Kaiser Franz". Feste und Feiern rund um den Wiener Kongress als patriotische Bühne', *Österreichische Musikzeitschrift* 70, no. 1 (2015): 10-19.

Hilscher, Elisabeth, 'Antonio Salieri und die Feste des Wiener Kongresses', *Römische Historische Mitteilungen* 58 (2016): 267-78.

Husslein-Arco, Agnes, Sabine Grabner, and Werner Telesko (eds.), *Europa in Wien, Wien in Europa, der Wiener Kongress 1814/1815*, exh. cat. (Munich: Hirmer, 2015).

Hof= und Staats=Schematismus des österreichischen Kaiserthums (Vienna: Aus der Kaiserl. Königl. Hof= und Staatsdruckery, 1813-48).

Jäger, Johann Christian, *Vollstaendiges Diarium der Römisch=Königlichen Wahl und Kaiserlichen Krönung Ihro nunmehr allerglorwürdigst regierenden Kaiserlichen Majestät Leopold des Zweiten* (Frankfurt am Main: Im Verlag der Jägerischen Buchhandlung; 1791).

Junk, Rudolf, and Emil Schiller (eds.), *Kaiser Jubiläums-Festlichkeiten, Vienna 1908. Der Huldigungsfestzug. Eine Schilderung und Erklärung seiner Gruppen* (Vienna: Verlag des Zentral-Komitees der Kaiserhuldigungs-Festlichkeiten, 1908).

Das Kaiserlich-Königliche Österreichische Museum und die Kunstgewerbeschule: Festschrift bei Gelegenheit der Weltausstellung in Wien Mai 1873, K.K. Österreichisches Museum für Kunst und Industrie (Wien: Verlag des Osterreichischen Museums, Druck von J.C. Fischer & comp., 1873).

Der Kaiser-Huldigungs-Festzug Wien 12. Juni 1908 (Vienna: R. Lechner (Wilh. Müller), 1908).

Kos, Wolfgang, Ralph Gleis, and Thomas Aigner (eds.), *Experiment Metropole: 1873: Wien und die Weltausstellung*, exh. cat. (Vienna: Czernin, 2014).

Kraus, Karl, *Die Fackel* (Vienna: Verlag die Fackel, 1899-1936).

Kroll, Frank-Lothar, 'Kaisermythos und Reichsromantik—Bemerkungen zur Rezeption des Alten Reiches im 19. Jahrhundert', in *Was vom alten Reiche blieb...Deutungen, Institutionen und Bilder des Frühneuzeitlichen Heiligen Römischen Reiches deutscher Nation im 19. und 20. Jahrhundert*, edited by Matthias Ascher, Thomas Nicklas, and Matthias Stickler (Munich: Bayerische Landeszentrale für Politische Bildungsarbeit, 2011), pp. 19-32.

Kugler, Georg, and Herbert Haupt, *Uniform und Mode am Kaiserhof. Hofkleider und Ornate, Hofuniformen und Livreen des 19. Jahrhunderts aus dem Monturdepot des Kunsthistorischen Museums Wien*, exh. cat. (Eisenstadt: Amt der Burgenländischen Landesregierung, 1983).

Kurdiovsky, Richard, 'Die Wiener Hofburg und der europäische Residenzbau des 19. Jahrhunderts', in *Die Wiener Hofburg 1835-1918. Der Ausbau der Residenz vom Vormärz bis zum Ende des Kaiserforums*, edited by Werner Telesko (Vienna: Verlag der Österreichische Akademie der Wissenschaften, 2012), pp. 504-19.

Kurdiovsky, Richard, 'Zeremonielle Räume in der Wiener Hofburg unter Kaiser Franz Joseph', in *Inszenierung und Gedächtnis. Soziokulturelle und ästhetische Praxis*, edited by Hermann Blume (Bielefeld: transcript, 2014), pp. 191–209.

Kurdiovsky, Richard, et al., 'Legitimacy through History and Architecture. The Vienna Hofburg as Dynastic Hub and Seat of Government between Tradition and Innovation', *The Court Historian* 20, no. 2 (2015): 109–36.

Lobkowicz, Erwein, *Erinnerungen an die Monarchie* (Vienna, Munich: Amalthea Verlag, 1989).

Lorenz, Hellmut, and Anna Mader-Kratky, *Die Wiener Hofburg 1705–1835. Die Kaiserliche Residenz vom Barock zum Klassizismus* (Vienna: Österreichische Akademie der Wissenschaften, 2016).

Macek, Bernard, *Kaiser Karl I. Der letzte Kaiser Österreichs. Ein photographischer Bilderbogen* (Erfurt: Sutton, 2012).

Mazohl, Brigitte, 'Gewinner und Verlierer der europäischen Neuordnung. Der Wiener Kongress als Wegbereiter der modernen Machtpolitik', in *Europa in Wien, Wien in Europa, der Wiener Kongress 1814/1815*, exh. cat., edited by Agnes Husslein-Arco, Sabine Grabner, and Werner Telesko (Munich: Hirmer, 2015), pp. 53–9.

Mazohl, Brigitte, and Karin Schneider, ' "Translatio imperii"? Reichsidee und Kaisermythos in der Habsburgermonarchie', in *Was vom alten Reiche blieb. . . Deutungen, Institutionen und Bilder des Frühneuzeitlichen Heiligen Römischen Reiches deutscher Nation im 19. und 20. Jahrhundert*, edited by Matthias Ascher, Thomas Nicklas, and Matthias Stickler (Munich: Bayerische Landeszentrale für Politische Bildungsarbeit, 2011), pp. 101–28.

Meisl, Carl, *Das Monument weiland Seiner Majestät des höchstseligen Kaisers [. . .] Franz des Ersten Festgedicht* (Vienna: Grund, 1846).

Meynert, Hermann, *Das königliche Krönungszeremoniell in Ungarn* (Wien: Beck, 1867).

Moos, Carlo, *Habsburg post mortem. Betrachtungen zum Weiterleben der Habsburgermonarchie* (Vienna, Cologne, Weimar: Böhlau, 2016).

Morpurgo de Nilma, Carl Marcus (Ritter von), and Joseph Valensi (Ritter von), *Welt-ausstellung 1873 in Wien: Abtheilung der tunesischen regentschaft, organisirt unter dem hohen schutze Seiner Hoheit Mohamed el Sadek, pascha-bey von Tunis, durch herrn commandeur Morpurgo ritter von Nilma aus Triest, general-commissär für Tunis bei der Welt-ausstellung, unter mitwirkung von S.E. Sidi Mustapha Hasnadar, premier-minister und minister des aeusseren und anderer hoher persönlichkeiten aus Tunis* (Wien: Im Selbstverlage von Morpurgo de Nilma, 1873).

Neue Freie Presse (Vienna: Oesterr. Journal A.G., 1864–1939).

Öhlinger, Walter, 'Kommunale Oligarchie. Der Wiener Gemeinderat in der liberalen Ära', in *Experiment Metropole: 1873: Wien und die Weltausstellung*, exh. cat., edited by Wolfgang Kos, Ralph Gleis, and Thomas Aigner (Vienna: Czernin, 2014), pp. 74–83.

Palmer, Alan, *Metternich* (London: Weidenfeld and Nicholson, 1972).

Pangerl, Irmgard, Martin Scheutz, and Thomas Winkelbauer (eds.), *Der Wiener Hof im Spiegel der Zeremonialprotokolle (1652–1800): Eine Annäherung* (Innsbruck: Studienverlag, 2007).

Paulmann, Johannes, *Pomp und Politik. Monarchenbegegnungen in Europa zwischen Ancien Régime und Erstem Weltkrieg* (Paderborn: F. Schöningh, 2000).

Perth, Matthias Franz, *Wiener Kongresstagebuch 1814/15*, edited by Franz Patzer (Vienna, Munich: Jugend und Volk, 1981).

Praschl-Bichler, Gabriele, *Das Familienalbum von Kaiser Franz Joseph und Elisabeth* (Vienna: Ueberreuter, 1995).

Rauchensteiner, Manfried, *The First World War and the End of the Habsburg Monarchy* (Vienna: Böhlau, 2014).

Rauchensteiner, Manfried, *An meine Völker* (Vienna: Amalthea, 2014).

Rehbock, A. G., *Festzug der Stadt Wien am 27. April 1879* (Vienna: Pollak, 1879).

Riesenfellner, Stefan, *Steinernes Bewußtsein* (Vienna: Böhlau, 1998).

Roider, Karl A. Jr., 'The Habsburg Foreign Ministry and Political Reform, 1801–1805', *Central European History* 22, no. 2 (1989): 160–82.

Rosenstrauch, Hazel, *Congress mit Damen. Europa zu Gast in Wien 1814–15* (Vienna: Czernin Verlag, 2014).

Roth, Markus, *Karl von Österreich: Kaiser—Kriegsherr—Kirchenmann. Politischer Heiliger in der Neuzeit?*, exh. cat. (Hamburg: Dr. Kovač, 2013).

Schneider, Karin, 'Das Wiener Zeremoniell im 19. Jahrhundert. Ein Ausblick', in *Der Wiener Hof im Spiegel der Zeremonialprotokolle (1652–1800): Eine Annäherung*, edited by Irmgard Pangerl, Martin Scheutz, and Thomas Winkelbauer (Innsbruck: Studienverlag, 2007), pp. 627–38.

Schorske, Carl, *Fin-de-Siècle Vienna—Politics and Culture* (Cambridge: Cambridge University Press, 1981).

Shedel, James, 'Emperor, Church and People: Religion and Dynastic Loyalty during the Golden Jubilee of Franz Joseph', *Catholic Historical Review* 76 (1990): 71–92.

Siemann, Wolfram, *Metternich: Staatsmann zwischen Restauration und Moderne* (Munich: C.H. Beck, 2010).

Siemann, Wolfram, *Metternich: Stratege und Visionär* (Munich: C.H. Beck, 2016).

Stadlin, Eduard, *Festzug der Stadt Wien den 27. April 1879* (Vienna: Moritz Perles, 1879).

Stickler, Matthias, 'Die Herrschaftsauffassung Kaiser Franz Josephs in den frühen Jahren seiner Regierung. Überlegungen zu Selbstverständnis und struktureller Bedeutung der Dynastie für die Habsburgermonarchie', in *Der österreichische Neoabsolutismus als Verfassungs- und Verwaltungsproblem*, edited by Harm-Hinrich Brandt (Vienna, Cologne, Weimar: Böhlau, 2014), pp. 35–72.

Straub, Eberhard, *Der Wiener Kongress: das große Fest und die Neuordnung Europas* (Stuttgart: Klett-Cotta, 2014).

Telesko, Werner, *Geschichtsraum Österreich. Die Habsburger und ihre Geschichte in der bildenden Kunst des 19. Jahrhunderts* (Vienna, Cologne, Weimar: Böhlau, 2006).

Telesko, Werner, Richard Kurdiovsky, and Dagmar Sachsenhofer (eds.), *Die Wiener Hofburg 1835–1918. Der Ausbau der Residenz vom Vormärz bis zum Ende des 'Kaiserforums'* (Vienna: Österreichische Akademie der Wissenschaften, 2012).

Telesko, Werner, Richard Kurdiovsky, and Dagmar Sachsenhofer, 'The Vienna Hofburg between 1835 and 1918A Residence in the Conflicting Fields of Art, Politics, and Representation', *Austrian History Yearbook* 44 (2013): 37–61.

Telesko, Werner, 'Kaiser und Reich in der habsburgischen Denkmalkultur des 19. Jahrhunderts. Die Funktion von Denkmälern in der Habsburgermonarchie des 19. Jahrhunderts', in *Was vom alten Reiche blieb. . . Deutungen, Institutionen und Bilder des Frühneuzeitlichen Heiligen Römischen Reiches deutscher Nation im 19. und 20. Jahrhundert*, edited by Matthias Ascher, Thomas Nicklas, and Matthias Stickler (Munich: Bayerische Landeszentrale für Politische Bildungsarbeit, 2011), pp. 373–98.

Thun-Salm, Christiane, *Des Kaisers Traum. Festspiel in einem Aufzuge 2. Dezember 1908* (Vienna: Druck von J. Weiner, k. u. k. Hoflieferant, 1908) (ebd[1] 1898).

Ujvári, Hedvig, 'Feuilletons über die Wiener Weltausstellung 1873 im *Pester Lloyd*'. http://www.kakanien.ac.at/beitr/fallstudie/HUjvari1.pdf

Unowsky, Daniel, 'Staging Habsburg Patriotism. Dynastic Loyalty and the 1898 Imperial Jubilee', in *Constructing Nationalities in East Central Europe*, edited by Peter M. Judson and Marsha L. Rozenblit (New York, Oxford: Berghahn, 2005), pp. 141–56.

Unowsky, Daniel, *The Pomp and Politics of Patriotism: Imperial Celebrations in Habsburg Austria, 1848–1916* (West Lafayette, Ind.: Purdue University Press, 2005).

Unowsky, Daniel, and Laurence Cole (eds.), *The Limits of Loyalty: Imperial Symbolism, Popular Allegiances, and State Patriotism in the Late Habsburg Monarchy* (New York: Berghahn, 2007).

Vick, Brian E., *The Congress of Vienna* (Cambridge, Mass.: Harvard University Press, 2014).

Vocelka, Karl, and Lynne Heller, *Die private Welt der Habsburger. Kultur- und Mentalitätsgeschiche einer Familie* (Graz, Vienna, Cologne: Styria, 1997).

Vocelka, Karl, and Michaela Vocelka, *Sisi. Leben und Legende einer Kaiserin* (Munich: C.H. Beck, 2014).

Vocelka, Karl, and Michaela Vocelka, *Franz Joseph I. Kaiser von Österreich und König von Ungarn 1830–1916* (Munich: C.H. Beck, 2015).

Vocelka, Karl, and Martin Mutschlechner, *Franz Joseph 1830–1916*, exh. cat. (Vienna: Brandstätter, 2016).

Vorschrift für die von Sr. K.K. Majestät sämmtlichen Staatsbeamten bewilligte Uniform (Vienna: Kaiserlich-königliche Hof- und Staatsdruckerey, 1814).

Watanabe-O'Kelly, Helen, 'The Last Habsburg Coronation and What it Means to be Anointed', in *More than Mere Spectacle. Coronations and Inaugurations in the Habsburg Monarchy during the Eighteenth and Nineteenth Centuries*, edited by Klaas Van Gelder (New York: Berghahn, 2021), pp. 303–12.

Weber, Christian Gottlieb, *Merkwürdigkeiten bei der römischen Königswahl und Kaiserkrönung; Im Anhange Kaiser Leopold II. Wahl und Krönung* (Hamberger, Julius Wilhelm, 1754–1813).

Wegweiser durch Wien und die Weltausstellung (Vienna: Lehmann und Wentzel, 1873).

Weltausstellung 1873 in Wien (Vienna: K.K. Hof u. Staatsdr., 1872).

Wiener Zeitung (Vienna: Hof- und Staatsdruckerei, 1857–1919).

Wiener Weltausstellungs-Zeitung (Vienna: J. Schuster, 1871–73).

Wilson, Peter H., 'Bolstering the Prestige of the Habsburgs: The End of the Holy Roman Empire in 1806', *The International History Review* 28 (2006): 709–36.

Wilson, Peter H., *The Holy Roman Empire 1495–1806*, 2nd rev. ed. (Basingstoke: Palgrave Macmillan, 2011).

Winkelhofer, Martina, *Der Alltag des Kaisers. Franz Joseph und sein Hof*, 3rd ed. (Innsbruck, Vienna: Haymon Taschenbuch, 2010).

Winkelhofer, Martina, '*Viribus unitis*'. *Der Kaiser und sein Hof. Ein neues Franz-Joseph-Bild* (Vienna: Amalthea, 2008).

Wölfling Leopold, *Habsburger unter sich. Freimütige Aufzeichnungen eines ehemaligen Erzherzogs* (Berlin-Wilmersdorf: Goldschmidt-Gabrielli, 1921).

Brazil

Ambile, Valdirene do Carmo and Luiz Roberto Fontes, 'O que pode ter matado D. Leopoldina', in *D. Leopoldina e seu tempo: sociedade, política, ciência e arte no século XIX*, edited by Aline Magalhães Álvaro and Rafael Zamorano Bezerra (Rio de Janeiro: Museu Histórico Nacional, 2016), pp. 200–13.

Araújo, Valdei Lopes de, *A Experiência do Tempo: conceitos e narrativas na formação nacional brasileira (1813-1845)* (São Paulo: Hucitec, 2008).

Avella, Aniello Ângelo, 'Teresa Cristina Maria de Bourbon, uma imperatriz silenciada' (Rio de Janerio: Associação Nacional de História, 2010).

Avella, Aniello Ângelo, *Teresa Cristina de Bourbon: uma imperatriz napolitana nos trópicos* (Rio de Janeiro: EDUERJ, 2014).

Barbosa Oriente, Esther, *Pedro II: Imperador da cultura* (Goiâna: Kelps, 2007).

Barman, Roderick J., *Brazil. The Forging of a Nation 1798-1852* (Stanford: Stanford University Press, 1988).

Barman, Roderick J., *Citizen Emperor. Pedro II and the Making of Brazil 1825-1891* (Stanford: Stanford University Press, 1999).

Barman, Roderick J., *Princess Isabel of Brazil. Gender and Power in the Nineteenth Century* (Wilmington: Scholarly Resources, 2002).

Barman, Roderick J., 'Imperial Cities and Seasonal Residences: Petrópolis, Summer Capital of Brazil (1843-1889) and its European Counterparts', *The Court Historian* 13 (2008): 3-20.

Bernstein, Harry, *Dom Pedro II*. (New York: Twayne, 1973).

Brune, Krista, 'Retranslating the Brazilian Imperial Project: *O Novo Mundo*'s Depictions of the 1876 Centennial Exhibition', *Journal of Lusophone Studies* 3, no. 2 (2018): 1-23.

Cizeron, David, *Les representations du Brésil lors des expositions universelles* (Paris: l'Harmatton, 2009).

Colson, Frank, 'On Expectations. Perspectives on the Crisis of 1889 in Brazil', *Journal of Latin American Studies* 13, no. 2 (1981): 265-92.

Debret, Jean-Baptiste, *Voyage pittoresque et historique au Brésil, ou séjour d'un artiste français au Brésil, depuis 1816 jusqu'en 1831 / époques de l'avénement et de l'abdication de S. M. D. Pedro Ier, fondateur de l'empire brésilien*, 3 vols. (Paris: Firmin Didot Frères 1834-1839).

Dias, Elaine, 'D'abord peindre le prince: les conflits de Jean-Baptiste Debret et Nicolas-Antoine Taunay à la Cour de Rio de Janeiro', *Brésil(s)* 10 (2016), mis en ligne le 30 novembre 2016. http://journals.openedition.org/bresils/1992; DOI: 10.4000/bresils.1992

Dussel, Inés, 'Between exoticism and universalism: educational sections in Latin American participation at international exhibitions, 1860-1900', *Paedagogica Historica. International Journal of the History of Education* 47, no. 5 (2011): 601-17.

Giberti, Bruno, *Designing the Centennial: A History of the 1876 International Exhibition in Philadelphia* (Lexington: University Press of Kentucky, 2002).

Gomes, Laurentino, and Andrew Nevins, *1808: The Flight of the Emperor: How a Weak Prince, a Mad Queen, and the British Navy Tricked Napoleon and Changed the New World* (Guilford, Connecticut: Lyons Press, 2013).

Ingram, J. S., *The Centennial Exposition, Described and Illustrated* (Philadelphia: Hubbard Brothers, 1876).

Kann, Bettina (ed.), *D. Leopoldina: cartas da uma imperatriz* (São Paolo: Estaçao Liberdade, 2006).

Karge, Henrik, and Bruno Klein (eds.), *1810-1910-2-10: independencias dependientes: Kunst und nationale Identitäten in Lateinamerika: arte e identidades nacionales en América Latina: art and national identities in Latin America* (Frankfurt and Madrid: Vervuert-Iberoamericana, 2016).

Kraay, Hendrik, *Days of National Festivity in Rio de Janeiro, Brazil, 1823-1889* (Stanford: Stanford University Press, 2013).

Leeb, Rudolf, *Geschichte des Christentums in Österreich: von der Spätantike bis in die Gegenwart* (Vienna: Überreuther, 2003).

Leenhardt, Jacques, 'Jean-Baptiste Debret: le livre comme « mission ». Autour du *Voyage pittoresque et historique au Brésil*', *Brésil(s)*, 10 (2016), mis en ligne le 30 novembre 2016. http://journals.openedition.org/bresils/1980; DOI: 10.4000/bresils.1980

Leopoldine, Archduchess of Austria, Empress of Brazil, 'Mes Resolutions', MS, Vienna 1817.

Magalhães Álvaro, Aline, and Rafael Zamorano Bezerra (eds.), *D. Leopoldina e seu tempo: sociedade, política, ciência e arte no século XIX* (Rio de Janeiro: Museu Histórico Nacional, 2016).

Mareschall von Bieberstein, Wenzel Philipp Leopold Freiherr von, 'Correspondência do Barão de Mareschal', *Revista do Instituto Histórico e Geográfico Brasileiro* 335 (1982): 147–68.

Moritz Schwarcz, Lilia K., *The Emperor's Beard: Dom Pedro II and the Tropical Monarchy of Brazil* (orig. Portuguese ed. 1998), (trans.) John Gledson (New York: Hill & Wang, 2004).

Moritz Schwarcz, Lilia K., 'The Banana Emperor: D. Pedro II in Brazilian Caricatures, 1842–89', *American Ethnologist* 40, no. 2 (2013): 310–23.

Norton, Luiz, *A Côrte de Portugal no Brasil: Notas, Documentos Diplomáticos, e Cartas da Imperatriz Leopoldina*, 2nd ed. (Lisboa: Empresa Nacional de Publicidade, 1966).

Oberacker, Carlos H., *Leopoldina. Habsburgs Kaiserin von Brasilien*, 2nd ed. (Vienna, Munich: Amalthea, 1988).

Oliveira, Mariana Luiza de, 'Festejos do Progresso: O Império Brasilerio e A colônia Blumenau nas exposições universais (1860–1883)', Anais do XXVI Simpósio Nacional de História—ANPUH, São Paolo, July 2011. http://www.snh2011.anpuh.org/resources/anais/14/1308063630_ARQUIVO_ArtigoEXPOSICOESUNIVERSAIS-MarianaL.deOliveira-1.pdf

Oriá, Ricardo, 'Construindo o Panteão dos Heróis Nacionais: monumentos à República, rituals cívicos e o ensino de História', *Revista História Hoje* 3, no. 6 (2014): 43–66.

Rezende, Livia, 'Of Coffee, Nature and Exclusion: Designing Brazilian National Identity at International exhibitions (1867 and 1904)', in *Designing Worlds. National Design Histories in an Age of Globalization*, edited by Kjetil Fallan and Grace Lees-Maffei (New York: Berghahn, 2016), pp. 259–73.

Rezende, Livia, 'Manufacturing the Raw in Design Pageantries: The Commodification and Gendering of Brazilian Tropical Nature', *Journal of Design History* 30 (2017): 122–38.

Rezzutti, Paulo, *D. Leopoldina: a história não contada: a mulher que arquitetou a independência do Brasil* (São Paulo: LeYa, 2017).

Romero de Oliveira, Eduardo, 'O império da lei: ensaio sobre o ceremonial de sagração de D. Pedro I (1822)', *Tempo* 13, no. 26 (2009): 147–75.

Rui Vilar, Emilio, 'A transferência da corte portuguesa para o Brasil', in *Um novo mundo, um novo império. A corte Portuguese no Brasil 1808–1822*, exh. cat. (Rio de Janeiro: Museu Histórico Nacional, 2008), pp. 12–13.

Schubert, Guilherme, *A coroação de D. Pedro I: comunicação apresentada durante o Congresso de História da Independência do Brasil, Rio de Janeiro, 28 de agosto a 6 de setembro de 1972* (Rio de Janeiro: Ministéro da Justiça, Arquivo Nacional, 1973).

Um novo mundo, um novo império. A corte Portuguese no Brasil 1808–1822, exh. cat. (Rio de Janeiro: Museu Histórico Nacional, 2008).

Villeneuve, Julio Constancio de (ed.), *Relatório Sobre a Exposição Universal de 1867* (Paris: Typographia de Julio Claye, 1868).

Wilcken, Patrick, *Empire Adrift. The Portuguese Court in Rio de Janeiro 1808–1821* (London: Bloomsbury, 2004).

France

Abrantès, Mme la Duchesse d', *Mémoires, ou, Souvenirs historiques sur Napoléon, la Révolution, le Directoire, le Consulat, l'Empire et la Restauration* (Paris: Lavocat, 1831–34).

Alletz, Pons-Augustin, *Cérémonial du sacre des rois de France où l'on voit l'ancienneté de cet acte de religion; les motifs de son institution; le pompeux appareil avec lequel il est célébré; le costume des habillements, & une table chronologique du sacre des rois. On y a ajouté la traduction de toutes les oraisons & prières qui font une grande partie de la cérémonie* (Paris: G. Desprez, 1775).

Alphand, Adolphe, *Les promenades de Paris: histoire, description des embellissements, dépenses de création et d'entretien des Bois de Boulogne et de Vincennes, Champs-Elysées, parcs, squares, boulevards, places plantées, études sur l'art des jardins et arboretum* (Paris: J. Rothschild, 1867–73).

Aston, Nigel, *Religion and Revolution in France, 1780–1804* (Basingstoke: Macmillan, 2000).

Babelon, Jean-Pierre, Myriam Bacha, and Béatrice de Andia (eds.), *Les expositions universelles à Paris de 1855 à 1937* (Paris: Action artistique de la ville de Paris, 2005).

Baguley, David, *Napoleon III and his Regime. An Extravaganza* (Baton Rouge: Louisiana State University Press, 2000).

Bajou, Valérie, *Louis-Philippe et Versailles*, exh. cat. (Paris: Établissement public du château de Versailles, 2018).

Biskup, Thomas, 'Napoleon's second Sacre? Iéna and the ceremonial translation of Frederick the Great's insignia in 1807', in *The Bee and the Eagle: Napoleonic France and the End of the Holy Roman Empire*, edited by Alan Forrest and Peter Wilson (Basingstoke: Palgrave Macmillan, 2008), pp. 172–90.

Biskup, Thomas, 'Zeremonielle Sattelzeit? Überlegungen zu einer Neuverortung der symbolischen Kommunikation am Ende der Frühen Neuzeit', *Repräsentation und Selbstinszenierung Friedrichs des Großen* (2012). http://www.perspectivia.net/content/publikationen/friedrich300-colloquien/friedrich_repraesentation/biskup_sattelzeit

Bossuet, Jean Bénigne, *Politique tirée des propres paroles de l'Écriture Sainte. Ouvrage posthume* (Paris: Pierre Cot, 1709).

Broers, Michael, *Napoleon*. Vol. I: *Soldier of Destiny, 1769–1805* (London: Faber & Faber, 2014).

Broers, Michael, *Napoleon*. Vol. II: *The Spirit of the Age, 1805–1810* (London: Faber & Faber, 2018).

Cabanès, Jean-Louis, and Vincent Laisney, *L'Année 1855. La littérature à l'âge de l'exposition universelle* (Paris: Classiques Garnier, 2015).

Caiani, Ambrogio A. 'Ornamentalism in a European Context? Napoleon's Italian Coronation, 26 May 1805', *English Historical Review* CXXXII, no. 554 (2017): 41–72.

Calonne, Alphonse de, *Exposition universelle de 1855* (Paris: n.pub., 1855).

Cogeval, Guy, Yves Badetz, Paul Perrin, and Marie-Paule Vial (eds.), *Spectaculaire Second Empire*, exh. cat. (Paris: Musée d'Orsay, 2016).

Corbin, Alain, et al., *Les usages politiques des fêtes aux XIXe-XXe siècles* (Paris: Publications de la Sorbonne, 1994).

Dabot, Henri, *Souvenirs et impressions d'un bourgeois du quartier latin de mai 1854 à mai 1869* (Péronne: E. Quentin, 1899).

Darjou, A., *À l'exposition nouvelle* (Paris: J. Voisvenel, 1855).

Décret Impérial concernant la fête de Saint Napoléon et celle du rétablissement de la religion catholique en France (19 février 1806) (Montpellier, de l'Imprimerie de Bonnariq, Félix Avignon et Migueyron. Rue Arc-d'Arène, N° 56, 1806).

'Décret portant qu'à l'avenir l'anniversaire du 15 août sera seul reconnu et célébré comme fête nationale', in *Bulletin des lois de la République française contenant des lois et décrets d'intérêt public et general publiés depuis le 1ᵉʳ janvier jusqu'au 30 juin 1852*, p. 345: 1852/ 01–1852/07, 16 Février 1852.

Dubroca, Louis, *Les Quatre fondateurs des dynasties françaises, ou Histoire de l'établissement de la monarchie française par Clovis, du renouvellement des dynasties royales par Pépin et Hugues Capet et de la fondation de l'Émpire par Napoléon le Grand* (Paris: Dubroca, 1806; Paris: Fantin, 1806).

Ducuing, F. (ed.), *L'Exposition Universelle de 1867 Illlustrée. Publication Internationale autorisée par la Commission Impériale*, 2 vols. (Paris: Commission Impériale, 1867).

Dusaulchoy de Bergemont, Joseph-François-Nicolas, *Histoire du Couronnement ou Relation des cérémonies religieuses, politiques et militaires, qui ont lieu pendant les jours mémorables consacrés à célébrer le Couronnement et le Sacre de Sa Majesté Impériale NAPOLEON I.er, Empereur des Français; dédiée à son altesse sérérenissime, M.gr Le Prince Murat, Grand amiral, maréchal de l'empire, gouverneur de Paris, etc.* (Paris: Imprimeur du Musée Napoléon, 1805), pp. 143–95.

Dwyer, Philip, '"Citizen Emperor": Political Ritual, Popular Sovereignty and the Coronation of Napoleon I', *History* (2005): 40–57.

Dwyer, Philip, *Napoleon: The Path to Power, 1769–1799* (London: Bloomsbury, 2007).

Dwyer, Philip, 'Napoleon and the Foundation of Empire', *The Historical Journal* 53, no. 2 (2010): 339–58.

Dwyer, Philip, *Citizen Emperor: Napoleon in Power* (New Haven: Yale University Press, 2013).

Dwyer, Philip, and Peter McPhee (eds.), *The French Revolution and Napoleon: A Routledge Sourcebook* (Abingdon: Routledge, 2002).

Étiquette du Palais Impérial (Paris: l'imprimerie impériale, 1806).

Exposition universelle de 1867 à Paris. Oeuvres d'Art. Catalogue general publié par la Commission Impériale (Paris: E. Dentu, 1867).

La France Politique, Scientifique et Littéraire (Paris: n.pub., 1862–1937).

Gazette nationale, ou le Moniteur universel (Paris, 1789–1811). See also *Le Moniteur Universel.*

George, Henri, 'Saint-Napoléon a-t-il existé?', *Le Vieux Papier* (Jan. 1990).

Grand Album de l'Exposition Universelle 1867: 150 Dessins par les premiers artistes de la France et de l'Étranger (Paris: Michel Lévy Frères, 1868).

Guide Général ou Catalogue indicateur de Paris. Indispensables aux Visiteurs et Exposants (Paris: au Siège de l'Administration, 1867).

Guide officiel à l'Exposition universelle de 1867: vade-mecum du visiteur (Paris: E. Dentu, 1867).

Hancock, Claire, '*Capitale du plaisir*: the remaking of imperial Paris', in *Imperial Cities: landscape, display and identity*, edited by Felix Driver and David Gilbert (Manchester: Manchester University Press, 2017), pp. 64–77.

Hanley, Wayne, *The Genesis of Napoleonic Propaganda* (New York: Columbia University Press, 2005).

Haussmann (Paris: impr. de A. Lainé et J. Havard, 1867).

Haussmann, Eugène, *Mémoires* (Paris: Victor-Havard, 1890).

Hazareesingh, Sudhir, *The Saint-Napoleon. Celebrations of Sovereignty in Nineteenth-Century France* (Cambridge, Mass.: Harvard University Press, 2004).

Hübner, Joseph Alexander, Graf von, *Neun Jahre der Erinnerungen eines Österreichischen Botschafters in Paris unter dem zweiten Kaiserreich 1851–1859* (Berlin: Gebrüder Paetel, 1904).

Hugo, Victor, *Napoleon le Petit* (London: Jeffs, 1852).

Journal Officiel de la République Française (Paris: Impr. des Journaux Officiels, 1871–2015).

Illustrated Catalogue of the Universal Exhibition: Published with the Art Journal (London: Virtue, 1868).

Isabey, Jean-Baptiste, *Le sacre de S.M. l'Empereur Napoléon dans l'église metropolitaine de Paris, le XI frimaire an XIII Dimanche 2 décembre 1804* (Paris: L'Imprimerie impériale. [1804]).

Isay, Raymond, *Panorama des Expositions universelles* (Paris: Gallimard, 1937).

Jones, Colin, *Paris. Biography of a City* (London: Allen Lane, 2004), pp. 344–68.

Kroen, Sheryl, *Politics and Theatre. The Crisis of Legitimacy in Restoration France, 1815–1830* (Berkeley: University of California Press, 2000).

Las Cases, Emanuel, *Le Mémorial de Sainte-Hélène: Le Manuscrit Original Retrouvé*, Texte établi, présenté et commenté par Peter Hicks, François Houdeck, Thierry Lentz, and Chantal Prévot (Paris: Perrin, 2017).

Lavisse, Ernest, and Philippe Sagnac, *Histoire de France contemporaine depuis la Révolution jusqu'à la paix de 1919*, 10 vols. (Paris: Hachette, 1920–22).

Lefort, Élodie, 'Les Aigles Premier Empire et Second Empire'. https://www.napoleon. org/histoire-des-2-empires/objets/les-aigles-premier-empire-et-second-empire/

Lentz, Thierry, 'Napoleon and Charlemagne', *Napoleonica, La Revue* 1 (2008): 45–78; DOI: 10.3917/napo.081.0002

Lentz, Thierry, *Napoléon et la France* (Paris: Vendémiaire, 2015).

Le Play, Fréderic, *Rapport sur l'exposition universelle de 1867 à Paris: précis des opérations et listes des collaborateurs avec un appendice sur l'avenir des expositions, la statistique des opérations, les documents officiels et le plan de l'exposition* (Paris: Imprimerie Impériale, 1869).

Loyer, François, 'La ville en représentation', in *Spectaculaire Second Empire*, exh. cat. edited by Guy Cogeval, Yves Badetz, Paul Perrin, and Marie-Paule Vial (Paris: Musée d'Orsay, 2016), pp. 171–83.

Lyons, Martyn, *Readers and Society in 19th Century France: Workers, Women, Peasants* (Basingstoke: Palgrave Macmillan, 2001).

McQueen, Alison, 'Women and Social Innovation during the Second Empire: Empress Eugénie's Patronage of the Fondation Eugène Napoléon', *Journal of the Society of Architectural Historians* 66 (2007): 176–93.

Malkowsky, Georg (ed.), *Die Pariserweltausstellung in Wort und Bild* (Berlin: Kirchhoff, 1900).

Mansel, Philip, *The Court of France 1789–1830* (Cambridge: Cambridge University Press, 1988).

Mansel, Philip, *Paris between Empires 1814–1852* (London: John Murray, 2001).

Mansel, Philip, *Dressed to Rule: Royal and Court Costume from Louis XIV to Elizabeth II* (New Haven: Yale University Press, 2005).

Mansel, Philip, *The Eagle in Splendour. Inside the Court of Napoleon*, 2nd ed. (London: I.B. Tauris, 2015).

Marx, Karl, *Der achtzehnte Brumaire des Louis Napoleon*, 2nd ed. (Hamburg: Otto Meißner, 1869).

Masson, Frédéric, *Le Sacre et Couronnement de Napoléon* (Paris: P. Ollendorf, 1908).

Matthieu, Caroline, 'Le Palais de l'Industrie et ses annexes', in *Les expositions universelles à Paris de 1855 à 1937*, edited by Jean-Pierre Babelon, Myriam Bacha, and Béatrice de Andia (Paris: Action artistique de la ville de Paris, 2005), pp. 64–7.

Mauduit, Xavier, *Le Ministère du Faste. La Maison de l'empereur Napoléon III* (Château de Versailles: Fayard, 2016).

Metternich, Pauline von, *My Years in Paris* (London: Nash, 1922).

Milza, Pierre, *Napoléon III* (Paris: Perrin, 2007).

Miot de Mélito, André François (1762–1841), *Mémoires du comte Miot de Mélito, ancien ministre, ambassadeur, conseiller d'État et membre de l'Institut*, 3 vols. (Paris: Michel-Lévy Frères, 1858).

Le Moniteur Universel (Paris, 1812–68). See also *Gazette nationale*.

Morrissey, Robert, 'The *Mémorial of Sainte Hélène* and the Poetics of Fusion', *MLN* 120, no. 4 (2005): 716–32.

Morrissey, Robert, *Napoléon et l'héritage de la gloire* (Paris: Presses Universitaires de France, 2010).

Murphy, Margueritte, 'Becoming Cosmopolitan: Viewing and Reviewing the 1855 Exposition Universelle in Paris', *Nineteenth-Century Contexts* 32 (2010): 31–46.

Napoleon I, *Memoirs*, see Las Cases.

Napoleon I, *Histoire sommaire de la vie de l'empereur Napoléon après lui-même* (Paris: Mangin et Busseuil, 1841).

Napoleon I, *Correspondance Générale*, edited by Gaspard Gourgaud (Paris: Fayard, 2004–17).

Napoleon III (Louis-Napoléon Bonaparte), *Des Idées Napoloniennes* (Paris: Henri Plon, 1860).

Napoleon III (Louis-Napoléon Bonaparte), *L'Extinction du paupérisme ou projet d'organisation agricole pour amélioration pour du sort des travailleurs* (Paris: n.pub., 1848).

Napoleon III (Louis-Napoléon Bonaparte), *Discours, messages et proclamations de Napoléon III, Empereur des Français: 1849–1860* (Paris: Mirecourt, 1860).

Oesterle, Günter, 'Die Kaiserkrönung Napoleons: eine ästhetische und ideologische Instrumentalisierung', in *Zeremoniell als höfische Ästhetik im Spätmittelalter und Früher Neuzeit*, edited by Jörg Jochen Berns and Thomas Rahn (Tübingen: de Gruyter, 1995), pp. 632–49.

Poisson, Georges, '1855. France's First International Exhibition', *Revue du Souvenir Napoléonien* 457 (2005). Reissued: https://www.napoleon.org/en/history-of-the-two-empires/articles/1855-frances-first-international-exhibition/

Porterfield, Todd Burke, and Susan L. Siegfried, *Staging Empire: Napoleon, Ingres, and David* (University Park: Penn State Press, 2006).

Price, Roger, *The French Second Empire. An Anatomy of Political Power* (Cambridge: Cambridge University Press, 2001).

Procès-Verbal de la Cérèmonie du Sacre et Couronnement de LL.MM. l'Empereur Napoléon et l'Imperatrice Joséphine (Paris: Imprimerie Impériale, 1805).

Radetz, Yves, 'L'Exposition de 1867 ou le triomphe de l'Empire', in *Spectaculaire Second Empire*, exh. cat. edited by Guy Cogeval, Yves Badetz, Paul Perrin, and Marie-Paule Vial (Paris: Musée d'Orsay, 2016), pp. 249–62.

Regnault, Jean *Les aigles impériales et le drapeau tricolore 1804–1815* (Paris: J. Peyronnet, 1967).

Roberts, William, 'Napoleon, the Concordat of 1801, and Its Consequences', in *Controversial Concordats: The Vatican's Relations with Napoleon, Mussolini, and*

Hitler, edited by Frank J. Coppa (Washington, DC: Catholic University of America Press, 1999), pp. 34–80.

Saint-Félix, René de, *Le Voyage de S.M. l'Empereur Napoléon III en Algérie et la Régence de S.M. l'Impératrice, mai-juin 1865* (Paris: Grande Librarie Napoléonienne d'Eugène Pick, 1865).

Sellali, Amina, 'Les habitations à bon marché', in *Les expositions universelles à Paris de 1855 à 1937*, edited by Jean-Pierre Babelon, Myriam Bacha, and Béatrice de Andia (Paris: Action artistique de la ville de Paris, 2005), pp. 73–6.

Seward, Desmond, *Empress Eugénie: The Empress and Her Empire* (Stroud: Sutton, 2004).

Smith, William H.C., *Napoleon III. The Pursuit of Power* (London: Collins and Brown, 1991).

Strauss-Schom, Alan, *The Shadow Emperor. A Biography of Napoléon III* (New York: St. Martin's Press, 2018).

Trabouillet, L. (éd.), *L'État de la France, contenant tous les Princes, Ducs & Pairs, & Marêchaux de France: les Evêques, les Juridictions du Roïaume; les Gouverneurs des Provinces, les Chevaliers des Ordres du Roy, &c. (. . .)* (Paris: Charles Osmont, 1702).

Tresca, Henri-Édouard, *Visite à l'exposition universelle de Paris, en 1855* (Paris: Hachette, 1855).

Truesdell, Matthew, *Spectacular Politics: Louis-Napoleon Bonaparte and the Fête Impériale, 1849–1870* (New York: Oxford University Press, 1997).

Tulard, Jean, *Le mythe de Napoléon* (Paris: A. Colin, 1971).

Vilmer, Jean-Baptiste Jeangène, 'Commentaire du Concordat de 1801 entre la France et le St-Siège', *Revue d'Histoire Ecclésiastique* 102, no. 1 (2007):124–54.

Viney, Zoe, 'The empress Eugénie and the imperial vestments at St Michael's Abbey, Farnborough', *Napoleonica. La Revue* 2, no. 11 (2011): 183–208.

Vittet, Jean, *L'appartement de Napoléon Ier à Fontainebleau. Histoire et Metamorphoses* (Paris: Chateau de Fontainebleau, n.d.).

Wairy, Louis Constant, *Recollections of the Private Life of Napoleon* (Paris: Ladvocat, 1830).

Zanten, David van, *Building Paris: Architectural Institutions and the Transformation of the French Capital 1830–1870* (Cambridge: Cambridge University Press, 1994).

Germany

Albisetti, James C., *Schooling German Girls and Women* (Princeton: Princeton University Press, 2014).

Asser, Saskia, and Liesbeth Ruitenberg (eds.), *Der Kaiser im Bild—Wilhelm II. und die Fotografie als PR-Instrument* (Zaltbommel: Europese Bibliotheek, 2002).

Baedeker, Karl, *Northern Germany. Handbook for Travellers*, 6th ed. (Leipzig: Karl Baedeker; London: Dulau and Co, 1877).

Barclay, David, 'Hof und Hofgesellschaft in Preußen in der Zeit Friedrich Wilhelms IV. (1840 bis 1857)', in *Hof und Hofgesellschaft in den deutschen Staaten im 19. und beginnenden 20. Jahrhundert*, edited by Karl Möckl (Berlin: De Gruyter, 1990), pp. 321–60.

Barth, Matthias, *Kaiserliches Berlin. Architektur zwischen 1871 und 1918* (Görlitz: Bergstadtverlag Wilhelm Gottlieb Korn, 2012).

Das Berliner Zeughaus, *Magazin des Deutschen Historischen Instituts* 2, no. 6 (1992).

Benner, Thomas Hartmut, *Die Strahlen der Krone Die religiöse Dimension des Kaisertums unter Wilhelm II. vor dem Hintergrund der Orientreise 1898* (Marburg: Tectum Verlag, 2001).

Bernet, Claus, 'The "Hobrecht Plan" (1862) and Berlin's urban structure', *Urban History* 31 (2004): 400–19.

Biefang, Andreas, Michael Epkenhans, and Klaus Tenfelde (eds.), *Politisches Zeremoniell im Kaiserreich* (Düsseldorf: Drost Verlag, 2008).

Bienert, Michael, and Elke Linda Buchholz, *Modernes Berlin der Kaiserzeit. Ein Wegweiser durch die Stadt* (Berlin: Berlin Story Verlag, 2016).

Bildliche Darstellung der königlich- preußischen Civil-Uniformen (Berlin: J.W. Schmidt, 1804).

Biskup, Thomas, and Martin Kohlrausch (eds.), *Das Erbe der Monarchie. Nachwirkungen einer deutschen Institution* (Frankfurt am Main: Campus, 2008).

Bisky, Jens, *Berlin. Biographie einer Grossen Stadt* (Berlin: Rowohlt, 2019).

Bösch, Frank, 'Das Zeremoniell der Kaisergeburtstage', in *Politisches Zeremoniell im Kaiserreich*, edited by Andreas Biefang, Michael Epkenhans, and Klaus Tenfelde (Düsseldorf: Drost Verlag, 2008), pp. 53–76.

Bouillon, Stefan, 'Das Kaiser-Wilhelm-Denkmal am Deutschen Eck in Koblenz wieder aufgestellt', *Kunstchronik* 46 (1993): 521–3.

Caspar, Helmut, *Die Beine der Hohenzollern, interpretiert an Standbildern der Siegesallee in Primaneraufsätzen aus dem Jahre 1901, versehen mit Randbemerkungen Seiner Majestät Kaiser Wilhelm II* (Berlin: Deutscher Verlag der Wissenschaften, 1990).

Clark, Christopher, *Kaiser Wilhelm II* (Harlow: Longman, 2000).

Clark, Christopher, *Iron Kingdom. The Rise and Downfall of Prussia, 1600–1947* (London: Penguin, 2006).

Dölemeyer, Barbara, 'Victoria in Homburg und Kronberg', in *Victoria Kaiserin Friedrich: Mission und Schicksal einer englischen Prinzessin in Deutschland*, edited by Rainer von Hessen (Frankfurt: Campus Verlag, 2007), pp. 114–33.

Duvernoy, Max von, *Festschrift zum fünfundzwanzigjährigen Regierungs-Jubiläum Sr. Majestät Kaiser Wilhelm II. für das deutsche Volk, sein Heer und seine Jugend*, 2nd aug. ed. (Berlin: Borussia Druck- und Verlagsanstalt, 1913).

Eichler, Inge, 'Victoria als Malerin, Sammlerin und Mäzenin', in *Victoria Kaiserin Friedrich: Mission und Schicksal einer englischen Prinzessin in Deutschland*, edited by Rainer von Hessen (Frankfurt: Campus Verlag, 2007), pp. 134–50.

Fischer, Robert-Tarek, *Wilhelm I. Vom preußischen König zum ersten deutschen Kaiser* (Vienna, Cologne, Weimar: Böhlau, 2020).

Förster, Michael A., *Kulturpolitik im Dienst der Legitimation. Oper, Theater und Volkslied als Mittel der Politik Kaiser Wilhelms II* (Frankfurt am Main: Peter Lang, 2009).

Franz, Eckart G., 'Victorias Schwester in Darmstadt', in *Victoria Kaiserin Friedrich: Mission und Schicksal einer englischen Prinzessin in Deutschland*, edited by Rainer von Hessen (Frankfurt: Campus Verlag, 2007), pp. 80–93.

Frowein-Ziroff, Vera, *Die Kaiser-Wilhelm-Gedächtniskirche: Entstehung und Bedeutung* (Berlin: Gebr. Mann Verlag, 1982).

Führer durch das Königliche Zeughaus in Berlin (Berlin: W. Moeser Hofbuchhandlung, 1887.

Fulford, Roger (ed.), *Dearest Mama. Letters between Queen Victoria and the Crown Princess of Prussia 1861–1864* (London: Evans Brothers, 1968).

Fulford, Roger (ed.), *Your Dear Letter. Private Correspondence of Queen Victoria and the Crown Princess of Prussia 1865–1871* (London: Evans Brothers, 1971).

Fulford, Roger (ed.), *Darling Child. Private Correspondence of Queen Victoria and the Crown Princess of Prussia 1871–1878* (London: Evans Brothers, 1976).

Fulford, Roger (ed.), *Beloved Mama. Private Correspondence Queen Victoria and the Crown Princess of Prussia 1878–1885* (London: Evans Brothers, 1981).

Gall, Lothar, *Bismarck: der weiße Revolutionär* (Frankfurt am Main: Ullstein, 1980).

Geisthövel, Alexa, 'Wilhelm I. am 'historischen Eckfenster': Zur Sichtbarkeit des Monarchen in der zweiten Hälfte des 19. Jahrhunderts', in *Die Sinnlichkeit der Macht. Herrschaft und Repräsentation seit der Frühen Neuzeit*, edited by Jan Andres, Alexa Geisthövel, and Matthias Schwengelbeck (Frankfurt, New York: Campus Verlag, 2005), pp. 163–85.

Giloi, Eva, *Monarchy, Myth, and Material Culture in Germany 1750–1950* (Cambridge: Cambridge University Press, 2011).

Giloi, Eva, 'Copyrighting the Kaiser: Publicity, Piracy, and the Right to Wilhelm II's Image', *Central European History* 45 (2012): 407–51.

Glatzer, Ruth (ed.), *Berlin wird Kaiserstadt* (Berlin: Siedler Verlag, 1993).

Göttert, Margrit, 'Victoria und die deutsche Frauenbewegung', in *Victoria Kaiserin Friedrich: Mission und Schicksal einer englischen Prinzessin in Deutschland*, edited by Rainer von Hessen (Frankfurt: Campus Verlag, 2007), pp. 94–113.

Gruhl, Bernhard, *Die Schlosskirche in der Lutherstadt Wittenberg* (Regensburg: Schnell + Steiner, 2016).

Gundermann, Iselin, *Ernst Freiherr von Mirbach und die Kirchen der Kaiserin* (Berlin: Evangelischer Kirchenbauverein, 1993).

Harden, Maximilian, *Die Zukunft*, vol. 18 (Berlin: Verlag der Zukunft, 1897).

Hasselhorn, Benjamin, 'Der Kaiser und sein Großvater. Zur politischen Mythologie Wilhelms II.', *Forschungen zur Brandenburgischen und preußischen Geschichte* 25 (2015): 321–35.

Hasselhorn, Benjamin, 'Nach dem Königstod. Zum Umgang Wilhelms II. mit seinem Erbe nach 1918', in *Preußendämmerung. Die Abdankung der Hohenzollern und das Ende Preußens*, edited by Thomas Biskup, Truc Vu Minh, and Jürgen Luh (Heidelberg: Universitätsverlag Göttingen, 2019).

Hein, Julius, Ludwig Bernhard Hopffer, *Barbarossa* (Berlin: Königl. Geh. Ober-Hofbuchdruckerey, 1871).

Herrig, Hans, *Luther. Ein kirchliches Festspiel zur Feier des 400-jahrigen Geburtstages Martin Luthers in Worms* (Berlin: Luckhardt 1883).

Hohenlohe-Schillingsfürst, Fürst Chlodwig zu, *Denkwürdigkeiten der Reichskanzlerzeit*, edited by Karl Alexander von Müller (Stuttgart and Berlin: Deutsche Verlags Anstalt, 1931).

Hull, Isabel V., *The Entourage of Kaiser Wilhelm II 1888–1918* (Cambridge: Cambridge University Press, 1982).

Kessler, Harry Graf, *Das Tagebuch (1880–1937), Gesamtausgabe*, 9 vols., edited by Roland Kamzelak (Stuttgart: Klett-Cotta, 2018).

Kessler, Harry Graf, and Oskar Klaußmann, *Kaiser Wilhelm der Große. Ein Lebensbild des großen Kaisers in ernsten und heiteren Episoden. Ein Buch für das deutsche Volk* (Minden: Wilhelm Köhler, 1897).

Kirschstein, Jörg (ed.), *Aus Allerhöchster Schatulle—Kaiserliche Geschenke*, exh. cat., (Potsdam: Potsdam-Museum, 2008).

Kleiner, Stephanie, 'Der Kaiser als Ereignis: Die Wiesbadener Kaiserfestspiele 1896–1914', in *Die Wirklichkeit der Symbole. Grundlagen der Kommunikation in historischen und gegenwärtigen Gesellschaften*, edited by Rudolf Schlögl, Bernhard Giesen, and Jürgen Osterhammel (Konstanz: UVK, 2004), pp. 339–67.

Kleiner, Stephanie, *Staatsaktion im Wunderland. Oper und Festspiel als Medien politischer Repräsentation (1890–1930)* (Berlin: De Gruyter, 2013).

Klingenberg, Karl-Heinz, *Der Berliner Dom: Bauten, Ideen und Projekte vom 15. Jahrhundert bis zur Gegenwart* (Berlin: Union-Verlag, 1987).

Koelges, Michael, 'Heroisches Kaiserdenkmal oder "Faustschlag aus Stein"? Das Deutsche Eck in Koblenz'. http://www.rheinische-geschichte.lvr.de/Epochen-und-Themen/Themen/heroisches-kaiserdenkmal-oder-%22faustschlag-aus-stein%22-das-deutsche-eck-in-koblenz/DE-2086/lido/57d129cb4966f6.01154517

König, Wolfgang, *Wilhelm II. und die Moderne. Der Kaiser und die technische-industrielle Welt* (Paderborn: Schöningh, 2007).

Kohlrausch, Martin, 'Monarchische Repräsentation in der entstehenden Mediengesellschaft: Das deutsche und das englische Beispiel', in *Die Sinnlichkeit der Macht. Herrschaft und Repräsentation seit der Frühen Neuzeit*, edited by Jan Andres, Alexa Geisthövel, and Matthias Schwengelbeck (Frankfurt, New York: Campus Verlag, 2005), pp. 92–122.

Kohlrausch, Martin, *Der Monarch im Skandal: die Logik der Massenmedien und die Transformation der Wilhelminischen Monarchie* (Berlin: Akademie, 2005).

Kohlrausch, Martin, 'Zwischen Tradition und Innovation. Das Hofzeremoniell der wilhelminischen Monarchie', in *Das politische Zeremoniell der wilhelminischen Monarchie*, edited by Andreas Biefang, Michael Epkenhaus, and Klaus Tenfelde (Dusseldörf: Droste Verlag, 2008), pp. 31–51.

Kohlrausch, Martin, 'The Workings of Royal Celebrity. Wilhelm II as Media Monarch', in *Constructing Charisma: Celebrity, Fame, and Power in Nineteenth-Century Europe*, edited by Edward Berenson and Eva Giloi (New York: Berghahn, 2010).

Kohlrausch, Martin, 'Loss of Control: Kaiser Wilhelm II, Mass Media, and the National Identity of the Second German Reich', in *Transnational Histories of the 'Royal Nation'*, edited by Milinda Banerjee, Charlotte Backerra, and Cathleen Sarti (London: Palgrave Macmillan, 2017), pp. 87–108.

Kohut, Thomas, *Wilhelm II and the Germans: A Study in Leadership* (New York and Oxford: Oxford University Press, 1991).

Laforgue, Jules, *Berlin. La Cour et la Ville* (Paris: Éditions de la Sirène, 1922).

László, Philip de, *Catalogue Raisonné*. http://www.delaszlocatalogueraisonne.com/home

Lehnert, Uta, *Der Kaiser und die Siegesallee. Réclame Royale* (Berlin: Reimer, 1998).

Lemburg, Peter, 'Julius Raschdorf und der Dom zu Berlin', in *Der Berliner Dom: Geschichte und Gegenwart der Oberpfarr- und Domkirche zu Berlin*, edited by Detlef Plöse (Berlin: Jovis, 2001), pp. 36–45.

Lepp, Claudia, 'Summus episcopus. Das Protestantische im Zeremoniell der Hohenzollern', in *Das politische Zeremoniell der wilhelminischen Monarchie*, edited by Andreas Biefang, Michael Epkenhaus, and Klaus Tenfelde (Dusseldörf: Droste Verlag, 2008), pp. 77–114.

Lindenberg, Paul, *Pracht-Album Photographischer Aufnahmen der Berliner Gewerbe= Ausstellung 1896 und der Sehenswürdigkeiten Berlins und des Treptower Parks* (Berlin: The Werner Company, 1896).

Mainzer, Udo, 'Denkmäler zwischen Traum und Wirklichkeit. Zum selektiven Umgang mit Geschichte', *Wallraf-Richartz-Jahrbuch* 57 (1966): 213–27.

Mann, Heinrich, *Der Untertan* (Munich: dtv, 1964).

Mann, Thomas, *Königliche Hoheit*, edited by Heinrich Detering and Stephan Stachorski (Frankfurt a. M.: S. Fischer Verlag, 2004).

Meinecke, Andreas, '"Zu den schönsten Freuden des Kaisers". Die Eingriffe Wilhelms II. auf dem Gebiet der Denkmalpflege', *Forschungen zur Brandenburgischen und preußischen Geschichte* 25 (2015): 247–75.

Meißner, Kathrin, 'Die Berliner "Mietskaserne". Zur Karriere eines Begriffs seit der Mitte des 19. Jahrhunderts', in *Stadtgeschichte als Zeitgeschichte. Berlin im 20. Jahrhundert*, edited by Hanno Hochmuth and Paul Nolte (Görringen: Wallstein, 2019), pp. 39–65.

Müller, Frank Lorenz, *Our Fritz. Emperor Frederick III and the Political Culture of Imperial Germany* (Cambridge, Mass.: Harvard University Press, 2011).

Müller, Frank Lorenz, '"Frauenpolitik". Augusta, Vicky und die liberale Mission', in *Frauensache. Wie Brandenburg Preussen wurde*, edited by the Generaldirektion der Stiftung Preußische Schlösser und Gärten (Dresden: Sandstein Verlag, 2015), pp. 252–9.

Müller, Frank Lorenz, and Heidi Mehrkens (eds.), *Sons and Heirs. Succession and Political Culture in Nineteenth-Century Europe* (Basingstoke: Palgrave Macmillan, 2016).

Nipperdey, Thomas, 'Nationalidee und Nationaldenkmal in Deutschland im 19. Jahrhundert', *Historische Zeitschrift* 206 (1968): 529–85.

Nipperdey, Thomas, *Religion im Umbruch. Deutschland 1870–1918* (Munich: C.H. Beck, 1988).

Peers, Juliet, 'The Emperor of signs? Representations of gender and governance in popular imagery of Wilhelm II and Auguste Viktoria of Germany', *Australian and New Zealand Journal of Art* 2, no. 1 (2015): 42–70.

Plöse, Detlef (ed.), *Der Berliner Dom: Geschichte und Gegenwart der Oberpfarr- und Domkirche zu Berlin* (Berlin: Jovis, 2001).

Pohl, Klaus-D., 'Der Kaiser im Zeitalter seiner technischen Reproduzierbarkeit', in *Der letzte Kaiser. Wilhelm II. im Exil*, edited by Hans Wilderotter and Klaus-D. Pohl (Berlin: Bertelsmann Lexikon Verlag, 1991), pp. 9–30.

Pollmann, Klaus Erich, *Landesherrliches Kirchenregiment und soziale Frage* (Berlin, New York: De Gruyter, 1973).

Rathenau, Walther, *Der Kaiser. Eine Betrachtung* (Berlin: Fischer, 1919).

Richie, Alexandra, *Faust's Metropolis. A History of Berlin* (London: Harper Collins, 1998).

Röhl, John C.G., *The Kaiser and His Court: Wilhelm II and the Government of Germany* (Cambridge: Cambridge University Press, 1994).

Röhl, John C.G., *Young Wilhelm. The Kaiser's Early Life, 1859–1888* (Cambridge: Cambridge University Press, 1998).

Röhl, John C.G., *Wilhelm II. The Kaiser's Personal Monarchy 1888–1900* (Cambridge: Cambridge University Press, 2004).

Röhl, John C.G., *Kaiser Wilhelm II, 1859–1941. A Concise Life* (Cambridge: Cambridge University Press, 2014).

Roth, Joseph, *Radetzkymarsch* (Berlin: Kiepenhauer, 1932).

Ruhmeshalle, Die., Magazin des Deutschen Historischen Museums 2, no.6 (1992).

Schneider, Eva Maria, *Herkunft und Verbreitungsformen der "Deutschen Nationaltracht der Befreiungskriege" als Ausdruck politischer Gesinnung*, PhD thesis, Bonn. Vol. I: Text; Vol. II: Illustrations. https://web.archive.org/web/20070702074923/http://hss.ulb.uni-bonn. de:90/ulb_bonn/diss_online/phil_fak/2002/schneider_eva_maria/0083_1.pdf

Schönpflug, Daniel, *Die Heiraten der Hohenzollern* (Göttingen: Vandenhoeck & Ruprecht, 2013).

Schwengelbeck, Matthias, 'Monarchische Herrschaftsrepräsentationen zwischen Konsens und Konflikt: Zum Wandel des Huldigungs- und Inthronisationszeremoniells im 19. Jahrhundert', in *Die Sinnlichkeit der Macht. Herrschaft und Repräsentation seit der Frühen Neuzeit*, edited by Jan Andres, Alexa Geisthövel, and Matthias Schwengelbeck (Frankfurt, New York: Campus Verlag, 2005), pp. 123–62.

Sieg, Ulrich, 'Wilhelm II.ein "leutseliger Charismatiker"', in *Zur Theorie des Charismatischen Führers im modernen Nationalstaat* (Berlin: De Gruyter, 2014), pp. 85–108.

Siegessäule Berlin (Berlin: Monument Tales, 2015), n. pag.

Simplicissimus, illustrierte Wochenschrift (Munich: Simplicissimus Verlag, 1896–1944).

Spitzemberg, Hildegard von, *Das Tagebuch der Baronin Spitzemberg. Aufzeichnungen aus der Hofgesellschaft des Hohenzollernreiches*, edited by Rudolf Vierhaus (Göttingen: Vandenhoeck & Ruprecht, 1976).

Staudinger, Burkhard (ed.), *Kaiser-Wilhelm-Gedächtnis-Kirche* (Berlin: publicon, 2012).

Steffens, Martin, *Luthergedenkstätten im 19. Jahrhundert. Memoria—Repräsentation—Denkmalpflege* (Regensburg: Schnell and Steiner, 2008).

Steinberg, Jonathan, *Bismarck: A Life* (New York: Oxford University Press, 2011).

Stern, Fritz, *Gold and Iron. Bismarck, Bleichröder, and the Building of the German Empire* (London: Allen and Unwin, 1977).

Stickler, Matthias '"Erneuerung der Deutschen Kaiserwürde?"—das Nachleben der frühneuzeitlichen Reichssymbolik in Preußen-Deutschland im Spannungsfeld von Tradition und Konstruktion neuer Geschichtsbilder', in *Was vom alten Reiche blieb. . . Deutungen, Institutionen und Bilder des Frühneuzeitlichen Heiligen Römischen Reiches deutscher Nation im 19. und 20. Jahrhundert*, edited by Matthias Ascher, Thomas Nicklas, and Matthias Stickler (Munich: Bayerische Landeszentrale für Politische Bildungsarbeit, 2011), pp. 319–43.

Stillfried-Alcántara, Rudolf Maria Bernhard von, *Ceremonial-Buch für den Königlichen-preußischen Hof. X. Hof-Rang-Reglement* (Berlin: Decker, 1878).

Verroen, Dick, *Huis Doorn. Kaiserliche Exilresidenz* (Doorn: Stichting Huis Doorn, 2011),

Vossische Zeitung, Königlich Privilegierte Berlinische Zeitung von Staats- und gelehrten Sachen (Berlin, 1721–1934).

Wagner-Gyora, Georg, 'Beruf Kaiserin. Die mediale Repräsentation der preußisch-deutschen Kaiserinnen 1871–1918', *Historische Anthropologie: Kultur, Gesellschaft, Alltag* 15 (2007): 339–71.

Wildenbruch, Ernst von, *Willehalm. Dramatische Legende in vier Bildern* (Berlin: Freund & Jeckel, 1897).

Wilhelm II, *Die Reden Kaiser Wilhelms II. in den Jahren 1896–1900*, 3 vols., edited by Johannes Penzler (Leipzig: Philipp Reclam jun., 1904).

Witte, Leopold, *Die Erneuerung der Wittenberger Schloßkirche, eine That evangelischen Bekenntnisses* (Wittenberg: Herrose, 1892).

Zeughaus, *Führer durch das Königliche Zeughaus in Berlin*, dritte, umgearbeitete und vermehrte Auflage (Berlin: W. Moeser, 1887).

Zweig, Stefan, *Die Welt von Gestern, Erinnerungen eines Europäers* (Cologne: Anaconda, 2013).

British India

Auerbach, Jeffrey, 'Empire under Glass: The British Empire and the Crystal Palace, 1851–1911', in *Exhibiting the Empire. Cultures of Display and the British Empire*, edited by John McAleer and John M. MacKenzie (Manchester: Manchester University Press, 2015), pp. 142–67.

Baker, Herbert, 'The New Delhi: Eastern and Western Architecture: A Problem of Style', *The Times*, 3 October 1912, pp. 7–8.

Banerjee, Jacqueline, 'British India and Victorian-Era Architecture'. http://www.victorianweb.org/history/empire/india/architecture.html

Bartie, Angela, Linda Fleming, Mark Freman, Tom Hulme, Alex Hutton, and Paul Readman, 'The Pageant of Empire', The Redress of the Past. http://www.historicalpageants.ac.uk/pageants/1302

Bonea, Amelia, The News of Empire. Telegraphy, Journalism, and the Politics of Reporting in Colonial India c.1830–1900 (New Delhi: Oxford University Press, 2016).

Bradley, John (ed.), Lady Curzon's India. Letters of a Vicereine (New York: Beaufort Books, 1985).

Byron, Robert 'I.-New Delhi: The First Impression', The Architectural Review 69, issue 410 (January 1931): 1–12.

Cannadine, David, 'The Context, Performance and Meaning of Ritual: The British Monarchy and the "Invention of Tradition", c. 1820–1977', in The Invention of Tradition, edited by Eric Hobsbawm and Terence Ranger (Cambridge: Cambridge University Press, 1983), pp. 101–64.

Cannadine, David, Ornamentalism. How the British saw their Empire (London: Penguin, 2001).

Codell, Julie, 'Photographic Interventions and Identities; Colonising and Decolonising the Royal Body', in Julie Codell (ed.), Power and Resistance: the Delhi Coronation Durbars 1877, 1903, 1911 (Delhi: Alkazi Collection of Photography, 2012), pp. 110–42. Reprinted at: http://www.victorianweb.org/history/empire/india/codell.html

Codell, Julie, Power and Resistance: the Delhi Coronation Durbars 1877, 1903, 1911 (Delhi: Alkazi Collection of Photography, 2012).

Cohn, Bernard S., 'Representing Authority in British India', in The Invention of Tradition, edited by Eric Hobsbawm and Terence Ranger (Cambridge: Cambridge University Press, 1983), pp. 165–210.

Cohn, Bernard S., Colonialism and its Forms of Knowledge. The British in India (Princeton: Princeton University Press, 1996).

Cook, Majorie Grant, The British Empire Exhibition 1924: Official Guide (London: Fleetway Press, 1925).

Cundall, Frank (ed.), Reminiscences of the Colonial and Indian Exhibition, illustrated by Thomas Riley (London: William Clowes and Sons, 1886).

Curzon, George, British Government in India. The Story of the Viceroys and Government Houses, 2 vols., (London: Cassell, 1925).

Dalrymple, William, The Last Mughal (London: Bloomsbury, 2006).

Davies, Philip, Splendours of the Raj. British Architecture in India 1660–1947 (Harmondsworth, Middlesex: Penguin, 1987).

Devi, Gayatri, A Princess Remembers. The Memoirs of the Maharani of Jaipur (Delhi: Rupa, 1995).

Eldridge, C.C., England's Mission: The Imperial Idea in the Age of Gladstone and Disraeli (London: Macmillan, 1973).

Ellis, Robert The Official Descriptive and Illustrated Catalogue of the Great Exhibition of the Works of Industry of all Nations, 1851 (London: William Clowes and Sons, 1851).

Evenson, Norma, The Indian Metropolis. A View Toward the West (New Haven: Yale University Press, 1989).

Finding, Susan, 'London 1911: celebrating the imperial', Observatoire de la société britannique 11 (2011): 1–12.

Fortesque, John, *Narrative of the Visit to India of Their Majesties, King George V. and Queen Mary, and of the Coronation Durbar Held at Delhi, 12ᵗʰ December, 1911* (London: Macmillan, 1912).

Geppert, Alexander C. T., 'Wembley 1924: The British Empire as Suburban Metropolis', in *Fleeting Cities. Imperial Expositions in Fin-de-Siècle Europe* (Basingstoke: Palgrave Macmillan, 2010), pp. 134–78 and notes: 310–15.

The Gentlewoman: The Illustrated Weekly Journal for Gentlewomen (London, 1890–1926).

Ghuman, Nalini, 'Elgar's *Pageant of Empire*, 1924: An imperial leitmotif', in *Exhibiting the Empire. Cultures of Display and the British Empire*, edited by John McAleer and John M. MacKenzie (Manchester: Manchester University Press, 2015), pp. 220–56.

Gilmour, David, *Curzon: Imperial Statesman 1859–1925* (London: John Murray, 1994).

Goyle, Sonakshi, 'Tracing a Cultural Memory of 1857 in the Delhi Durbars, 1877, 1903, and 1911', *The Historical Journal* 59 (2016): 799–815.

Hassam, Andrew, 'Portable iron structures and uncertain colonial spaces at the Sydenham Crystal Palace', in *Imperial Cities. Landscape, Display and Identity*, edited by Felix Driver and David Gilbert (Manchester: Manchester University Press, 1999), pp. 174–93.

The Historical Record of The Imperial Visit to India 1911 (London: John Murray, 1914).

The Illustrated London News, 1842–2003. https://www.gale.com/intl/c/illustrated-london-news-historical-archive

India. Catalogue. British Empire Exhibition 1924 (London: Sanders Phillips and Company, 1924).

Indian Court. Festival of Empire 1911. Guide Book and Catalogue (London: Bemrose, 1911).

The International Exhibition of 1862: The Illustrated Catalogue of the Industrial Department, volume 3: Colonial and Foreign Division (London: Her Majesty's Commissioners, 1862).

Jeffrey, Robin (ed.), *People, Princes and Paramount Power: Society and Politics in the Indian Princely States* (Oxford Delhi: Oxford University Press, 1978).

Khilnani, Sunil, *The Idea of India*, 2nd ed. (London: Penguin, 2012).

The King Emperor and His Dominions. Souvenir of the Coronation Durbar of H.I.M George V., Delhi, December 1911 (London: Burroughs Wellcome & Co, 1911).

Lambert, David, 'Reflections on the Concept of Imperial Biographies. The British Case', *Geschichte und Gesellschaft* 40 (2014): 22–41.

Lethbridge, Roper, *The Golden Book of India: A Genealogical and Biographical Dictionary of the Ruling Princes, Chiefs, Nobles and Other Personages, Titled or Decorated, of the Indian Empire* (London: Macmillan, 1893 and 1900).

Lomas, Sophia Crawford, *Festival of Empire, Souvenir of the Pageant of London* (London: Bemrose, 1911).

The London Gazette, 1666–present. https://www.thegazette.co.uk/

Lucas, E.V., *The Pageant of Empire. Souvenir Volume*, with illustrations by Frank Brangwyn, Spencer Pryse, and Macdonald Gill (London: Fleetway Press, 1924).

MacKenzie, John, 'Exhibiting Empire at the Delhi Durbar of 1911: Imperial and cultural contexts', in *Exhibiting the Empire. Cultures of Display and the British Empire*, edited by John McAleer and John M. MacKenzie (Manchester: Manchester University Press, 2015), pp. 194–219.

McGarr, Paul M., ' "The Viceroys are Disappearing from the Roundabouts in Delhi": British symbols of power in post-colonial India', *Modern Asian Studies* 49 (2015): 787–831.

Menpes, Mortimer, *The Durbar*. Text by Dorothy Menpes (London: Adam and Charles Black, 1903).

Metcalf, Thomas, *An Imperial Vision. Indian Architecture and the British Raj* (London: Faber and Faber, 1989).

Misra, Maria, 'Lessons of Empire', *SAIS Review* 23, no. 2 (2003): 133–53.

Misra, Maria, 'From Nehruvian neglect to Bollywood heroes; the memory of the Raj in post-war India', in *Sites of Imperial Memory. Commemorating Colonial Rule in the Nineteenth and Twentieth Centuries*, edited by Dominik Geppert and Franz Lorenz Müller (Manchester: Manchester University Press, 2015), pp. 187–206.

Mitter, Partha, *Much Maligned Monsters. A History of European Reactions to Indian Art* (Oxford: Oxford University Press, 1977).

Morris, Jan, and Simon Winchester, *Stones of Empire. The Buildings of the Raj* (Oxford: Oxford University Press, 1983).

Official Report of the Calcutta International Exhibition 1883–84 (Calcutta: Bengal Secretariat Press, 1885).

Peers, Douglas M., and Nandini Gooptu (eds.), *India and the British Empire* (Oxford: Oxford University Press, 2012).

Plunkett, John, *Queen Victoria. First Media Monarch* (Oxford: Oxford University Press, 2003).

Port, Michael Harry, *Imperial London. Civil Government Buildings in London 1850–1915* (New Haven: Yale University Press, 1995).

Prinsep, Val C., *Imperial India: An Artist's Journals, Illustrated by Numerous Sketches Taken at the Court of the Principal Chiefs in India* (London: Chapman and Hall, 1879).

Ryan, Deborah S., 'Staging the imperial city: The Pageant of London, 1911', in *Imperial Cities. Landscape, Display and Identity*, edited by Felix Driver and David Gilbert (Manchester: Manchester University Press, 1999), pp. 117–35.

Sayer, Derek, 'British Reaction to the Amritsar Massacre 1919–1920', *Past & Present* 131 (May 1991): 130–64.

Sharma, Arvind, *The Ruler's Gaze. A Study of British Rule over India from a Saidian Perspective* (Noida: HarperCollins, 2017).

Shears, Jonathon, *The Great Exhibition 1851: A Sourcebook* (Manchester: Manchester University Press, 2017).

Simonelli, David, '"[L]aughing nations of happy children who have never grown up": Race, the Concept of Commonwealth and the 1924–5 British Empire Exhibition', *Journal of Colonialism and Colonial History* 10, no. 1 (2009); DOI: 10.1353/cch.0.0044

Smith, Tori, '"A grand work of noble conception": the Victoria Memorial and imperial London', in *Imperial Cities. Landscape, Display and Identity*, edited by Felix Driver and David Gilbert (Manchester: Manchester University Press, 1999), pp. 21–39.

Statham, H. Heathcote, 'London as a Jubilee City', *The National Review* 1897 (172): 594–603.

Steggles, Mary Ann, *Statues of the Raj* (London: BACSA, 200).

Talmeyr, Maurice, 'L'école du Trocadéro', *Revue des Deux Mondes* (November 1900): 198–213.

Taylor, Robert, *The Princely Armory: Being a Display of the Arms of the Ruling Chiefs of India After Their Banners as Prepared for the Imperial Assemblage Held at Delhi on the First Day of January 1877* (Calcutta: Office of the Superintendent of Government, 1877).

Taylor, Miles, *Empress. Queen Victoria and India* (New Haven: Yale University Press, 2018).

Tharoor, Shashi, *Inglorious Empire. What the British did to India* (London: Penguin, 2017).

The Times, Exhibition Supplement, 23 April 1924.

Trendell, Herbert A. P. (ed.), *Dress and Insignia Worn at His Majesty's Court Issued with the Authority of the Lord Chamberlain* (London: Harrison and Sons Ltd, 1921).

Tunzelmann, Alex von, *Indian Summer. The Secret History of the End of an Empire* (London: Simon & Schuster, 2007).

Vijayaraghavacharya, Thiruvalayangudi, *The British Empire Exhibition, 1924. Report by the Commissioner for India for the British Empire Exhibition* (Calcutta: Government of India Press, 1925).

Warrant of Precedence for India. https://en.wikisource.org/wiki/The_Indian_Biographical_Dictionary_(1915)/Appendix_I

Wheeler, James Talboys, *The History of the Imperial Assemblage at Delhi* (London: Longmans, Green, Reader, and Dyer, 1877).

Wheeler, Stephen, *History of the Delhi Coronation Durbar held on the First of January 1903 to Celebrate the Coronation of his Majesty King Edward VII Emperor of India* (London: John Murray, 1904).

Willcock, Sean, 'Composing the Spectacle: Colonial Portraiture and the Coronation Durbars of British India, 1877–1911', *Art History* 40 (2017): 133–55.

Mexico

Acevedo-Valdés, Esther, 'La Historia: Los ciclos iconográficos del Palacio Imperial'. https://www.academia.edu/14882945/LA_HISTORIA_LOS_CICLOS_ICONOGR%C3%81FICOS_DEL_PALACIO_IMPERIAL

Advenimiento de SS. MM. Maximiliano y Carlota al trono de México. Documentos relativos y narración del viaje de nuestros soberanos de Miramar a Veracruz y del recibimiento que se les hizo en este último puerto y en las ciudades de Córdoba, Orizaba, Puebla y México (México: Imprente de J. M. Andrade y F. Escalante, 1864).

Alberro, Solange, 'Los efectos especiales en las fiestas virreinales de Nueva España', *Historia Mexicana* 59, no. 3 (2010): 837–75.

Anna, Timothy E., 'The Rule of Agustín de Iturbide: A Reappraisal', *Journal of Latin American Studies* 17 (1985): 79–110.

Anna, Timothy E., *The Mexican Empire of Iturbide* (Lincoln, University of Nebraska Press, 1990).

Archer, Christon I., 'Royalist Scourge or Liberator of the Patria? Agustín De Iturbide and Mexico's War of Independence, 1810–1821', *Mexican Studies* 24, no. 2 (2008): 325–61.

Arenal Fenochio, Jaime del, *Un Modo de Ser Libres: Independencia y Constitución en México* (Zamora, Michoacán: El Colegio de Michoacán, 2010).

Barta, Ilsebill (ed.), *Maximilian von Mexiko. Der Traum vom Herrschen* (Vienna: Museen des Hofmobiliendepots, 2013).

Beltrán, Rosa, *La Corte De Los Ilusos* (México: Grupo Editorial Planeta, 1995).

Caneque, Alejandro, *The King's Living Image: The Culture and Politics of Viceregal Power in Colonial Mexico* (Abingdon: Routledge, 2013).

Carbajal López, David, 'Una liturgia de ruptura: el ceremonial de consagración y coronación de Agustín I', *Signos Historicos* 25 (2011): 68–99.

Ceremonias de la Iglesia en la Uncion y coronacion del nuevo Rey ó Emperador, Escritas en latin por D. Andres Castaldo y traducidas al Castellano (Mexico: En la Oficina del Sr. Valdés, Impresor, de Cámara, 1822).

Chust, Manuel, and Víctor Minguéz (eds.), *La Construcción del Héroe en España y México, 1789-1847* (València: Universidad de València, 2003).

Constituciones de la Imperial Orden de Guadalupe: instituida por la Junta Provisional del Imperio, á propuesta del Sereníssimo Señor Generalísimo Almirante Don Agustín de Iturbide, en 18 de febrero de 1822 (México: En la Oficina de D. Alejando Valdes, impresor de Cámara del Imperio, [1822]).

Corti, Egon Caesar, *Maximiliano y Carlota* (Mexico City: Fondo de Cultura Económica, 1944).

Cuervo Álvarez, Benedicto, 'Maximiliano I y el Segundo Imperio Mexicano', *La Razón Histórica. Revista Hispanoamericana de Historia de las Ideas* 28 (2014): 82–116.

Cunningham, Michele, *Mexico and the Foreign Policy of Napoleon III* (Basingstoke: Palgrave Macmillan, 2001).

Demm, Eberhard, and Jean-Marie Steinlein, *Kolonialpäläste in Mexico* (Cologne: Benedikt Taschen Verlag, 1991).

Il Diario del Imperio, see Hernández Sáenz.

Duncan, Robert, *Political Legitimation and Maximilian's Second Empire in Mexico 1864-1867)* (Mexico: Ponencia IX, Reunion de Historiadores Canadienses, Mexicanos y de los Estados Unidos, 1994).

Duncan, Robert H., 'Embracing a Suitable Past: Independence Celebrations under Mexico's Second Empire, 1864-67', *Journal of Latin American Studies* 30, no. 2 (1998): 249–77.

Entrada pública en Valladolid de la señora doña Ana Huarte de Iturbide, Digna esposa del immortal héroe mexicano. Impresa en Valladolid y por su original en México en la imprenta de los ciudadanos militares independientes D. Joaquín y D. Bernardo de Mira. . . a expensas del capitán D José Guadalupe Palafox y Lozada (Valladolid [1821]).

Fabiani, Rosella, and Luca Caburlotto, *L'Arte di Massimiliano d'Asburgo. Dipinti, sculture et arredi nel Castello di Miramare* (Milan: Solvana, 2013).

Gaceta Imperial Extraordinaria de México (Impr. Imperial de Alejandro Valdés, 1821-22; Imp. del Supremo Gobierno, 1822-12).

Galeana de Valadés, Patricia, *El Nacimiento de México* (Mexico, D.F.: Archivo General de la Nación, 1999).

Gutierrez de Estrada, José Maria, *Méjico y el Archiduque Fernando Maximiliano de Austria* (Paris: Librería Española de Garnier Hermanos, 1862).

Hernández Sáenz, Luz María, *Espejismo y Realidad: Maximiliano y El Diario del Imperio 1865-1867* (Mexico, D.F.: Secretaría de Gobernación; AGN, 2012). The accompanying CD contains a digitized version of the *Diario del Imperio*.

Humboldt, Alexander von, *Versuch über den politischen Zustand des Königreiches Neu-Spanien*, vol. 2 (Tübingen: J.G. Cotta, 1810).

Ibsen, Kristine, *Maximilian, Mexico and the Invention of Empire* (Nashville: Vanderbilt University Press, 2010).

Iturbide, Agustín de, *Proclamación del Excmo. Señor Don Agustín de Iturbide* (Mexico: C. de la Torre, 1821).

Iturbide, Agustín de, *Manifiesto al mundo de Agustín de Iturbide, o sean, Apuntes para la historia*, edited by Laura B. Suárez de la Torre (Tlalpan, D.F.: Fideicomiso Teixidor, 2000). http://bdmx.mx/documento/manifiesto-agustin-iturbide

Iturbide, Agustín de, and Vito Alessio Robles, *La Correspondencia de Agustín De Iturbide Después de La Proclamación del Plan de Iguala.* Archivo Histórico Militar Mexicano; no 1. (Mexico: Taller Autográfico, 1945).

Johnson, Lynam (ed.), *Death, Dismemberment, and Memory: Body Politics in Latin America* (Albuquerque: University of New Mexico Press, 2004).

Kühn, Joachim, *Das Ende des maximilianischen Kaiserreichs in Mexico. Berichte des königlich preußischen Ministerresidenten Anton von Magnus an Bismarck, 1866–1867* (Göttingen: Musterschmidt, 1965).

McAllen, M.M., *Maximilian and Carlota: Europe's Last Empire in Mexico* (San Antonio Texas: Trinity University Press, 2014).

Navarro Méndez, José María, 'La mujér del emperador: Ana María Huarte de Iturbide. Un perfil biográfico (1786–1822)', *Legajos. Boletín del Archivo General de la Nación* 16 (mayo–agosto 2018): 11–34.

Orden del accompañamiento desde Palacio á la Santa Iglesia Catedral Metropolitana; y desde esta á su regreso al mismo Palacio en la mañana del dia de la inauguracion, bendicion y coronacion de SS. MM. el Emperador AGUSTIN PRIMERO, y su Esposa ANA MARIA, Emperatriz del Imperio de Anahuac, arreglado por el Gefe del Ceremonial. MS. Archivo General Nacional (AGN), Mexico City, Gobernacion, Sin Sección, caja 27, exp. 2.

Pani, Erika, 'El proyecto de Estado de Maximiliano a través de la vida cortesana y del ceremonial público', *Historia Mexicana* 45, no. 2 (1995): 423–60.

Pani, Erika, 'Dreaming of a Mexican Empire: The Political Projects of the "Imperialistas"', *Hispanic American Historical Review* 82, no. 1 (2002): 1–31.

Perotti, Eliana, *Das Schloss Miramar in Trieste (1856–70)* (Vienna, Cologne, Weimar: Böhlau, 2002).

Proyecto del ceremonial que para la inauguración y coronación de Su Majestad, el emperador Agustín Primero, se presentó por la comisión encargada de formarlo al Soberano Congreso en 17 de junio de 1822 (Mexico, Imprenta de D. José María Ramos Palomera en el Convento Imperial de Santo Domingo, 1822).

Pruonto, David, 'Did the Second Mexican Empire under Maximilian of Habsburg (1864–1867) have an "Austrian Face"?', *Austrian Studies* 20 (2012): 96–111.

Pruonto, David, *Das mexikanische Kaiserreich. Ein französisches Kolonialabenteuer?* (Bochum: Dr. Dieter Winkler Verlag, 2016).

Ratz, Konrad, and Amparo Gómez Tepexicuapan, *Los Viajes de Maximiliano en Mexico (1864–1867)* (Mexico City: Direccion General de Publicaciones, 2012).

Reglamento para el Servicio y Ceremonial de la Corte (Mexico, D.F.: José Manuel Lara, 10 April 1865). https://scholarship.rice.edu/jsp/xml/1911/26931/1/aa00034.tei.html

Rodríguez Moya, Inmaculada, 'Augustín de Iturbide: Héroe o emperador?', in Manuel Chust and Víctor Mínguez (eds.), *La Construcción del Héroe en España y México (1789–1847)* (València: Universidad de València, 2003), pp. 211–28.

Rodriguez O., Jaime E., 'Los caudillos y los historiadores: Riego, Iturbide y Santa Anna', in Manuel Chust and Víctor Mínguez (eds.), *La Construcción del Héroe en España y México (1789–1847)* (València: Universidad de València, 2003), pp. 309–35.

Romero de Terreros y Vinent, Manuel de, 'Don Agustín de Iturbide, emperador de México y su corte', *Memorias de la Academia Mexicana de la Historia* 28, no. 3 (1969): 225–87.

Rydjord, John, 'La Correspondencia de Agustín de Iturbide después de la Proclamación del Plan de Iguala. (Book Review)', *The Hispanic American Historical Review* 26, no. 2 (Durham: Duke University Press, 1946): 206–7.

Santiago Burgoa, Nizza, 'Forjando la cara del imperio. Los arquitectos del Emperador Maximiliano (1864–1867)', in *España y América en el Bicentenario de las Independiencias*, edited by Lucía Casajús and Francisco José Fernández Beltrán (Castello de la Plana: Publicaciones de la Universitat Jaume, 2012), pp. 375–90.

Tenenbaum, Barbara, 'Streetwise history: The Paseo de la Reforma and the Porfirian State, 1876–1910', in *Rituals of Rule, Rituals of Resistance: Public Celebrations and Popular*

Culture in Mexico, edited by William Beezley et al. (Lanham, Maryland: Rowman and Littlefield 1994), pp. 127–50.

Uribe-Uran, Victor, 'The Birth of a Public Sphere in Latin America during the Age of Revolution', *Comparative Studies in Society and History* 42, no. 2 (2000): 425–57.

Vázquez Mantecón, María Del Carmen. 'Las Fiestas Para El Libertador y Monarca de México Agustín De Iturbide, 1821–1823', *Estudios de historia moderna y contemporánea de México*, no. 36 (2008): 45–83.

Vega Juanino, Josefa, *Agustín de Iturbide* (Madrid: Historia 16, Ed. Quorum, 1987).

Iturbide, Augustín de, *Proclamación*, MS, Mexico, 1823.

Villalpando, José Manuel, *El juicio de la historia: Maximiliano* (Mexico City: Penguin Random House, 2017).

Zarate Toscano, Verónica, 'El papel de la escultura conmemorativa en el proceso de construcción nacional y su reflejo en la ciudad de México en el siglo XIV', *Historia Mexicana* 52, no. 3 (2003): 417–46.

Index

For the benefit of digital users, indexed terms that span two pages (e.g., 52–53) may, on occasion, appear on only one of those pages.